THE SCAPULAR OF OUR LADY OF MOUNT CARMEL

THE CARMELITE ORDER

THE CONFRATERNITIES OF OUR LADY OF MOUNT CARMEL

and THE WEDNESDAYS OF UDIENZA

First published in 2022 by
New Life Publishing, Luton,
Bedfordshire LU4 9HG

British Library Cataloguing in Publication Data
A catalogue record for this book is available
from the British Library

ISBN 978 1 912237 38 8

Front cover image
The Miraculous Painting of Our Lady
of Mount Carmel in The Basilica of Valletta
(Credit: Mark Micallef Perconte)

Typesetting by New Life Publishing,
Luton, UK www.goodnewsbooks.co.uk
Printed and bound in Great Britain

THE SCAPULAR OF OUR LADY OF MOUNT CARMEL

THE CARMELITE ORDER

THE CONFRATERNITIES OF OUR LADY OF MOUNT CARMEL

and THE WEDNESDAYS OF UDIENZA

COLLATED FROM NUMEROUS SOURCES BY

MARK AGIUS

Rector of the Confraternity of
Our Lady of Mount Carmel, Valletta

CONTENTS

Foreword 1

To Set the Scene 3

Introduction 8

PART ONE: EARLY HISTORY 16

1. The Early History of the Carmelite Order 17
2. Saint Simon Stock and the Scapular Vision 26
3. The Sabbatine Privilege 31
4. The development within the Carmelite Order of devotion to Our Lady and the wearers of the Scapular and the Carmelite Saints 40
5. Why is Saturday dedicated to Our Lady? 49
6. The development of Scapular Confraternities in and Europe and in Malta 68
7. The history of the scapular as a sign on consecration to Mary 84
8. The beginnings of the Feast of Our Lady of Mount Carmel 90
9. What Saints have said about the Scapular 101
10. What Popes have said about the Brown Scapular 106
11. The relationship between the Confraternities of the Scapular, the Carmelite Order, and our Lady of Mount Carmel 113
12. Some practicalities 119

PART TWO: CATECHESIS OF THE SCAPULAR OF OUR LADY OF MOUNT CARMEL 122

13. The use of the Scapular of Our Lady of Mount Carmel in giving honour to Our Lady 123
14. The devotion of the Carmelite Scapular 130
15. The Carmelite Scapular and our consecration to Our Lady 140
16. The Carmelite Scapular as a collection of virtues 148
17. The Carmelite Scapular and prayer 154
18. The Carmelite Scapular - a pledge of salvation 162

contents continued...

...contents continued

PART THREE: STORIES AND TRADITION LINKED WITH THE DEVOTION OF OUR LADY OF MOUNT CARMEL 169

19. Stories of the Brown Scapular 170
20. Our Lady of Mount Carmel and sailors and fishermen 185
21. Our Lady of Mount Carmel, patroness of builders 197
22. Our Lady of Mount Carmel as a general and patron of countries and regions of South America 202
23. Our Lady of Mount Carmel in Spain... in the footsteps of Saint Teresa 214
24. Italy: a land of miracles and apparition of Our Lady of Mount Caemel 218
25. The pardon of Notre Dame 233
26. Ireland, Penal Times, and a Missionto Africa 235
27. Icons of Our Lady of Mount Carmel 239
28. The Feast of Our Lady of Mount Carmel in Haifa, Israel 248
29. The celebration of Our Lady of Mount Carmel in the Philippines 256
30. Two celebrations of Our Lady of Mount Carmel in the Andes 262
31. The Italian migrants take Our Lady of Mount Carmel to New York 280
32. Images of Our Lady of Mount Carmel crowned by the Pope or the Vatican Chapter 287
33. Cathedrals dedicated to Our Lady of Mount Carmel 295
34. Carmelite devotion to Our Lady of Sorrows 301

PART FOUR: THE WEDNESDAYS OF OUR LADY (L-Erbghat Tal-Udienza) 303

Introduction 309

35. The Joys of Our Lady 313
36. The Joys of Our Lady in Europe 318
37. Is this a devotion proper to the Carmelites? 348
38. The golden age of the devotion of the Joys of Our Lady in Carmel (XVII and XVIII centuries) 364
39. A serious crisis in the devotion of the Joys of Our Lady in Carmel 379
40. The devotion of the Joys of Our Lady in Mount Carmel in the 19th and 20th centuries 387

contents continued...

...contents continued

41. The Carmelite Chaplet of the seven Joys of Mary at the present day 396

42. Listing the Joys in the Carmelite tradition 401

43. The chaplet of the Joys of Our Lady in the Italian popular Carmelite tradition 420

44. The seven Joys of Our Lady and the Franciscans: the Franciscan Crown or Rosary 446

45. Why does Wednesday have a special significance in the Mediterranean 450

46. The Madonna Bruna of Naples and the devotion to Our Lady of Mount Carmel on Wednesdays 453

47. The seven Wednesdays after Easter - Wednesdays 'of audience' (Tal-Udienza) 459

48. The relationship between the Carmelite Order and Our Lady 461

49. A special name for the seven Wednesdays after Easter 468

50. Other places in Italy in which the title The Madonna dell'Udienza is used 478

51. Our theory about the origin of the name, Wednesdays dell'Udienza 484

52. Malta: Where the Wednesdays Tal-Udienza 490

53. Conclusion by Fr. Borg Gusman 493

54. The link between the Joys of Our Lady, the Scapular, and the Rosary 497

55. The Crowned Icon of Our Lady of Mount Carmel in the Valletta Basilica 502

56. The sanctuary of Our Lady of Mount Carmel in Valletta 504

57. Conclusions of the translator 519

PART FIVE: THE CARMELITE, THE SCAPULAR WEARER, AND THEIR RELATIONSHIP WITH GOD 526

58. The Carmelite and his relationship with God - the Carmelite Rite and the Scapular now 527

59. The contribution of the Carmelites to the concept of the Immaculate Conception 532

60. Some Carmel Saints and Consecration to the Virgin Mary 540

61. The Carmelite Mystics, models of the human person, and relationship with God 553

contents continued...

...contents continued

62. Some Carmelite Saints, consecration to the Virgin Mary, living in Union with God and the Scapular of Carmel 562

63. Carmel, the Scapular, and Love 579

Afterword: Conclusions from this book 585

Appendix: The Scapular of Our Lady of Mount Carmel 592

FORWORD

DEVOTION TO OUR LADY OF MOUNT CARMEL HAS BEEN A VERY widespread devotion within the Maltese Islands since the Carmelites first arrived in Malta in 1418. Indeed it has become part of the National Character of the Maltese Islands.

Large numbers of Maltese wear the Scapular or become Carmelite Tertiaries. But what does the Scapular mean? Our Newest National Saint, Saint George Preca insisted that all members of his Society of Christian Doctrine should wear the Scapular. But what does the Scapular mean? The Scapular signifies a deep spiritual link between the wearer and Mary, and thence between the wearer and her Son Jesus. It is in fact a link which means that the wearer lives constantly in the presence of God, who lives with us, as Saint Teresa of Avila described so well in her 'Interior Castle'. Thus this book argues that wearing the scapular implies an ever deepening commitment to a relationship with Christ , who abides within us; a relationship which is facilitated by our relationship with His Mother Mary. This is the reality which explains the promises which , since Simon Stock's vision of 1251, are attached to the scapular.

The Centre in Malta for the Devotion of the Scapular is the Basilica of Our Lady of Mount Carmel in Valletta. In it is the historic painting of Our Lady of Mount Carmel, the first painting in Malta to e crowned by the Vatican Chapter. To all Maltese this painting signifies Our Lady, enthroned as Queen of Heaven and the will of

Jesus that all humanity should receive Graces through His Mother. Hence, not only do the Maltese celebrate her feast on the sixteenth of July, but also each week on Wednesday and Saturday, and especially on the Wednesdays between Easter and Pentecost, when, in Maltese Tradition , Our Lady as Queen receives her supplicants in 'Audience' to impart Graces. This book describes how this devotion came about, and it shows how it is related to the even earlier medieval devotion to the Joys of Our Lady. The author suggests that the devotion to the Joys evolved into many forms in different parts of the world, including that of the rosary, as we know it today, while in Malta it evolved into the devotion that we know as the 'Erbghat ta'l-Udienza'.

But we should look wider to experience the impact of the scapular on humanity. Thus we find the widespread devotion to the scapular by the sailors and fishermen of the Mediterranean, the peoples of Chile and the rest of South America, the population of the Philippines and Italian Immigrants in the USA among others. All are devoted to Our Lady of Mount Carmel and all express their joy at this devotion in their own national ways. Surely, this joy is well placed, because , as this book explains, it is the Joy of living the reality of 'God with Us as experienced through our relationship with His Mother', and therefore of living as Human Beings as God intended us to be.

+Charles Jude Scicluna, Archbishop of Malta

TO SET THE SCENE

THIS BOOK IS ABOUT OUR LADY OF MOUNT CARMEL. HOWEVER, it is not just about a devotion. It is about the historical development of a Religious Order as an order of Prayerful Persons, but not only about that, but it is about the impact of that Order on huge numbers of persons, those persons who wear the Carmelite Scapular, so that they constitute a huge mass movement, whose numbers are in millions, who celebrate Our Lady of Mount Carmel all over the world.

These persons do not necessarily know each other, and they celebrate their relationship with Mary in their own way, each according to their own culture - they may be Native Americans in Peru, Maltese and Neapolitans praying in famous shrines, English who have reclaimed the ancient home of the Order in Aylesford, Arab Christians who boast having saved the statue of Our Lady during the first world war, Spanish sailors, Chilean Soldiers, or so many others. Some are organised in confraternities, others are in the Third Order, many others are part of the Confraternity simply because they have chosen to wear the scapular after it was given to them by a priest. But all are united in a relationship with Our Lady. While I have written this book primarily about these lay persons, I have had to write a great deal about the development of the Religious of the Order, but not in detail; the great historian of the Order, Joachim Smet O.Carm. wrote four volumes on that, and his work could have filled many more. What I have done is to describe in simple terms how the understanding of the Order developed over the centuries, so that their understanding of themselves as relating to Mary as their Queen, Mother and Sister, developed into their becoming a group of persons living in deep union with God as a result of their living in union with Mary, as has been described so well by Emanuele Boaga O.Carm.

In parallel with this development were two other processes; one was the increasing association between the friars and the ordinary people- including the rich and Noble like John of Gaunt but most of all the ordinary workers- the Sailors, Builders, Soldiers we have mentioned before, who became associated with the Order as the Order moved from a group of Hermits to a Mendicant order, and, when the Order could not be there, continued, as members of Confraternities or Tertiaries, to relate to their Mother Mary.

Finally, there is an ongoing saga of unusual events - Visions, Miracles, Graces received, which accompanied these other two developments. True, some of these events, especially those of early times, are inadequately documented by today's standards, but others, such as the Fatima Apparitions, are certainly well examined in modern times. But this flow of events, while not being the basis of belief, served to confirm the belief of the people, and encourage their relationship with Mary, their Mother and Sister.

In this 'Post Truth' or 'Fake News' era, we find ourselves faced with a difficulty in understanding the nature of truth. On the one hand, when choosing a medicine to take, we require incontrovertible proof that a medicine will improve our health, on the other, we seem to be willing to accept that anything on the Internet must be true. We fail, sometimes, to understand that every group of persons needs a 'founding story' in order to give the group coherence. So we happily label traditions handed down from one generation to next as 'unproven' without any concern for the ordinary person who learnt stories at his Mother's knee, so that a person's very existence and identity may be threatened when deeply held beliefs are challenged. But for us, the stories we are told do not depend on themselves, but are stories which have been held with conviction by huge numbers of persons over the centuries, and most important of all, the truths behind the stories have been independently accepted as doctrinally true by the teaching 'Magisterium' of the Catholic Church. When what my mother taught me is exactly the same as what the Church's authority tells us, then I can certainly believe in Confidence.

Hence, the story in this book indeed shows that those countless thousands of persons who over the centuries have celebrated Our Lady of Mount Carmel do indeed have something to celebrate. They can celebrate the fact that they are Human Beings, made each one with the dignity of being in the Image of God. They can celebrate that they have a Mother and Sister and Queen- Mary – who loves them and who is also the Mother of God and the spouse of the Holy Spirit. They can celebrate that, if they are faithful to Mary and Jesus, at the end of their lives they will find eternal life in Heaven.

This book was compiled from many sources. For the history of the Carmelite Order I depend a great deal on Fr. Emanuele Boaga's book 'The Lady of the Place'. For the doctrine of the Scapular I depend on a translation of a Maltese Carmelite, Fr. Ewgenju Tonna, who in turn depends on Fr. Ludovico Saggi. For the history of the Joys of Mary and the Wednesdays of Our Lady, I depend on my friend Fr. Valentin Borg Guzman, but I have used and quoted many other authors, Carmelite and otherwise. This book in fact was originally a translation of Father Borg Guzman and Father Tonna's work, before I began adding much more material to it. I also included Fr. Charlo Camilleri's work about the Painting in the Valletta Basilica.

After I had worked on four parts to this book, in which I used Carmelite Authors to describe the development of the Order, the history and theology of the Scapular, and the impact of the Scapular on those devotees who use it across the world, a fifth part almost wrote itself. In it I argue, using the writings of Carmelite Theologians, and Saints who have worn the scapular, that the centre of the Message of the Scapular is living in union with or in the presence of God all the time, and that this is achieved by being united with Mary and through her with Jesus. This seems to me the ultimate way in which we should always live our lives; open to the will of God, guided by Him but also doing things to the best of our ability. What I realised is that it is not simply a few Great Carmelite Saints but in fact everyone who wears the scapular, indeed all Christians, who are called to live this life; the scapular is simply a reminder of the commitment we made when we agreed to wear it. Given that this is so, indeed all those who are devotees of Our Lady and the scapular have much to celebrate.

I dedicate this book to Anna and Sophie, two Catholic students of mine to whom I attempted to introduce the scapular in Cambridge, and to their families. Also I dedicate this to Molly, another of my students whose interest in my work always makes it possible to share it with her, and to Hannah, Michaela, and Elin, whose singing in praise of God is so beautiful, and to Annalisa and Beppe and to Claranne and her family , for their friendship, Most of all, I also dedicate it to Anne, my wife, who has put up with me while I worked on this text for many years.

INTRODUCTION

A brief account of the origins of the Carmelite Order and of its development of Devotion to Our Lady, to put in perspective both the development of the devotions of The Scapular of Carmel and the Wednesdays 'Tal-Udienza' and the presence of the Carmelite Order in Malta

(Based on Boaga, The Lady of the Place, and the Website of the Maltese Carmelite Province)

This book is about the development of the devotion of Our Lady of Mount Carmel, with Her Scapular, as well as the devotion to the Wednesdays of Our Lady, called l-Erbgħat Tal-Udienza, however it is necessary, if these devotions are to be understood, to put them within the context of the history of the Carmelite Order and the development of its devotion to Our Lady, as well as the history of the entry of the Carmelites into Malta. Here, then, is a brief account of the development of the Order.

Mount Carmel is a promontory near Haifa, Israel. After the first crusade, Western Hermits, struck by its beauty, settled there. They built a church dedicated to Our Lady, in the center of their settlement. They saw themselves as being Mary's own order, and Carmel as being Mary's own Place; they received a rule from the Ordinary of the Diocese of Jerusalem, Saint Albert, some time between 1206 and 1214[1], thus they became the Carmelite Order. The rule was one designed for hermits.

The new Order had two great influences on Mount Carmel; on the one hand, there were numerous historical references on Mount Carmel to the Prophet Elias, who had lived on Mount Carmel and driven out the False Prophets of Baal, and had seen within the cloud rising from the sea a vision of Our Lady. On the other hand, was Our Lady, patroness of the Chapel of Mount Carmel, in which her Icon stayed. She was linked with Mount Carmel by numerous legends, such as the idea that she used to bring the Child Jesus to Carmel to visit the 'Sons of the Prophets', followers of Elias. The story of Elias' vision of Our Lady in the cloud linked these two influences.[1]

Hence the first Carmelites saw themselves as being Mary's own order, and Carmel as being Mary's own Place, a place of beauty, they defended this affiliation with Mary against all other orders.[1,6]

As the Carmelites moved from the Holy Land into Europe, their rule was adapted so that they became mendicant friars, and thus better able to mix with the common people and to evangelise. This brought them into 'competition' with the other mendicant orders such as the Franciscans and the Dominicans. However, some aspects of their rule, such as that each lived in a cell, remained that of hermits.[1,2]

At the end of Saint Louis' first crusade to the Holy Land in 1254, he took six Carmelites back to France with him and the Order had begun to found houses throughout Europe from 1238 onwards. However, when Saint Jean d'Acre fell in 1291, they were forced to withdraw from Mount Carmel by the Saracens.[1]

One very important route by which the Carmelites came to Europe was via England. Aylesford Priory, or 'The Friars' to give it its traditional name, was founded in Kent in 1242 when the first Carmelites arrived from the Holy Land.[3] They came under the patronage of Richard de Grey, a crusader, who gave them a small piece of land at his manor of Aylesford. Other patrons gave the Carmelites Hulme in Northumbria, and they spread throughout England.

The third route by which the Carmelites came to Europe was Sicily and Italy. It is likely that they arrived in Sicily at Messina, brought by ships from Amalfi, probably in 1238. They spread through the Island. The other site of entry to Italy was Naples, **Santa Maria del Carmine** (Our Lady of Mount Carmel), or the Carmine Maggiore is a church in Naples, Italy. It is at one end of Piazza Mercato. The church was founded in the 13th century by Carmelite friars driven from the Holy Land in the Crusades, presumably arriving in the Bay of Naples aboard Amalfitan ships.[4] Some sources, however, place the original refugees from Mount Carmel as early as the eighth century. Within this Church is an Icon, the Madonna Bruna, said to have been brought from Mount Carmel.

Once they had arrived in Europe, the Carmelites developed from Hermits into Mendicant Friars, in direct competition with the Franciscans and the Dominicans. These orders also had great devotion to Our Lady, but the Carmelites tenaciously defended their claim to be Our Lady's Order.

In 1251, **St Simon Stock** (died 1265), Prior General of the Order, was said to have had a vision of Our Lady promising her protection to those who wore the Carmelite habit. She promised that those who died wearing it would be safe from the fires of Hell. The part of the Habit which she gave Simon Stock in the vision was the scapular, a piece of the habit worn by serfs to show which Lord they belonged to.[5]

However, in the meantime, the tensions with the other Mendicant Orders continued. Here we show a timeline which illustrates over what period tensions with the other mendicant orders lasted.Over that period, as a defence, the Carmelites insisted that they were 'Mary's Order' par excellence.[6]

- *On 30 January 1226 Pope Honorius III approved their rule of life in the bull Ut vivendi normam.*
- *About 20 years later on 1 October 1247, in consultation with Dominican theologians Cardinal Hugh of Saint Cher and William -Bishop of Tortose, Pope Innocent IV revised the Rule slightly in the decree Quae Honorem to reflect the realities of the mendicant and monastic life to which the original hermits had been forced to adapt due to the threat of Muslim attacks in Palestine. It later underwent mitigations which were not in the original text.*
- *The Second Council of Lyon in 1274 decreed that no order founded after 1215 should be allowed to continue. However, the Carmelites were allowed to continue under certain restrictions.*
- *However later Carmelite apologists, from the fourteenth century onwards, interpreted the Second Council of Lyon as a confirmation of the Order.*
- *Such tensions may in part explain why, at a General Chapter*

in London in 1281, the order asserted that it had ancient origins from Elijah and Elisha at Mount Carmel.

- *In 1286, Honorius IV confirmed the Carmelite Rule,*
- *In 1298 Boniface VIII formally removed the restrictions placed on the Order by the Second Council of Lyon.*
- *In 1326, John XXII's bull Super Cathedram extended to the order all the rights and exemptions that existed for the older existing Franciscans and Dominicans, signalling an acceptance of the Carmelites at the heart of Western religious life.*

Until now, the Carmelites continued to deepen their commitment to Mary, It is worth following Boaga's timeline to describe development of Marian Devotion in the early Order;[6]

- ***In the Beginning*** *Allegiance to Mary – Protection, Dedication, Allegiance to the Lord and to the Lady of The Place.*
- *Then Patronage of Mary; Dedication of Churches, Title of the Order (bull 1252), Marian Apostolate (Toulouse 1264), Profession made to God and to Mary (1281) Habit; a sign and symbol of the virgin Mary, Liturgical regulations, Imitation of Virtues, Remembrance and prayer. Prayer of supplication, Imitation of her Virtues, Exemplary nature of Mary's Maternity for those who would conceive Jesus in their Hearts, Marian devotion (liturgical regulations, pilgrimages, shrines, images)*
- *Mary - The Patroness-'Domina Loci' - 'De Institutione', Baconthorpe, Arnold Bostius*
- ***XIV century*** *Mary IMMACULATE; Virgo Purissima Mary - seen as Sister and Mother of the Carmelites; (The Carmelites changed their cloak to white from striped in Honour of the Immaculate Conception)*
- *Sister, so Virginity,Listening to the word, Imitation, Faith*

- *Mother, so Filial Love, Praise to the mother, Prayer in time of need, Contemplation of the life and virtues of Mary. A life of dependence upon Mary, Imitation of Mary's Virtues*
- ***XV Century**, Imitation of Mary's Virtues, Imitatio Christi*
- ***XVI Century** Mary model of Perfection on the Journey into God; Teresa of Jesus, John of the Cross, Mary Magdalene de' Pazzi, Mystical union with Mary*
- ***XVII Century** Mystical union with Mary in perfect harmony with the central position of Christ Michael of St. Augustine /Marie Peyt*
- ***XVIII Century**, XIX-XX Century Our Lady of the Scapular Emphasis on the Holy Scapular as a pastoral instrument, Privileges and Popular devotion*
- ***XIX-XX** Century Exemplarity of Mary; Teresa of the Child Jesus, Elizabeth of the Trinity, Edith Stein, Titus Brandsma Imitation as the best form of devotion, recovery of the Biblical Approach, Mary, a way to holiness, To be 'Theotokos' like Mary*
- ***Vatican II Council**.*

What happened is that over the 13th to 17th Century, the whole thrust of development of Carmelite Devotion is about deepening the Carmelite's relationship with Mary and with God, while it is only in the 16th and Seventeenth Century that the Scapular Vision, and therefore the general use of the scapular, becomes generally talked about as being important.[6]

In 1322, it was said that Pope John XXII had experienced a vision in which Our Lady had announced the Sabbatine Privilege, but the debates around this lasted till 1613, so it was only after this date that the Carmelites could preach about the privilege, and thus definitively preach the scapular devotion. The scapular, however, remains a sign of the wearer's devotion to Mary.

This is reflected in the Iconography of the Order; the Madonna Bruna, and other early Icons, such as the Florence Madonna del Popolo are 'Mother and Child' Icons - of the type referred to as Our Lady of Tenderness, **Eleoúsa**, without any sign of the scapular, which becomes very important from the 16th century onwards.[6]

Where does the entry of the Carmelites into Malta fit with these timelines of the development of Carmelite Devotion? Here is, from the Carmelite Website, the account of the development of the Maltese Convents[7];

'The Carmelites arrived in Malta in 1418, when the noblewoman, Margaret d'Aragon, deeded the chapel and surrounding land of Lunzjata (Rabat) to any religious Order that would undertake the incumbent religious duties. The Carmelites accepted the offer.

- *Subsequently, they opened priories in*
- *Valletta (1570),*
- *Vittoriosa (1582-1652),*
- *Mdina (1659),*
- *Balluta - Sliema (1892),*
- *Santa Venera (2 houses: 1913 and 1980),*
- *Fgura (1945)*
- *Fleur-de-lys (1947).*

Thus, the early Carmelite Church is named after the Annunciation (Not Our Lady of Mount Carmel), and the Valletta Church was built in 1570, and Mdina in 1659. Valletta and Mdina are also named for the Annunciation (Later the dedication of the Valletta church was changed to Our Lady of Mount Carmel). Later, from the nineteenth Century, subsequent foundations can be named for Our Lady of Mount Carmel, that is, of the Scapular. Thus, the naming of the Carmelite Churches in Malta reflects the development of devotion to Mary in the Order in General.

References.

1 *https://en.wikipedia.org/wiki/Carmelites*
2 *https://en.wikipedia.org/wiki/Louis_IX_of_France*
3 *https://en.wikipedia.org/wiki/Aylesford_Priory*
4 *http://www.santuariocarminemaggiore.it/*
5 *https://en.wikipedia.org/wiki/Simon_Stock*
6 *Emanuele Boaga O.Carm. The Lady of the Place, Mary in the History and in the life of Carmel Edizioni Carmelitane Roma 2001.*
7 *www.ocarm.org/en/content/ocarm/province-malta*

Dr Mark Agius
Rector of the Archconfraternity of Our Lady of Mount Carmel, Valletta

Part One

History

Dr. Mark Agius M.D.

ONE

THE EARLY HISTORY OF THE CARMELITE ORDER

THE ORIGINS OF THE CARMELITES LIE ON MOUNT CARMEL IN THE Holy Land. Unlike most Religious Orders the Carmelites have no one founder[1,2.]

Earliest historical accounts find the first Carmelites already settled as Christian hermits on Mount Carmel - a mountainous ridge in Israel-Palestine - around the year 1200 (i.e. some 800 years ago)[1,2].

The hermits lived by the fountain or well of the prophet Elijah (whose exploits on Carmel are described in the Bible's *Books of the Kings*).The hermits took as their particular model the prophet Elijah, a model of inspiration for religious life in the Churches of both East and West[1,2].

> *At the time of the Crusades to the Holy Land, hermits settled in various places throughout Palestine. Some of these, 'following the example of Elijah, a holy man and a lover of solitude, adopted a solitary life-style on Mount Carmel, near a spring called Elijah's Fountain. In small cells, similar to the cells of a beehive, they lived as God's bees, gathering the divine honey of spiritual consolation.'* (Carmelite Constitutions 1995)[3]

The date of the foundation of the Order of Our Lady of Mount Carmel has been under discussion from the fourteenth century to the present day, the order claiming for its founders the prophets Elias and Eliseus, whereas modern historians, beginning with Baronius, deny its existence previous to the second half of the twelfth century[1,2].

All of Mount Carmel was surrounded with a host of Sacred Traditions related to Elijah and Mary. The book 'On the Institution of the First Monks' as well as a letter said to be from St. Cyril of Constantinople 'On the progress of his Order', written about 1230, connects the order with the Prophets of the Old Law. The book 'On the Institution of the First Monks', was mentioned for the first time in 1342, and was published in 1370. It purports to be written by John, the forty-fourth (more accurately the forty-second) Bishop of Jerusalem (A.D. 400)[1,2].

The silence of Palestine pilgrims previous to A.D. 1150, of chroniclers, of early documents, in one word the negative evidence of history has induced modern historians to disregard the claims of the order, and to place its foundation in or about the year 1155 when it is first spoken of in documents of undoubted authenticity. Even the evidence of the order itself was not always very explicit. The General Chapter of 1287 (unedited) speaks of the order as of a plantation of recent growth (*plantatio novella*)[1,2].

The Greek monk John Phocas who visited the Holy Land in 1185 relates that he met on Carmel a Calabrian (i.e. Western) monk who some time previously, on the strength of an apparition of the Prophet Elias, had gathered around him about ten hermits with whom he led a religious life in a small monastery near the grotto of the prophet[1,2]. Rabbi Benjamin de Tudela had already in 1163 reported that the Christians had built there a chapel in honour of Elias. Jacques de Vitry and several other writers of the end of the twelfth and the beginning of the thirteenth centuries give similar accounts[1,2].

The exact date of the foundation of the hermitage may be gathered from the life of Aymeric, Patriarch of Antioch, a relative of the 'Calabrian' monk, Berthold; on the occasion of a journey to Jerusalem in 1154 or the following year he appears to have visited the latter and assisted him in the establishment of the small community; it is further reported that on his return to Antioch (c. 1160) he took with him some of the hermits, who founded a convent in that town and another on a neighbouring mountain; both of these monasteries were destroyed in 1268[1,2].

The first Carmelite community on Mount Carmel was unusual in that most of the hermits were laymen, living as solitaries in a community. Hospitality was no doubt one of the original values for the early Carmelites, thus Mount Carmel served as a place of rest for pilgrims in the Holy Land, and this encouraged new members, since some pilgrim were so impressed by the beauty of Carmel and the simple lifestyle of the community of hermits who lived there that they stayed[1,2].

A notice written between 1247 and 1274 (Mon. Hist. Carmelit., 1, 20, 267) states that hermits, the 'sons of Elias', dwelt on Mount Carmel, and that their successors after the Incarnation built there a chapel in honour of Our Lady, for which reason they were called in papal

Bulls 'Friars of Blessed Mary of Mount Carmel'. Thus, The chapel which stood in the midst of the hermits' cells was dedicated to Mary, the Mother of Jesus[1,2]. The oratory was dedicated to the Virgin in her aspect of Our Lady, Star of the Sea, (Latin: *Stella Maris*)[1,2].

Stretching out into the deep blue of the Mediterranean Sea, Mount Carmel in the springtime of the year is aglow with the vivacious colouring of flowering shrubs and plants. The early hermits saw the sheer beauty of Mount Carmel itself as a symbol of Mary's spiritual beauty. Thus Mary increasingly became a spiritual companion for the hermits on their interior journey to the Lord[1,2].

There are many witnesses to the presence of the Carmelites on Mount Carmel, and The Church dedicated to Our Lady; They include; La Citez de Hierusalem written between 1220 and 1231, Le chemins et les peregrinages de La Terre Sante redaction A before 1265, Le chemins et les peregrinages de La Terre Sante redaction B, 1268, Brother Philip Bussero between 1285-1291, Umberto of Dijon 1332, Giacomo of Verona 1335, Robert of S.Severino 1458[1,2].

Numerous Legends Linked Mary with Carmel[1,2]; these included; Elijah, Elisha and the sons of the Prophets observe virginity. (Patristic literature), The origin of Elijah and Mary from one Tribe of Aaron (Patristic literature), The dream of Sabac, father of Elijah (Patristic and Medieval literature). The visits of Mary and her virgin Companions to Mount Carmel (Hebrew literature) The frequent visits of Mary to the religious on Mount Carmel because of its closeness to Nazareth, and including the suggestion that she would bring her son, Jesus, with her to Mount Carmel, the founding of a house in Jerusalem, near the house of saint Anne, where the Virgin was conceived, by the Golden Gate, the membership of St. Cyril of Alexandria of the Order, and the concession to him by the council of Ephesus to wear the white cloak in honour of Mary[1,2].

This dedication of their first chapel to Our Lady had a fundamental influence on the later development of Marian Spirituality in the Order. The cause of this dedication is in the hearts of the hermits. Dedicating a church to Mary in the Holy land always had something to do with the belief of Mary's Connection to the place dedicated to her[2].

The Fathers of the Church, and later, Carmelite Writers linked the beauty of the place with Mary, quoting; 'Your Head is adorned like Carmel' (Sg.7, 6), 'The glory of Lebanon was given to her, the beauty of Carmel and Sharon' (Is.35, 2), Thus, Mary became the Lady of the Place, Domina Loci[2].

The Carmelites would know, that according to the rules of Chivalry and in the Feudal System, it was possible (rarely) for a Lady in her own right to own an estate and castle and to manage her affairs, with Knights and Vassals acknowledging her as their Lady and carrying out her wishes, and honouring her in a chivalrous manner. This attitude sets the scene for the Carmelite claim of a Marian Title of their order, in other words that they were Mary's Order Par Excellence. Carmelite writers consistently defended this claim[2].

Under Berthold's successor, Brocard, some doubts arose as to the proper form of life of the Carmelite hermits. Between the years 1206 and 1214, the community on Mount Carmel petitioned Albert, the Latin Patriarch of Jerusalem for a rule of life. Thus, the Patriarch of Jerusalem, Albert de Vercelli, then residing at Tyre, settled the difficulty by writing a short rule, part of which is literally taken from that of St. Augustine (c. 1210). This 'formula for living' that Carmelites follow to this day as the *Rule of Saint Albert*[1].

> *Later, St. Albert, Patriarch of Jerusalem brought the hermits together, at their request, into a single 'collegium'; he gave them a formula for living which expressed their own eremitical ideals ('propositum') and reflected the spirit of the so-called pilgrimage to the Holy Land and of the early community of Jerusalem. Moved by 'their love of the Holy Land', these hermits consecrated themselves in this Land to the One who had paid for it by the shedding of his blood, in order that they might serve him, clothed in the habit of religious poverty, 'persevering 'in holy penance' and forming a fraternal community.* (Constitutions 1995)[3]

The hermits were to elect a prior to whom they should promise obedience; they were to live in cells apart from one another, where they had to recite the Divine Office according to the Rite of the church of the Holy Sepulchre, or, if unable to read, certain other prayers, and to spend their time in pious meditation varied by manual labour. Every morning they met in chapel for Mass, and on Sundays also for chapter. They were to have no personal property; their meals were to be served in their cells; but they were to abstain from flesh meat except in cases of great necessity, and they had to fast from the middle of September until Easter. Silence was not to be broken between Vespers and Terce of the following day, while from Terce till Vespers they were to guard against useless talk. The prior was to set a good example by humility, and the brothers were to honour him as the representative of Christ. This was the originating act of the Order, who took the name 'Order of the Brothers of Our Lady of Mount Carmel' or Carmelites[2].

Therefore, because they were without a specific founder, the Carmelites have continually looked to the great figures of Elijah and Mary for inspiration on the basis that they had first settled by the Well of Elijah on Carmel and dedicated the first chapel to the Mother of God. Throughout their history, these key figures have helped the Carmelites clarify their identity and renew their spirit[1,2].

Mary and Elijah provided a wonderful integration of the two streams of the contemplative Carmelite tradition: prayer blended with active service; meditation combined with prophecy; reflection informed by and informing apostolic work[1,2].

Elijah and Mary provide Carmelites with an example to imitate. The Carmelites struggled with fear, stood in the face of very difficult questions, and deeply felt the pains of human life. They, being human, may appear fragile and vulnerable, but they were filled with a deep conviction which lies at the heart of the Carmelite spirit: God is alive! God is present! God is with us! - in the words of the Prophet Elijah 'God lives, in whose presence I stand'[1,2].

Within a few decades, these monastic hermits left the troubled Holy Land and the Carmelite order spread throughout Europe[1]. Initially, no provision was made for any further organisation beyond the community on Carmel itself, whence it must be inferred that until 1210 no other foundation had been made except those at and near Antioch, which were probably subject to the patriarch of that city. After that date new communities sprang up at Saint Jean d'Acre, Tyre, Tripoli, Jerusalem, in the Quarantena, somewhere in Galilee *(monasterium Valini)*, and in some other localities which are not known, making in all about fifteen. Most of these were destroyed almost as soon as they were built, and at least in two of them some of the brothers were put to death by the Saracens. Several times the hermits were driven from Carmel, but they always found means to return; they even built a new monastery in 1263 (in conformity with the revised rule) and a comparatively large church, which was still visible towards the end of the fifteenth century. Finally, Mount Carmel was taken by the Saracens in 1291, the brothers, while singing the Salve Regina, were put to the sword, and the convent was burnt[1].

So, soon after they received Albert's Rule, the Carmelites were forced to leave the known slopes of Carmel and settle in Europe. In all probability many of the first Carmelites had been crusaders or pilgrims and they naturally headed for their own countries. Carmel spread first to Cyprus, then to France, and then to England in 1241. Colonies of hermits were sent out to Cyprus, Sicily, Marseilles, and Valenciennes (c. 1238). St. Louis, King of France, visited Mount Carmel in 1254 and brought six French hermits to Charenton near Paris where he gave them a convent. Some brothers of English nationality accompanied the Barons de Vescy and Grey on their return journey from the expedition of Richard, Earl of Cornwall (1241), and made foundations at Hulne near Alnwick in

Northumberland, Bradmer (Norfolk), Aylesford, and Newenden (Kent)[1]. From Sicily, the Carmelites arrived in Naples. With them they brought an icon, now known as the Madonna Bruna[2]. It was said to have been brought directly from Mount Carmel[2]. Possibly it may have been a copy of the Icon of the Chapel of Mount Carmel, The Mother of God called 'La Bruna' belongs to the 'Eleousa' or 'Mother of Tenderness' type of Icon, which, through the flow of the prayer that accompanies her presence in Naples since the thirteenth century, offers to those who contemplate the Icon a singular story of faith and the proclamation of 'The Word made man' (St. Mary Magdalene de' Pazzi), through the testimony of the family of Carmel[2]. There is no doubt that the icon of the Mother of God 'La Bruna' was made in the east, one cannot specify whether the source of the prototype was the Byzantine iconography school rather than the Adriatic: Cypriot Cretan or Venetian-Cretan[2].

The first prior generals were St. Berthold, St. Brocard, St. Cyril, Berthold (or Bartholomew), and Alan (1155-1247). At the first chapter which was held at Aylesford, St. Simon Stock was elected general (1247-65)[1,3].

References

1 *https://en.wikipedia.org/wiki/Carmelites*

2 *Emanuele Boaga O.Carm. The Lady of the Place, Mary in the History and in the life of Carmel Edizioni Carmelitane Roma 2001.*

3 *https://www.ocarm.org/en/content/ocarm/brief-history-carmelites*

TWO

Saint Simon Stock and the Scapular Vision

It was in this atmosphere during which the Carmelites struggled to establish their existence within the church as a mendicant religious order and to establish themselves as the Mary's Order that St. Simon Stock is said to have had a vision of Our Lady.

Saint **Simon Stock**, an Englishman who lived in the 13th century, was an early prior general of the Carmelite religious order. Little is known about his life with any historical certainty.[1] The Blessed Virgin Mary is traditionally said to have appeared to him and given him the Carmelite habit, the Brown Scapular, with a promise that those who die wearing it will be saved. Thus, popular devotion to Saint Simon Stock is usually associated with devotion to Our Lady of Mount Carmel.

He is believed to have lived at Aylesford in Kent, a place that hosted in 1247 the first general chapter of the Carmelite Order held outside the Holy Land, and where there is still a monastery of Carmelite friars.[2] Saint Simon was probably the fifth or sixth prior general of the Carmelites (historical evidence suggests perhaps from about 1256-1266), and died in Bordeaux, France, where he was buried[3].

According to traditional accounts, the Blessed Virgin Mary appeared at Cambridge to St. Simon Stock, who was Prior General of the Carmelite Order in the middle of the 13th century.[4] The earliest reference to this tradition, dating from the late 14th century, states that 'St. Simon was an Englishman, a man of great holiness and devotion, who always in his prayers asked the Virgin to favour his Order with some singular privilege. The Virgin appeared to him holding the Scapular in her hand saying, 'This is for you and yours a privilege; the one who dies in it will be saved[3].'

In other words, Mary's promise to an early Carmelite, Saint Simon Stock, is that anyone who remains faithful to the Carmelite vocation until death will be granted the grace of final perseverance. In answer to his appeal for help for his oppressed order she recommended the Brown Scapular of the Our Lady of Mount Carmel to him and promised salvation for the faithful who wore it piously[2].

This promise was based on the Carmelite tradition that the Blessed Virgin Mary appeared to St. Simon Stock at Cambridge, England in 1251[3].

Historicity of the Vision

However, this issue is subject to debate among scholars. Today historians question whether this Marian apparition took place at all, others argue that it was another Carmelite brother who witnessed the apparition. The Carmelite Order states on their website 'Although the historicity of the scapular vision is rejected, the scapular itself has remained for all Carmelites a sign of Mary's motherly protection and as a personal commitment to follow Jesus in the footsteps of his Mother, the perfect model of all his disciples.[6]'

The great Carmelite authors of the 14th century do not mention the scapular at all. Challenges to the historicity of the scapular vision (and passionate defences of it) are not a new phenomenon; a notable challenge came in 1653, from a scholar at the University of Paris, Fr. Jean de Launoy. In response, a Carmelite named Fr. John Cheron published a fragment of a letter which he purported to be an account by Saint Simon Stock's secretary Peter Swanington (or Swanyngton), giving details of the Saint's life, and the scapular vision.[1,3,4] This document was also the origin of the date that has become traditional for the vision, July 16, 1251 (July 16 was already in the 17th century the feast of Our Lady of Mount Carmel, though that liturgy made no reference to the scapular). Today, scholars affirm that this document was a forgery and Fr. Cheron himself the likely author[1,3,4].

The Place in which the Apparition happened

Thus, it is said that Simon Stock lived at Aylesford as prior general, and his relic – his skull brought from Bordeaux – is presently at Aylesford, but the tradition, based, of course on Chinon's Document, is that the site of the vision was Cambridge, but not the old Carmelite Monastery at Friar's Court in Queens' College, as this monastery was built later than 1251, in 1292. We can imagine Simon Stock travelling to Cambridge in 1251 to dispute with the other religious orders already established there – the Franciscans were involved in the founding of the University, and the Dominican convent was founded in 1238. Tired after his Journey, in unfamiliar accommodation, and stressed before his disputations, he prays the 'Flos Carmeli' fervently, and then experiences the Apparition of Our Lady.

Although many believe that the apparition occurred in Aylesford, the first evidence available- even if possibly tainted- suggests Cambridge as the site of the Apparition, and the website of Aylesford Priory itself says 'Some believe the vision happened at Aylesford but it is more commonly thought to have occurred in Cambridge.[5]'

It is worth looking at the timescale of the apparition in relation to the development of the University of Cambridge. The University of Cambridge got its Royal Charter in 1209. The Scapular vision is said to have occurred in 1251. The University received Papal Approval from Pope John the Twenty Second on 9th June 1318.

The Institution of the Feast of Our Lady of Mount Carmel, or of the Scapular

The discussion about whether the Carmelites were Our Lady's Order continued, Pope Honorius III approved the order in 1226 and In 1374 the Carmelite John Hornby defended the Marian Title of the order [and the Immaculate Conception] against the Dominican, John Stokes in the University of Cambridge, The University senate judged in Favour of the Carmelites. It was this that led to the feast of 16th July being instituted in the Order in England to celebrate this victory and the approval of the order by the Second Council of Lyon (1272), so Cambridge continued an important place for the history of the order and the scapular.

In 1609, after Robert Cardinal Bellarmine examined the origins of the feast, it was declared the patronal feast of the Carmelite order. From then on, the celebration of the feast began to spread, with various popes approving the celebration in southern Italy, then Spain and her colonies, then Austria, Portugal and her colonies, and finally in the Papal States, before Benedict XIII placed the feast on the universal calendar of the Latin Church in 1726[1,3,4]. It has since been adopted by some Eastern Rite Catholics as well[1,3,4].

References

1 *https://en.wikipedia.org/wiki/Carmelites*

2 *Emanuele Boaga O.Carm. The Lady of the Place, Mary in the History and in the life of Carmel Edizioni Carmelitane Roma 2001.*

3 *https://en.wikipedia.org/wiki/Simon_Stock*

4 *https://en.wikipedia.org/wiki/Our_Lady_of_Mount_Carmel*

5 *https://www.flickr.com/photos/john_berghout/8218257350*

6 *https://ocarm.org/en/item/107-st-simon-stock-religious*

THREE

THE SABBATINE PRIVILEGE

THE SECOND APPARITION OF OUR LADY OF MOUNT CARMEL LINKED specifically with the scapular is that of the 'Sabbatine Privilege'.

In 1322, seventy one years after she had made her promise to Saint Simon Stock, she is said to have appeared to Pope John XXII and promised in favour of those who wear her Scapular speedy release from Purgatory, particularly on Saturday, provided certain conditions are fulfilled[1, 2,3].

This second promise in favour of those who wear Mary's Scapular is known as the Sabbatine Privilege. It is called the Sabbatine Privilege because of Our Lady's special mention of Saturday (in Latin, Sabbatum means Saturday) as the day when she will come to the assistance of her children[1].

Saturday is traditionally honoured as Our Lady's day—the liturgy provides special Masses in her honour and we are encouraged to turn our thoughts and prayers to her on that day.

Historical research has shown that the alleged fourteenth-century appearance of the Blessed Mother to Pope John XXII is without historical foundation. As a matter of fact, in the year 1613 the Holy See determined that the decree establishing the 'Sabbatine Privilege' was unfounded and the Church admonished the Carmelite Order not to preach this doctrine. Unfortunately, the Order did not always comply with this directive of the Holy See[1].

At the time the Carmelites were instructed to stop mentioning the 'Sabbatine Privilege' the Holy See acknowledged that the faithful *may* devoutly believe that the Blessed Virgin Mary by her continuous intercession, merciful prayers, merits, and special protection will assist the souls of deceased brothers and sisters and members of the confraternity, especially on Saturday, the day which the church dedicates to the Blessed Virgin[1].

The Carmelites were forbidden to preach the Sabbatine privilege — a prohibition they did not always honour — although the faithful were to be allowed to believe, with certain conditions, 'that the Blessed Virgin by her continuous intercession, merciful prayers, merits and special protection will assist the souls of deceased brothers and members of the confraternity (of the Scapular), especially on Saturday, the day which the church dedicates to the Blessed Virgin[1].'

Boaga confirms that indeed the Portuguese Inquisition banned the teaching about the Sabbatine Bull. In the subsequent Appeal to Rome, the Carmelite wish to preach the privilege was strongly defended by Cardinal (Later Saint) Robert Bellarmine, as well as by Cardinal Sfrondati, and as a result, though the Sabbatine Bull was condemned, the preaching of the Sabbatine Privilege was permitted to the Carmelites. However It was also forbidden that pictures be made of Our Lady descending to Purgatory, in the midst of the flames, but only the angels would go there to assist the holy souls and lead them to heaven through the intercession of Mary[1].

Christian P. Ceroke, O. Carm discusses the Sabbatine Privilege further...

> 'The devotion also teaches that the aid of Mary may be confidently expected in purgatory by all those who have faithfully worn the Scapular and have fulfilled two other conditions: the practice of chastity according to one's state of life and the daily recitation of the Little Office of the Blessed Virgin[3].'

This privilege of the Scapular devotion is believed to originate from an apparition of Mary to Pope John XXII, who then announced this spiritual benefit to the faithful in 1322[3].

The Bull attributed to John XXII, stated that the devotee of the Scapular would be released from purgatory on the Saturday after death.

Because of the allusion to Saturday, the document of John XXII is referred to as the 'Sabbatine Bull' and its Marian privilege is called the 'Sabbatine Privilege[3].'

The Sabbatine Bull was of great importance in the spread of the Scapular devotion during the sixteenth and seventeenth centuries[3]. Throughout this period the popes repeatedly promulgated the Sabbatine Privilege in allusion to the Bull of 1322 attributed to Pope John XXII: Clement VII (1530); Paul III (1534; 1549); Pius IV (1561); Pius V (1566); Gregory XIII (1577); Urban VIII (1628); Clement X (1673; 1674; 1675); Innocent XI (1678; 1679; 1682; 1684)[3].

Since according to the Sabbatine Privilege the souls of the faithful departed would benefit in purgatory from the intercession of the Blessed Virgin, the Church found it useful to stress this privilege in order to demonstrate the legitimacy of the doctrine of indulgences and of Marian devotion[3].

The tradition of the Sabbatine Bull appears to have been first spread during the fifteenth century[3,4].

The Bull was known to the Carmelites Calciuri in 1461 and Leersius in 1483[3].

It was referred to by the Carmelite General Chapter of 1517[3].

Historically, however, the tradition of the Sabbatine Bull is clearly vulnerable to attack[3].

There is no evidence of the Bull in the registers of John XXII[3].

One accepts that the absence of a papal document from the medieval registers is not necessarily a conclusive argument against its authenticity, but there is no other positive historical evidence from other sources to support the papal origin of the Bull. (It is now believed to have originated from an inauthentic papal Sicily bull forged in Sicily in the first half of the fifteenth century). Its literary character is too atypical to suggest that it is the work of John XXII[3].

For these reasons, historians have rejected the authenticity of the Sabbatine Bull[3].

The fact that it is probable that the Bull is spurious casts serious doubt on the belief that the Sabbatine Privilege originated from a Marian apparition to Pope John XXII.

Three theories have been proposed to explain how the tradition of the apparition and the Bull arose[3].

One view is that the tradition originated from an oral statement by John XXII[3]. This theory could explain the spurious nature of the Bull and its unusual style. However, this explanation is too conjectural to win credence[3].

A second theory suggests that the Sabbatine Bull is derived from an original authentic document of John XXII which became corrupt over the course of time[3]. However, no evidence has been produced from existing copies of the Bull to demonstrate a gradual corruption of its text[3].

A third theory suggests that the Bull is a theological interpretation of the Marian promise to St. Simon Stock[3]. Since Mary's Mediation of Grace, of which her promise of eternal salvation is a reflection, embraces the final goal of the Christian life, which is union with God, it is logical to conclude that her maternal assistance makes itself felt in purgatory[3].

This third theory, that is that the Sabbatine Privilege is a more developed understanding of the significance of the Marian promise to St. Simon Stock, is the most likely explanation of the origin of the Sabbatine Bull[3].

The Bull shows a close relationship between the promise to St. Simon Stock and the Sabbatine Privilege'. Thus the Bull states, 'One who perseveres in holy obedience, poverty and chastity — or who will enter the Holy Order — will be saved.'[3]

Then follows the declaration of the Sabbatine Privilege concerning release from purgatory for 'others' who wear the holy 'habit' of the Order[3].

Therefore it appears that the Sabbatine Privilege arose historically from a fuller understanding of the Marian promise to St. Simon Stock[3]. None the less, since the early seventeenth century, Carmelite preaching of the Sabbatine Privilege has been theologically independent from the historical authenticity on the Sabbatine Bull[3].

In 1603 a book containing the privileges of the Carmelite Order, including the Sabbatine privilege, was condemned by the Portuguese Inquisition. Six years later all books mentioning the Sabbatine privilege were put on the Index of Forbidden Books in Portugal. An appeal to Rome ended when the Roman authorities supported the Inquisition's ban[4].

The appeal of the Carmelites against this ban was supported strongly by Cardinal St. Robert Bellarmine, Finally, in 1613 the Holy Office under Pope Paul V issued a decree on the Sabbatine Privilege which took account of the papal bulls of the sixteenth century.

These Bulls had promulgated the privilege according to the tradition of the Sabbatine Bull[4].

The decree of the Holy Office made no reference to the Bull of John XXII or to the tradition of the Marian apparition to him. It simply affirmed the privilege itself[3]. The decree of the Holy Office is as follows:

> The Carmelite Fathers may preach that the Christian people can piously believe in the aid of the souls of the brethren and [confratres] of the Sodality of the Most Blessed Virgin of Mount Carmel. Through her continuous intercessions, pious suffrages, merits, and special protection the Most Blessed Virgin, especially on Saturday, the day dedicated to her by the Church, will help after their death the brethren and members of the Sodality who die in charity. In life they must have worn the habit, observed chastity according to their state, and have recited the Little Office. If they do not know how to recite it, they are to observe the fasts of the Church and to abstain from meat on Wednesdays and Saturdays, except for the feast of Christmas[3].

This decree of Paul V stated in effect that the spiritual authority of the popes of the sixteenth century had sanctioned the Marian teaching of the Sabbatine [3].

This aspect of the devotion of the Brown Scapular was thus declared spiritually fruitful for the laity. (Christian P. Ceroke, O. Carm)[3]

In effect, as Emanuele Boaga O.Carm, says in his book 'The Lady of the Place' (page 108), 'Therefore the Term 'Sabbatine Bull' and reference to it were outlawed in preaching as a support and explanation of the privilege.[1]'

On the other hand, as a result of the decision of the Inquisition, supported by St Robert Bellarmine, and later by several popes, the Sabbatine Privilege was permitted to the Carmelites[1].

After the decree of the Holy of Office of 1613…

- The University of Paris supported the Sabbatine Privilege…
- The decree was reconfirmed in the 17th century…
- It was included in the Summary of Indulgences edited in 1678 under Pope Innocent XI
- Benedict XIV referred to it as a 'Very Wise Decree'
- The decree was reformulated during the pontificate of Pius X in the Summary of Indulgences of July 1908 and the Decree of the Holy Office of 16th December 1910.
- Finally, it was again reconfirmed by Pius XII in his Apostolic Letter Neminem profecto latet of 11th February 1950[1].

Hence the Sabbatine Privilege no longer depends on a spurious bull but on the Magisterium of the Church[4].

It is clear that in the thinking of the Pontifical Magisterium that a proper presentation of the Scapular and the privileges attached to it has to be based on a good theology of Mary's role in the mystery of Christ and of the Church.

Indeed, the power of Mary to help those who wear the scapular is in substance, from the theological point of view, the application of the doctrine of her spiritual motherhood and her role as mediatrix of graces, properly understood…

Mary acts in us but we have to be willing to accept what she does and respond fully by coming to Christ, offered to us by Mary[2].

The scapular devotion then should be understood as a consecration, or, more precisely, an entrusting of oneself to Mary by means of the Carmelite habit and the observance of its conditions.

It thus becomes an effective form and means for fostering fidelity to Christ and to a full acceptance of him in our lives, following the example of Mary[1].' Emanuele Boaga O.Carm, 'The Lady of the Place' (page 109)

References:

1 *Emanuele Boaga O.Carm. The Lady of the Place, Mary in the History and in the life of Carmel Edizioni Carmelitane Roma 2001.*
2 *Rev. Eamon R. Carroll, O. Carm., S.T.D. An Explanation of the Sabbatine Privilege https://www.ocarm.org/en/content/ocarm/explanation-sabbatine-privilege*
3 *Christian P. Ceroke, O. Carm The Scapular Devotion https://www.ewtn .com/library/mary/scapular.htm*
4 *Father Sam Anthony Morello. OCD and Father Patrick McMahon, O.Carm A Catechesis on the Brown Scapular 2000 https://laudateomnes. wordpress.com/2019/07/09/catechesis-on-the-brown-scapular/*

FOUR

The Development Within the Carmelite Order of Devotion to Our Lady and the Wearers of the Scapular and the Carmelite Saints

PRESENTLY, EMANUELE BOAGA O.CARM IS PROBABLY THE LEADING historian of Marian Devotion of the Order. In his book 'The Lady of The Place', he describes the devotion of the Carmelite Order as developing over a number of stages.

In the beginning, he says that the Carmelite Devotion to Mary was characterised by their Allegiance to Mary, their devotion to Mary due to their first Chapel on Mount Carmel implying their Dedication to Mary, her Protection, and their Allegiance to the Lord and to the 'Lady of The Place.'[1]

In the Thirteenth Century, their emphasis was on the Patronage of Mary,[1] and this was evidenced by the Dedication of Churches of the Order to Her, their defence of the Title of the Order (bull 1252), their adopting a Marian Apostolate (Miracle of Toulouse, 1264), the profession they made to God and to Mary (1281), by their seeing their Habit, including their cloak and their scapular as a sign and symbol of the virgin Mary, and by Liturgical regulations, by Imitation of Her Virtues, Prayer of supplication to her, Imitation of her Virtues. They emphasised the Exemplary nature of Mary's

Maternity for those who would conceive Jesus in their Hearts, and they encouraged Marian devotion including promoting pilgrimages, and the veneration of shrines and images of the Virgin Mary. Baconthorpe and Arnold Bostius, the original writers of the Carmelite Order, described Mary as the Patroness of the Carmelites. In the Fourteenth century, The Carmelites are describing Mary as the Immaculate Conception, as Virgo Purissima.[1] They say her as their Sister, imitating her Virginity, especially in listening to the word, imitating her faith in the Lord. They also saw her as their Mother, relating to her with Filial Love, giving Praise to her as the Mother, they promoted Prayer to Her in time of need, they encouraged Contemplation of the life and virtues of Mary, and lived A life of dependence upon Mary. This led to devotion to Mary as the Mother of Sorrows and Mercy.[1]

In the Fifteenth Century, this contemplation on Mary's Virtues developed into Imitation of Mary's Virtues. This led onto Imitation of Christ, Imitatio Christi, and Intimacy with and total giving of self to Mary, and through her to Jesus (Imitation and Union with Mary and Jesus).[1]

In the Sixteenth Century, in the writings of Teresa of Jesus and John of the Cross, Mary is seen as the model of Perfection on the Journey into God, while Mary Magdalene de' Pazzi was, in the same way, describing a Mystical union with Mary and thence with God.[1]

In the seventeenth Century, Michael of St. Augustine and his directee Marie Peyt exemplified Mystical union with Mary in perfect harmony with the central position of Christ.[1]

From the seventeenth Century onwards till the twentieth century, there is emphasis on Our Lady of the Scapular, with Emphasis on the Holy Scapular as a pastoral instrument, its Privileges and on the Popular devotion to Our Lady of Mount Carmel.[1]

Contemporaneously, in the nineteenth and twentieth centuries, there is emphasis on the Exemplarity of Mary,[1] in other words, on Mary as an example, especially in the writings of Teresa of the Child Jesus, Elizabeth of the Trinity, Edith Stein and Titus Brandsma, The Imitation of Mary is seen as the best form of devotion, there is recovery of the Biblical Approach. Mary is seen as a way to holiness, to the extent that the aim is to be 'Theotokos' (Christ Bearing) like Mary.

Finally, in recent Documents of the Order, between 1971-1989, Mary is seen in the context of the mystery of Christ and of the Church and as a source of Inspiration to Christians.[1]

Thus, during these developments, there was a stage, starting with the 17th century, when the use of the scapular became very important in popular devotion,[1] for instance Our Archconfraternity of Our Lady of Mount Carmel in Valletta was founded in 1621. However the popularity of the Brown Scapular antedated this; Pope Paul V had endowed the Brown Scapular with many indulgences in 1606, and had decided that the feast of the Brown Scapular should be on July the sixteenth, and this was extended to the whole church in 1726.[1] In 1609, the Chapter General of the order ordered that the feast of the Brown Scapular or Our Lady of Mount Carmel should be the principal feast of the whole Order.[1] However, the promotion of the Brown Scapular as a major popular devotion antedated this. In the sixteenth century, the chapter general of the Order had decided in 1593 that there should be a monthly procession in honour of Our Lady of Mount Carmel 'in every convent where the Confraternity of Our Lady of Mount Carmel was instituted.'[1]

However, also, it is likely that ever since the coming of the friars to Europe, founders of convents and benefactors would be affiliated with the Order as Confratres, which gave them a right to participation in the prayers and good works of the order, and to suffrages after their death[4] (New Advent Catholic Encyclopaedia). There were no obligations incumbent on the Confratres[4] (New Advent Catholic Encyclopaedia). By the end of the fifteenth century these letters of affiliation as Confrates were very common[4] (New Advent Catholic Encyclopaedia). Out of this confraternity, which stood in no organic connection with the order, arose in the sixteenth century, according to all probability, the Confraternity of the Scapular[4] (New Advent Catholic Encyclopaedia). These developments were acknowledged by the church with the institution of the feast of the Brown Scapular. So there was a gradual development, almost from the beginning of the Order's appearance in Europe till the seventeenth Century of popular devotion to Our Lady and which was evidenced by the development of the Brown Scapular Confraternities[2, 3] and WHICH WAS UNDERPINNED by the development of the devotion to Our Lady within the Order which was described after Boaga above.

All of these Carmelites wore the scapular. This is a description of the habit of the order soon after the Order appeared in Europe. When the Carmelites first arrived in Europe, the habit consisted of a tunic, girdle, scapular, and hood of either black, brown or grey colour (the colour became subject to numberless changes according to the different subdivisions and reforms of the order), and of a mantle composed of four white and three black vertical stripes or rays, whence the friars were popularly called *Fratres barrati, or virgulati, or de pica* (magpie). Under Peter de Millaud (1274-94) a change was made in the habit. In 1287 this variegated mantle was exchanged for one of pure white wool which caused them to be called Whitefriars. The change was made in honour of the Immaculate Conception.[1]

Therefore, we have a picture of an order, in which all wore the scapular, which from the Thirteenth century at least had writers who constantly deepened their relationship with Mary. These authors, who over time continued to deepen the relationship of themselves and their readers with Christ and His Mother, were surrounded, almost from the beginning, with a growing throng of lay persons, who became Confrates and enrolled in the Confraternity of the Brown Scapular, so that the devotion to Our Lady and Her Brown Scapular grew more and more until this devotion became recognised as being part of the worship of the Whole Church, Thus the popular devotion of the scapular and the union of the Human Person with Jesus Christ through Mary his Mother came to be 'two sides of the same coin' in the work of the Carmelite Order.

It was not necessary for the Medieval Carmelite Authors to write about the Scapular Vision of Simon Stock. They were describing other aspects of their relationship with Mary, Arnold Bostius, as well as seeing Mary as Mother, also sees her as sister, since there is a connection between her virginity and that of the Carmelites which makes a deep loving fraternal relationship between them.[1]

Paleonidorus, John Baconthorpe, John of Cheminot, John of Hildesheim, John Baptist de Lezana, Daniel of the Virgin Mary give similar arguments. John Baconthorpe at the beginning of the 14th century called the white cloak 'Mary's Mantle'.[1] For John of Hildesheim, Philip Ribot, John Grossi (14th Century) the white cloak symbolised the Purity and Virginity of Mary.[1] For Ribot, the use of the white cloak meant conserving purity of mind and body. In the Mantuan Congregation, the white cloak was a sign of the Immaculate Virgin. In a sermon on the feast of the Immaculate Virgin in the Carmelite church of Avignon, Bishop Richard Fitzralph said 'This holy and ancient order of Carmelites, which celebrates this feast with special solemnity, underlines it and relates it, prudently and devoutly, to the whiteness of the cloak.'[1] In 1370, John of Hildesheim related the white cloak to the purity of the followers of Elijah and in praise of Mary, who also used the white cloak to be like the angels and in honour of her son in the Transfiguration.[1]

The most important Carmelite Theologians who defended the Immaculate Conception were John Baconthorpe in England (Cambridge), Michael Aiguani in Italy (Bolognia), Francis Marti (Spain).[1] The Argument of John Baconthorpe to support the Immaculate Conception was as follows and was an elaboration of Gensis:

> Mary had a unique position in the realm of grace because of her predestination to be Mother of God. Thus in order to be the habitation of the Son of God, Mary was destined to be holy and without the stain of sin.[1]

The Argument of Michael Aiguani to support the Immaculate Conception was based on St. Augustine and St. Anselm. At the time there was seen to be two parts to conception; first material conception, then the infusion of the soul. Mary, he said, was 'purified and sanctified before the infusion of the soul, in the first moment of her conception'.[1]

Other Carmelites who wrote about the Immaculate Conception were Philip Ribot, John of Hildesheim, and John of Chemont. They saw imitating Mary in her Purity as important in imitating her in her Union with God by means of Prayer and their faithful listening to the Word of God.[1] Thus, the Carmelites were moving from their discussion of the Immaculate Conception to the deep relationship between Man and God 'via Mary' which Teresa of Jesus, John of the Cross and Mary Magdalene de' Pazzi would expand in the sixteenth century.[1]

All of these writers in the thirteenth and Fourteenth Centuries, who all defended first the particular relationship of the Carmelite Order with Mary, and then defended the Immaculate Conception - like all Carmelites wore both the Scapular and the White Cape. The scapular vision also occurred in the thirteenth century. There was no need for these men to discuss this event in their writing, more importantly they were describing their relationship with Mary and with Jesus, which was a consequence of their belonging to her order, and this belonging was symbolised by the scapular. We can expect then that the Scapular Vision would have been an oral tradition in the Order, and they wore the scapular as they wrote.

Also wearing the scapular before the onset of popular devotion in the seventeenth century are a number of Carmelite Saints and Blessed. These include in the thirteenth century Saint Angelus (1185–1220) , Albert of Trapani (c. 1240 – August 7, 1307), in the fourteenth century Peter Thomas (1305-1366), Andrew Corsini, O.Carm. (1302 – January 6, 1374), in the fifteenth century *Angelus Mazzinghi* (1385?-1438), *Blessed Archangela Girlani* (1460 – 25 January 1494), Bl. *Baptist Spagnoli,* (1447-1516), *Bl. Bartholomew Fanti* (died 1495), Bi. Aloysius Rabata, (1443- 1490). They included Bishops, Cardinals, Founders of Religious Congregations, and persons who had great pastoral impact.[2] Thus, their being in the Carmelite Order, and thus wearing the Scapular had a great impact on many lives.

Nor can it be said that the number of Carmelites was small; many people joined the Carmelite Order. Often, the fact that there were many reformed congregations of the order, such as those of Mantua and Albi meant that there could be more than one convent of the order in a single city, so, given that there was an oral tradition about the scapular and the apparition to Saint Simon Stock, this was a tradition which will have been known to large numbers of people throughout the order.

From all this evidence it can be argued that, as the Scapular gained in popularity and spread, the Carmelite Order deepened its relationship with Mary and Her Son Jesus, and the popular devotion to Our Lady of Mount Carmel contemporaneously further expanded. To understand the development of the story and devotion of the scapular, we should see it therefore in this context.

References:

1 *Emanuele Boaga O.Carm. The Lady of the Place, Mary in the History and in the life of Carmel Edizioni Carmelitane Roma 2001.*

2 *Joachim Smet O.Carm The Carmelites A History of the Brothers of Our Lady of Mount Carmel Vol III The Catholic Reformation 1600-1750*

3 *Joachim Smet O.Carm The Carmelites A History of the Brothers of Our Lady of Mount Carmel Vol IV The Modern Period 1750-1950*

4 *https://www.newadvent.org/cathen/13508b.htm Brown Scapular*

FIVE

Why is Saturday Dedicated to Our Lady?

What is the relationship of Saturday to the Sabbatine Privilege and Our Lady of Mount Carmel?

A preliminary note on the ancient custom of Fasting on Saturdays

It appears that the beginning of the identification of Saturday as an important liturgical day goes back to the custom in the early church of Rome of having Saturday as a day of fasting[14]. *The issue of fasting on particular days was linked with the days on which worship and the Eucharist was celebrated*[14]. *By the end of the fifth century, the Latin church replaced Wednesday with Saturday as a fasting day*[15].

Regarding why in the fourth century, Wednesday and Friday were fast days, but not Saturday, the Apostolic Constitutions explain; 'But let not your fast be with the hypocrites; for they fast on the second and fifth days of the week. But do you either fast the entire five days, or on the fourth day of the week (Wednesday), and on the day of the Preparation (Friday), because on the fourth day the condemnation went out against the Lord, Judas then promising to betray Him for money; and you must fast on the day of the Preparation, because on that day the Lord suffered the death of the cross under Pontius Pilate. But keep the Sabbath (Saturday), and the Lord's day (Sunday) festival; because the former is the memorial of the creation, and the latter of the resurrection.'[24]

Despite this, by the end of the fifth century, the Latin church replaced Wednesday with Saturday as a fasting day[16].

The Western church, in order to oppose and be distinguished from Jews and Judaists (Christians of Jewish background or leanings), adopted the practice of observing Saturday as a day of fasting. However, Augustine, Ambrose of Milan, and Jerome claimed that this matter had not been decided by divine authority and pointed out that this had no particular connection with the essence of faith and of sanctification. They believed that 'in such matters each individual should follow the custom of his own church, or of the country in which he resided, and strive that the bond of charity might not be broken by differences in such unimportant matters.'[17] *Augustine wrote 'God did not lay down a rule concerning fasting or eating on the seventh-day of the week, either at the time of His hallowing that day because in it He rested from His works, or afterwards when He gave precepts to the Hebrew nation concerning the observance of that day.'*[18] *Innocent, bishop of Rome issued a declaration to the Spanish bishop Decentius, 'that the Sabbath, like Friday, must be observed as a fast day.' 'Sabbato jejunandum esse ratio evidentissima demonstrate.'*[19]

On the other hand, The Eastern Church followed Apostolic Constitutions, which were compiled in the fourth century probably in Antioch, states similarly that Christians should keep the Sabbath (Saturday) and the Lord's day (Sunday) festivals 'because the former is the memorial of the creation, and the latter of the resurrection.'[20] *Thus, they did not fast on Saturdays. In the Eastern churches it was a general rule that there should be no fasting on Saturday and, specifically, that Saturday as well as Sunday should be exempt from fasting in the period before Easter.*[21]

Easter.*A number of ancient historians record this difference in practice, Socrates Scholasticus of Constantinople, a church historian of the fifth century, wrote that 'For although almost all churches throughout the world celebrate the sacred mysteries on the Sabbath of every week, yet the*

Christians of Alexandria and at Rome, on account of some ancient tradition, have ceased to do this'[22], *Also 'The people of Constantinople, and almost everywhere, assemble together on the Sabbath, as well as on the first day of the week, which custom is never observed in Rome or at Alexandria.*

There are several cities and villages in Egypt where, contrary to the usage established elsewhere, the people meet together on Sabbath evenings, and, although they have dined previously, partake of the mysteries'[23]

It is worth noting that although Christians in the East did not fast on the Sabbath and on the Sundays of Lent, they did abstain from 'everything which is killed... from eggs and cheese, which are the fruit and produce of those animals.'[25]

This difference in practice regarding fasting lasted at least until the Great Schism of 1054, because differences in practices regarding fasting were one of the points of difference raised by either side in the exchange of letters which initiated the schism. The Patriarch of Constantinople Michael Cerularius and Leo of Achrida,[26,27] *as well as Nicetas Stethatos accusing the Romans of fasting on the Sabbath, While Cardinal Humbert in reply emphasised the Roman tradition of not fasting on the Sabbath in order to be distinguished from Jewish tradition; 'Therefore, in such observance of the Sabbath, where and in what way do we [Latins] have anything in common with the Jews? For they are idle and keep a holiday on the Sabbath, neither ploughing nor reaping, and by reason of custom do not work, but they hold a festivity and a dinner, and their menservants, maidservants, cattle, and beasts of burden rest. But we [Latins] observe none of these things, but we do every [sort of] work, as [we do] on the preceding five days, and we fast as we [are wont to] fast on the sixth day [Friday] next to it.'*[28]

What is of very great interest is that the reason given for the Greeks not fasting on Saturday is that Saturday 'is the memorial of the creation'. This seems to be consonant with the argument for making Saturday the day for honouring Our Lady in the fifteenth century in that 'Saturday is the day when creation was completed. Therefore it is also celebrated as the day of the fulfilment of the plan of salvation, which found its realisation through Mary.'[1] *Thus the ideas of the Early Church might have resurfaced again in the Latin Church several centuries later.*

Also, it is worth noting that two fast days at different times- Wednesday and Saturday- became days where abstinence was held in honour of Our Lady of Mount Carmel. One wonders what part the 'folk' religion of Southern Italy, for long under Greek influence, albeit in union with Rome, might have had in this, given also the importance of Carmelite influence in Sicily, Calabria and Campania.

Now with this background, we can discuss why Saturday became the day to celebrate Our Lady.

That Saturday should be dedicated to Our Lady is an ancient custom.

Its origin goes back to the belief in the Ancient Church that on Saturday, the risen Christ appeared to His Mother, because on that day, no other person of the Apostles and disciples continued to believe in Jesus except Mary alone.[1] So, Jesus appeared to Mary to reward her for her steadfast faith in His divinity, which did not waver under the Cross.[1] Thus from the time Our Lord died on the Cross on Good Friday until Resurrection Sunday only Our Lady believed in His divinity[2], therefore she alone had perfect faith, for as Saint Paul says, 'Without the Resurrection our Faith would be vain.'[2,6] Therefore, that Saturday only Our Lady personified the Catholic Church throughout the Earth and medieval men praised her especially on that day.[2,6] Thus Saturday is a sign that the 'Virgin Mary is continuously present and operative in the life of the Church.'[4,8,9]

Another tradition to explain why Saturday is dedicated to Our Lady is that Divine Wisdom, becoming flesh of the Virgin Mary, *rested* (Saturday=Sabbath=day of rest) in Mary as on a bed.[1]

Saturday is the day when creation was completed; therefore it is also celebrated as the day of the fulfillment of the plan of salvation, which found its realisation through Mary.[4] In parallel, Jesus rested in the womb and then in the loving arms of Mary from birth until she held His lifeless body at the foot of the Cross; thus the God-head rested in Mary.[4]

One of the oldest customs related to honouring Mary on Saturday in the Roman Church of Rome was that on the Saturday before 'Whitsunday' (White Sunday), newly-baptised members of the Church would be led from St. John's baptistry of the Lateran to St. Mary Major, Mary's great shrine on the Esquiline Hill (built under Pope Liberius 352-66).[1]

St. Innocent I who reigned from 401-417 wrote the faithful a letter decreeing that each Saturday was to be observed as a day of abstinence in honour of the Sorrows of the Blessed Virgin Mary (10). In the Eastern Church, St. John of Damascus' († 754) writings prove the celebration of Saturdays dedicated to Mary in the Church of the East.[1]

The liturgical books of the ninth and tenth centuries contain Masses in honour of Mary on Saturday.[1]

Over time, the fast which existed in early times on Saturday became associated with Mary.[1]

The most important characteristic of Mary's relationship with Saturday occurs in the Liturgy. Saturday is dedicated to Mary by a Mass or Office of the Blessed Virgin Mary.[1] This is so even today. Through these liturgical acts, Christians exalt the person of Mary in the mass, which is the action that renews the sacrifice of Christ and in the action that prolongs his prayer.[1]

The liturgy of Saturday being in honour of Mary was largely the work of Alcuin (735-804), the Benedictine monk at the court of Charlemagne and who contributed in a decisive manner to the Carolingian liturgical reform.[1] Alcuin composed six formularies for Votive (or devotional) Masses – one for each day of the week. And he assigned two formularies to Saturday in honour of Our Lady. This practice was quickly and joyously embraced by both clergy and laity.[1]

Cardinal Peter Damian († 1072) also fostered this Marian Saturday celebration (1), the custom of dedicating Saturday Masses to Mary was fostered specially in the cloister churches of the various orders, and quickly spread throughout the whole Church.[1] Devotion to Our Lady received a great impulse in the beginning of the tenth century with the monastic reform led by Cluny, the Order that built medieval civilisation.[2] It was then that the habit of dedicating Saturday especially to her became widespread. For example, Saint

Hugh (Abbot of Cluny) determined that when no immovable feast occurred on a Saturday, in all monasteries of Cluny should be sung the Office of the Blessed Virgin Mary and celebrated the Mass 'De Beata Virgine,' that is, the liturgy especially composed in her praise.[2] Pope Urban II ordered that the Little Office of Our Lady be added to the Office of the Church on Saturdays. This shows the impulse that the Order of Cluny gave to devotion to Our Lady, and particularly on Saturdays.[2]

The custom of celebrating Mary on Saturdays became more popular during the time of the crusades. Peter of Amiens preached the first crusade and started out with a vanguard for Constantinople on a Saturday, March 8, 1096.[1] Pope Urban II admonished the faithful to pray the hours of the liturgy in honour of the most holy Virgin for the crusaders.[1] At the Synod of Clermont the year before, Blessed Pope Urban II had prescribed priests to pray the hours of the liturgy in honour of the most holy Virgin as well.[1] He required priests and monks to pray the Office of the Blessed Virgin on Saturday, and 'Votive Masses of the Blessed Virgin were decreed for every Saturday of the year unless prohibited by explicit rubrics to the contrary.'[10]

The theologians of the twelfth and thirteenth centuries, including St. Bernard, St. Thomas, and St. Bonaventure explained the dedication of Saturdays to Mary by pointing to the time of Christ's rest in the grave. Everyone else had abandoned Christ; only Mary continued to believe.[1]

A Dominican missal of the fifteenth century listed an additional reason for dedicating Saturday to Mary in a hymn: Saturday is the day when creation was completed.[1] Therefore it is also celebrated as the day of the fulfilment of the plan of salvation, which found its realisation through Mary.[1]

Since Sunday is the Lord's Day, it seemed appropriate to name the day preceding it as Mary's day.[1]

In the centuries to follow, the Marian Saturdays were expressed in several devotions. This was the day the faithful selected to go on pilgrimages.[1] Sodalities held their meetings on Saturdays and called them Fraternity Saturdays or Sodality Saturdays.[1]

The seven dolors or sorrows of Mary were commemorated on seven consecutive Saturdays.[1]

The fifteen Saturdays before the liturgy in honour of Mary as Queen of the Rosary (October 7) recalled the fifteen decades of the rosary.[1]

In some areas, as in parts of Germany, this was the day that the crops and harvests were blessed and celebrated.[1]

The growing devotion in honour of the Immaculate Conception by the Franciscans contributed to furthering the Marian Saturdays.[1] In 1633 the Order's Chapter determined that a Holy Mass in honour of the Immaculate Conception was to be celebrated on Saturday.[1]

Over time, it became customary for Catholics everywhere to consider Saturday Mary's day just as Sunday is the Lord's Day.[1] Many of the faithful commemorated the day by attending Mass, receiving the Eucharist, and praying the rosary as a family or attending an evening devotion at the Church, as well as performing works of neighbourly love in many forms.[1]

Vatican II with its liturgical reforms did not abolish the practice of Masses in honour of Our Lady.[1]

In the early centuries a widespread type of Marian devotion on Saturday, particularly in Germany, was the three Golden Saturdays which followed the Feast of St. Michael at the end of October.[1]

Thus, a document from 1387 found in the town of Bischofsdorf near Mattighofen, Germany sets the date for the 'next three golden Saturdays.'[1] This custom was well-known by the fourteenth century and widespread in Austria, Bohemia, Bavaria and Württemberg.[1] These golden Saturdays were celebrated festively with reception of the sacraments and with pomp and circumstance especially at places of pilgrimage.[1] Some of these festivities are still found in these cultural areas today.[1]

The origin of the three golden Saturdays is unclear.[1] A document from 1765 recounts that Emperor Ferdinand received the following promise from Mary.[1] She said: 'Whoever will honour me on three Saturdays after the feast of the Archangel Michael – who always guarded my virginal pure conception, without stain of original sin – with a devotion of zealous prayer, especially with the holy rosary, shall have the consolation of all my graces for a joyfully blessed little hour of death, without any struggle with evil powers and temptations.'[1] This report cannot be proven and is only a legend[1], however it shows how the connection between St. Michael and Mary was explained at the time.[1]

Earlier and more frequently than in the West, the art and popular devotion in the East depict St. Michael as the protector of Mary and the Child Jesus.[1] Here, too, ancient legends connect St. Michael to Mary's death and assumption into heaven, and therefore St. Michael was long considered the patron of the dying.[1]

The reason these Saturdays were called golden is that golden is the term often used to explain something especially valuable, important and effective.[1] The Quatember Weeks (fourth of the ember weeks) was called the golden week, the Quatember fast days were called the Gold Fast, the following Sunday, the golden Sunday, and a jubilee year a golden year.[1] There were also golden rosaries, a golden Mass which was considered especially rich in blessings and was therefore used for extraordinary intentions.[1]

The reason there were three Saturdays was that the Masses were not celebrated all in one place, but at three different places to which the people could walk on a pilgrimage on three consecutive Sundays.[1] They were limited to three Saturdays possibly to emphasise their specialness.[1]

It is worth saying that in Malta, Confraternities of Saint Michael still exist to celebrate the feast of Saint Michael in late September.

Rosary Saturdays

Rosary Saturdays, that is, saying the rosary on Saturday, have been popular since the seventeenth century and continued to the present at places of pilgrimage.[1] Both Pope Pius IX and Pope Leo XIII fostered this custom.[1] Grignion de Montfort fostered the rosary in connection with his missions, which often encompassed Saturdays.[1]

The Sabbatine Privilege

Within this situation where Saturday was a definite day dedicated to Our Lady, the Carmelite Order developed the Privilege of the Scapular known as the Sabbatine Privilege.

This developed from a legend that in 1322, Seventy-one years after her scapular vision to Saint Simon Stock, Our Lady is said to have appeared to Pope John XXII and promised in favour of those who wear her Scapular speedy release from Purgatory, particularly on Saturday, provided certain conditions are fulfilled.[11]

The conditions approved by the church, after much discussion are:

1. To wear the Scapular faithfully after valid enrolment;
2. To observe chastity according to one's state;
3. To recite daily the Little Office of the Blessed Virgin;

OR, to observe the fasts of the Church while additionally abstaining from meat on Wednesdays and Saturdays;

OR, *as is the common practice in our day, to have this third* condition commutated to the daily recitation of five decades of the Most Holy Rosary (this commutation must be given by a priest — ordinarily it is done at the time of enrolment).[11]

The story of the vision of the Blessed Virgin Mary to Pope John XXII at Avignon conferring the Sabbatine Privilege of her promise to deliver from purgatory on the Saturday following death the souls of any who died in the scapular has been shown by scholars to be based on an inauthentic papal bull forged in Sicily in the first half of the fifteenth century.[12] Thus the Sabbatine Vision and Privilege too are without any historical foundation. Moreover, in 1603 a book containing the privileges of the Carmelite Order, including the Sabbatine privilege, was condemned by the Portuguese Inquisition.[12] Six years later all books mentioning the Sabbatine privilege were put on the Index of Forbidden Books in Portugal.[12] An appeal to Rome ended when the Roman authorities supported the Inquisition's ban regarding the Bull.[12]

In 1613 the Holy Office under Pope Paul V issued a decree on the Sabbatine Privilege which took account of the papal bulls of the sixteenth century.[12] These Bulls had promulgated the privilege according to the tradition of the Sabbatine Bull.[12] The decree of the Holy Office made no reference to the Bull of John XXII or to the tradition of the Marian apparition to him. It simply affirmed the privilege itself.[12]

> In the subsequent Appeal to Rome, the Carmelite wish to preach the privilege was strongly defended by Cardinal (later Saint) Robert Bellarmine, as well as by Cardinal Sfrondati, and as a result, though the Sabbatine Bull was condemned, the preaching of the Sabbatine Privilege was permitted to the Carmelites… It was also forbidden that pictures be made of Our Lady descending to Purgatory, in the midst of the flames, but only the angels would go there to assist the holy souls and lead them to heaven through the intercession of Mary…[13]

The Carmelites were forbidden to preach the Sabbatine privilege — a prohibition they did not always honour — although the faithful were to be allowed to believe, with certain conditions, 'that the Blessed Virgin by her continuous intercession, merciful prayers, merits and special protection will assist the souls of deceased brothers and members of the confraternity (of the Scapular), especially on Saturday, the day which the church dedicates to the Blessed Virgin.'[13]

Thus, since the early seventeenth century, Carmelite preaching of the Sabbatine Privilege has been theologically independent of the historical authenticity of the Sabbatine Bull.[12]

Given the long development of Saturday as a day dedicated to Our Lady, it is no surprise that Carmelite Confessors and other priests should choose to commute the obligations of the Sabbatine Privilege to abstaining from meat on Wednesdays and Saturdays. The reason for Wednesday as a day dedicated to Our Lady of Mount Carmel has been discussed already; it is linked with the devotion to the Madonna Bruna in Naples.

First Saturday Communion of Reparation

The custom of dedicating First Saturdays of the month as days of Reparation to the Immaculate Heart of Mary was originated by a Servite Nun at Rovigo, Italy in the latter half of the nineteenth century. In this town, was a family called Ronconi.[1] The seven sons in the family all died a saintly death at a very early age. The last to die – he was nineteen – received an apparition from Our Blessed Lady just before his death.[1] Our Lady told the dying youth that she wanted his father to become a Servite tertiary. Mister Ronconi did become a Tertiary and had the Servite Order canonically erected in the Parish of St. Michael at Rovigo in 1890.[1] The Servite Tertiaries at Rovigo purchased a large oleograph of Murillo's *Sorrowful* Mother and mounted it over one of the side altars in St. Michael's church, where they held their meetings.[1] On May 1, 1895, it was noted that 'the Sorrowful Mother of St. Michael's is moving her eyes!' The eyes of the image were moving, looking up to heaven, then looking down as if in great sorrow.[1] One witness was Maria Inglese, a Servite Tertiary for the past four years. She knew immediately that Our Lady was asking for reparation and love.[1] At that point the whole practice of Marian Reparation seemed revealed to her in a flash.[1] In February 1889,moved by an irresistible interior revelation, she instituted among her friends the pious practice of 'Communion in Reparation to the Immaculate Heart of Mary.'[1] The bishop of the diocese not only approved of the practice, but also recommended it most warmly to his people.[1] So the devotion spread rapidly in Italy. The plan at that time was to have members take turns in uninterrupted daily Communions and Hours of Adoration in Reparation to the Immaculate Heart of Mary.[1] In 1905 St. Pius X approved the practice. That year, Our Blessed Lady appeared to Maria Inglese[1] at Rovigo. No words were spoken during the Apparition, but Our Lady showed the girl a nun's habit.[1] Maria Inglese was advised by the bishop to join the Servite Nuns,founded in 1890 by Sister Mary Elisa Andreoli, and when she visited them, she found that they wore the habit that Our Lady had shown her.[1] The congregation of nuns changed their name to 'Servants of Mary of Reparation.'[1] The new Rule was that each day would be a series of uninterrupted hours of Reparation before Our Lady's altar, and that the First Saturday of each month be the most solemn day of Reparation.[1] On each first Saturday the community would engage in special penances and prayers and would renew its Consecration to the Immaculate Heart of Mary.[1] The miraculous picture of Our

Lady was then moved from St. Michael's Church to the novitiate of the Sisters, and a *Marian League of Reparation* was founded as a magazine to spread the concept of Marian Reparation.[1] Through this, the nuns spread their apostolate of the First Saturday Communion of Reparation to the Immaculate Heart of Mary.[1]

The Fifteen Saturdays of the Rosary

An Irish version of Saturday devotions to Mary is known as the Fifteen Saturdays of the Rosary.[1] The devotion consists in receiving holy communion and saying at least five decades of the rosary sometime during the day or evening on fifteen consecutive Saturdays – or Sundays, when Saturday is not possible – or to meditate in some other way on its mysteries (1), Specific to the devotion is to meditate on one of the mysteries each Saturday (or Sunday) when preparing for communion as well as praying for personal intentions The intention of the devotion is to honour Jesus and Mary by meditating on the fifteen mysteries represented in the traditional decades of the rosary.[1]

The First Saturdays Devotion

The First Saturday's devotion before the apparitions of Fatima. had already been an established custom in the Catholic Church.[3] On July 1, 1905, Pope Pius X approved and granted indulgences for the practice of the First Saturdays of twelve consecutive months in honour of the Immaculate Conception.[3]

Fatima, Saturday, and Reparation to the Immaculate Heart of Mary During her July apparition at Fatima, Our Lady said to Lucia, 'I shall come to ask... that on the First Saturday of every month, Communions of reparation be made in atonement for the sins of the world.'[6,7]

In the message of Fatima, especially in the apparitions of June 13 and July 13, 1917, Mary drew attention to the custom of devoting Saturdays to her and praying the rosary in reparation.[1] Lucia, the eldest of the three children heard the following on June 13:

> My child, behold my heart is surrounded with thorns which ungrateful men place therein at every moment by their blasphemies and ingratitude. You, at least, try to console me, and tell them that I promise to help, at the hour of death, with the graces needed for salvation, whoever, on the First Saturday of five consecutive months, shall confess and receive Holy Communion, recite five decades of the Rosary, and keep me company for fifteen minutes while meditating on the fifteen Mysteries of the Rosary with the intention of making reparation to me.[1]

On July 13, the children were again asked to say the rosary. At this time, the Blessed Mother asked for the consecration of the world to her Immaculate Heart, and for communion of reparation on the first Saturday of each month.[1] These messages were accompanied by an appeal and a promise – an appeal for prayer and reparation by the people for their transgressions against the divine law; a promise of peace and love in this life and eternal happiness in the next on the twofold condition of prayer and amendment·[1] Sister Lucia later reported that on December 10, 1925, the Virgin Mary appeared to her at the convent in Pontevedra, Spain, and by Her side, elevated on a luminous cloud, was the Child Jesus. At this point Lucia was a postulant in the Sisters of St. Dorothy.[3] In 1925, Lucia vouched for this message, saying that Mary would assist us at the hour of death if the first Saturdays of five consecutive months were sanctified with confession, communion, praying the rosary and meditation.[1] After that time, Lucia had become a Carmelite Nun. Also, in the last apparition of Fatima, Our Lady had appeared wearing the Carmelite Habit. Hence this again associated Carmel and the Scapular with both the Fatima Apparitions and Saturday as a day set aside for Devotion to Mary.

References

1 *Saturday Devotions in Honour of Our Lady – M. Jean Frisk, S.S.M. https://udayton.edu/imri/mary/s/saturday-devotions.php*

2 *Why Saturday Is Dedicated to Our Lady Plinio Corrêa de Oliveira 2018 The American TFP (About Our Lady) Why Saturday Is Dedicated to Our Lady*

3 *First Saturdays Devotion Wikipedia*

4 *Why are Saturdays dedicated to the Blessed Mother? Eastside Parishes eastsideparishes.org › Home › Parish Blog*

5 *Why Saturday Is Dedicated to Our Lady Plinio Corrêa de Oliveira Tradition In Action, Inc. 2009 (TIA) https://www.traditioninaction.org/religious/d020rpSaturdays.htm*

6 *The Five First Saturdays Devotion www.themostholyrosary.com › appendix2*

7 *A Short History of the First Saturday Devotions - Priestly, ..fssp.com › a-short-history-of-the-first-saturday-devotions*

8 *Saturday Devotions to the Virgin Mary http://archive.wf-f.org/SaturdayDevotions.html*

9 *Vatican web site: DIRECTORY ON POPULAR PIETY AND THE LITURGY*

10 *Proof That Saturday Is Mary's Special Day 2019 JOSEPH PRONECHEN National Catholic Register https://www.ncregister.com/blog/joseph-pronechen/proof-saturday-is-marys-special-day*

11 *Fr. Peter Davis O.Carm Our Lady's Brown Scapular Sign of Consecration to Mary www.ecatholic2000.com › cts › untitled-328.*

12 *A Catechesis on the Brown Scapular Father Sam Anthony Morello, OCD and Father Patrick McMahon, O.Carm. https://laudateomnes.wordpress.com/2019/07/09/catechesis-on-the-brown-scapular/*

13 *The Lady of the Place: Mary in the History and in the Life of Carmel (Carmelitana) by Emanuele Boaga, J Chalmers, et al. | 31 Dec 2001*

14 *Radiša Antic The Controversy over fasting on Saturday Between Constantinople and Rome, Andrews University Seminary Studies, Vol. 49, No. 2, 337-352.*

15 *Tia M. Kolbaba, The Byzantine Lists: Errors of the Latins (Urbana: University of Illinois Press, 1995), 34-35.*

16 *Augustus Neander, General History of the Christian Religion and Church (Edinburgh:T.& T. Clark) 3:402.*

17 *Augustine, Epistle 36, to Casulanus, in NPNF1 1:265-270.*

18 *Augustus Neander, General History of the Christian Religion and Church (Edinburgh:T.& T. Clark) 3:403*

19 *Apostolic Constitutions 7.23, titled 'Constitutions of the Holy Apostles' (ANF 7:469)*

20 *Augustus Neander, General History of the Christian Religion and Church (Edinburgh: T. & T. Clark, 1847-1855), 3:402.*

21 *Socrates, Ecclesiastical History 5.22, (NPNF2 2:132).*

22 *Sozomen Ecclesiastical History 7.19 [NPNF2 2:390]*

23 *Apostolic Constitutions 7.23*

24 *'The Canons of the Council in Trullo,' NPNF2 14:391.*

---

25 *Michael Cerularius and Leo of Achrida, 'Epistle to John of Trani,' in Patrologia graecea, ed. J.-P. Migne, 162 vols. (Paris, 1857-1886), 120:835-845.*

26 R. L. *Odom, 'The Sabbath in the Great Schism of 1054,' AUSS 1 (1963): 74-80.*

27 *Nicetas Stethatos, 'Libellus Contra Latinos,' (PG 120:1011-1022).*

28 *Humbert, 'Adversus Calumnias Graecorum,' (PL 143:936, 937)*

SIX

THE DEVELOPMENT OF SCAPULAR CONFRATERNITIES IN EUROPE AND IN MALTA

THE CARMELITES DEVELOPED INTO THREE BRANCHES; THESE WERE the First Order of Priests, the Second Order of Enclosed Nuns, the Third Order regular of Nuns, who were not enclosed, and the third order Secular of men and women, who were lay persons who were members of the order. They also cared for the Confraternities of the scapular, who were groups of lay persons who were affiliated to the order. In the Middle Ages, clergy and Religious Orders often organized the faithful into confraternities, that is brotherhoods or sisterhoods, to help them lead a more spiritual life. This started with Lay confraternities who used the churches of the Order to meet.

Probably ever since the coming of the friars to Europe, founders of convents and benefactors were admitted to the order under the title of Confratres, which gave them a right to participation in the prayers and good works of a section or of the entire order, and to suffrages after their death. Neither such Confratres, nor even the text of confraternity letters, contain any mention of obligations incumbent on them (New Advent. The Catholic Encyclopaedia). The letters were at first granted only after mature consideration, but from the end of the fifteenth century it was less difficult to obtain them; in many cases the general handed numerous blank forms to provincials and priors to be distributed by them at their own discretion. Out of this confraternity, which stood in no organic connection with the order, arose in the sixteenth century, according to all probability, the Confraternity of the Scapular (New Advent; The Catholic Encyclopaedia). Another example of a confraternity established in a Carmelite Church was a guild established in 1280 at Bologna, and perhaps elsewhere, which held its meetings in the Carmelite church and from time to time made an offering at a certain altar, but otherwise was entirely independent of the order. (New Advent; The Catholic Encyclopaedia). The Ancient Confraternity of the Battuti Di Modena, dated 1300, is an early example of a Confraternity based in a Carmelite Church, but not specifically linked with the Carmelite Order.

Confraternities are of very great importance in the history of the church, starting in the middle ages. They were groups of lay persons who met for a number of different reasons. Some of these confraternities existed to perform charitable works, as does the Misericordia in Florence, and they still do. In Malta a good example is the confraternity of Our Lady of Charity in the parish of Saint Paul in Valletta. Other Confraternities originated as Guilds of Tradesmen, as happened with the London Guilds. In Malta these Trade Guilds were important, and existed in the 'three cities' and Valletta;[12] They included those of

- Of Saint Joseph = Carpenters
- Of Saint Homobonus = Taylors
- Of Saint Crispin and Crispinian = Shoemakers
- Of Saint Michael = Greengrocers
- Of Saint Martin = Tavern keepers
- Of Saints Cosmas and Damian = Doctors

- Of Saint Ivo = Lawyers
- Of Saint Catherine = Rope makers
- Of Saint Helena = Goldsmiths
- Of Saint Eligius = Ironsmiths
- Of Saint Demetrius = Chalkers

Other confraternities were organised to be penitential brotherhoods or, more rarely, sisterhoods. They often held processions, usually during Holy Week, in which they went through the streets barefoot and half naked, carrying crosses, scourging themselves, and even wearing crowns of thorns. The Confraternity of the Crucifix at Ta' Ġieżu Church in Valletta, which organises the Procession of Good Friday is an example of this type. On the other hand, there were the 'Laudensi' confraternities, such as those of the Immaculate Conception or the Rosary whose function was to praise God, Our Lady, or the saints. Another sort of Confraternity are the Confraternities of the Blessed Sacrament, whose main aim was to Honour The Blessed Sacrament. They became important after the Council Of Trent, as their role was to implement the teaching of that Council on the Blessed Sacrament. They were introduced into Malta in the Apostolic Visitation of Mgr. Dusina, in 1575. He established this Confraternity in every town including Porto Salvo Parish, Valletta. In Malta, As well as looking after the feast of Corpus Christi, the Confraternities of the Blessed Sacrament look after the feast of the Parish Patron Saint. As will be seen later, our Archconfraternity of Our Lady of Mount Carmel in Malta also reflects some characteristics of a Blessed Sacrament confraternity, although not based in a parish Church, because of its association with the Altar of the Blessed Sacrament in Our Basilica.

The Mendicant Orders, that is, the Franciscans, Augustinians, Carmelites, and Dominicans—saw great value in these Confraternities. They viewed the Confraternities as ways of associating the laity in the mission and ministry of their Orders. The Mendicants all had their 'Third Orders' in which the laity actually became members of the Order, but not all those who wished to associate with the Orders wanted to, or were able to, make this level of commitment. So the Confraternities were a way of incorporating the faithful into an affiliation to the Orders without giving them full membership. Thus, the Franciscans were linked with the Confraternities of the Immaculate Conception, reflecting the work and teaching of their theologian Duns Scotus, the Augustinians were linked with Confraternities of Our Lady of the Cincture, the Dominicans were linked with Confraternities of Our Lady of the Rosary.One can see these confraternities reflected in the confraternities of the parishes of Malta. Hence, not surprisingly, the Carmelites began to set up Confraternities of the Scapular, or of Our Lady of Mount Carmel.[11]

The members of the various Confraternities were bound by the rules of a statute. They would meet regularly at the Church of the Order to which they were affiliated for prayers. The Confraternity members would meet regularly, participate in devotions together, and had a sense of identity with one another and identification with the Order. At their meetings, they often wore a habit that was similar to the habit of the Religious Order to which they were affiliated. In Carmelite, or scapular confraternities, the habit often included the white cloak that marked the Carmelites as the Whitefriars, since this cloak would have given them the most immediate identification. In

Valletta we still wear this white cloak or muzzeta. However, when the stories of the vision of Simon Stock and the promises made to the Carmelites began to spread at the beginning of the fifteenth century, the scapular became the desired badge of affiliation to the Order. Thus, it too became part of the habit of the members of the Confraternity. Thus, in Valletta, the members of the Confraternity wear a brown 'Great Scapular' similar to that of the friars. The Confraternity members would say their prayers together and receive instruction from the friars. The confraternities had certain rights including participation in processions and ceremonies within the churches of the friars. The confraternity members also usually had certain rights about being buried in the church as well, or having the friars assist at their funerals.[11]

In the eighteenth century, under the influence of the ideas of the Enlightenment, many of the religious orders, including the Carmelites, were suppressed in various places in Europe. Thus the Carmelites, who had already lost their English and some of their German houses because of the Reformation, now lost houses in many parts of Europe. The suppressions of Religious Orders were even more widespread after the French Revolution, and well into the nineteenth century. The Carmelites were wiped out from France and all ceased to exist in Germany, the Netherlands, and the Austrian empire. They were suppressed for several decades in Spain and Portugal, and, by the time of the Italian Risorgimento, they lost their houses in Italy. However, while the religious were banished, the Confraternities were often able to continue, and often, they took responsibility for the churches where they met, which had previously belonged to the various orders. Without the religious directing them, the Confraternities achieved a certain independent identity. They continued devotion to Our Lady of Mount Carmel and to Her Scapular. They continued organising the feast on the sixteenth July and continued repeating, spreading, and performing the prayers and rituals they had long practiced but without the living spirituality of the Order.

Some Confraternities of Our Lady of Mount Carmel, such as that in Taranto, look after the Good Friday Processions. In Valletta, Our Confraternity collected a complete set of paintings of the stages of the passion of Our Lord Jesus Christ. At Taranto, as in Valletta, the Confraternity of Our Lady of Mount Carmel is Particularly known for its Devotion to the Blessed Sacrament, as exemplified by their visits to the altars of repose or Sepolcri on Maundy Thursday.

The Carmelites in Malta

The Carmelites came to Malta in 1418, when the noblewoman, Margaret d'Aragon, deeded the chapel and surrounding land of Lunzjata (Rabat) to any religious Order that would undertake the incumbent religious duties. The Carmelites accepted the offer, and so the first monastery was founded. Subsequently, they opened priories in Valletta (1570), Vittoriosa (1582-1652), Mdina (1659), Balluta - Sliema (1892), Santa Venera (2 houses: 1913 and 1980), Fgura (1945) and Fleur-de-lys (1947). In 1944 a secondary school, later named Saint Elias College, was inaugurated.[1]

The Maltese Province was erected on May 7, 1892. Previously, the Maltese foundations had formed part of the Sicilian Province of St. Angelus, but when the English took over the island, the government of the day was anxious that Maltese groups should not be linked with governance from abroad. Therefore, the Maltese Convents became an independent vicariate, and later became a full province, in 1892. In 1987 the Province assumed the care of the church and convent of Milazzo in Sicily (Italy), It is worth saying that, while, because of the Reformation, the Enlightenment, The French Revolution, Napoleon, and the Unification of Italy, huge numbers of Carmelite Convents closed throughout Europe, In Malta our Convents never closed.

The Discalced Carmelite Friars arrived in Malta to make their first foundation in the year 1625. This was St. Teresa's Missionary College. Thus the church of St. Theresa in Cospicua was probably the first in the Christian world to be dedicated to Saint Teresa, the founder of the Discalced Carmelites. It was for this reason ultimately that Maltese Lay Brothers decorated Stella Maris Monastery Church, on Mount Carmel. Later the Discalced Carmelites founded convents in Birkirkara in 1896, Tas-Silġ in 1933 and Ta' Xbiex in 1948.

The Arch-Confraternity of Our Lady of Mount Carmel Valletta

The Arch-Confraternity of Our Lady of Mount Carmel in Valletta[8,9] is a Scapular Confraternity which is linked with the Basilica of Our Lady of Mount Carmel in Valletta. It is mentioned for the first time in 1622, the last year in which Alof de Wignacourt was Grandmaster of the Order of St John. It was on the thirteenth of February of that year when the Confraternity was officially founded, and on the same day the members of the confraternity took part in a procession in Valletta for the first time. This, 1622, was the first year that the procession of Our Lady of Mount Carmel was held in Valletta.[1,2]

The Confraternity was quick to develop its own Oratory. The first oratory was composed of two rooms that were acquired from the friars by a contract which was made before Notary Ambrogio Sciberras on the tenth of July 1622. On the sixteenth of May 1642 in the acts of Notary Vella, the Carmelite community assigned to the Confraternity another area near the main Altar of the church which had a door opening on to Old Mint Street, for a rent of six scudi a year, Thus the Oratory was originally located in the area where the apse of the Basilica is now. Many works of art existed in this oratory, including Giuseppe D'Arena's painting of the Immaculate Conception and Stefano Erardi 's Adoration of the shepherds and Adoration of the magi, both of the Erardi paintings are now in the Basilica Shrine of Our Lady of Mount Carmel, and have featured in Maltese Postage Stamps. D'Arena was a rector of the Confraternity.[1,2]

There were other Paintings which were in the old Oratory; Saverio Bartolo donated a painting of the Madonna liberating souls from Purgatory. There was a whole series of paintings of scenes of the Passion, including an Agony in the Garden and a 'Kiss of Judas' donated by Fra Enrico Savona of the Order of Saint John.Saverio Bartolo donated the Scourging at the Pillar, and also a Crucifixion and a Madonna Addolorata.The surgeon Gabriele Henin gave a Crowning with Thorns painted by Gio.Nicola Buhagiar. There is also an Ecce Homo.Fra Alfonso Pace may have donated Christ Carrying the Cross. All these paintings are now in a corridor of the monastery or in the sacristy of the present oratory.[9]

It is recorded that some knights joined the Confraternity, such as Grand Masters Raphael and Nicholas Cotoner, and Balis Pinto and Pappalardo, Major benefactors were the painter Giuseppe d'Arena (1712), the leading silversmith Michele Pianta (1725) and Gabriele Henin, professor of surgery and anatomy.[5,9]

Baron Cesare Passalaqua was the founder of the confraternity and also one of the greatest benefactors who are remembered to this day. In 1664 he donated to the Confraternity the exceptional necklace (called a Sincill) which exists to this day and is worn by the statue of Our Lady of Mount Carmel in the Oratory. This necklace contains 28 rubies, 5 diamonds and 94 pearls.[9]

When in 1895 the Carmelite church was raised to the dignity of a Minor Basilica, the friars asked the Confraternity to give them their oratory in order that they could enhance the apse and build a canopy mounted on pillars over the altar, as is usual with minor basilicas. One year later an agreement was reached between the Friars and the Confraternity by which the confraternity was given in exchange a new oratory which was, in fact, a corridor of the Monastery. This is the oratory we have today.[2]

In the present Oratory is the oldest extant Processional Statue of Our Lady of Mount Carmel in the Maltese Islands.[2] It is Modelled on Melchiorre Gafa's Rabat Madonna of the Rosary....and was thought to have come from Rome. It has recently been attributed to Pietro Paolo Troisi , who besides being a Sculptor was also Master of the Mint of the Knights of Saint John. This statue wears the Passalaqua 'Sincill' or necklace during the feast of the sixteenth July.

The Confraternity has always been generous to the friars and the Sanctuary of Our Lady of Mount Carmel. Among other objects which the Confraternity have donated to the Sanctuary are the bronze Via Sagra (1852), the new damask of the church in 1900. They also donated the silver pedestal of the statue, made in 1931 for the fiftieth anniversary or Golden Jubilee of the Solemn Coronation of the Miraculous Painting in 1931. This Pedestal was designed by Abram Gatt and sculpted by Vincent Apap in 1931, it was manufactured by electroplating by the German firm Wurtenbergischer Metallwarenfabrik. In 1949 the Confraternity donated the silver tabernacle that is used during the feast of the sixteenth July.

The Oratory contains many important silver artefacts, often donated by members of the Confraternity. It also contains Numerous silver ex-Votos arranged in designs decorating the pilasters of the Oratory. This type of ex-Voto, depicting parts of a Healed body, is frequently seen in Malta, but is a Byzantine custom, common in Greece.

The Confraternity also gave a bell – Il-Fustanija – to the Carmelite Church, on condition that it be tolled when a member of the confraternity was dying. Death of members was of great importance to confraternities. The Confraternity now owns graves at the Addolorata Cemetery so that poor members can receive a decent burial.

The Confraternity is the duty bound to spread the devotion of Our Lady of Mount Carmel, so that it was at the request of the Confraternity in 1791 that the Novena began to be held before the feast.

The confraternity participates in the procession of the translation, which generally begins in the Oratory, and in the main procession of the feast of our patroness, Our Lady of Mount Carmel, on the sixteenth July.

Furthermore the confraternity is responsible for the altar of the Blessed Sacrament in the Sanctuary, otherwise known as the Altar of Saint Agnes, with an altarpiece which is said apocrifically to be by Guido Reni, and ensures that it is properly adorned for every necessity which occurs during the liturgical year, Therefore the confraternity has special devotion to the Blessed Sacrament and is responsible for all the liturgical utensils required by this altar.[6] It also participates in a procession for the feast of the Sacred Heart and used to participate in the Corpus Christi Procession which takes place from Saint John's Co-Cathedral.

In the oratory, besides many other works of art, there is oldest extant processional statue of Our Lady of Mount Carmel in the Maltese Islands,[1,2] going back to at least 1657, when it was said to have been brought from Rome and participated in the procession of the 16th July of that year, This is the statue which surmounts the altar of the Oratory. The confraternity has now been advised by Art Expert Sandro Debono that it in fact is to be attributed to Pietro Paolo Troisi.

Subsequently, the Confraternity acquired another processional statue of Our Lady of Mount Carmel from Naples, Sculpted by Gennaro Reale, This was later given by the members to the Church and convent of Our Lady Of Mount Carmel in Balluta, where it is used as the processional statue today.[3,7]

The third statue, the one used at present during the feast, was acquired by the order, not the confraternity. It was made in 1781 by Vincenzo Dimech,[4] and its Silver Pedestal was donated by the Confraternity in 1931- for the fiftieth anniversary of the Canonical Coronation of the Icon. This pedestal was designed by Abram Gatt, and modelled by Vincent Apap.[2]

Until 1790, the Confraternity used to hold a second procession of Our Lady of Mount Carmel, using their statue, on the octave of the feast. In that year, it petitioned the Prior to replace this Octave procession with a Novena leading to the feast. This novena is held to this day.[2]

At Balluta Bay, in St. Julians, since 1859 (architect Giuseppe Bonavia) there was a church dedicated to Our Lady of Mount Carmel, built by the Confraternity of Our Lady of Mount Carmel of Valletta; the church was rebuilt in 1877 (Architect Emanuel Galizia) and given to the Carmelite friars who rebuilt it in 1900. In 1958 it was rebuilt again and in 1974 it became the parish church of the locality. To celebrate this, the Rector of the Arch-Confraternity is annually invited to attend the High Mass on the Feast of Our Lady of Mount Carmel on the last Sunday of [3].

The Confraternity had given to the Friars the church they owned in Balluta and also the land on which to build their convent there. Thus the Confraternity, by helping the friars, did work which led to the development of an important parish community and thus gave an important contribution to the development of the social history of the Sliema area of Malta.

The Oratory of the Confraternity also contains other notable statuary. There is the statue of Jesus Christ as Captive-In-Nazzarenu, which is often placed on the main altar, and wears the scapular of the Trinitarian Order, which is an order which used to be dedicated to the redemption of Christian Slaves. There is great devotion to this statue.[9] It was probably sculpted by Karlu Darmanin, there is a recently Restored Our Lady of Sorrows, also by Karlu Darmanin, and two very well loved and much bejewelled statues of children - a statue of the child Mary in the clothes of a child of a noble Maltese Family (this is used in the feast of the birth of Our Lady) and a statue of the Child Jesus which is known as the Child of Prague, and to which there is much devotion.[9] It is worth noting that this Child of Prague, during a recent restoration, was in fact found to be a nineteenth century copy of the Child Jesus of Aracoeli in Rome.

Within the sacristy of the Oratory are the archives of the Confraternity, which go back to at least 1722, and appear in good state of preservation. It is the intention of the Confraternity to digitalise its archive, so as to make it accessible to scholars. So far this has been achieved only in part.

The Confraternity of Valletta is known as an Arch-Confraternity because another Confraternity of Our Lady of Mount Carmel, that of Żurrieq, was founded from it. This was founded in 1801 by episcopal decree within the church of Saint Catherine in Żurrieq, however there had been an altar dedicated to Our Lady of Mount Carmel in the Parish Church of Żurrieq. The founder of the confraternity of Żurrieq was Giovanni Maria Borg, a member of the Valletta Confraternity and a business-man, who took refuge in

Żurrieq during the Napoleonic War.[10] The statue used by the Żurrieq Confraternity was sculpted in wood by Salvatore Psaila in 1842. The members of the Confraternity wear a white habit and a brown great scapular, as well as a violet cape (mozzetta) on which is embroidered a picture of Our Lady.

There is record of another confraternity having been set up in the Church of Our Lady of Mount Carmel in the Church in Mdina.

In Birkirkara, a confraternity of Our Lady of Mount Carmel existed in the Church of Saint Helen. When the Discalced Carmelites arrived in Birkirkara, its name was changed into that of All Souls, so that the Carmelites could set up a Confraternity in their monastery.

There are also Confraternities of Our Lady of Mount Carmel founded in Senglea and Siġġiewi. In Tarxien, the Confraternity of Our Lady of Doctrine is founded on the Altar of Our Lady of Mount Carmel.[11]

However, to return to Valletta, Father Valentin Borg Gusman argues that the devotion to Our Lady of Mount Carmel and her scapular was most enhanced by a sodality, which dates back to at least 1696. It was known as 'the sodality of the four farthings'.[1] Through this sodality, a Carmelite Friar would go daily to a city or village to enrol people and families in the sodality and the Carmelite Scapular, so that it came about that most of the population of these islands had a great affection for Our Lady of Mount Carmel.

Apart from the Confraternities of Our Lady of Mount Carmel, a number of Catholic organisations in Malta and across the world expect their members to wear the Brown Scapular. These include The Blue Army of Our Lady of Fatima, The Legion of Mary and the MUSEUM, whose founder, Saint George Preca was deeply devoted to the Carmelite Scapular and was also a Carmelite Tertiary.

References:

1 *BORG GUSMAN, V. 1983. Marian Devotion in the Maltese Carmelite province during the 17th and 18th Centuries, in V. BORG (ed.) Marian Devotions in the Islands of Saint Paul (1600-1800). Malta.*

2 *SAMMUT, L.M. 1952. Is-Santwarju Tal-Karmnu. Malta*

3 *ABELA, S. 2006. Il-Karmelitani fil-Balluta 1890-2006. Malta.*

4 *DEBONO, J. 2006. L-Istatwi tal-Madonna tal-Karmnu ta'l-1871 u ta' l-Anġlu Kustodju u l-Iskulturi Tagħhom. Programm Tal-Festa tal-Madonna tal-Karmnu 2006: 31-45. Malta.*

5 *BONELLO, G. II-Fratellanza tal-Madonna tal-Karmnu 1622 2014. Programm Tal-Festa, Festa tal-Madonna tal-*
Karmnu Valletta 2014: 27-35. Malta.

6 *MAGRO CONTI, E. 2015. Il-Fided tal-Festa tal-Artal tal-Fratellanza tal-Karmnu. Programm Tal-Festa 2015:117-125.Malta.*

7 *PACE GOUDER, A. 2016. F'Għeluq il-120 sena mill-Ewwel Festasal-lum 1896-2016. Malta.*

8 *FARRUGIA, J., C. PACE & M. AGIUS, 2016. Mill-Oratorju tal-Karmnu. Malta.*

9 *The Archconfraternity of Our Lady Of Mount Carmel and its Oratory in Valletta. Agius M, Farrugia J, Pace C. Vigilo - DIN L-ART HELWA December 2016.*

---

10 *https://www.talkarmnuŻurrieq.org/il-fratellanza*
11 *Vincent Borg Marian Devotions in Maltese Diocesan Churches in V. BORG (ed.) Marian Devotions in the Islands of Saint Paul (1600-1800). Malta.*
12 *Karmenu Ellul Galea, Fratellanzi u Xirkiet Tas-Snajja', Stamperija Il-Ħajja, 1981, Malta*

SEVEN

THE HISTORY OF THE SCAPULAR AS A SIGN OF CONSECRATION TO MARY

WE HAVE ALREADY DESCRIBED HOW THE EARLY CARMELITES SAW Our Lady as 'The Lady of the Place' in Mount Carmel, and how the church in which they prayed was dedicated to Our Lady. We have seen how the 'Madonna Bruna' of Naples was said to have been brought to Europe from Mount Carmel. We have seen how the Carmelites began to see themselves as being particularly the Order of Our Lady, more so than the other orders of friars. Throughout the middle ages they distinguished themselves as being assiduous in defending the privileges of Mary, their Mother, Guide and Sister, such as the privilege of the immaculate Conception, in honour of which they wore the white cloak, as well as and their privilege of being Mary's Order.[1]

Like many religious, they wore a scapular. This was a single piece of cloth, which was worn over the shoulders, front and back, so that it looked like an apron. Monks wore this, at least from the beginnings of the Benedictines, and serfs wore scapulars of different colours, which denoted to which master they belonged - in other words, a scapular was part of the livery of a particular lord.

The Carmelites, who wore a brown scapular, began to see themselves as wearing the livery of Our Lady, the Domina Loci - the Lady of the place - to whom they owed allegiance.[1]

When it became known that Our Lady had appeared to Saint Simon Stock and given him the Scapular of the order, promising that whoever wore it at the time of his death, would be saved from Eternal Fire, the scapular of the order became the sign of a special link, both of the whole order and of each individual member with Our Lady. This was so for Order, both Male and Female members, and the members of the third Order (lay persons affiliated with the Order and who shared its life) and the members of the Confraternity of the Scapular, who were lay persons who wore the scapular as a devotion and a sign of having a link to the order.

For the convenience of lay persons, the scapular was shrunk into two small pieces of cloth linked by white ribbon. This is the scapular we know today.

Because of the link between Mary and the Carmelite Order and the Carmelite scapular, the scapular began to be seen as a sign of Consecration to Mary and thence to Jesus, in other words, of a person fully belonging to Mary in the same way as Carmelite friars saw themselves as being, since this is the special charism of their order.

Consecration to Jesus through Mary was strongly advocated by such saints as St. Louis de Montfort (1673 - 1716),[4] so since the brown scapular was seen as an important sign of Consecration to Mary, Wearers of the scapular belonged to Mary, the Lady of the Place, and therefore to her son Jesus.

In even more recent times, the idea of Consecration to Mary through the scapular became linked with the apparitions of Our Lady at Fatima in 1917, when she reproached the world for its laxity and commanded us all to pray for sinners. She promised peace to the world if only the world would turn to her, and she requested the consecration of ourselves and of Russia to her Immaculate Heart. The link with the scapular was accentuated because in the last vision to the children of Fatima, on 13th October 1917, the children saw Our Lady clad in the Carmelite habit and holding her Brown Scapular down towards the crowd. The story of this vision was an eloquent sign of her desire that all should wear the Scapular in her honour, and as a sign of their consecration to her.

The Visionaries reported that Our Lady herself promised that the conversion of Russia was linked to the consecration and devotion of the world to Her Immaculate Heart. She is reported to have said: 'If my requests are heard, Russia will be converted, and there will be peace.'

It seems clear that Pope Pius XII had this in mind when he wrote these words in his letter on the Brown Scapular:

> May it (the Scapular) be a sign of their consecration to the Most Pure Heart of the Immaculate Virgin, which consecration we have so strongly recommended in recent times.

This apparent request by Our Lady to commit both individuals and indeed the whole World to Consecrate themselves to Her Immaculate Heart has led to organisations such as the Blue Army, and indeed the Legion of Mary and the MUSEUM recommending both the Brown Scapular and Consecration to the Immaculate Heart of Mary to their members. The Brown Scapular became the sign of that Consecration.

Christian P. Ceroke, O.Carm describes the symbolism of the scapular as follows:[2]

> As a symbol it possesses a twofold import, one in relation to the Blessed Virgin, one in relation to its wearer. As a sign of consecration to Mary, the Scapular is a reminder of the spiritual prerogatives enjoyed by her in the economy of the redemption, and it is a pledge that her role be activated in favor of the wearer of the Scapular. In relation to its wearer, the Scapular is a sign that one has resolved to dedicate himself to the service of Christ and Mary according to his station in life.The Scapular symbolises both the recognition of the spiritual maternity of Mary and an acceptance of the spiritual duties that Christians, as children of Mary, are obligated to undertake in the service of God.

Emanuele Boaga O.Carm, in 'The Lady of the Place' (page 109), says of the idea of the Scapular as a sign of Consecration to Mary,[1]

> It is clear that in the thinking of the Pontifical Magisterium that a proper presentation of the Scapular and the privileges attached to it has to be based on a good theology of Mary's role in the mystery of Christ and of the Church. Indeed, the power of Mary to help those who wear the scapular is in substance, from the theological point of view, the application of the doctrine of her spiritual motherhood and her role as mediatrix of graces, properly understood. Mary acts in us but we have to be willing to accept what she does and respond

fully by coming to Christ, offered to us by Mary. The scapular devotion then should be understood as a consecration, or, more precisely, an entrusting of oneself to Mary by means of the Carmelite habit and the observance of its conditions. It thus becomes an effective form and means for fostering fidelity to Christ and to a full acceptance of him in our lives, following the example of Mary.

Father Sam Anthony Morello, OCD and Father Patrick McMahon, O.Carm., in their *Catechesis* on the Brown Scapular say:[3]

'The Brown Scapular of Our Lady of Mount Carmel is best understood in the context of our Catholic faith. It offers us a rich spiritual tradition that honours Mary as the first and foremost of her Son's disciples. This scapular is an outward sign of the protection of the Blessed Virgin Mary, our sister, mother, and queen. It offers an effective symbol of Mary's protection to the Order of Carmel — its members, associates, and affiliates — as they strive to fulfil their vocation as defined by the Carmelite Rule of Saint Albert: 'to live in allegiance to Jesus Christ.' While Christ alone has redeemed us, the Blessed Virgin Mary has always been seen by Catholics as a loving mother and protector. The Blessed Virgin has shown her patronage over the Order of Carmel from its earliest days. This patronage and protection came to be symbolised in the scapular, the essential part of the Carmelite habit. Stories and legends abound in Carmelite tradition about the many ways in which the Mother of God has interceded for the Order, especially in critical moments of its history. Most enduring and popular of these traditions, blessed by the Church,

---

> concerns Mary's promise to an early Carmelite, Saint Simon Stock, that anyone who remains faithful to the Carmelite vocation until death will be granted the grace of final perseverance. The Carmelite Order has been anxious to share this patronage and protection with those who are devoted to the Mother of God and so has extended both its habit (the scapular) and affiliation to the larger Church.'

Thus, the Carmelite scapular signifies Our Lady's protection of the wearer, but it also signifies the commitment of the wearer to live the Christian life, since as *Morello and McMahon* say,

> The Brown Scapular of Our Lady of Mount Carmel is a reminder to its wearers of the saving grace which Christ gained upon the cross for all: *All you who have been baptised into Christ have clothed yourselves in him* (Galatians 3:27). There is no salvation for anyone other than that won by Christ.[3]

References:

1 *Emanuele Boaga O.Carm. The Lady of the Place, Mary in the History and in the life of Carmel Edizioni Carmelitane Roma 2001.*
2 *Christian P. Ceroke, O. Carm. The Scapular Devotion https://www.ewtn.com/library/mary/scapular.htm*
3 *Sam Anthony Morello, OCD. and Patrick McMahon, O.Carm. The Brown Scapular of Our Lady of Mount Carmel A Catechesis. https://www.meditationsfromcarmel.com/content/scapular-catechesis*
4 *St. Louis de Montfort, True Devotion to Mary, 1712*

EIGHT

The Beginnings of the Feast of Our Lady of Mount Carmel

The Carmelites of the Middle ages always defended their right to be seen as the 'Brothers of the Blessed Virgin Mary' par excellence. Their leading writers, such as Baconthorpe and Boetus defended the Immaculate Conception of Our Lady, and they changed their cloak from striped to white in Honour of this privilege of the Blessed Virgin.

Here are three medieval stories which emphasised the belief of the Carmelites that they were the 'Brothers of the Blessed Virgin Mary', or 'Our Lady's Order'.

During the period when the Carmelites were strongly challenged regarding their claim to be 'the Brothers of the Virgin Mary', three miracles were quoted by Carmelite writers to support their claim.

Baconthorpe and Thomas Bradley recorded that, during a votive procession in Chester, a miraculous statue of Our Lady spoke as the Carmelites went past and said 'These are my brothers. These are my beloved and chosen brothers.' It is known that as a result, John of Gaunt, Duke of Lancaster (6 March 1340 – 3 February 1399) wrote to the Pope requesting that the Carmelites should be given that title.[15]

John of Hildesheim records miracles surrounding the founding of the Carmelite House in Toulouse between 1242 and 1264, an eminent Jew, walking in his garden saw, at the leafy top of a particular tree a woman of rare beauty holding a child in her arms, who disappeared as he came nearer. This was interpreted by a holy priest thus '*This is a true sign that Our Lady wants to receive permanent homage in this house in which she has so often been blasphemed*', '*The Brothers of the Blessed Virgin Mary as yet do not have a house in this city. Offer them some land to construct a house. Be baptised and become a member of her Order.*' The Jew did as he was bidden. Later, the prefect of the King of France, deeming the house unauthorised, blockaded it with a wall. The Carmelites prayed the 'Ave Stella Mattutina' and the wall collapsed, and the prefect's eyes fell out of their sockets. The Carmelites then sang the Salve Regina, and his eyes returned to their sockets.[15]

A third miracle occurred in Montpellier, described by Baldwin Leers. A large relic of the Holy Cross had fallen to the ground. Every attempt to return it to its place failed till a Carmelite told his brethren in the Monastery Let us also go to take the wood of the Lord because last night, in a vision, the Blessed Virgin said to me, '*I want only my brothers to carry the cross of my son.*' The Carmelites retrieved the relic. They indeed went out in procession and retrieved the relic. In all these stories, the Carmelite's claim to be Mary's brothers was emphasised.[15]

The solemn liturgical feast of Our Lady of Mount Carmel was probably first celebrated in England in the later part of the 14th century. Its aim was to give thanksgiving to Mary, the patroness of the Carmelite Order, for the benefits she had accorded to it through its difficult early years. In particular, the institution of the feast is likely to have come about as a result of the vindication of their title 'Brothers of the Blessed Virgin Mary' at Cambridge England in 1374, when the Carmelite John Hornby defended the Marian Title of the order [and the Immaculate Conception] against the Dominican, John Stokes in the University of Cambridge, and also the approbation of its name and constitution from Honorius III on 30 Jan., 1226. This feast was instituted by the Carmelites between 1376 and 1386 under the title 'Commemoratio B. Marif Virg. duplex', The date originally chosen was 17 July, but on the European mainland this date conflicted with the feast of St. Alexis, so there was a shift to 16 July, which remains the Feast of Our Lady of Mount Carmel throughout the Catholic Church. The Latin poem '*Flos Carmeli*' (meaning 'Flower of Carmel') first appears as the sequence for this Mass. Thus, originally, there was no special link of the feast with the scapular of Carmel.[15]

However, a tradition first attested to in the late 14th century says that Saint Simon Stock, an early English prior general of the Carmelite Order, had a vision of the Blessed Virgin Mary in which she gave him the Brown Scapular. The scapular formed part of the Carmelite habit after 1287. In the vision, Mary promised that those who died wearing the scapular would be saved.[16]

In 1606, Paul V enriched the Confraternity of Our Lady of Mount Carmel with many indulgences and placed its patronal feast on July 16. Three years later (1609), the General Chapter of the Carmelite Order chose July 16 as the principal feast of the whole Order. A monthly procession in honour of Our Lady of Mount Carmel had been already prescribed by the decrees of the General Chapter of 1593. It had to take place on a Sunday in each of the convents where the Confraternity of the Brown Scapular was instituted. It is worth commenting that Processions, originally to the tomb of Christ in Jerusalem, and in His honour, were very prominent in the Rite of the Holy Sepulchre, which was the Carmelite rite.[16]

In 1642, a Carmelite named Fr. John Cheron published a document which he said was a 13th-century letter written by Saint Simon Stock's secretary, Peter Swanington. This document, later argued to be a forgery, claimed that 16 July 1251 was the date of the vision (16 July being the date of the Feast of Our Lady of Mount Carmel), which led for centuries to a strong association between this feast day and the scapular devotion. So, although originally, the liturgical feast of Our Lady of Mount Carmel did not have a specific association with the Brown Scapular or the tradition of Stock's vision of the Blessed Virgin Mary, this tradition grew gradually. Once the controversy regarding the Sabbatine privilege had been settled by the decisions of the Church in 1613, the way was open to the development of the feast of the 16th July into the Feast Of Our Lady of Mount Carmel, with particular emphasis on the scapular of Carmel, as we know it today.[16]

By 1638, members of the Diocesan clergy in the Neapolitan kingdom, and in some regions of Spain and Sicily, began also to celebrate this feast. The Sacred Congregation of Rites, at the request of the Queen of Spain extended the celebration of the feast to all countries under Spanish rule on the 21st November 1674, and to the kingdoms of Austria and Portugal in 1679. Subsequently the feast was approved in the Papal States, and Benedict XIII placed the feast on the universal calendar of the Latin Church in 1726.[16] It has since been adopted by some Eastern Rite Catholics, as well.

How, then, did the Feast of the sixteenth July develop in Malta? The development of the feast of the sixteenth July in Malta is also the development of the convents of the Carmelites in Malta. The first convent was that of the Old Annunciation church outside Rabat. It was founded in 1418. In it, the monthly procession in honour of Our Lady of Mount Carmel which had been already prescribed by the decrees of the General Chapter of 1593 was held on the third Sunday of the month. It was certainly being held in 1612, and was very popular, with devotees from all over Mdina, Rabat and the neighbouring villages participating. It is not known whether another procession used to be held there on 16th July, but to celebrate the feast, a painting of Our Lady of Mount Carmel was acquired in 1612.[1]

In Valletta, the Carmelite Church began to be built in 1570. It was designed by the famous Maltese architect Girolamo Cassar and was intended originally to be dedicated to the Annunciation of the Blessed Virgin Mary. However, when it was completed it was renamed for Our Lady of Mount Carmel. The solemn procession of July 16 held by the Carmelites at Valletta was the first procession ever to take place there, in 1622. It grew to become one of the most famous and popular processions in Malta. By 1828 all the different Religious Orders in Valletta used to take part in it as well as all Confraternities which were canonically erected in that church, namely those of Our Lady of Mount Carmel, St Joseph, The Guardian Angel, The Blessed Franco, St Louis Gonzaga and St Louis, King of France. There is no evidence of any picture of the statue of Our Lady of Mount Carmel being carried during that procession until 1657, when a statute of this Madonna was taken out processionally on July 16 and July 23 of that year.[1,2,4,5]

Until the year 1790, besides the solemn procession of July 16, another procession of Our Lady of Mt. Carmel used to take place in Valletta, It was organised by the Confraternity of Our Lady of Mount Carmel and was held on July 23, the octave day of the feast. Between the years 1657-1790, three different statues of the same Madonna were used. Two of them belonged to that Confraternity. The first of which was brought from Rome about the year 1657. Till 1779, it was this statue that was carried out processionally on July 16 and 23. In 1780, the Confraternity brought a new statue from Naples,sculpted by Gennaro Reale,making use of it for the first time in the above-mentioned processions of that same year.[1]

Problems between the Friars and the members of the Confraternity regarding the place to store the second statue led the Friars deciding to acquire a statue of their own in 1781, the one that is used today. This has been sculpted by Vincenzo Dimech. Ever since 1781, this statue has been carried out during the July 16th procession. The members of the Confraternity, on their part, used to carry their own statue during the procession held on July 23 until 1790.[1]

On the 12th October 1790, the Confraternity of Our Lady of Mount Carmel made a written petition to the Friars, wherein they suggested a novena preceding the feast of July 16 instead of the procession of July 23, under the following conditions: during that novena, starting on July 7, there was to be a daily high Mass with the exposition of the Blessed Sacrament and a sermon on the Virgin Mary during the same mass. The evening service was to include the *Salve Regina*, the Litany and sacramental benediction with the pyx. This is the origin of the Novena held every year before the feast[1] of the 16th July in Valletta. Eventually the statue by Gennaro Reale was given, by the Confraternity, to the Carmelite Community of Balluta.[3]

In Mdina, the Carmelite Community solemnised the feast of July 16 a month after they took residence in the Old City, in 1659, they celebrated that feast with music. It is uncertain whether they organised a procession that year, but certainly did so the following year. The Processional statue of the Virgin of Mount Carmel is by the Maltese sculpture Andrea Imbroll in 1721.[14]

In the meantime, within the diocese of Malta, two churches dedicated to Our Lady of Mount Carmel had been built. The Fawwara Church, built beside a spring in the limits of Siġġiewi, was founded in 1616, and is to this day looked after by the Confraternity of Our Lady of Charity of Valletta, which organises the feast in July while the Vittoriosa church, previously owned by the Carmelites, reverted to the diocese when the Carmelites had to give it up because of the small size of the community in 1653.

Many altars were dedicated to Our Lady of Mount Carmel in Parish Churches; these included Żurrieq in 1630, Birkirkara in 1646, Siġġiewi, Naxxar in 1634, Għargħur in 1668.[14] Three confraternities in her honour were founded within the diocese, one at Senglea in 1722, another one at Siġġiewi in 1745[9] and finally the Żurrieq confraternity whose statues were duly approved in 1801. This Żurrieq Confraternity, wearing their distinctive great Brown Scapulars over their white sack, and their violet Muzzetta (small cape) with a picture of Our Lady embroidered on it, is still very strong today. It had been founded by a merchant from Valletta, called Giovanna Maria Borg, who, in 1800 had taken refuge in Żurrieq during the Napoleonic War and siege of Valletta by the Maltese. The Confraternity was founded in 1801, with 90 founder members. This confraternity commissioned a polychrome wood processional statue from Salvu Psaila in 1842 for use in the Procession of the feast, which is held on the third Sunday of July.[7]

In all the places we have mentioned, the feast was celebrated, either by the confraternities or by fraternities of tertiaries.

Big boosts to the popularity of devotion to Our Lady of Mount Carmel were the arrival of the Discalced Carmelites in Malta in 1625, and the approval of Pope Sixtus V for the celebration of her feast on the 16th July in 1587. The Discalced Carmelites built their first Monastery in the city of Cospicua. From it, many missionaries went to the Middle East, and even re-settled on Mount Carmel itself.

A Marian Sodality with a very strange name contributed a great deal to the popularity of the Scapular in Malta: 'The Sodality of the four farthings', whose name derived from the four farthings its members were to pay monthly for the celebration of masses and prayers after their death. This Sodality played a very important part in the history of the devotion of Our Lady of Mount Carmel in our Islands. It is reckoned that it was through this Sodality that the Scapular devotion was mostly enhanced.[14]

In 1790, a niche in Fgura was rebuilt into a church by Klement Darmanin. The Carmelites took over care of the church in 1945.

This developed into a full parish which celebrates the feast on the first weekend of July.[10]

In 1892, the Carmelites were given the small church at Balluta by the Confraternity of Our Lady of Mount Carmel, who had built it. This church was rebuilt on three occasions. It has grown into a full parish, and the Confraternity has also given the Carmelites the Gennaro Reale statue which had previously been in Valletta. This parish celebrates with great pomp the feast of Our Lady of Mount Carmel on the last weekend of July, and the Valletta Confraternity still participates.[3]

The Gżira parish developed as a result of an unusual occurrence in 1902. Three soldiers were trying to rouse a barman to open his shop and give them more drinks. One of them threw a stone, which stuck in the protective glass of a picture of Our Lady of Mount Carmel. For this reason, here Our Lady is called 'Tal-Ġebla' 'of the stone'. This event led to the building of a church, which became a parish and which celebrated the feast of Our Lady of Mount Carmel on the second weekend of July.[8]

The Carmelites took over the convent of Santa Venera in 1913,[13,6] which led to the development of further convents at Fleur-de-Lys in 1947 and at the new parish church in 1980. The feast in Fleur-de-Lys is held in early July, while in Santa Venera it is held as a pilgrimage in October- linked with the last apparition in [12].

In Birkirkara, the Discalced Carmelites also celebrate the feast from their shrine of Saint Therese. Here there also exists a Confraternity. Before the Discalced Carmelites came to Birkirkara, in the Basilica of Saint Helena there existed a Confraternity of Mount Carmel whose name was changed to Confraternity of the Holy Souls so as to distinguish it from the Confraternity of Mount Carmel which was moved to the Carmelite Monastery.[14]

In Gozo there are churches of Our Lady of Mount Carmel in Ta' Hamet and in Xlendi. In both these churches, the feast is celebrated, in Ta-Hammet as a pilgrimage on the 16th July, and in Xlendi as a fisherman's feast later in the summer. It appears that much land around Xlendi was owned at one time by the Monastery of Our Lady of Mount Carmel in Mdina.

The result of all these locations and feasts is that The Feast of Our Lady of Mount Carmel is one of the most widely celebrated in the Maltese Islands, and Malta has been called 'Malta Karmelitana'.

References:

1 *BORG GUSMAN, V. 1983. Marian Devotion in the Maltese Carmelite province during the 17th and 18th Centuries, in V. BORG (ed.) Marian Devotions in the Islands of Saint Paul (1600-1800). Malta.*

2 *SAMMUT, L.M. 1952. Is-Santwarju Tal-Karmnu. Malta*

3 *ABELA, S. 2006. Il-Karmelitani fil-Balluta 1890-2006. Malta.*

4 *DEBONO, J. 2006. L-Istatwi tal-Madonna tal-Karmnu ta' l-1871 u ta' l-Anġlu Kustodju u l-Iskulturi Tagħhom. Program Tal-Festa tal-Madonna tal-Karmnu 2006: 31-45. Malta.*

5 *The Archconfraternity of Our Lady Of Mount Carmel and its Oratory in Valletta. Agius M, Farrugia J, Pace C. Vigilo - DIN L-ART ĦELWA December 2016.*

---

6 *www.ocarm.org/en/content/ocarm/province-malta*

7 *https://www.talkarmnuŻurrieq.org/il-fratellanza*

8 *https://en.wikipedia.org/wiki/Gżira*

9 *http://www.Siġġiewiparish.com/parrocca/?q=node/83*

10 *http://fguraparish.org/storja/storja.htm*

11 *Patri Serafin Abela O. Carm 'Il-Karmelitani fi Fleur-de-Lys'*

12 *http://www.fleurdelysparish.com/rizorsi/storja*

13 *https://it.wikipedia.org/wiki/Santa_Venera_(Malta)*

14 *Vincent Borg Marian Devotions in Maltese Diocesan Churches in V. BORG (ed.) Marian Devotions in the Islands of Saint Paul (1600-1800). Malta.*

15 *Emanuele Boaga O.Carm. The Lady of the Place, Mary in the History and in the life of Carmel Edizioni Carmelitane Roma 2001.*

16 *Fr. Sam Anthony Morello, OCD. And Father Patrick McMahon, O.Carm r The Brown Scapular of Our Lady of Mount Carmel A Catechesishttps://www.meditationsfromcarmel.com/content/scapular-catechesis*

NINE

What Saints Have Said About the Scapular

Many great Saints, not only Saints of the Carmelite Order, have written and spoken about the Carmelite Scapular and had great devotion to it.[1,2]

Blessed Pope Gregory X died in 1276. was buried wearing the Scapular, 25 years after the traditional date of the scapular vision. When his tomb was opened 600 years after his death, in 1830, his Scapular was found intact. It can be seen, perfectly preserved in the Arezzo museum, in Italy.

Similarly, St. John Bosco and St. Alphonsus Liguori had both got a deep devotion to Our Lady of Mount Carmel. When their graves were opened, although everything else in their graves that was corruptible had decayed, their Carmelite Scapulars were found intact.

St. Alphonsus Liguori's Brown Scapular is still miraculously intact and on exhibit in his Monastery in Rome.

The Jesuit Saint Claude de la Colombiere, who was spiritual director of St. Margaret Mary, the visionary of the Sacred Heart of Jesus and the 'First Friday Devotion' says 'Because all the forms of our love for the Blessed Virgin and all its various modes of expression cannot be equally pleasing to Her, and therefore do not assist us in the same degree to reach Heaven, I say, without a moment's hesitation, that the Brown Scapular is the most favoured of all!' He also adds, 'No devotion has been confirmed by more numerous authentic miracles than the Brown Scapular.' Furthermore, Claude de la Colombiere says, 'I know well that the Saints have spoken most encouragingly on the powerful protection of Mary, but enlightened and holy as they have been, they are, after all, only men'. Here it is the Queen herself who in that celebrated revelation, reveals all the tenderness of her heart to Saint Simon Stock! Those great Saints have assured me that with Mary to protect my interests I need fear nothing. That does not suffice me. I wish to know if she does protect my interests. Yes. She gives me proof unequivocal. I have but to glance at my Scapular, tangible proof before my eyes, and re-call the promise attached to its devout wearing: 'Whosoever dies wearing this shall never suffer eternal fire.' Where his devotion to the scapular originated from is said by Claude de la Colombiere ' I learned to love the Scapular Virgin in the arms of my mother,' Saint Claude de la Colombiere further says: 'It is not enough to say that the habit of the Blessed Virgin is a mark of predestination. Because of the alliance which Mary contracts with us, and which we enter into with her, no other devotion renders our salvation so certain.' These quotes are quoted by Fr. Peter Davies, O. Carm.

According to Rev. Howard Rafferty, O. Carm., Venerable Francis Ypes used to say that there are three things of which the demons are most afraid: the Holy Name of Jesus, the Holy Name of Mary, and the Holy Scapular of Carmel.

St. Peter Claver - apostle of the negro -used the Scapular to ensure the salvation of his converts, when he converted to Christianity the slaves who arrived regularly in Cartegena, South America. Peter Claver organised catechists to give them instruction, and before they were sold, he saw that they were baptised. Many ecclesiastes accused the Saint of indiscreet zeal but Peter reminded them that he had baptised and enrolled all in Our Lady's Scapular. He was confident that Mary would watch over each one of his converts.

The Cure of Ars is another great saint who had a devotion to the Carmelite Scapular. This is a story about him. One day a young woman, before entering the religious life, went to see the Curé of Ars, and during the conversation, he asked her, 'Do you recall, my child, at the certain evening of dancing, where you were? There was a very young man, very pretty, unknown, distinguished, admired, and all the girls wanted to dance with him.' 'Yes, I recall when he never came to ask me, I was sad, yet all the other girls were privileged to dance with that young man.''You would have liked to dance with him, wouldn't you?' 'Yes.' 'Do you recall, when that young man was leaving the dance hall, you saw under his feet two blue flames? And you thought it was an illusion of your eyes? When you saw that young man leave the dance hall, you saw fire under his feet! It was not an illusion of your eyes, my daughter. That man was a demon. And if he did not come to you to ask you to dance, it's for one reason: you were wearing the vestment of Our Lady of Mount Carmel.'

Saint John of the Cross, the great Carmelite mystic, said of the Scapular or Habit of the Order when he received it: 'I desire to practice with fervour all the virtues of Mary which this holy habit symbolises.' He used to pray for the grace of dying on Saturday, and his prayers were answered. Before he died, in the year 1591, he said: 'The Mother of God and of Carmel hastens to Purgatory with grace on Saturday and delivers those souls who have worn her Scapular. Blessed be such a Lady who wills that, on this day of Saturday, I shall depart from this life!'

It is worth recording the famous story from an old Carmelite book which describes a link between Saint Angelo, Saint Francis and Saint Dominic. In the pages of an ancient history of the Carmelite Order (written in mediaeval Latin by a priest named Fr. Marianus Ventimiglia), published in 1773 in Naples, we find this historical account[3]: Three famous men of God met on a street corner in Rome. They were Friar Dominic, busy gathering recruits to a new Religious Order of Preachers; Brother Francis, the friend of birds and beasts and especially dear to the poor; and Angelus, who had been invited to Rome from Mount Carmel, in Palestine, because of his fame as a preacher. At their chance meeting, by the light of the Holy Spirit each of the three men recognised each other and, in the course of their conversation (as recorded by various followers who were present), they made prophecies to each other. Saint Angelus foretold the stigmata of Saint Francis, and Saint Dominic said:

> *'One day, Brother Angelus, to your Order of Carmel the Most Blessed Virgin Mary will give a devotion to be known as the Brown Scapular, and to my Order of Preachers she will give a devotion to be known as the Rosary.* **ONE DAY, THROUGH THE ROSARY AND THE SCAPULAR, SHE WILL SAVE THE WORLD.**'

Finally, we should mention Malta's own saint, Saint George Preca. He was greatly devoted to Our Lady of Mount Carmel and was a

Carmelite Tertiary. There are numerous pictures of him wearing the scapular. He insisted that all members of the Society of Christian Doctrine, which he founded, should be enrolled in, and wear the Carmelite Scapular.

References:

1 *Fr. Peter Davies. O.Carm Our Lady's Brown Scapular Sign of Consecration to Mary www.ecatholic2000.com › cts › untitled-328*

2 *Howard Rafferty, O. Carm Stories of the Brown Scapular https://www.tldm.org/news7/miraculousstoriesscapular.htm*

3. *https://fsspx.uk/en/news-events/news/story-scapular-our-lady-mount-carmel-67490*

TEN

What Popes Have Said About the Brown Scapular

I have collected from the internet all the quotes by popes which I could find which discuss the brown scapular. As good Catholics, we always look to the Holy Father for a lead in matters of devotion, and we know that what is approved by the Pope is safe for us to follow. For many centuries, the Popes have publicly voiced their approval of the Scapular, and have themselves worn it faithfully and lovingly.[1,2]

When Leo XI (2 June 1535 – 27 April 1605) was being crowned as Pope, his Scapular was accidently removed from his shoulders, and he said: 'Leave me Mary lest Mary should leave me'—an eloquent tribute to his faith in Our Lady's promises.

Pope Pius IX was notable for his special love for the Mother of God. It was he who defined the Dogma of the Immaculate Conception in 1854. This saintly Pontiff said:

> This most extraordinary gift of the Scapular from the Mother of God to St. Simon Stock, brings its great usefulness not only to the great Carmelite family of Mary, but also to all the rest of the faithful who wish, affiliated to that family, to follow Mary with a special devotion.

Leo XIII, (born March 2, 1810, Carpineto Romano, Papal States — died July 20, 1903, Rome), said of the scapular of Carmel:

> The Carmelite Scapular, because of its nobility of origin, its extra-ordinary spread among Christian peoples for many centuries, the spiritualising effects produced by it and the outstanding miracles worked in virtue of it, render the Scapular of Carmel commendable to a wondrous degree. In his last illness he said, 'Let us now make a novena to Our Lady of Mount Carmel and I shall be ready to die.'
>
> Pius X was pope from August 1903 to his death in 1914. wore the Scapular — he was also a Carmelite Tertiary, a member of the Third Order of Carmel.

Pope Benedict XV ascended the throne of St. Peter in 1914, the year in which the terrible First World War broke out. His pleas for peace fell on deaf ears— but his stirring appeal for the wearing of the Scapular should be heard by every Catholic. He declared:

> Let all of you have a common language and a common armour; the language, the sayings of the Gospel; the common armour, the Scapular of the Virgin of Carmel which you all ought to wear, and which enjoys the extraordinary privilege of protection even after death.

Benedict XV full quote is as follows:

> Prompted by Our constant love for the tender Mother of God, and mindful also of Our own enrolment from boyhood in the Confraternity of this same Scapular, most willingly do We commend so pious an undertaking, and We are certain that upon it will fall an abundance of divine blessings. **For not with a light or passing matter are we here concerned, but**

> **with the obtaining of eternal life itself, which is the substance of that promise of the most blessed virgin, which has been handed down to us.** We are concerned with that which is of supreme importance to all, and with the manner of achieving it safely. For the Holy Scapular, which may be called the Habit or Garment of Mary, is a sign and a pledge, of the protection of the Mother of God. But not for this reason, however, may they who wear the Scapular think that they can gain eternal salvation while remaining slothful and negligent of spirit, for the Apostle warns us: 'In fear and trembling shall you work out your salvation.'
>
> Let all of you have a common language and a common armour; the language, the words of the Gospel; the armour, the Scapular of the Virgin of Carmel, which enjoys the singular privilege of protection even after death.

Pope Pius XI died in 1939. It was he who canonised the great Carmelite Saint, Therese of Lisieux, the Little Flower, and made her the Patroness of Missions throughout the world. But long before he knew little Therese, he was devoted to the Scapular. He said: 'I learned to love the Scapular Virgin in the arms of my mother.' He never tired of urging the faithful to wear the Scapular faithfully and so obtain the protection and promises of Our Lady. He said 'The munificent goodness of the heavenly Mother towards her children; it surely ought to be sufficient merely to exhort those who belong to the scapular confraternity to persevere in the holy exercises which have been prescribed for the gaining of the indulgences to which they are entitled.'

Pope Pius XII shared the devotion of his predecessors to the Scapular — a devotion which went back to his boyhood days. He called the Scapular 'the keepsake of the Queen herself, and the Garment of Mary.' His very beautiful letter on the occasion of the 700th anniversary of the Scapular is quoted here:

'The Scapular is, in a true sense, a 'habit'. Those who receive it are, by their clothing, associated in a more or less intimate way with the Order of Carmel. Those who wear it profess to belong to Our Lady in the same way as the Knight of the Thirteenth Century, the century of the Scapular Vision, felt that he was ever under the watchful eye of his Lady. He was valiant and sure in battle, and when wearing his 'Colours', would rather have died a thousand times than allow them to be tarnished'.

> Therefore, all Carmelites, whether they live in the cloisters of the First and Second Orders, or are members of the Third Order Regular or Secular, or of the Confraternities, belong to the same Family of our Most Blessed Mother and are attached to it by a special bond of love. May they all see in this Keepsake of the Queen herself, a mirror of humility, and purity; may they read in the very simplicity of the Garment a concise lesson in modesty and simplicity; and above all, may they behold in this same Garment, which they wear day and night, the eloquently expressed symbol, of their prayers for the divine assistance; finally may it be to them a Sign of their Consecration to the most Pure Heart of the Immaculate Virgin, which (consecration) in recent times We have so strongly recommended. 'And certainly this most gentle Mother will not delay to open, as soon as possible, through her inter-

> cession with God, the gates of heaven for her children who are expiating their faults in Purgatory — a trust based on that Promise known as the Sabbatine Privilege.

Saint Pope John XXIII has spoken:

> of the Mother of God, who is honoured in this Church of Our Lady of Mount Carmel. Devotion to her becomes a necessity; towards Our Lady of Mount Carmel we are drawn with a most tender, yet irresistible, attraction. It becomes clearer day by day that the way for men to return to God is assured by Mary, that Mary is the basis of our confidence, the guarantee of our security, the foundation of our hope.

Saint Pope Paul VI speaking of Marian devotions, especially of the Scapular, says:

> Let the faithful hold in high esteem the practices and devotions to the Blessed Virgin approved by the teaching authority of the Church (Vatican II). It is Our conviction that the Rosary of Mary and the Scapular of Carmel are among these recommended practices. The Scapular is a practice of piety, which by its very simplicity is suited to everyone.

In the Message of Saint Pope John Paul II to the Carmelite Family on the 750th Anniversary of the Bestowal of the Scapular 25 March 2001:[4]

> Carmelites have chosen Mary as their Patroness and spiritual Mother and always keep before the eyes of their heart the Most Pure Virgin who guides everyone to the perfect

> knowledge and imitation of Christ. In Carmel therefore and in every soul moved by tender affection for the Blessed Virgin and Mother, there has thrived a contemplation of her, who from the beginning knew how to open herself to hearing God's Word and to obeying his will (Lk 2: 19, 51).

Saint Pope John Paul II, in a General Audience, at Castelgandolfo July 16, 2003:[3]

> I, from my youngest days, have worn around my neck the Scapular of Our Lady and I take refuge with trust under the mantle of the Blessed Virgin Mary, Mother of Jesus. I hope the Scapular will be for everyone, especially the faithful who wear it, a help and defence in times of danger, a seal of peace and a sign of Mary's care.

When Pope John Paul II was shot and operated on in 1981, he told doctors not to remove the brown scapular he was wearing.

On July 16th, 2011, at Castel Gandolfo, speaking to Pilgrims, Benedict XVI referred to wearing the scapular as,

> a particular sign of union with Jesus and Mary. For those who wear it, it is a sign of filial abandonment to the protection of the Immaculate Virgin. 'In our battle against evil, may Mary our Mother wrap us in her mantle.'

Addressing Chile's president, government, civil organisations, and the diplomatic corps at the La Moneda Palace on 16th January 2018 when visiting Chile, Pope Francis praised the scapular and concluded his remarks by saying: 'I pray that Our Lady of Mount Carmel, Mother and Queen of Chile, will continue to accompany and bring to birth the dreams of this blessed nation.'[5]

Thus for 700 years the popes have loved the Scapular and trusted its protection. We need to have no fear of doing what they have done, and what they have so constantly urged us to do. We should wear the scapular with confidence and love for our Heavenly Queen, since in doing so we are honouring her, and in return, we can be confident that she will do all she has promised for us.

References:

1 *Fr. Peter Davies. O.Carm Our Lady's Brown Scapular Sign of Consecration to Mary www.ecatholic2000.com › cts › untitled-328*

2 *Howard Rafferty, O. Carm Stories of the Brown Scapular https://www.tldm.org/news7/miraculousstoriesscapular.htm*

3 *https://ocarm.org/en/content/ocarm/scapular-devotion-pope-john-paul-ii*

4 *ocarm.org › content › ocarm › pontiff-praises-wearing-scapular*

5 *www.carmelite.org › news › popes-visit-chile-highlights-devotion-our lady of Mount Carmel.*

ELEVEN

The Relationship Between The Confraternities of the Scapular, the Carmelite Order, and Our Lady of Mount Carmel

In the Middle Ages, it was customary for the Carmelites to give their scapular to those who collaborated with them as a sign of affiliation to the order. Thus, For Instance, John of Gaunt, Duke of Lancaster, received the scapular in this way.

Often, the Carmelites would organise these affiliates into confraternities — brotherhoods or sisterhoods — to help them lead a more spiritual life.[1] (Scapular Catechesis The Brown Scapular of Our Lady of Mount Carmel *Father Sam Anthony Morello, OCD and Father Patrick McMahon, O.Carm.*)

Later, when because of the Reformation, the Enlightenment, The French Revolution, Napoleon, and the Unification of Italy, whole provinces of the Order were suppressed, the devotion to Our Lady of Mount Carmel was continued by these confraternities alone, who often, especially in Italy, maintained the old Carmelite Churches and with them Carmelite Devotions.[7]

Initially, the first Confraternities were ones, such as the 'Battuti' of Modena (1300), which met in Carmelite churches. Later specific scapular Confraternities were set up.

The members of the various Confraternities would meet regularly at the Church of the Order to which they were affiliated for prayers. At their meetings, they often wore a habit — most Confraternities had a habit of some sort — that was similar to the habit of the Religious Order to which they were affiliated. They would say their prayers together and receive pious instruction from the friars. They had certain rights to participate in processions and ceremonies in the friars' churches. They usually had certain rights about being buried in the church as well, or having the friars assist at their funerals. It is worth noting that the members of the Confraternities were affiliated to the Order but their obligations were (and are) not as great as those of the Members of the Third Order, since the members of the third order were actually members of the Carmelite Order who lived at home with their families, while the members of the Confraternities were not members of the order, but simply enrolled in the scapular and members of a confraternity local group[1,7].

The Archconfraternity of Our Lady of Mount Carmel of Valletta (founded 1622) and the Confraternity of Our Lady of Mount Carmel in Żurrieq (founded 1801) are two examples of Scapular Confraternities of this type.[3,4,5] There is also a Confraternity of Our Lady of Mount Carmel in Birkirkara.

Clearly, so many confraternity groups spread first around Europe and then throughout the world constitute a huge number of persons involved is working to promote the Scapular of Our Lady of Mount Carmel. It is impossible in a book of this size to list all the confraternities of Our Lady of Mount Carmel. We will limit ourselves to describing a few important confraternities of Our Lady of Mount Carmel which we have come across in our travels in Italy and Spain, and one or two very important ones in South America. In Taranto, Italy, the Arciconfraternita di Maria SS. Del Carmine has its own church and numerous members. As well as the feast of Our Lady of Mount Carmel it famously organises the Holy Week festivities in the town.[9,10] In the same region there are also the Confraternita Santa Maria del Carmine — Talsano and the Confraternita della Madonna del Carmine in Grottaglie. In Gallipoli, the Confraternita di Maria Santissima del Monte Carmelo e della Misericordia - Orazione e Morte - is an ancient confraternity which also celebrates the feast of the Vergine Addolorata in Holy week. So also, with its own Church, Does the Confraternita del-Carmine of Ostuni.[13]

In Palermo Church of the Carmine Maggiore and at the Church of Madonna della Traspontina in Rome,[11] there are Confraternities of the Madonna del-Carmine which are linked with the Carmelite Communities of those churches. The Nobile congrega di Maria Santissima del Carmelo at Palmi is likewise linked with the Carmelite Community of the Church.[12]

The church of S.Agatha in Trastevere, Rome, is the Seat of the Venerabile Arciconfraternità del Santissimo Sacramento e Maria Santissima del Carmine in Trastevere, which organised the Festa de'Noantri in Rome every July. In Venice the Confraternity of the Great Scuola del Carmine has recently been revived.[14]

In Santu Lussurgiu in Sardegna,[15] the Confraternity is in charge of the Sanctuary of Our Lady of Mount Carmel.

All the above confraternities are only a random sample of the huge number of Confraternities in Italy.

Spain is also a very fertile ground for the discovery of Scapular Confraternities, We only need to Quote the city of Seville. Here there are 9 confraternities dedicated to Our Lady of Mount Carmel and celebrating the 16th July; Calatrava, San Gil, Santa Catalina, Triana, San Leandro, Santo Ángel, Su Eminencia, San Pablo and el Buen Suceso, and all these hold ceremonies and processions on that day[8]. Furthermore, there is a Confraternity of the 'Carmen Doloroso' which participates in the celebrations of Holy Week.[18] Such fervor is reflected in the rest of Spain.

Also of great importance are the Archicofradía del Carmen of San Cayetano of Cordoba[16] **and the Antigua y Venerable Archicofradía de Nuestra Señora del Carmen Coronada of Malaga,[17] who both organise the Feast of the 16th July in honour of their crowned statues, the one in Malaga being a seaborn procession linked with the devotion of the sailors and fishermen.**

Meanwhile, in the Countries of the old Spanish Empire, we have mentioned elsewhere in this book the Confraternities of Santiago del Cile and Lima, among others.

Why is it necessary to quote this long list of Organised Confraternities? While many of these have many members because each confraternity is autonomous, linked with its own customs and Location, it is difficult for them to be seen collectively as a transnational movement such as Catholic Action or Focolare. In

Malta, the two most important Confraternities of Our Lady of Mount Carmel are alive and growing. However, in general there are many in Malta who see confraternities in general as gradually dying out, with their patrimony unlikely to survive. This is not so; seen globally the confraternities of the scapular are a vast untapped resource for local churches, both in terms of the presence of the faithful, in terms of making spirituality available to them, and in terms of their making real every day the pius traditions of their fathers.

References:

1 *Fr. Sam Anthony Morello, OCD. And Father Patrick McMahon, O.Carm r The Brown Scapular of Our Lady of Mount Carmel A Catechesis https://www.meditationsfromcarmel.com/content/scapular-catechesis*

2 *BORG GUSMAN, V. 1983. Marian Devotion in the Maltese Carmelite province during the 17th and 18th Centuries, in V. BORG (ed.) Marian Devotions in the Islands of Saint Paul (1600-1800). Malta.*

3 *SAMMUT, L.M. 1952. Is-Santwarju Tal-Karmnu. Malta*

4 *The Archconfraternity of Our Lady Of Mount Carmel and its Oratory in Valletta. Agius M, Farrugia J, Pace C. Vigilo - DIN L-ART HELWA December 2016.*

5 *https://www.talkarmnuŻurrieq.org/il-fratellanza*

6 *Vincent Borg Marian Devotions in Maltese Diocesan Churches in V. BORG (ed.) Marian Devotions in the Islands of Saint Paul (1600-1800). Malta.*

7 *Emanuele Boaga O.Carm. The Lady of the Place, Mary in the History and in the life of Carmel Edizioni Carmelitane Roma 2001.*

---

8 *Juan Martinez Alcalde Hermandades de Gloria de Sevilla 1988 Boletin de las Confradias de Sevilla.*

9 *Nicola Caputo, Alfredo Majorano Nunziato Le Poste, L'Addolorata i Misteri Mandese Editore 1998 Taranto*

10 *Nicola Caputo I giorni del Perdono Scorpione Editrice 1995 Taranto. carminemaggiorepa.blogspot.com/p/confraternita.html*

11 *romanchurches.wikia.com/wiki/Santa_Maria_in_Traspontina*

12 *https://it.wikipedia.org/wiki/Santuario_di_Maria_Santissima_del_Carmelo*

13 *http://www.arciconfraternitadelcarmine.it/laconfraternita/*

14 *www.scuolagrandecarmini.it/*

15 *http://www.santulussurgiucomunitaospitale.it/confraternita_del_carmine*

16 *processionsofcordoba.com/category/carmen-de-san-cayetano/*

17 *carmenperchel.blogspot.com/*

18 *https://en.wikipedia.org/wiki/Hermandad_del_Carmen_Doloroso*

TWELVE

Some Practicalities

The Brown Scapular of Our Lady of Mount Carmel is in the habit of the Carmelite Order. For the religious members of the Order it takes the form of two long, undecorated panels of brown cloth joined at the shoulders and falling, one to the front and one to the back. For the laity it takes the form of two smaller pieces of brown or dark cloth, either plain, or often also decorated with pictures of Our Lady and the Sacred Heart, joined over the shoulder by ribbons, and falling, one to the back, the other to the front. Because it is the Order's habit, the scapular signifies some degree of affiliation to the Carmelite Order.

The various Carmelite confraternities practiced a devotion to Our Lady of Mount Carmel and usually maintained traditional Carmelite disciplines, such as abstaining from meat on Wednesdays and Saturdays as well as Fridays.

Persons are intended to be Enrolled in the Scapular, and therefore this should be done in a ceremony, and the names of the new persons enrolled should be recorded in a book. In recent years, the discipline of the Church has changed world-wide so that any priest may enrol persons in the scapular. The problem with this is that, because many priests are not located close to a Carmelite Monastery, it is often the case that the names are not passed on to the Carmelite Order. Often, in Malta, Children, while still very young, are enrolled in the Scapular when they are presented to Our Lady. This is a laudable practice, but there is the risk that they may not remember whether they have been enrolled in the scapular or not. Equally, it is important that, when persons are enrolled in properly set up Scapular Confraternities, such as the Arch-Confraternity of Valletta, it is important that the new member is formally enrolled in the Brown Scapular; there have been cases when the new member is unsure whether he is enrolled or not. Records must be kept, and be accessible. Nowadays, the scapular can be substituted by a medal on one side of which is Our Lady and on the other side of which is the image of the Sacred Heart. It is important however that the cloth scapular is used to enrol persons. *The Catechesis on the Brown Scapular produced by the Carmelite Institute Washington D.C. comments;*

> In the end, when all is said and done, the scapular is the Carmelite habit. Carmelite tradition declares, not so much from a vision as from the living faith of the men and women of Carmel over eight centuries, that we — the Carmelites — enjoy a special protection by the Mother of God as a sign of her love for us and her appreciation of our trust and confidence in her and our devotion to however as our model for living a life of allegiance to her Son. We Carmelites are willing — even anxious — to share this protection and favour that Mary shows us as we are anxious to share the trust and confidence we place in her and our devotion to her. A visible sign of our sharing this protection and this devotion is the scapular. It is the Carmelite Order— not the Blessed Virgin — who gives the scapular to the faithful and invites the faithful to share our charism in expectation of the graces won by Christ and bestowed on Carmel and its members through the

intercession of the Mother of God. The Graces are bestowed on the Family of Carmel; the scapular is a sign of belonging in some way and to some varying degree to the family of Carmel.

Reference:

Fr. Sam Anthony Morello, OCD. And Father Patrick McMahon, O.Carm r The Brown Scapular of Our Lady of Mount Carmel A Catechesishttps://www.meditationsfromcarmel.com/content/scapular-catechesis

PART TWO

CATECHESIS OF THE SCAPULAR OF OUR LADY OF MOUNT CARMEL

BY

P. EWGENJU TONNA,

O.CARM, S.TH. D.

First Published Malta 1979.
Based on the *Novena del Carmine*
by P.Ludovico Saggi O.Carm.

Note. The Constitutions and Decrees of the Second Vatican Council mentioned in this second part are abbreviated in this way:

AA = 'Apostolicam Actuositatem'; AG = 'Ad Gentes';
LG= 'Lumen Gentium'; OT = 'Optatam totius';
PC = 'Perfectae Caritatis'; PO = 'Presbyterorum Ordinis';
SC = 'Sacrosanctum Concilium'; UR = 'Unitas Redintegratio'.

THIRTEEN

THE USE OF THE SCAPULAR OF OUR LADY OF MOUNT CARMEL IN GIVING HONOUR TO OUR LADY

EVERYONE KNOWS THAT THE CHURCH LOVES AND HONOURS MARY. Openly and without hesitation, it urges Christians 'Let us honour above all else the remembrance of the most Glorious Ever Virgin Mary, Mother of God and of our Lord Jesus Christ.'

A) WHY THE CHURCH HONOURS MARY

The honour of the Church to Our Lady is Christocentric. She loves and honours Mary because she loves and honours Christ. Christ is the centre of the liturgy. In truth therefore the Church, throughout the year, celebrates the main mysteries of His life. However, because Mary had a strong link with these mysteries, the church also gives her the honour which she deserves.

Therefore, because:

- Christ became a man through Mary, the Church presents us with the feast of the Annunciation;
- Christ, when he was still in Mary's womb, made holy Saint John the Baptist on the occasion when Mary visited her relative Elizabeth, the Church presents us with the feast of the Visitation;
- Christ was born of Mary, so the feast of Christmas is also a feast of Our Lady;
- Christ was presented in the Temple from the hands of Mary, so, the Church presents us with the feast of the Purification (Candlemas);

- Christ carried out His first miracle at the request of Mary, so the Church honours Her as Mediatrix of all Graces;
- Christ, when he died on the cross, had Mary beside Him 'Suffering profoundly with Him, and joining, with a Mother's heart in His sacrifice while with love agreeing with the offering of the Victim born of Her' (LG, n.58), the church honours her as Our Lady of Sorrows and Mother of all human persons in the Order of Grace (LG., n.61).

Together with the reasons which we have mentioned why the Church honours Mary, we can add another: because in Her, in this Mother of God united with Her Son in the work of salvation, the Church sees Herself, that is, she sees how she wishes and hopes to be (SC, n.103).

Therefore, Christians should keep their eyes on Mary, who shines as an example of virtue before the community of the redeemed. While they announce her greatness and honour her, she draws them closer towards Her Son (LG, n.65).

So, while we love, praise and give honour to Mary, we come to know better, love, and give honour to Her Son Jesus and to follow his teaching.

B) What sort of Honour does the Church give to Mary?

The sort of honour which the Church gives to Mary is essentially different from that which the Church gives to Jesus, the Son of God made man, and the two other Divine Persons: the Father and the Holy Spirit. To each of these three persons, since they are truly God, the church gives the honour of adoration, that is the cult of latria

(LG, n.66). Nor is it the same as the cult given to the saints, the honour or cult of dulia. The cult given to Mary is 'entirely singular or unique'(LG, n.66), because it is the highest sort of dulia. The church gives Mary the honour or cult of hyperdulia.

Cult is an action of honour or reverence which is given to someone to recognise his greatness or dignity[1] . Therefore, since Mary, in her unique dignity as Mother of God, surpasses all the saints, theologians call this special honour hyperdulia, that is honour which is higher than that given to the Saints.

Mary deserves this honour not only because she is the Mother of God, but also because she participated in the mysteries of the life of Christ.

Whosoever gives honour to Our Lady as is right does not need to believe in or give importance to stories, miracles, or visions about which the Church does not speak. True devotion does not consist of empty sentimentalism which passes, or of unnecessary beliefs, but comes from true faith which leads us to recognise the pre-eminence of the Mother of God (LG, n.67).

In our honouring Our Lady, what is important is our love as children of this loving, powerful Mother, linked with a sincere desire to follow her example in everything and to imitate her virtues (LG, n.67).

C) Mary is honoured by those who are not Christians or Catholics

People seem drawn to the concept of Honouring Our Lady. Indeed, it is not only Catholics who honour her, but also many others, including Moslems, Orthodox Christians, and Protestants.

- Moslems have great esteem for Mary and often pray to her with great fervour.
- Orthodox Christians, although not Catholics, have a very great devotion to Our Lady. They received this tradition from the first Ecumenical Councils, especially that of Ephesus. They compose to Her and sing to Her beautiful hymns. In their churches, there are always images of Mary to be venerated. (LG, n.15; UR, n.15)
- Protestants do not agree with us about the role of Mary in the work of redemption (UR, n.20). However, the very author of Protestantism, Luther, often gave honour to Mary in his writings and never challenged any of the Marian dogmas which existed in his time. Regarding the Anglican church, one often sees chapels dedicated to Our Lady, as in Westminster Abbey and Canterbury Cathedral.

D) The Second Vatican Council urged Catholics to honour Mary.

The Second Vatican Council wished that all the children of the Church should honour the Blessed Virgin and have great esteem for the practices and exercises which are carried out in Her honour, and which have been recommended from time to time by the Magisterium of the Church (LG, n.67). Therefore it encourages all sorts of Catholics with these words:

- The Religious are reminded that, with the help of the Virgin Mary, whose life is a model for everyone, they should move forward in the road to holiness so that their fruit of salvation will be more plentiful (PC, n.25).

- Seminarists, that is, those who are preparing for the priesthood, are advised to have the confidence of children and have love and devotion to the Blessed Virgin Mary, who Jesus Christ gave the beloved disciple as a Mother, when He was dying on the cross (OT, n.8),

- Priests should be enthusiastic in carrying out all that their mission expects of them. To achieve this the example of Our Lady is put before their eyes. Led by the Holy Spirit She dedicated Herself entirely to the salvation of mankind. She, the mother of the High Priest, the Queen of the Apostles, is the help of the priest in the accomplishment of his mission. That is why they should honour her and love her like children (PO, n.18).

- Missionaries are promised that the fathers of the council as well as all Christians will pray for them, so that through the intercession of the Virgin Mary, Queen of the apostles, all people will soon come to acknowledge the truth (AG,n.42).

- All Christians are encouraged to pray fervently to the Mother of God and of men, so that as She helped the Early church with her prayers, so, now that She is raised above all the angels and saints in Heaven, she will intercede for the church before Her Son. Through Her prayers and help, we hope that all people and families, whether Christian or not, join together as one people of God and live happily in peace together.(LG, n.69).

E) We honour Mary through the Scapular of Carmel.

If one reads carefully the words of Vatican II it must be clear that the Scapular of Carmel is very helpful for us to express honour to Our Lady. In the decree on the Apostolate of the Lay People, the Council says clearly to those lay persons who, led by a special call, have enrolled themselves in an organisation or institute approved by the Church should do all they can to develop holiness according to the appropriate characteristics of that organisation or institute (AA, n.4).

Persons who are enrolled in the Carmelite scapular are linked with the Carmelite Order. Therefore, such persons are part of the Carmelite family, the family of Mary. Because of this they share the same privileges and duties that Carmelite religious have. Among these duties, they have that of loving and honouring Our Lady as Mother and powerful Patroness of all those who have been redeemed by the Blood of Christ and the Hope of all Christians. And this is the importance or usefulness of the Carmelite Scapular because it

- Reminds us of the connection which we have with Our Lady.
- It gives us hope and confidence in Her help.
- It reminds us of our duties towards such a great, beloved Mother.

He who follows Our Lady moves more rapidly towards Christ to join with Him. Our Lady is the best example of this union with Christ, because She, the greatest among the saints and the most full of the Grace of God, developed rapidly in Her spiritual life. It was Mary, the Queen of the apostles, who worked most with Jesus on earth to save all mankind.

The Scapular, therefore, while reminding us of Our Lady, reminds us of the duty we have to do all that we can to unite even more deeply with Christ. Furthermore we must work for the spiritual salvation of our brothers in mankind, whether they are our relatives or not, both in our country and in faraway lands.

The Scapular also reminds us of something else. This is that Mary in heaven never stops taking care of us and supporting us even though we are poor men. She keeps on helping us until she can bring us to join Her in eternal Glory (Heaven). Therefore, we must honour Her, because she is the ladder which leads us from earth to Heaven. The Scapular is a sign that he who trusts in Our Lady will gain eternal life.

F) Conclusion

This is why the Carmelite Order has worked and continues to work to spread honour everywhere to Our Lady through the Scapular. All Catholics are a brotherhood, are one family, The Scapular reminds us that we are all children of the same Mother who has cried and suffered like us, and who wants us to love each other and live as one family.

He who wears the Carmelite Scapular with faith and hope in the Virgin Mary must love Our Lady, love his neighbour, and be at peace with everyone.

Reference:

1 *St. Thomas, Summa Th., i-ii,q.2, a.2*

FOURTEEN

THE DEVOTION OF THE CARMELITE SCAPULAR

THE DEVOTION OF THE CARMELITE SCAPULAR IS A VERY WIDESPREAD way of giving praise and honour to Our Lady. Its basis are the great privileges with which God chose to adorn Mary when he chose Her to be Mother of His dearest Son. By this choice He raised Her to a dignity which no man or angel has ever had. Because she is the Mother of God and the most generous co-operator with the divine saviour (LG, n.61), Mary is also Mother of humanity, the Mediatrix of Grace and the Queen of heaven and earth.

Whoever wears the Scapular of Our Lady of Mount Carmel shows that he/she believes in these privileges of Our Lady. Through this blessed Scapular Our Lady shares all sorts of Graces with Her devotees.

A) SACRAMENTS AND SACRAMENTALS

The sources of Grace are the Seven Sacraments founded by Jesus Christ. These are signs which mean and give grace, which mean friendship with God (Council of Trent, sess.7, kan.6).[1] In other words, through them man becomes indeed an adoptive son of God, taking part in His divine life, and in the merits that Christ received when He redeemed us.

However, as well as the Sacraments, there are also Sacramentals.

These are things or actions which the Church uses, in a similar word of the Sacraments, to receive from God the effects of the Redemption, especially the spiritual effects (Code of Canon Law, kan.1144; SC, n.60).[2]

The sacraments and the Sacramentals are to be distinguished from each other for four essential reasons:

- Origin or Author. As opposed to the Sacraments, sacramentals do not owe their origin directly to Christ, in that He is not their direct author. Instead, the Church founded them with the authority given to Her by Christ.

- Effect. Sacraments and sacramentals differ in their effect. While sacraments directly cause or increase sanctifying grace, sacramentals give us directly actual grace. [definitions; Sanctifying grace is a state in which God allows us to share in his life and love. Actual grace is to remember that it enables us to act. It is the strength that God gives us to act according to his will.]

- Mode of action. Sacramentals have their effect in a different way from sacraments. Sacraments 'ex opera operato' that is they act of themselves, while sacramentals 'ex opera operantis', that is they act in view of the Church which instituted them, and as a result of the belief and prayers of those who give them and those who receive them. Sacramentals are, however, similar to sacraments in that they usually consist of a matter or form which produces a spiritual effect on the subject [person].

- Number. Finally, there is a difference in number - There are only seven sacraments –no more no less - (Council of Trent, esss.7, can.1)[3], while the number of sacramentals is not fixed or definitive. The Church can increase or decrease the number of sacramentals according to the needs of the times.

B) The Carmelite Scapular is one of the permanent sacramentals.

According to whether they last for a long or a short time, sacramentals can be divided into transitory or permanent. The majority are transitory, that is they are sacred actions which come to an end quickly. (such are blessings or exorcisms). Others are permanent, that is, things which remain (such as Holy Water, the consecration of a Church, a religious profession, etc.).

The Carmelite Scapular is classed as a permanent sacramental. It cannot be called 'the sacrament of Mary', as some have said, except in the very widest sense.

Etymologically, the word sacrament (from the verb 'sacrare' and the substantive suffix 'mentum'), suggests something sacred. Over the years, this rather vague generic sense began to become narrower and more specific. It began to be felt that 'sacrament' was something holy and visible, which is a sign of something which is invisible, that is, of grace. In this sense, one can call the Carmelite Scapular' the sacrament of Mary', because it is the sign of Our Lady's mercy for humanity. Through it She gives all sorts of graces, spiritual and material to those who deserve Her help.

For her part, the Church has not hesitated to welcome and spread the devotion of the Scapular of Carmel. The Church believes that the Carmelite Scapular is a useful source of graces.

C) The proper nature of the Scapular of Our Lady of Mount Carmel.

In order to properly understand the Scapular of Our Lady of Mount Carmel we should understand its proper nature in a historical and theological perspective. If we do so, it becomes clear that the imposition and wearing of the scapular is not a simple ceremony but is the Habit of a Religious Order which is dedicated to Our Lady.

(i) It is a blessed habit.

On the occasion of the seventh centenary of the Scapular, Pius XII sent a letter to the General of the Carmelite Order (Neminem profecto latet)[4]. In it he says, 'The Blessed Scapular, being the garment of Mary, is a sure sign and proof of the protection of the Mother of God over us'.

We find this same concept of a holy garment, the garment of Mary in the words of the form of investment. When he is clothing us with the scapular, the priest prays in the name of the Church: 'Lord Jesus Christ, Redeemer of mankind, bless this Scapular which your servant is going to wear for your love and that of your mother the Virgin Mary...' and later he says, 'Wear this blessed Scapular...' (Manwal tat-Terz' Ordni ta' Sidtna Marija tal-Karmnu, Il-Belt, 1954, p.77)[5].

A garment has more than one use. In the Bible we can find several used for a garment: (i) To cover, as when God covered Adam and

Eve (Gen.3, 21); (ii) as a sign of great love, when Jacob gave the coat of many colours to his son Joseph (gen.37, 4); as a sign of power, as when the Prophet Elias threw his cloak over the prophet Elishua as a sign that he had endowed him with a double portion of his spirit (4 Kings 2, 9); (iv) as a sign of forgiveness and love, as when in the parable of the prodigal son, the father dresses his son with new clothes (Luke 15, 22).

Mary, too, as any other woman who is about to become a mother, would have prepared some clothes with much love and care for the child she was expecting. When He was born, she would have immediately wrapped Him in them (Luke, 2, 12). Who knows, later, how carefully she must have treasured Him and wrapped him up well in clothes to protect Him from all harm during her flight at dead of night into Egypt! (Matt.2, 14) It is only natural. A mother clothes her children because she loves them and takes care of them. A Maltese proverb says 'Your Clothes make you a man', and this is true, because another function of clothes is to show what we are - including our trade or profession. Often, poor people and rich people can be distinguished by their dress. By their uniform, one can identify soldiers, sailors, policemen and many others. Apart from social conditions or employment, often a person's taste in fashion is demonstrated by his clothes.

Often, in the spiritual sphere, one can tell by their dress whether someone has committed himself to God for the good of souls. One can tell from his Habit or Cassock who is a friar and who is a priest, and, on the altar, one can identify a priest by his vestments.

(ii) It is the Habit of a Religious Order.

From the earliest times, from the beginning of Monasticism, a form of dress was used to identify the obligations that many committed themselves to for the love of Jesus Christ. This dress, or habit, was for the monks a living reminder that they did not belong to the world but to Christ.

The scapular was used by many religious orders and was part of the Religious Habit. Sometimes it would be taken to be a sign of the Monk's dress, that is to represent the whole habit.

In the Middle Ages, in Feudal Times, when monasticism was developing further with the establishment of the Mendicant Orders, this form of dress (scapular) also signified the link between the owner and the serf. The poor would commit themselves entirely to the service of the rich, and these latter would undertake to protect them and guarantee them their livelihood. But first there would be a ceremony, an oath of fealty given by one side (the poor) and the giving of a garment - the scapular - by the nobleman. The nobleman would give a dress – a scapular - to the person who knelt before him and promised to serve him in everything. This dress would act as a sort of uniform, which distinguished him and showed to which owner he belonged.

This ceremony was taken up by the Religious Orders. For them it consists of the vows which the novices make to the superior before the altar and the dress or habit which the superior gives them. The dress serves to distinguish and protect those who join the Order and to remind him or her that he/she is completely dedicated to God.

Thus, the Scapular is part of the blessed Habit of a Religious Order, and often is used to signify the whole habit.

(iii) It is the Habit of an Order which is dedicated to Mary. The Carmelites, too, used to wear the Scapular; it was an essential part of their habit. Whoever used to wear the Habit of the Carmelite Order used to be stating openly that he was a member of the Family of Carmel, and therefore was ready to serve God and Our Lady with his prayer and work for the good of souls according to the spirit of that Order.

The devotion of the Carmelite Order to Our Lady is a historical fact. Since the time that the Holy Land had been liberated from the enemies of Christianity (in the First Crusade), the Carmelites had built a chapel on Mount Carmel in honour of the Virgin Mary. In it they used to come together to pray and to praise Mary as Mother of God and of all mankind. So whoever wore the Carmelite Habit would join this religious family and with them praise God and His Blessed Mother.

One should understand that in the Middle Ages, it was understood that the titular of a church, that is the saint to whom it was dedicated, was seen as the owner of that church. Thus, the name of a church could be used to distinguish one order from another or one religious' group from another. Therefore, since the Carmelites had dedicated their chapel on Mount Carmel to Our Lady, therefore Mary was seen by them as their lord or patron. It is not therefore surprising that they often called on Mary to show them that she is indeed their patron and to bring them aid in all the difficulties which they came across, especially when they began to spread across Europe. Many real documents of that time show us clearly that they used to honour Mary as their Patroness (in the feudal sense which we have mentioned) and that they specifically set up their Order in Her honour.

The popes recognised the Marian title of the Carmelite Order, and they even gave indulgences to those who referred to the Carmelite Order as 'the Brothers of the Blessed Virgin Mary'.

Mary always helped them. As a loving Mother and a Powerful Patroness, she always protected them and made them victorious over their enemies. Therefore, the Carmelites were right to accept the vision of Mary to Saint Simon Stock when the Order, surrounded everywhere by enemies, appeared to be close to being extinguished. They saw this vision as an act of protection by their patroness to whom they had dedicated their order, and themselves. Since the garment was the sign of the lifetime protection which the lord gave to his servants, they saw in the blessed scapular, their Habit, the sign that Mary would make them victorious.

The apparition of Our Lady to Saint Simon Stock is, for them, a confirmation of this, their belief. While he was praying devoutly to Her, with anxiety in his heart to ask her for Her help for the Order which by right and law was Hers, since she was the Protector and Patroness of the Order, she appeared to him and told him that the Scapular was to be the sign of their being freed from danger. She would not ever break Her word. Thus Mary showed this saint and everyone else that the Carmelite Habit, the Scapular, is the certain sign of Her help and Her protection from danger, especially as regards danger to the soul.

(iv) Conclusion

This then is the scapular of Our Lady of Mount Carmel in the historical and theological setting of its origin. It is the blessed habit of a Religious Order, the Carmelite Order, which is dedicated to Our Lady. It is the sign of the link between Mary and those who wear it: Mary is with us and we are with Her.

This is why the Carmelite religious and all the devotees of Our Lady of Mount Carmel always loved the blessed Scapular

It was as a sign of their love and of their great honour towards the Blessed Virgin that so many Christians entered the Carmelite family, All sorts of persons were enrolled in the Scapular, whatever their social condition or their age or gender: rich or poor, old or young, men or women, even good and holy persons, Popes and Kings. Mary helped them all with her graces, protected them from danger, and kept them united in love towards Jesus, for in the same way that the sacraments are the sources of God's grace, so the Carmelite Scapular is the source of the mercy of Mary.

The sacraments are the signs of the redemption and of the merits of Christ; the scapular is a sign of the distribution of the graces won by these merits. Jesus entrusted the distribution of these graces to His Mother Mary; in other words he passes them on to us through Her. Because Mary is our spiritual Mother, and the Mediatrix of all graces, she recognises us, who wear the scapular as her special children and so she always protects us, in life and in death, until we are in Her arms forever, as children in the arms of a dear Mother.

References:

1 *(council of Trent, sess.7, kan.6).*
2 *Code of Canon Law Can. 1144; SC, n.60*
3 *Council of Trent, esss.7, can.1*
4 *Pius XII Neminem profecto latet*
5 *Manwal tat-Terz'Ordni ta' Sidtna Marija tal-Karmnu, Il-Belt, 1954, p.77*

FIFTEEN

THE CARMELITE SCAPULAR AND OUR CONSECRATION TO OUR LADY

CONSECRATION TO OUR LADY IS A FORM OF DEVOTION GIVEN TO Mary and strongly recommended by the Popes. Before we discuss the meaning of the Consecration it is worth discussing the meaning and need for devotion.

A) THE DEVOTION

Religion is that quality or moral virtue through which we give God the honour which he is due because of his greatness. The main act of this virtue is devotion, which is nothing more than our will to serve God with all our commitment.

This sort of devotion is very necessary in the Christian life. Without it we cannot serve God well. Leo the thirteenth speaks of it in the encyclical 'Libertas praetantissimum' (20th January 1888)[1], He says that among the duties of the human race, without any doubt the greatest and most holy is that which braves humankind to honour God with love and devotion.

Besides this sort of (essential) devotion, there is another sensible devotion, through which we feel joy and pleasure when we think of God. The usefulness of this is that it helps us and encourages us to serve God better. In other words, it makes essential devotion much easier.

One needs to bear in mind that all devotion has God as its ultimate aim, even when we give honour to Our Lady and the saints. We give them honour because they are friends of God and because they help us come closer to Him. Honouring God, Our Lady and the saints can be shown in many different ways, such as prayer, works of charity, etc. These are what we call devotions, those concrete acts by which we show our devotion.

B) Devotion to Our Lady

We feel that we are not mistaken if we say that devotion to Our Lady originates from God Himself. Indeed, Jesus Christ owes his body and blood to Our Lady, because She conceived Him and gave Him birth. Furthermore, He was united to Her with the great Love and obedience which He had towards Her, as every good son has towards his mother. Jesus Himself is the best example of how we should honour Mary.

We can discuss Marian devotions in three ways - Her point of view, our point of view, and how they are spread:

- From Her point of view, Our Lady brings about certain devotions to Herself in order to show Her goodness and Her Care as a Mother and her greatness and power in the Kingdom of Grace.
- From our point of view, these devotions can be transitory, that is acts of praise which end quickly (such as saying the Rosary or other prayers), or permanent, that is a form of honour which is more full and long lasting, such as our consecration to Our Lady. Thus, seen from this aspect, these devotions show how we wish to give ourselves over to honouring Mary.

- Finally, we can consider the spread of these devotions. Indeed, there are private and individual devotions, such as visiting certain churches or other prayers. There are also public devotions, organised by the Church, liturgical, recommended over time by the Magisterium of the Church and spread throughout the world.

C) CONSECRATION

One permanent form of devotion to Our Lady recommended by the Church is indeed Consecration. So now let us consider what this Consecration means.

To consecrate means to make something holy by giving it to God in a special way. Thus, we say that religious or priests are consecrated to God because they have given themselves in a special way to Him. We understand the same thing when we talk about the consecration of a chalice or of a church, in that these things are reserved to God, for His honour.

Consecration is made to God alone, since He alone is the absolute Lord of everything. It is part of the cult or honour of adoration; it is a sign or expression of it. Therefore, since Adoration can only be given to God, consecration is only made to Him.

Consecration is carried out by saying some prayers. If the consecration is of a person, who is endowed with understanding and free will, as well as the prayer there needs to be the internal intention and will to adhere to and do all that consecration entails.

Everything which is consecrated must serve God alone, according to the purpose of the object consecrated is. Thus, if it is a chalice, a church, or some other sacred object, then these can only be used in order to serve God. However, if it is a person, then this person must always use its intelligence in order to seek to discern what the consecration demands of her /him and do her/his best to live the consecration. Because Jesus was consecrated to the Eternal Father, He was totally given over to Him: wisdom, heart and will. In the same way, Mary was totally consecrated to God.

D) Consecration to Our Lady.

This form of devotion - Consecration to Our Lady - is now very much in use. It has even been recommended by the Popes. It was Pius XII (in 1942) who consecrated the world to the Immaculate Heart of Mary. One can mention as examples the consecration of Italy to Mary - renewed in the Eucharistic Congress of Catania - and the consecration of our Island - Malta - to the Sacred Heart of Jesus and the Heart of Mary which took place some years ago.

However, is Consecration to Our Lady Right and can it be done? Have we not said that consecration can only be made to God? If we truly understand what we mean by consecration to Our Lady, we find that there is nothing wrong here, and that all we have said is true.

By consecration to Our Lady we mean that, in the same way as God wanted to become man and live among us through Her, so we can give ourselves entirely to God through Her.

Consecration to Our Lady means that someone promises that he will do his best to live according to the example of Mary, especially in Her love for Her neighbour, Her unceasing prayer, and Her complete accordance with the Divine Will.

E) The Carmelite Scapular is a sign of Consecration to Our Lady

The Carmelite Scapular implies and means that the person who wears it is consecrated or given over entirely to Our Lady in the way that we have just described. To show this we can quote the words of Pope Pius XII and of Lucia, the seer of Fatima.

- Pope Pius XII writes: 'all the Carmelites, religious, tertiaries, or those enrolled in the Carmelite Scapular, have in this garment (the Scapular) which they wear, a proof of that consecration to the Blessed Heart of the Immaculate Virgin Mary which we have recently fervently recommended'.[2]
- Lucia: Although in Fatima Our Lady did not ask for any particular form of consecration, in the last apparition of the 13th of October 1917, she appeared dressed as a Carmelite, holding the scapular. Thus, she showed how close to Her heart is the traditional devotion of the Scapular of Carmel. A long time later, on the 15th August 1950, Lucia said to a Carmelite Religious: 'There is no doubt, and the Pope himself has said it, that the Scapular of Carmel is a sign of Consecration to Mary.'[3]

Why is the Scapular a sign of this consecration? The scapular of Carmel is, as we have said before (in the sermon about 'The Devotion of the Scapular'), is the habit of a Religious Order which is totally committed to Mary - the Carmelite Order. Therefore it is necessary that Mary will give this Order all Help and Heavenly Graces.

Every Religious Order, as well as all other virtues, attempts to copy and follow particularly closely a special virtue of Our Lord Jesus Christ. Hence the Franciscans imitate his poverty, the Salesians imitate his love of children and the Dominicans imitate his commitment to save souls. The special virtue which the Carmelites imitate is the love of Jesus Christ for His dear Mother.

Now, to wear the scapular or the Habit of an order implies that one should follow the example and try to achieve the goal of that Order. Therefore it means that one should imitate the virtues, especially the characteristic virtue of the chosen Order, so as to achieve its goal. Therefore, to wear the Carmelite Scapular means that one must follow the special way which leads to the goal for which the Carmelite Order was founded. This means imitating the virtues especially the characteristic one of that Order. Therefore, when you decide to wear the scapular, as well as its dignity, you also shoulder the commitment of the Carmelite Order, that is to exercise the virtues, and especially the special virtue, which is the imitation of the love that Jesus Christ had for His Mother Mary. This is the consecration to Our Lady which is signified by the Carmelite Scapular.

The act of consecration is carried out during the vestition, that is, when we receive and wear the Scapular for the first time. When we wear it- as indeed, we should wear it forever - we are showing everyone that we have a particular devotion to Our Lady. At the same time, it reminds us that we have been given to Our Lady and that we belong to Her. Therefore, we should exercise those virtues required by the Scapular, that is by our consecration through the scapular of Carmel.

We can see which virtues a wearer of the Scapular should profess can be found in the words of Pius XII. He says:

> The Carmelites and all those who in one way or another are members of the family of the Virgin Mary must remember that the Scapular is for them a sign and remembrance of humility and purity. In its shape they have a teaching of modesty and simplicity. Since they should wear it night and day, the scapular is a symbol of constant prayer which they raise to God to receive His Help. Finally, in the Scapular they have a witness of their consecration to the Immaculate Heart of Mary. ('Neminem profecto latet').[2]

Therefore, the virtues which the Carmelite Scapular reminds us of are: Humility, purity, modesty, simplicity, prayer and consecration. Consecration is the 'climax', the peak of the 'crescendo', or the friction of these virtues. Whoever wears the scapular has a duty to practice these virtues, of which consecration to Our Lady is, as it were, the Queen.

F) Conclusion.

From what we have said, it is clear that the Scapular of Carmel does not simply give privileges, indulgences, and that Our Lady should help us with grace because we wear her garment. This is an incorrect concept. We need to work ourselves as well. This is a warning which Pius XII makes, using the words of Saint Paul:

Those who wear the Carmelite Scapular should not think that simply because of this they will receive eternal life. They should also work and not be lazy, as Paul warns: 'Work out your salvation with fear and trembling.' (Philippians 2, 12).

In this world we must all serve each other or make sacrifices for someone or something. If we are good servants of Mary, and serve Her in all things, She will certainly not fail to remember us. She will help us achieve the aim for which we were created by giving us help to carry out our duty, so that we will then go and enjoy eternal life with her.

References:

1 *Leo XIII 'Libertas Praetantissimum' (20th January 1888)*
2 *Pius XII Neminem profecto latet*
3 *Howard Rafferty O.Carm. The Brown Scapular and the Fatima Message https://www.scapularofmountcarmel.com/fatima.html*

SIXTEEN

THE CARMELITE SCAPULAR AS A COLLECTION OF VIRTUES

HOLINESS OR CHRISTIAN PERFECTION IS EVERYBODY'S DUTY. Everyone without exception is asked by Jesus Christ to be perfect: 'Be perfect as your heavenly Father is perfect' (Matt. 5, 48).

A) JESUS AND MARY ARE THE TWO BEST EXAMPLES OF HOLINESS

We achieve perfection if we live in the Love of God, by imitating the faithfulness and generosity of Jesus Christ. He is the Way the Truth and the Life, and no one can go to the Father if not by Him (John14, 6).

Jesus walked the way of sacrifice and the cross, but the basis of all His work was the complete conformity of His will with that of God the Father: 'I always do that which pleases Him' (John 8, 28): 'Thy will be done, not mine' (Luke 22, 42).

After Jesus, Our Lady is the most shining example of holiness. She leads us to Jesus, most of all by showing us that we too can, like Her, do what Her Son requires of us.

B) THE CARMELITE SCAPULAR REMINDS US OF THE HOLINESS OF MARY

The Carmelite Scapular, as we have seen, is the garment of Mary. Therefore, it is inevitable that it brings before our mind Her two greatest virtues: humility and purity, since it was because of them that she was chosen to be the Mother of God.

Since, in its form, the Carmelite Scapular is as simple as can be, it reminds us of modesty and simplicity, two virtues which we see well exemplified in the life of Mary.

Finally, because we wear the scapular all the time, night and day, it reminds us of the prayer without ceasing and of our union with God, two other virtues which Mary is a great example of.

These six virtues are those which Pius XII saw as being linked with the scapular. He warned those who wear the Scapular always to remember the duty they have to observe the following virtues: Humility, chastity, modesty, simplicity, prayer and consecration. Therefore, we can call the Carmelite Scapular a collection of Virtues.

C) Humility and Purity

It was because of Mary's two virtues of humility and purity that she found favour before God and she was chosen to be the Mother of His Son.

(i) Humility. Two texts from scripture are sufficient to assure us of Mary's humility. We find the first on the lips of Our Lady when she unites Her will with the will of God and accepts the Divine Motherhood. Although now Her dignity as Mother of God raises Her above all creatures, she recognises Her nothingness and declares Herself the servant of the Lord (Luke, 1, 38), The second text is found in the canticle called the 'Magnificat', where she herself states that the Lord had 'cast His eyes upon the lowliness (=Humility) of His servant.' (Luke, 1, 48)

It is worth reflecting that Mary did not take part in the triumphs of

Her son, as when He entered Jerusalem among shouts of happiness and praise. However, when Christ was coming out of the same town carrying the cross, insulted and cursed...then she was there. She went to meet Him, to comfort Him, to console Him,...and stood by the cross till He died.

Humility consists of recognising our nothingness before others and most of all before God. We recognise that everything good that we have was given, or rather leant to us by Him. Therefore, we have no right to boast about ourselves or about what we have. On the other hand, we should say with Mary 'The Powerful has done great things with me' (Luke 1, 49).

(ii) Chastity. Mary possessed the highest grade of chastity, that is virginity. In the old testament it was not of any honour for a woman not to bear children. However, Mary wanted to be forever virgin and to protect her virtue of virginity in order to please God. We are more impressed and appreciate this virtue more especially when we consider why Jewish women would want to marry early and have children. It was because they hoped that the Messiah might be born from them. And how did Mary react regarding this? Even though God had chosen Her to be Mother of the Saviour, she did not give Her consent before the angel had reassured Her that Her virginity would not be affected (Luke 1, 34).

Virginity consecrated to God is giving to Him the entire person, body and soul, so that, as Saint Paul says, our thoughts will be only in the Lord, without sharing one's love with any other person (I Corinthians 7, 32). Jesus promises the beatific vision to those who are pure of heart. (Matt. 5, 8). Furthermore, according to Saint John, they will, in heaven, have the names of Jesus and God the Father written on their foreheads and they will learn to sing a new song before the throne of God and they will follow the Lamb (Jesus) wherever He goes (Apoc.14, 1-4).

Those who wear the Brown Scapular should imitate Mary and observe the virtue of chastity according to their state in life. Indeed during the vestition of Carmelite Novices or Tertiaries, the priest says to them: 'Take this cincture and bind it round your waist as a sign of mortification of the senses and chastity.' And while the cape is given to the novice, the priest says: 'Wear this white cape as a sign of chastity and mortification of your body. 'And when enrolling devotees in the scapular the celebrant says 'Wear this blessed Scapular and pray to the Virgin Mary so that through Her Merits you keep it without stain......'[1] (Manwal tat-Terz'Ordni ta' Sidna Marija tal-Karmnu, il-Belt, 1954, pp.45-46, 77).

D) A SPECIAL DEVOTION OF THE CARMELITE ORDER TO MARY'S PURITY

Our Lady was given two great privileges related to Her virtue of Purity. These are her being conceived without any original sin, that is, her Immaculate Conception and Her Impeccability, that is the impossibility of Her ever falling into sin. Thus Mary is completely pure.

The Carmelite Order has always been especially devoted to Mary's Purity. Thus:

- The Chapter General of 1306 issued an order that the feast of the Immaculate Conception should be celebrated across the whole Order.

- In the Curia of Papal Palace, the feast of the Immaculate Conception was celebrated officially by the Carmelites.
- In the year 1384, Pope Clement VII gave the right to the prior of the Carmelites of Lyons (France) that only the Carmelites, and no other mendicant order could preach about the Immaculate Conception.
- In Paris, on all Saturdays of the year and on the Eves of the Feasts of Our Lady, the Carmelites used to sing the antiphon 'Inviolata' which said: 'Our Lady is a pure virgin, without stain, chaste, without original sin.'
- Carmelite Authors always proclaimed and defended the privilege of Mary's Immaculate Conception
- In the sixteenth century, the Carmelites of Spain and Portugal bound themselves by a vow to defend the Immaculate Conception.
- Saint Maria Maddalena de' Pazzi had a great devotion to the purity of Mary.
- From the middle of the sixteenth century onwards, all Carmelites used to see their white cloak as a symbol of Mary's Immaculate Conception and purity.

E) Modesty and simplicity

The Carmelite Scapular is not a luxury item, nor is it complicated. It is as simple as possible: a small piece of woollen cloth without any decoration or extra adornment. Therefore, it is well suited to remind us that in the spiritual life we should be 'little' and simple and live in a humble and childlike way, without complicating things, because the Christian life is essentially simple. Since everybody is called to the Christian life, big and small, rich and poor, wise and unlettered, it is necessary for the Christian Life to be simple and uncomplicated, so that even those who are young, poor and unlettered can achieve it and live it...

Here we should remember what Saint Therese of the Child Jesus, the Saint of the 'Little Way' and spiritual childhood said: 'When I read that perfection is something difficult and complicated, I close these books of wisdom which confuse my mind and take up the Gospels. Then everything seems simple to me.'

This is why the dress of those who wear the Scapular of Carmel should be what is appropriate to their state and condition. They should avoid all excess and follow Christian Modesty, as befits the followers of the Immaculate Conception. They should observe modesty in everything, including their words. As we read in Scripture (Proverbs 10, 19) and we know from experience, sin often occurs because of inappropriate talk. We will need to account on the day of judgement for every empty word they have spoken (Matt. 12, 36).

F) CONCLUSION

Mary was filled with all virtues. Following Her example, those who wear the Carmelite Scapular should unite the virtues of modesty and simplicity. We should be wise like serpents but simple like doves (See Matt. 10, 16). We must not forget the saying of Jesus that 'unless we are (simple) like children we will not enter the Kingdom of Heaven' (See Matt. 18, 3; 19, 14; Mark 10, 15; Luke 18, 17).

References:

1 *Manwal tat-Terz'ordni ta' Sidna Marija tal-Karmnu, il-Belt, 1954, pp.45-46, 77*

SEVENTEEN

THE CARMELITE SCAPULAR AND PRAYER

On the closure of the celebrations for the seventh centenary of the Scapular, Pius XII sent a letter to the Prior Generals of the Carmelite Order. In it, among other things, he said that all Carmelites (Religious, Tertiaries and those enrolled in the Scapular), have, in the garment which they wear, a sign that they should pray without ceasing, night and day, to call upon the help of God.

Without a doubt, we can claim that whosoever wears the Carmelite Scapular will find it easier to follow the command of the Lord to 'Pray without ceasing'(see Luke 18, 1), since, if we live according to the true devotion of the Scapular, we will be in constant contact with God - and this is true Prayer.

Prayer is the raising of our minds and hearts to God, and therefore, it is our contact with Him, in order to praise Him as Lord of all creation, Redeemer of mankind, and Joy of Eternal Life. The Carmelite Scapular is an effective sign of this virtue of prayer, because it does not only remind us of our duty to pray but it helps us to fulfil this duty.

A) We have a duty to pray

Jesus used to teach us our duties to God not just by His words but by His example. As we say in Maltese proverb 'A word encourages, but example drives us on.' Therefore He not only told us about prayer, but He himself prayed.

- The example of Jesus: Jesus, who was in constant contact and in perfect union with the Eternal Father said: 'I and the Father are One' (John 10, 30). He often used to spend the whole night in prayer (Luke 6, 12). His example is a command to us. This is why we should pray.

- The word of Jesus: Jesus imposed the obligation of Prayer on us when He told us to 'Pray without ceasing' (Luke 18, 1). He repeats to us: 'Stay awake then and pray constantly' (Luke 21, 36). He even taught us Himself how to pray when He taught us the 'Pater Noster' (Luke 11, 2-4).

And it was Jesus who taught us how our prayer should be: with humility (not like the Pharisees - Luke 18, 9-14); with simplicity, and not as the pagans thought, that the more words were said, the more likely they were to be heard (Matt.6, 7); in secret: 'When you pray, enter your inner room close your door, and pray to your Father in secret, and your Father, who sees what is in secret, will answer you' (Matt.6, 6): with sincerity, that is, from the Heart, not just with the lips, so that you will not deserve the reproach of Jesus to the Pharisees: 'Double Faced, rightly declared the prophet Isaiah (29, 13) when he said: this people honour me with words but its heart is far from me' (Matt. 15, 7-8).

B) Prayer is necessary

Let us give some examples why prayer is necessary:

- In order to live every creature requires air and the ambience which is appropriate to it, as in water for fish and air for birds. This is how prayer is for the Christian. Prayer is the life of our soul. Through prayer our soul breathes the air of the Grace of God and so we live as true Christians.

- In the same way as man becomes ill when he breathes bad air and dies without air, the Christian cannot live well with God if he does not pray.

Thus, Saint Alphonsus Maria de' Liguori writes correctly 'He who prays will be saved and he who does not pray will be condemned.' We need the help of God if we are to live well the life of Grace, and to resist the enemies of our souls, and we normally receive this help through prayer.

C) The Scapular and prayer

Now that we have understood our duty to pray and the necessity of prayer, we must now discuss who we should pray to and the part which the Scapular of Carmel has in prayer.

From the very definition of prayer, it is clear that we should pray to God. Prayer is the raising up of the mind and heart to God so that we can adore Him, thank Him, ask His forgiveness, and ask Him for everything we need. In this way we live in contact with Him and talk to him. So much so that many believe that prayer is a discussion between two persons: man, and God.

However, it is also good that we should pray to the saints, who are the friends of God. In them we see reflected the Face of God, from whom the holiness of the saints derives, and out of all the saints first comes Mary, the mother of God.

We should pray to Mary not only because of the greatness of Her Maternity, but also because she is our mediatrix. Although God is the beginning and end of everything and Jesus Christ is our only Mediator (1 Tim. 2, 5-6), because of her subordinate function in our redemption, Our Lady is also the mediatrix of all graces. God has wished that we should receive all graces through Her.

When we are enrolled in the Carmelite Scapular, the priest invites us to pray to the Virgin Mary, so that, through the merits of Her Son, we receive from Her help so that we can live life without sin, we are protected from all anxiety, and She will guide us to eternal life[1] (See Manwal tat-Terz'Ordni ta' Sidna Marija tal-Karmnu. Il-Belt, 1954, p.77). In these words, we have all that we need to live a truly Christian life. This is why the constant wearing of the scapular, day and night, reminds us of our duty to pray without ceasing to God so that, through Mary, we will receive from Him everything we need so that we can live as true Christians.

D) Imitating the prayer of Mary

The Carmelite Scapular does not only remind us of our duty to pray, but also, as the habit of an Order dedicated to Mary, teaches us that we should imitate Mary's virtue of prayer. If prayer unites us with God and gives us the help we need to live in His grace, then who more than Mary was united with God and full of grace? This is why Her talks with God were dear and full of goodness and sweetness, even before She became the Mother of God. Later, when what the angel had announced to Her came to pass, she was even more united with God and grew further in grace.

Prayer exists not only so that we can receive graces, but most of all it is so that we can adore God, praise Him and give Him thanks.

Therefore it is useful to consider here Our Lady adoring and honouring the Son of God, hidden in her pure womb, as she travels over the hills and plains of Judea: deep in thought, only thinking about the Word of God who lives within Her, so that nothing can remove from Her mind her internal vision of Him. We can glimpse a view of her deep interiority and depth of prayer from the words of the 'Magnificat': 'My soul magnifies the Lord....'

Think further of Her at the birth of Jesus, of Her carrying out all Her duties to Him as His Mother, of her union with Him in His Boyhood and His Youth, throughout His hidden life, and on Calvary. Praying means being united with God. Who more than Mary could be united with God? She was not only united with Her Son as His Mother but was also united with the Father as his dearest Daughter and with the Holy Ghost as His spouse.

The Carmelites always saw Mary as their teacher in the life of prayer. They never forgot the teaching which She left us in the 'Magnificat', nor did they forget what the Gospel tells us - that She used to keep in Her Heart every word that the Lord said (Luke 2, 52). They also remembered Her suffering beneath the cross John 19, 25; Lumen Gentium, n.61) and Her praying in the Cenacle (Acts1, 14; LG, n.59).

Finally, the Carmelites felt that they should have a special devotion to the Annunciation, because (by tradition) the angel found Her alone, deep in prayer when He announced to Her the mystery of Her divine Motherhood. Therefore, initially they had lived as hermits on Mount Carmel, and they dedicated their churches to the Annunciation when they spread across Europe.

As well as this life of prayer, they wished to imitate Mary's great virtues of Virginity and Purity, so that they could be more united with God and their thoughts would be only of Him, as Please Him (1 Cor.7, 32-34), since, as Jesus tells us, 'blessed are the pure of heart for they shall see God.' (Matt. 5, 8). It is for these reasons that the Carmelites had great devotion to Mary, who is so pure and chaste.

E) The Rule and the Carmelite Saints on prayer

When we move from the theory about prayer to practice, we see that indeed the Carmelites, on the example of Mary, were committed to prayer and became experts on prayer. To take an example, let us see what the Rule of the Order and the Saints of the Order say about prayer.

- The Carmelite Rule: The rule advised the Religious that they should, to the best of their possibility, stay in their cells and contemplate day and night on the law of the Lord and in prayer[2] (See chapter 7: 'De mansione in cellulis').
- The Carmelite Saints: Both the Carmelite Saints and the whole order are well known in the Church because of their life of prayer. Examples are Saint John of the Cross, Saint Teresa of Jesus, Saint Mary Magdalene de' Pazzi, Saint Teresa Margaret Redi, Saint Therese of the Child Jesus, and many others.

One should also mention Saint Elizabeth of the Trinity, canonised on 16th October 2016. She wrote:

> Let us unite with God who is within us; this divine and intimate union is, so to say, the essence of our Carmelite life. This is the essence of the Carmelite life: our life in God. Then all the sacrifices, offerings, all becomes divine.[3]

> This gift of prayer is what consists of the essence of the Carmelite life; this heart to heart union never ceases, because when we love something more than ourselves we live more within it than within ourselves (and this thing is God).'[3]

We should not forget in the end those who are less well known, but are great teachers about the life of prayer: the Venerable Brother John of Saint Sampson (Du Moulin: 1571-1636), who according to Bremont, we can call the Saint John of the Cross of the Ancient Observance, and the Venerable Father Michael of Saint Augustin (1621-1684), on whom Saint Louis Grignion de Montfort depends for his teaching on Consecration to Mary.

F) Conclusion

Prayer is not, as some think, muttering words without sense. Prayer is the resting and the consoling of the soul in Christ, the Divine Teacher. It also helps us to overcome the difficulties which we meet with. Saint Elizabeth of the Trinity, who we have mentioned, once wrote this to a friend:

> Try as I do, to build a small cell in your heart. Think of God who resides there.... When you feel nervous and troubled... enter that cell quickly and entrust everything to Jesus. If you confide in Him, prayer will not trouble you anymore. Prayer is rest, relaxation, a visit by us in simplicity to the person who we love. Let us stay beside Him as a child stays in his mother's arms and lets his heart become one with hers.[3]

This is the message of the Carmelite Scapular, which is appropriate for our time, the Twenty-first century: that we should pray to Mary, but above all, to imitate Her in our union with God. This is what the Carmelite Saints and all true devotees of Our Lady of Mount Carmel have always done. In the Scapular they found a useful and effective way to unite with God and Our Lady.

References:

1 *Manwal tat-Terz'ordni ta' Sidna Marija tal-Karmnu. il-Belt, 1954, p.77*

2 *carmelite rule chapter 7: 'de mansione in cellulis'*

3 *Elizabeth of the Trinity Complete Works ICS 1984*

EIGHTEEN

THE CARMELITE SCAPULAR - A PLEDGE OF SALVATION

God wants all Human Persons to be saved and Jesus Christ gave Himself as the price for the redemption of everyone (1 Tim.1, 4-7). The Carmelite Scapular is a pledge of this salvation.

A) Final Perseverance

When a person is being enrolled in the Scapular, before the priest imposes the Scapular, he prays to God that, through the prayers of His Mother, the Virgin Mary, we should be protected from the lies and deceptions of the enemy and that we should live in God's Grace until death. When The priest then imposes the Scapular on us, He tells us to take the Holy Scapular and pray to the Blessed Virgin so that through Her merits, she gives us the grace to wear it without blame, so that she should protect us from all anxiety and bring us to eternal life[1] (See Manwal tat-Terz' Ordni ta' Sidna Marija tal-Karmnu. Il-Belt, 1954, p.77).

So that this will be accomplished more effectively, the priest says this formula to whoever receives the scapular: 'I, by the power given to me, include you in all the spiritual benefits obtained through the mercy of Jesus Christ by the Religious Order of Mount Carmel... and we beseech The Blessed Virgin Mary of Carmel that at the hour of your death she will crush the head of the ancient serpent so that you may receive the palm and the crown of eternal life' (O.c., p.78).

Therefore, the Scapular of Carmel is a pledge of final perseverance and therefore of salvation: 'the one who stands firm to the end will be saved.' (Matt. 24, 13).

But we should not forget what we have said before that the Carmelite Scapular is one of the Sacramentals. These do not operate their effects of their own accord, but through the Church which founded them and the disposition of those who receive them. Hence the Scapular of Carmel is a pledge of salvation through the will of the Church and the dispositions, belief and prayer of those who wear it on their chest. If one of these two conditions is not met, then the effect will not occur.

As far as the Church is concerned, there is certainly no obstruction or difficulty. It prays for us through the merits of Jesus Christ and his Mother Mary, so that she (the Church) can give us the graces which she promises us when through the priest she enrols us in the Scapular. However there may be difficulties and obstruction on our part. Therefore, so that the Scapular of Carmel should be a pledge of salvation, it is necessary for us to wish or want to truly achieve salvation and work for it, by doing all that the Scapular of Carmel requires of us.

Eternal life is the most important thing. 'What good will it be for someone to gain the whole world, yet forfeit their soul?' (Matt. 16, 25). It is not, therefore, for nothing that Pius XII encourages us to find the most certain way to receive eternal life, such as the scapular[2] (See the letter Neminem profecto latet, 1950).

How great is the grace of final perseverance of which the Scapular of Carmel is a pledge! The Council of Trent teaches us that no one can be absolutely certain of this grace. The Council even excommunicates those who say that they can be certain of final perseverance in grace, unless through a private revelation, and also excommunicates those who say that one can persevere till the end without special help from God or that because of this gift of grace they need not persevere[3] (Session 6, chapter 13, canon 16, 22) The saints themselves used to be fearful when they thought about this. On final perseverance depends whether we are saved or whether we are lost for ever.

B) The Sabbatine Privilege

As well as being saved, everyone wishes to go to enjoy God as soon as possible. The Scapular of Carmel is an efficacious way of achieving this goal.

It is certain that one of the main reasons for great popular devotion to Our Lady of Mount Carmel is the so-called 'Sabbatine Privilege'. By a decree of the year 1613, the Church gave the right to the Carmelite Order to preach this privilege, which, according to certain historians, Our Lady gave to all who wear the scapular[4] (see Bullarium Carmelitanum, I, 62; II, 601). She appeared to Pope John XXII and told him that if persons die in the grace of God and during their lives they had worn the Scapular, those devotees of Our Lady of Mount Carmel who had lived in purity according to their state of life and had said certain prayers or observed certain fasting, would be freed purgatory soon and especially on the first Saturday after their death.

We all hope that after our deaths someone will remember us and pray for us. However, we need to look after ourselves. It would be wiser if we look after ourselves during our lives. Therefore it is wise for us to always keep our scapular on us and carry out the conditions given us by Our Lady, so that after our death, the mother of God will look after us.

The basis of the Sabbatine privilege is the doctrine about the universal mediation of Our Lady. Indeed, the decree which we have mentioned says: ' Our Lady helps those enrolled in the Scapular of Carmel by interceding for them (before Her Son Jesus) through Her prayers and merits, and because She gives them special protection'[2]. It is true that our only mediator before God is Jesus Christ. 'For there is one God and one mediator between God and mankind, the man Christ Jesus, who gave himself as a ransom for all people' (I Tim.2, 5-6). He is enough. But the unique mediation of the Redeemer does not exclude the mediation of Mary, because every help through the influence of the Blessed Virgin to help mankind does not arise from necessity, but by the wish of God and as a result of the superabundant merits of Jesus Christ. Therefore it in no way reduces the value of the unique mediation of Christ, but instead it shows how important it is. It neither increases nor decreases the dignity or efficacy of the unique Mediation. Mary's mediation is subordinate to that of Christ. The Church has no doubt about Mary's mediation; it openly recognises it, feels it and recommends it to the faithful, so that, upheld by this motherly support, the faithful should be more closely bound to the Mediator and Redeemer (LG, nn.60, 62).

Our Lady, like Christ, supported us when she was in this world.

She helped in our redemption by accepting to become the Mother of the redeemer, she brought Him into the world, she enabled Him to grow, she presented Him to the Father in the temple, and she suffered with Him when He was dying on the Cross (LG, n.61). In Heaven, also, like Christ, She does not cease this work of redemption. By Her intercession She continues to bring us graces to bring us to eternal life, and as a true Mother she looks after us until she leads us into the kingdom of Heaven (LG, n.62).

There are different ways in which Our Lady carried out this office over the years. Therefore She is given various titles by the Church-Advocate, Auxiliatrix, Adjutrix, and Mediatrix (LG, n.62). One way is the Scapular of Carmel, the 'Marian garment, a sign and pledge of the protection of the Mother of God'.

The mediation of Mary also extends to purgatory because it is the will of God that, through her motherly love, she will continue to take care of the brothers of her Son until she leads them to the kingdom of Heaven (LG, n.62) , and therefore care for those who die in the grace of God and are being purified so as to be purged from their sin (LG, nn.49, 50).

The souls in purgatory are cleansed from their sins in two ways: by suffering and by intercession. The suffering is caused by the temporary denial of the vision of God. The central idea of purgatory is love. Now, love causes suffering in those who cannot be united for some time with their beloved person, and the greater the time of separation the greater the suffering. We can say this of the souls who are being cleansed of their sins.

Intercession also has its part to play in the purification of the souls in purgatory. The Church, in the Councils of Florence and Trent, teaches us that Christians who are still alive, can, through their intercession, that is, by prayer, charity, and other acts of mercy, especially by masses, can help these souls be cleansed from their sins (see DS.,*1304, 1820).

How does Mary help the souls in purgatory by Her intercession? By more than one way, including:

- Through the untold merits of which she is the depository and especially through the great merits which she earned on earth.
- By reminding living Christians to pray and intercede for these souls.
- By receiving from God the possibility to apply to these suffering souls the intercessions made by those souls who have already been cleansed from their sins and have entered the kingdom of Heaven.
- By receiving from God the possibility of applying to the souls of Her devotees the intercessions made in a generic way for the Souls in purgatory.

C) Conclusion

We believe that Our Lady, while observing the rule required by the Holiness of God that no soul can enter the kingdom of Heaven unless it is purified entirely from its sins, helps all her children in Purgatory and especially her devotees, such as those who in their life had properly warn the Scapular of Carmel. It is inevitable that Mary, as the Mother of Mercy, will help her suffering children given that she can.This is the belief and hope of all of us in the Scapular of Carmel and Her Scapular. We hope that she will help them enter the Joy of Heaven as soon as possible,

Let us therefore be true children of Mary. There is moral certainty that those who live as true children of Mary will not be lost. Let us wear the Holy Scapular as a sign of our total giving of ourselves, that is our consecration, to Mary, and let us do the duties required from us.

Our hope is strengthened by these words of Pius XII: 'Our Blessed Mother will certainly not allow her children, suffering for their sins in purgatory, not to enter Heaven as soon as possible, She does this through her intercession, according to the Sabbatine Privilege, given to us by tradition.'[2] (the letter 'Neminem profecto latet', 1950)

P. Ewġenju Tonna, O.Carm
Carmelite Convent
Saint Julian's (Balluta)

References:

1 *Manwal tat-Terz' ordni ta' Sidna Marija tal-Karmnu. il-Belt, 1954, p.77*
2 *Pius XII Neminem profecto latet, 1950*
3 *Council of Trent Session 6, chapter 13, canon 16, 22*
4 *Bullarium Carmelitanum, i, 62; ii, 601*

PART THREE

STORIES AND TRADITIONS LINKED WITH THE DEVOTION OF THE SCAPULAR OF OUR LADY OF MOUNT CARMEL

The Anthropology of the Scapular

Dr. Mark Agius M.D.

Devotion to Our Lady of Mount Carmel is extremely popular throughout the World, especially across the Mediterranean and the countries of the old Spanish Empire. Here we discuss the numerous groups of people who have particularly fostered the devotion, the major images of Our Lady under this title, Churches and Cathedrals dedicated to Our Lady of Mount Carmel, and so on.

NINETEEN

Stories of the Brown Scapular

Here we are not at all looking at doctrine about Our Lady or the Scapular or the Carmelite Order, but at the anthropology of popular devotion surrounding the Scapular of Mount Carmel. People do believe that the scapular can be linked with miracles. After all, wearing the scapular is, for the wearer, a prayer, a constant sign of commitment to Our Lady,[3] and prayers are often answered in a remarkable way. When I was young, such stories used to be told to us on retreats and in other meetings, however sadly today such stories are seen as outmoded, but when we, as young persons heard them, they brought our faith to life, and they showed us God's presence in the world.

In the sanctuary of Our Lady of Mount Carmel in Valletta, as well as in other sanctuaries in Malta, such as tal-Ħerba, Żabbar and Mellieħa, we see ex-voto pictures which tell of miracles which have been witnessed by ordinary people and in them often, our lady holds the scapular of Carmel. Interestingly, a recent book on Our Lady of Mellieħa records that this sanctuary used to be referred to as 'La Madonna del Carmine'.[4,5]

In 1657, on the Island of Malta,[1] a five year old girl who wore the Holy Scapular of Our Lady of Mount Carmel fell into a deep well which contained a great deal of water. This well was close to the palace of the bishop, and he ran to the well, and looked in, expecting to find her drowned. Instead he found her floating on the water, asleep, with her head resting on her hand. She was pulled out of the well and handed over to her mother. When her clothes, which were soaking wet, were taken off, it was found that her scapular was dry. The girl was unharmed.

This miracle was related by Padre Maestro Giuseppe Maria Fornari in his book *Anno Memorabile de Carmelitani* , Published in Milan in 1690[1]. It was brought to our attention by Dr. Anna Borg Cardona.

Here then are some stories of recorded interventions linked with the scapular which I have gleaned from the Internet.

Edward II of England had a very tumultuous reign;[2] he was defeated by the Scots at Bannockburn, and in the retreat from that battle he made a vow to found a Carmelite religious house at Oxford if he survived, This is how the incident is reported. Edward II, King of England, hearing about some miracles that were happening in all parts of his kingdom by virtue of the sacred habit, was one of the first princes to once again wear the Scapular, and he received with devotion this precious proof of Mary's love; shortly thereafter, he experienced the effect of the protection of the Blessed Virgin, to whom he was devoted. His army, which had already suffered two defeats, was on the verge of complete surrender. He invoked Mary and promised Her that he would establish a monastery of the Order of Mount Carmel. Immediately, by a miraculous assistance, he won a complete victory over his enemies, who at that point thought they had already won the battle. Edward, wanting to perpetuate the memory of this powerful protection and to keep his vow, gave to the Carmelites his palace at Oxford to establish a monastery.

The following story refers to the Battle of White Mountain,[2] outside Prague, During the Thirty Years War In the year 1618, Maximilian, Duke of Bavaria and general of the imperial army in the war with Prague, in order to acquire God's benediction on his armies, put himself under the protection of the Blessed Virgin by receiving the holy Scapular with his whole army. Full of confidence in this precious shield of the Queen of Heaven, he gave battle against prince Palatine, who had usurped the crown from Ferdinand II, and the Duke won a complete victory with very few losses of his own. The Emperor Ferdinand II, desirous of giving a public witness to Our Lady for Her protection, received, along with the Queen and the princes, the Blessed Scapular from the hands of Father Dominique, a Discalced Carmelite. The Battle of White Mountain led to the Discalced Carmelites settling in Prague in the Church of Our Lady of Victories, which now is the shrine of the famous Child Jesus of Prague.

In France, the following was reported:[2] As the town of Montpellier was in a state of siege, in 1622, there occurred a miracle in the sight of the entire army and under the eyes of the King of France, Louis XIII. In a general assault, one of his officers, Champrond De Beauregard, received a bullet wound in the chest. The wound should have been fatal, but the bullet, after piercing the clothing, flattened out against the Scapular, without doing the least bit of harm to the officer. Astonished by the miracle, the officer told all that were around him. Those who surrounded him, witnesses to this wonder, spread it through the army from rank to rank. Eventually news of the miracle reached the monarch's ear. Louis XIII came forward to see this wonder that had been brought to his attention. He examined the facts very carefully, and after having convinced himself with his own eyes of the reality of the wonder, he wanted to dress himself in this heavenly armour, to receive the Scapular from the hands of the Carmelites and be enrolled as one of the members of the Confraternity.

On August 27th, 1602 Barthelemi Lopez,[2] a Spanish soldier, on duty in the Castle of Saint Elmo, in Naples, was saying prayers in honour of Our Lady of Mount Carmel whose Scapular he was wearing, when all of a sudden lightning and thunder exploded above his head. The lightning bolt hit his shoulder, and without making any sort of injury, left on his shoulder the print of a cross — as a sign of salvation which demonstrates that it was to a special help from Heaven that he owed the favour of having been preserved from the terrible effects of the lightning.

Howard Rafferty, O. Carm. Recounts another story; A French priest on pilgrimage to Einsiedeln, Switzerland[2] was on his way to Mass when he remembered that he had forgotten his Scapular. Although late, he returned to his room for it. While saying Mass, a young man approached the altar, pulled out a revolver and shot him in the back ... but the priest continued to say Mass. In the sacristy the abbot exclaimed, 'I thought the man missed you.' When the vestments were removed, the bullet was found, adhering to his little brown Scapular.

Rev. Howard Rafferty, O. Carm. Recounts; In 1845, the English ship, King of the Ocean, was lashed by a wild hurricane.[2] The Rev. Fisher, a Protestant minister, together with his wife and children and other passengers, struggled to the deck to pray for mercy and forgiveness as the end seemed at hand. Among the crew was a young Irishman, John McAuliffe. He opened his shirt — took off his Scapular — made the Sign of the Cross over the angry waves, then threw the Scapular into the ocean. At that very moment the wind calmed, only one more waves washed over the deck, bringing with it the Scapular which landed at the boy's feet. The Rev. Fisher and his family had observed what he had done. They questioned the boy. He told them about the Virgin and Her Scapular and Her Promise of protection in time of danger. So impressed were they that they determined to enter the Church and enjoy alike protection.

Here is another story from France;[2] In 1834, an elderly soldier living in Angouleme, France, no longer able to bear certain sorrows, resolved to take his own life. He decided to kill himself with poison, thinking that he could more easily hide his crime from the public. Upon taking the poison, he did not have to wait long to suffer the effects. Immediately he went to the hospital and asked to spend the night, thinking that the cause of his death would be undiscovered and his name would not be blackened because of commission of the cowardly sin of suicide. But the hospital supervisor would not allow him to be admitted without an administration pass — which would mean discovery of his impending death by his own hand. The unhappy soldier was forced to abandon the idea of spending the night in the hospital. While wondering what course of action to take, he suddenly heard a voice telling him to go to Saint Peters and confess to Father ***. The soldier went to the designated church and asked Father *** to hear his confession. Father ***, overcome with fatigue, told the man to wait — it was Lent and it was three o'clock in the afternoon and he had not yet had a bite to eat. The unhappy soldier made a new plea and assured the priest that there was no time to wait. The priest entered the confessional and the penitent confessed that he had just poisoned himself. The confessor showed him his obligation before God, which included divulging the penitent's secret. The soldier, touched by this grace, gave the priest permission, and like the fire which burned his insides, the sufferings he felt threw him into a state of perfect hopelessness. The charitable priest pulled him out of the confessional and took him to the hospital. He immediately asked for an antidote, but while they were preparing it, he took the pulse of the sick man, and no longer found any: a deathly pale complexion, misty eyes — everything heralded the coming death. His heart pierced with sadness, but full of confidence in the Divine Mercy, the fervent priest threw himself to his knees, and recited the Litany of the Blessed Virgin. At the first invocation, he sensed the pulse of the dying man's return, and a short time later he heard the soldier speak a few words. 'O my good Father', he said in a weak voice, 'my Father, pray, pray some more!' And he let out a breath and said: 'Holy Mary, pray for me!' And soon his consciousness returned. Father ***, in his enthusiasm over such a marvellous change, asked the soldier if he hadn't kept some pious practices — 'No, my Father, I have not said any prayers in a long time.' But after having reflected for an instant, he showed a Scapular: 'Here is the only sign of piety that I have preserved.' — 'Ah! My friend, 'notes the priest, 'I am no longer surprised by the miracle which just occurred; it's Mary who protected you, it's to Her that you owe being alive.' Nevertheless the doctor arrived, and after having heard the necessary details on the condition of the patient, he assured them that only a superior power could prolong his life for longer than two hours after having taken the poison, one of the most active that we know; and five hours had gone by since the fatal moment! ... The antidote became useless. The doctor proposed to record a statement to attest the truth of the miracle; but the humble priest, fearing that they would perhaps attribute the miracle to the fervour of his prayers, did not think about making the miracle public. It was told to me by others, that it may give you a new confidence in Mary.

Rev. Howard Rafferty, O.Carm. then recounts the following personal story;[2] I saw Her keep it one day in a town near Chicago where I was called to the bedside of a man away from the Sacraments for many years. He did not want to see me; he would not talk. Then I asked him to look at the little Scapular I was holding, 'Will you wear this if I put it on?' I asked nothing more. He agreed to wear it. Within the hour he wanted to go to confession and make his peace with God. It did not surprise me because for over 700 years Our Lady has been working in this way through Her Scapular. Another story is as follows; 'We should even give the Scapular to non-Catholics, for Our Lady will bring conversions to those who will wear it and say one Hail Mary each day, as the following true story will show. An old man was rushed to the hospital in New York City, unconscious and dying. The nurse, seeing the Brown Scapular on the patient, called the priest. As the prayers were being said for the dying man, he became conscious and spoke up: 'Father, I am not a Catholic.' 'Then why are you wearing the Brown Scapular?' asked the priest. 'I promised my friends to wear it, 'the patient explained, and say one Hail Mary a day.' 'You are dying,' the priest told him. 'Do you want to become a Catholic?' 'All my life I wanted to be one,' the dying man replied. He was baptised, received the Last Rites, and died in peace. Our Lady took another soul to Heaven under Her mantle through Her Scapular!'

This story from the Second World War describes how a scapular saved two lives.[2] 'My battalion was a member of the Irene Brigade (Royal Netherlands Motorised Infantry Brigade). We were just about to advance. After we passed Eindhoven, our trucks and tanks went through Uden. In the evening we camped on an old farm near Nijmegen. Behind the house there was an old wooden pump surrounded by bricks, to wash away the sweat and dust of hours of fighting. You can well imagine that we made good use of this opportunity. I was one in the group and so I tossed my jacket on the ground and hung my Scapular on the pump while I washed.

An hour later we received orders to proceed about a mile and a half further and to occupy a trench there. We were looking forward to being able to get a peaceful night's sleep in that trench. I was about to lie down and was unbuttoning my collar when to my horror I realised that I no longer had my Scapular. It had been a gift from my mother. I had it with me all during the war and now that we were approaching the lion's den was I to be deprived of it? To go fetch it was unthinkable, so I tried not to think about it anymore and to go to sleep. I pitched and tossed from side to side, but I couldn't get to sleep. All round me, my buddies were sleeping like logs even though from time to time shells fell dangerously close. Finally, I was overcome by the desire to get my Scapular back and I crept out among my sleeping companions. It wasn't so easy to get past the sentry, but I managed to do it and ran back the way we had come.

It was pitch dark, but nevertheless I had good luck and in a short time I was back on the farm and at the pump. My hands gilded searchingly all over the pump, but the Scapular was gone. I was just about to strike a match when there was the sound of a dreadful explosion. What was I to do? Was that the sign of an enemy attack? As fast as I could I ran back to our trench. Maybe I could do something for my buddies there.

Near the trench I saw the engineers busily removing piles of dirt and barbed wire. At the very spot where my companions had been sleeping there yawned a gigantic shell-hole. Before the enemy had vacated this trench, the enemy had placed a time bomb in it and it had exploded during my absence. Nobody survived the explosion. If I had not set out to fetch my Scapular, I would have been buried under that rubble too.The following morning, I went to the field kitchen and met a buddy there. He looked at me with astonishment. 'I thought you were in that trench!' 'And I thought you were buried there!'

My friend continued, 'I was lying in the trench, but before I went to sleep, I went looking for you. But I couldn't find you. The corporal saw me hunting around and asked me what I wanted.

When I told him what I was doing there he said, 'Be sensible! Instead go to that inn nearby and get me a bottle of water.' And while I was on the errand the explosion occurred.

'Well, I escaped it by a hair's breadth too, 'I replied. 'But why on earth were you looking for me so late at night?' 'To give you this,' he replied, and handed me my Scapular, which he had taken from the old pump.

Another story is about how Our Lady of Mount Carmel saved a life during a Japanese Kamikaze attack,[2] Mr. Sisto Mosco of North Providence, Rhode Island, is a veteran of World War II, who survived, unscathed, the invasion of Normandy, and later, the 7th fleet war with the Japanese fleet, the taking of Iwo Jima and Okinawa, and other bloody battles in the South Pacific. Sisto affirms that his miraculous escape is another perfect example of the powerful protection of Our Blessed Mother of Mount Carmel, through Her Brown Scapular. 'I was on the battleship the U.S.S. Nevada as chaplain's yeoman during WWII in the Pacific. (I always wore my Scapular because I was brought up close to the Church, and I kept it on me all through the war.) The ship was loaded with dynamite. A suicide plane hit the deck real close to where I was positioned. The blast blew open the bolted steel doors of the compartment. I alone was left uninjured after the explosion. The rest were all dead or seriously mangled. I was the only one untouched and I attribute it to the wearing of my Scapular.'Mr. Mosco later received a commendation from the Admiral of the fleet for bravery, but in his heart he firmly believes that the credit goes to Our Lady, the Virgin most powerful, who works such wonders through Her Habit of Salvation.

Rev. Howard Rafferty, O. Carm. Recounts another story from the 1950s, which therefore is easily verified;[2] In May of 1957, a Carmelite priest in Germany published the unusual story of how the Scapular saved a home from fire. An entire row of homes had caught fire in

Westboden, Germany. The pious inhabitants of a two-family home, seeing the fire, immediately fastened a Scapular to the main door of the house. Sparks flew over it and around it but stayed unharmed. Within 5 hours 22 homes were reduced to ashes and ruins. This one stood unharmed amidst the destruction. Hundreds of people came to see the place Our lady had saved.

Another story is about a train accident.[2] One of the most extraordinary of all Scapular incidents took place right here in the United States. It happened around the turn of the century in the town of Ashtabula, Ohio, that a man was cut in two but a train; he was wearing the Scapular. Instead of dying instantly, as would be expected he remained alive and conscious for 45 minutes - just enough time until a priest could arrive to administer the Last Sacraments. These, and other such incidents, tell us that Our Blessed Mother will take personal care of us in the hour of our death. So great and powerful a Mother is Mary that She will never fail to keep the Scapular contract, i.e. to see that we die in God's grace.

Rev. Howard Rafferty, O. Carm. recounts another story originating in Aylesford.[2] In 1951 the ancient home of St. Simon Stock at Aylesford, England was rededicated, and the relics of the Scapular saint returned. Since then thousands of Scapular wearers have come on pilgrimage. In 1957 little Peter came. He was suffering from leukaemia. His arms and legs were covered with ugly sores. He had only a few days to live. When he returned that very evening, the sores were gone, and his strength had returned. His family realised that he was cured. Doctors confirmed his complete cure.

Rev. Howard Rafferty, O. Carm. also recounts another story from the Holy Land.[2] One day in 1944, a Carmelite missionary in the Holy Land was called to an internment camp to give the Last Rites. The Arab bus driver made Father get off 4 miles from the camp because the road was dangerously muddy. After 2 miles had been covered, his feet sank deeper and deeper in the mud. Trying to get solid footing he slipped into a muddy pool. Sinking to death in a desolate place he thought of Mary and Her Scapular, for he was wearing the full habit, and looked toward Mt. Carmel. There, in the distance, was the holy mountain of Carmel, the birthplace of devotion to God's Mother. He cried out, 'Holy Mother of Carmel, help me! Save me!' A moment later he found himself on solid ground. He told me, 'I know I was saved by the Blessed Virgin through Her Brown Scapular. My shoes were lost in the mud and I was covered with it but I walked 2 miles more through that desolate country praising Mary.'

Also recounted by Howard Rafferty, O. Carm. is a story of a deepening of the spiritual life through the scapular.[2] In October of 1952, an Air Force officer in Texas wrote the following: 'Six months ago, shortly after I started wearing the Scapular, I experienced a remarkable change in my life. Almost at once I started going to Mass every day. After a short time, I started to receive Holy Communion daily. I kept Lent with a fervor I had never experienced before. I was introduced to the practice of meditation and found myself making feeble attempts on the way to perfection. I have been trying to live with God. I credit Mary's Scapular.

A Jesuit missionary in Guatemala[2] tells of an incident of Our

Lady's Scapular protection. In November of 1955 a plane carrying 27 passengers crashed. All died except one young lady. When this girl saw that the plane was going down, she took hold of her Scapular, and called on Mary for help. She suffered burns, her clothing was reduced to ashes, but the flames did not touch her Scapular.

In the same year of 1955, a similar miracle occurred in the Midwest.[2] A 3rd-grader stopped in a gasoline station to put air in his bicycle tires, and at that very moment an explosion occurred. The boy's clothing was burned off, but his Brown Scapular remained unaffected: a symbol of Mary's protection. Today, although he still bears a few scars from the explosion, this young man has special reason to remember the Blessed Mother's protection in time of danger.

A priest recounted the following which occurred about 1980[2] in Ontario, Canada, in a small city near Toronto. 'A woman whose son I had recently enrolled in the Brown Scapular relayed the following: She told me that she was very grateful because I had enrolled her son in the Scapular. That same day, after the enrolment, she went somewhere with her son. She had put him in the back seat and closed the door and drove away down the highway. But she didn't close the door very well, and when she turned the corner the door opened, and her son rolled out onto the highway. She was terrified and horrified and she came back to pick him up and discovered that he did not have a scratch on him. He was, of course, wearing his Scapular.'

The priest also recounted;[2] 'There was a man in Baltimore who told me this himself in about 1990. As he was driving down the highway, someone threw a rock through his window. He didn't know where from. It knocked his glasses that were in his shirt-pocket onto the seat beside him. He didn't need the glasses, so he left them where they landed. When he arrived home, he remembered his glasses. He went to pick them up to put them back in his pocket, but they wouldn't go in. He thought it was because the rock was still in his pocket. So he pulled the rock out, but it wasn't a rock. It was a bullet. He had been shot at. He was uninjured. He was wearing his Scapular.'

To end this collection of stories I would like to add a story recounted in a recent panigiric on Our Lady of Mount Carmel in Valletta, Malta. It regards the Maltese Saint George Preca.[2] When he was a child, he was with a servant by the sea at Valletta when he fell into the water, which was deep at that point. As always, he was wearing his scapular. A boatman who was rowing a group of musicians to the Basilica to celebrate the feast of Our Lady of Mount Carmel saw him, jumped in, and saved the little boy. Years later, now a priest, Father George was walking past an Old People's Home, when a nun came out of the door, accosted him, and asked him urgently to come in and give the Last Rites to a dying man. It was the boatman who had saved him years before.

I have collected from a much broader collection of graces received through the Scapular some which are well documented historically, or which come from our own times, and so can be easily checked. It seems clear that Our Lady does give graces of Conversion, deepening of the Spiritual life, and saving from serious danger, through the scapular.

References:

1 *Anno Memorabile de Carmelitani , Milan 1690 Giuseppe Maria Fornari O. Carm.*

2 *Stories of the Brown Scapular. (Whosoever dies clothed in this Scapular shall not suffer eternal fire - 1251) Pamphlet – 1995 O. Carm. Rev. Howard Rafferty (Author)*

3 *Our Lady's Brown Scapular Sign of Consecration to Mary, Fr. Peter Davies O.Carm https://www.ecatholic2000.com/cts/untitled-328.shtml*

4 *In peril on the sea Marine Votive Paints in the Maltese Islands A.H.J. Prins Said 1989*

5 *Ex Voto Sanctuary of Our Lady of Mellieha -Malta J. Muscat 2009 Mellieha Sanctuary*

6 *https://en.wikipedia.org/wiki/George_Preca*

TWENTY

Our Lady of Mount Carmel and Sailors and Fishermen

It is said that Saint Louis of France, when on Crusade, was saved from shipwreck when his crew heard the bells of the monastery of Mount Carmel, and this led to his choosing to take a group of friars with him to France to found a monastery.[1] Indeed, even today, a lighthouse stands beside the Monastery on Mount Carmel.

It is also said that when the friars decided to leave Mount Carmel because of the Saracen Attacks, Our Lady Appeared in their midst, and promised them that she would be their Star of the Sea. Later, in the Prayer of Saint Simon Stock, the Flos Carmeli, he referred to Our Lady as Star of the Sea.[2] We should remember that sailors use Stars to help them to navigate - to guide them.

Presumably, it was this association with 'The star that gives us safe passage to port' that led to Our Lady of Mount Carmel becoming the patroness of Sailors and Fishermen everywhere throughout the Mediterranean. This is true in Sicily and Italy, in Istria, Dalmatia, and the Croatian Islands, but most of all, in Spain, and this devotion spread with the Spanish Empire to South America, the Caribbean, and the Philippines.

Even more deeply, it appears that the words Maria and Marea or Mare, that is sea, have the same root.[3]

Thus, in Sicily and Calabria, the feast of 16th July is celebrated in many seaports. In Trapani, the Carmelite Basilica of Our Lady of Trapani has a Chapel of the Brotherhood of Sailors,[4] and beside it are many ex-Voto paintings, including one of a boat which had been holed, but a large fish had come and blocked the hole, preventing it from sinking. In Trani, it is specifically the feast of the sailors, who participate in uniform in the Procession around the Port, and, as in Spain, part of the procession happens at sea, with the Statue sailing round the port in a boat- 'La Sagra del-Mare',[5] At Porto Empedocle (Agrigento): The feast is organised by paranzari (fishermen) on the third Sunday of July; there is a sea procession with the statue of the Madonna and of San Simon Stock, accompanied by fireworks and the sirens of the boats present in the port.[6]

In Terracina (Latina) the feast is celebrated on the Sunday after July 16th. The statue of the Madonna is carried in procession through the streets to the port, the procession then embarks on a fishermen's boat, illuminated for the occasion. At the Circeo promontory a crown of laurel and flowers is thrown into the sea in memory of those who fell into the sea. It returns to port accompanied by fireworks, and a fair for the Sagra del Pesce is held.[7]

At Torre Melissa (Crotone) the feast is held in early August.[8] The Madonna del Carmelo is venerated here in thanksgiving for the protection of the small fishing village during the bombings in the Second World War. The statue of the Madonna is carried in procession through the streets, then, the procession embarks and is taken to sea accompanied by the boats of fishermen lit for the occasion.

In Taranto, a major fishing and naval[9], organised by the brotherhood of Maria Santissima del Carmine, happens in the city Centre, with up to 500 persons participating in front of the statue of the Virgin of the Carmel.

At Gallipoli during the Second World War, then, a prodigious fact occurred, which increased its devotion. A ship was sunk with the whole crew by enemy bombardment. Only one sailor, who came from Naples was saved and swam to shore on July 16, He landed just opposite the church of the Madonna del Carmine, where the inhabitants were celebrating the feast. His rescue was attributed to the miraculous intervention of the Madonna, and the sailor returned every year till the 1980s to help organise the celebrations.[10]

In Rome, in the Festa Dei Noantri, the last weekend of July, the Statue of the Madonna del Carmelo is embarked on a boat for a procession on the Tiber.[11]

In Caria the feast of Our Lady of Mount Carmel has been celebrated every year since 1897,[12] when the Virgin of Carmelo miraculously saved Giuseppe Pugliese, from a terrible shipwreck while returning from America. In the midst of a frightful storm he invoked the help of Our Lady, under the title of Carmel, ... suddenly the storm subsided and the ship on which he was traveling was saved.

In Naples, the Famous Carmine Maggiore in Naples[13] is on Piazza Mercato, where the fishermen sell their catch, and of course, Venice has its famous Scuola del-Carmine,[14] seat of the Confraternity of Our Lady of Mount Carmel of that city.

I have witnessed in Postira,[19] on the Croatian Island of Brac, the fishermen organising bonfires around the port for the eve of the feast of 16th July with choirs and other singing groups around the port, and later, singing through the early hours before the statue of Our Lady in the church, and then the procession in the evening. There are a number of other churches of Our Lady of Mount Carmel in Croatia, many in fishing villages, and there are 'Associations of Our Lady of Mount Carmel', previously confraternities, which organise the Feast.

However Spain is where the devotion of Sailors to Our Lady of Mount Carmel is most evident. There Our Lady of Mount Carmel is honoured as an admiral in the Navy.[15] On the feast of the 16th July, in some places the statue of Our Lady is placed in a boat to sail around the port to bless the other boats, or a whole procession of boats is formed. In other places, the statue of Our Lady of Mount Carmel is ceremonially carried into the sea by its bearers so as to bless the boats, of course accompanied by fireworks.[17]

In particular, The Spanish Navy 's devotion to Our Lady of Mount Carmel is linked with the Image of Nuestra Señora del Carmen de San Fernando in San Fernando, near Cadiz,[15] This image is crowned by the Vatican Chapter. The Devotion of the Navy is organised by a Confraternity, the 'Venerable y Real Hermandad de Nuestra Señora del Carmen Coronada Patrona y Alcaldesa Perpetua de la Ciudad de San Fernando –Patrona y Capitán General de la Armada Española'.[15]

One Spanish website describes the feast of Our Lady of Mount Carmel thus:

> On the day of the feast of Our Lady of Mount Carmel, sailors and fishermen decorate their boats with flowers, ribbons and flags, and after carrying the Virgin in procession through the streets, embark and drive a few miles into the sea, to bless the waters,[17] which is where they carry out their work and live their lives, all in an atmosphere of great emotion, surrounded by numerous boats of all kinds, equally decorated, that do not stop sounding horns and sirens, in a manifestation of pride and joy. In the religious acts there is also a lot of emotion and feeling towards the Virgin of Carmen. It is the day when many people make offerings, and ask for protection for relatives who are absent at sea, so that they return without incident. It is also time to pray for those who disappeared or who did not return alive.

In the 18th century, when the feast of the Virgen del Carmen in Spain was very popular, the Mallorcan admiral Antonio Barceló Pont de la Terra, (1716- 1797),[18] encouraged his crew to celebrate the 16th July feast, From then on the Spanish navy adopted the patronage of the Virgen del Carmen, and now sailors salute her on parades by singing the 'Salve marinera',[16] whose words are the following:

Hail, star of the seas,
of the seas of eternal happiness
save, oh phoenix of beauty
Mother of Divine Love

From your people, to the sorrows
your clemency of consolation
fervent, get to heaven,
and to You, to our cry.

Hail, Hail, star of the seas
Hail, star of the seas
Yes, fervent, get to heaven
and to You, and to You, our cry.

Hail, Hail, Star of the Seas
Star of the seas,
salve, salve, salve, salve.

Again, the Spanish website reports the celebrations in the Spanish Navy:

> The military Navy also celebrates this festivity and collaborates on many occasions together with the fishermen in the organisation of the events. On the day of the feast, the sailors wear their white dress uniform, as white represents the purity of their patron, and wear their decorations on their chests, in fact it is one of the few celebrations in which they are proud to exhibit them. Naturally, ships that are in port are decorated, and that day the entire crew receives a special meal.[20]

In Malta, the National Shrine of Madonna tal-Mellieħa, used in the past, to be referred to as 'Madonna del Carmine'[21] (Ex Voto J Muscat Santwarju tal-Madonna tal-Mellieħa, 2009), and it has been suggested that there was a relationship between this shrine and the Carmelite one of Our Lady of Trapani[22] (in Peril on the Sea AHJ Prins 1989). Some Ex-Voto paintings in Mellieħa show Our Lady with a scapular in her hands.

Many of the stories regarding Our Lady of Mount Carmel, Sailors and Fishermen come from Central America. Here are some of them: In Colombia, in the riverside towns of the Great Magdalena River, the people go in procession by the river, escorting the image with hundreds of boats. Our Lady of Mount Carmel is the Patroness of Puerto Colombia[23], Department of the Atlantic, where there is a story that some sailors left a box forgotten in the port and sometime later, when the people noticed it and opened it, they found inside an image of Our Lady of Mount Carmel, which from that time , became the Patron of the municipality.

In Costa Rica, Our Lady of Mount Carmel became famous because of the Miracle of Puntarenas. In 1913 , the small town of Puntarenas, received the sad news that the 'El Galileo',[24] a pearl-shell ship, had been shipwrecked near Isla del Caño with all its crew on board. Don Hermenegildo Cruz Ayala, the owner of the shipwrecked vessel, driven by concern for the relatives of the crew of his ship, went to the Church of the town to ask Our Lady of Mount Carmel to help his workers. He was joined by Father Carmona, the parish priest, and many people. They all prayed for the men of whom there was no news. The miracle was reported a few days later, when a ship brought the crew of the Galileo back to Puntarenas, having found them on dry land. They talked about a woman who, in the middle of the storm, fed and accompanied them so that they found sufficient strength to swim to land, where they were rescued. They, with their family and friends went to the Church, and knelt before the Virgin of Carmel, while the captain and one of the sailors narrated the miracle of the apparition of the Virgin and their rescue in the midst of the storm.

Since that time, the port workers call the Virgin of Carmel the Virgin of the Sea, and she is honoured by all the fishermen of the Gulf of Nicoya. They thank her for the fruit of their work and ask her confidently to protect them every time they go out to sea to find sustenance for their children, while every year, on July 16, Costa Ricans from all over the country come to Puntarenas to thank her. The procession on the 16th July is one of fishing boats decorated with ribbons, flags and flowers, mostly in the yellow and white colours of the Catholic Church.

In Panama, the fishermen from the coastal towns of the districts of Chame and San [25] in the western sector of the province of Panama, in El Puerto beach, in the district of Guararé and Playa[26], in the province of Los Santos, as well as of the coastal sector of the province of Coclé[28] (Farallón, Santa Clara, Juan Hombón among others), organise processions at sea with their fishing boats. In La Palma de Darién,[27] the Virgen del Carmen is also venerated, with the fishing boats arriving at the town to process the virgin through the mouth of the Tuira river. In Táboga,[29] this patron saint of the sea is celebrated with a similar procession of boats.

In Nicaragua, also, processions of boats in honour of Our Lady of Mount Carmel are held in the city and port of San Juan del Sur, and in the city of Río Blanco on July 16th.[30,31] Here she is called 'Regina del Mary los Ríos '(Stella Maris) and 'Protectora de Los Pescadores'. In Mexico, Nuestra Señora del Carmen is venerated in Ciudad del Carmen, in Campeche.[32] The devotion of this town arose from the expulsion of pirates from the island in the morning of July 16, 1717. This victory was attributed to the Patron Saint of the Mariners. Later a fort was built to defend the population and within it was built a chapel in honour of the Virgen del Carmen. At the beginning of 1900, the fishermen of the city donated a golden crown to the Virgin, and a smaller one to the Child Jesus. In 1956, the image was pontifically crowned by order of Pope Pius XII. There is a legend that when hurricanes or storms approach the island, the Virgin walks around it to ward off the storms, leaving her habit wet and full of sea sand. There is also a legend that the finding of Oil off the island was due to intervention by Our Lady of Mount Carmel. She is also venerated in the city of Catemaco, in the state of Veracruz,[33] where there is a basilica in his honour and where she is said to have appeared in 1664 in a place on the shore of Lake Catemaco called Tecalli or Tegal (Stone House) to the fisherman Juan Catemaxca. Here the feast begins on July 14 when the Virgin, accompanied by folk music, processes through the main streets of the city to then go round the lake, past the place of the apparition. In Gutiérrez Zamora (Veracruz) every year the Feast of Our Lady of Carmen is celebrated with a procession of the Virgin by the Tecolutla River. The feast of the 16th July is also celebrated at Playa del Carmen, Quintana Roo,[34] in the Municipality of Solidaridad. According to tradition, the Virgin of Carmen appeared to fishermen who were lost on the high seas and saved them. This led to this fishing village becoming called Playa del Carmen. The festa is celebrated with much folklore. In

Perote (Veracruz) and in Teziutlan (Puebla)[35] nearby, the Virgen del Carmen is taken to the Cathedral from her sanctuary on July 6 and returns to her sanctuary on July 16. The story is that she arrived by boat, so she is always taken in a simulated 'ship', and she is always accompanied by her honour guard.

Thus, the tradition that Our Lady of Mount Carmel is the patroness of fishermen and sailors has been taken from the old world to the new, where it flourishes.

References:

1 *https://bluehearttravel.com/places-to-see/mount-carmel-in-the-holy-land-carmelites-10*
2 *http://www.preces-latinae.org/thesaurus/BVM/FlosCarmel.html*
3 *https://en.wiktionary.org/wiki/mare*
4 *https://www.tititudorancea.com/z/madonna_of_trapani_basilica_ sanctuary_maria_santissima_annunziata.htm#:~:text=The%20Basilica%2DSanctuary%20of%20Maria,1332%20and%20rebuilt%20in%201760.*
5 *https://www.charminly.com/popular-festivals-and-traditions-of-trani-a-bridge-between-sacred-and-profane/*
6 *https://sicilyintour.com/en/luogo/festa-della-madonna-del-carmine-a-porto-empedocle/*
7 *https://www.laziosociale.com/2020/07/16/terracina-festa-della-madonna-del-carmine-processione-in-mare/*
8 *https://www.e-borghi.com/it/ev/ricorrenze-religiose/crotone/melissa/9-agosto-2022/150/madonna-del-carmelo,-a-torre-melissa.html*
9 *http://www.confraternitadelcarmine.it/*

10 *https://www.facebook.com/ComitatoFestaMadonnadelCarmineGallipoli/*
11 *https://it.wikipedia.org/wiki/Festa_de_Noantri#:~:text=La%20Festa%20de%20Noantri%20(%22di,pi%C3%B9%20sentite%20dal%20popolo%20romano.*
12 *http://www.poro.it/caria/cariafesta2011.htm*
13 *https://en.wikipedia.org/wiki/Santa_Maria_del_Carmine,_Naples*
14 *http://www.scuolagrandecarmini.it/*
15 *https://hermandaddelcarmencoronada.org/*
16 *https://armada.defensa.gob.es/ArmadaPortal/page/Portal/ArmadaEspannola/multimediahimnos/prefLang-es/091Salve*
17 *https://www.surinenglish.com/lifestyle/201707/11/seaside-devotion-20170711124033.html*
18 *http://www.secrettenerife.co.uk/2007/07/tenerife-fiestas-in-july.html*
19 *https://www.adriatic.hr/en/guide/dalmatia-island-brac-postira/pl-142*
20 *https://armada.defensa.gob.es/ArmadaPortal/page/Portal/ArmadaEspannola/iniciohome/prefLang-en/*
21 *ex Voto J Muscat Santwarju tal-Madonna tal-Mellieħa, 2009*
22 *In peril on the Sea AHJ Prins Said 1989*
23 *https://upatrimonio.wordpress.com/santuario-mariano/*
24 *https://puntarenas.com/puntarenas-information/virgen-del-mar/*
25 *https://www.telemetro.com/nacionales/2013/07/16/devotos-virgen-carmen-celebran-pescadores/1853755.html*
26 *https://www.panamaamerica.com.pa/nacion/devotos-de-la-virgen-del-carmen-le-rendiran-honores-827896*
27 *https://panoramacatolico.com/celebran-a-la-virgen-del-carmen/*
28 *https://elcapitalfinanciero.com/cooperativa-virgen-del-carmen-de-farallon-apuesta-al-turismo/*
29 *https://www.efe.com/efe/america/sociedad/la-isla-panamena-de-taboga-rinde-tributo-a-su-protectora-virgen-del-carmen/20000013-4024473*

---

30 *https://diocesisdematagalpamedia.org/rio-blanco-asi-se-vivio-la-festividad-de-nuestra-senora-del-carmen/*
31 *https://www.laprensani.com/2013/07/17/departamentales/155121-celebran-a-la-virgen-del-carmen-en-san-juan-del-sur*
32 *https://www.flickr.com/photos/eltb/5791807879*
33 *https://www.flickr.com/photos/eltb/8696789939*
34 *http://newsite.iglesiadelcarmen.org.mx/wp/*
35 *https://luisignaciosan.com/blog/turismo/puebla/teziutlan/virgen-del-carmen-en-teziutlan/*

TWENTY ONE

Our Lady of Mount Carmel Patroness of Builders

In Italy, Our Lady of Mount Carmel is the Patroness of Builders (Muratori). It is fascinating to see how this came about. It appears to have begun in the town of Foggia.

The church in honour of the Blessed Virgin of Carmel, was built in 1646 by a group of builders (muratori)[1,2] who, prayed together, asked the Virgin to drive away from the city the epidemic of cholera that was killing a considerable number of people. The builders who were constructing the Church were so impressed by the power of Our Lady of Mount Carmel in keeping the illness away that they decided to adopt her as their protector. They were 'Mastri Fabbricatori' and they organised themselves into a congregation (or Confraternity). It is said that every mason contributed to its construction of the church by offering their own means, which sometimes consisted of workdays offered for free for pure devotion.

The feast is also held on the 16th of July each year at Poggio Imperiale nearby.[3,4] The festivities begin with a solemn mass celebrated in the Mother Church of San Placido Martire, which follows the procession through the streets of the town and ends with a firework display at the end of the evening. There, as in Foggia and many other places in Italy the tradition – of the 'Carmine' feast – depends on the initiative of the mason of Poggio Imperiale, and more precisely the few young people who still follow this type of activity. In the past, the 'Mastri Fabbricatori' in this part of the world, were known to be excellent. However fewer people are now willing to do this sort of work.

During the last century the mason was among the poorest social classes, as he often worked on piecework and was penalised because he did not earn during the bad weather that raged in the winter.

In Foggia and in almost the whole province, Madonna del Carmine is the patron saint of masons so much that in ancient times there was no family of masons who did not have a daughter named Carmela (Melina).

The Masons collect funds for the feast and carry the statue in Procession. Special masses are organised for the Muratori during the feast.

In Siponto, near Manfredonia[5], up to the early 60s of the 20th century, the Festa was always organized by the Carmine Confraternity, as well as having the active participation of construction builders, masons and carpenters engaged in raising funds for the organisation of the Feast in honour of the Madonna del Carmine, protector masons. Most of the construction workers do not work on the day of the Feast, first of all as a sign of respect and devotion for the Virgin of Carmel and also because of an ancient popular belief considers July 16 an unlucky day, during which, accidents may occur in the workplace.

So much so that the sipontese by popular belief that this day is 'Pònde de Stèlle!' (Star point, danger, especially for those who work on that day of celebration). I remember that my mother, on the Feast of Our Lady of Carmine, forbade us to go to the beach to take a bath and scolded us saying: 'jògge jì a Madònne u Carmine, je pònde de stèlle and ngiavute jì a mére, succedene desgrazzje, capute ninde! Attinde a vuje se ve muuijte da qua' (today is the Madonna del Carmine, and it is a star point, and you do not have to go to the beach to bathe, because misfortunes happen, we are aware! if you move near home).

Despite this, the main reason, for which the sipontini, on the Feast of the Madonna del Carmine did not work, and did not exercise any other activity, should certainly be sought in spirituality and devotional fact, because they believed that this sacred recurrence had to be exclusively dedicated to Virgin of Carmine. In Laterza, the builders stop work for three days, from the 15th to the 17th July.

Also on July 16, in Siponto the carpenters once used to celebrate (now in a minor form).

Other places where 'muratori', masons, have Our Lady of Mount Carmel as their patron[6], are Rignano Garganico, San Severo, Trani, Palo, Lacedonia, Manfredonia, Agnione, Grumo Appula, Lungobuco, San Paolo di Civitate, Cerignola,Casalvecchio di Puglia (FG), San Marco in Lamis (Foggia),Torremaggiore (FG),Canosa di Puglia, Martina Franca (where they join the Archconfraternity of Carmel), Grumo Appula, Laterza,Sant'Agata di Puglia, Castellaneta, San Giovanni Rotondo, Palo del Collo (BA), Lucera,Capaccio, San Nicandro Garganico,

---

In Piacenza, in the old church of Our Lady of Mount Carmel[7], an emblem of the corporations of Builders and Carpenters has been found and is exhibited in a local museum.

In some places, Our Lady of Mount Carmel is patroness of other work groups. In Angione, she is patroness of the Coal Merchants. In Martina Franca[8], groups of other workers join the confraternity, including carters, makers of nails for shoes, carpenters, butchers, farm workers, In Castellaneta Reapers and Bakers also see her as their Patron.[10]

In Agnone Our Lady of Mount Carmel is also seen as Protectress against Earthquakes.[9]

References:

1 *https://www.ilmattinoquotidiano.it/news/almanacco-dauno/38423/oggi-16-luglio-festa-della-madonna-del-carmine-patrona-dei-muratori.html?id=0*
2 *https://www.foggiacittaaperta.it/news/read/la-madonna-del-carmine-protettrice-dei-muratori*
3 *http://www.paginedipoggio.com/?p=3890*
4 *https://poggioimperialefg.wordpress.com/2013/07/17/festivita-della-madonna-del-carmine-2/*
5 *https://www.ilsipontino.net/la-madonna-del-carmine-ponde-de-stelle/*
6 *https://www.materanews.net/il-materano-oggi-celebra-la-madonna-del-carmine-protettrice-dei-muratori-auguri-a-tutti-coloro-che-portano-il-suo-nome-2/*
7 *https://www.ilpiacenza.it/cronaca/riapre-al-pubblico-la-chiesa-di-santa-maria-del-carmine.html*

---

8 *http://martinacultura.altervista.org/wordpress/?p=1566*
9 *https://www.altosannio.it/maria-ss-del-carmine-16-luglio-di-domenico-meo-2/*
10 *http://www.laterza.org/contenuti.asp?IDP=36&page=7-17-Luglio-Festa-Madonna-Del-Carmine*

TWENTY TWO

OUR LADY OF MOUNT CARMEL AS A GENERAL AND PATRON OF COUNTRIES AND REGIONS OF SOUTH AMERICA

OUR LADY OF MOUNT CARMEL IS GREATLY REVERED IN SOUTH America. This is the result of devotion brought by the Spanish, but Our Lady of Mount Carmel is very much the Madonna who is loved by the ordinary people.

In Chile, she is the Patroness of the country.[1] In Chile, Our Lady of Mount Carmel is also called Chinita, Mother of Chile, Augusta patrons of Chile, Queen of the Tamarugal or simply Carmelita.

The Devotion was brought from Spain to America in 1595 (or 1680) by the Augustinians friars[1], who brought with them the first image. In northern Chile, as a result, there began to occur the first Christian festivities with pagan origins, whence started the celebrations of La Tirana in honour of the Virgin of Carmen[1] at the beginning of the sixteenth century. On the other hand, the Brotherhood (Confradia) of the Virgin of Carmen was founded in Concepción, in southern Chile, around 1640.

The devotion was strongly associated with the military.[1] This was especially so in the Concepción area, which was considered the frontier of Spanish rule and there were constant battles with the Mapuches (indigenous residents), so that the military was especially entrusted to the Virgin of Carmen.

Most of the soldiers and their families were members of the Confraternity of Our Lady of Mount Carmel, and it was as a consequence of this that, during the struggle to establish national independence, Our Lady of Mount Carmel was established as the 'Patron of Chile.'[1] This is because José de San Martín, general of the Liberation Army, proclaimed that the Virgin of Carmen received the title of 'Patron of the Army of the Andes'[1]. Thus, the Liberation Army, led by José de San Martín, chose the Virgin of Carmen as protector and patron of the liberation of America and swore fidelity to Her. On January 5, 1817, San Martin handed her his baton as an offering to achieve the liberating victory in the subcontinent.

Bernardo O'Higgins, general of the Chilean army, called her 'Patron and Generala de las Armas Chilenas' - 'the most important patron saint of the arms of Chile'- on the eve of the decisive battle of Chacabuco.[1]

Despite the victory in the battle of Chacabuco, the royalist army was very close to the city of Santiago, so O'Higgins called a meeting in the cathedral and implore the protection of the Virgen del Carmen to obtain the final victory over the forces of the Spanish crown. Therefore, on March 14, 1818, together with the religious authorities, the people performed an act of prayer where they implored the protection of heaven.[1] They vowed to erect a temple to the Virgin of Carmen in the place where the battle for the independence of Chile was decided. This place was Maipú, and there was the votive temple of Maipú.[1]

The main images that are venerated are the one located in the altar of the Parroquia del Sagrario, that is the Cathedral in Santiago which is the seat of the Archbishopric of the Chilean Armed Forces. This statue was carved in France in the 19th century, and the one that is found on the main altar of the Votive Temple of Maipú, was carved in Quito in 1765. This temple is a votive temple which celebrated the decisive victory in the battle of Maipú, where the Chileans achieved independence from Spain.[1]

In order to find the temple, and because of his promise, Bernardo O'Higgins wrote a supreme decree on May 7 that ordered the construction of a temple in honour of the Virgen del Carmen. It stated:

> *La Inmaculada Reina de los ángeles, en su advocación de Nuestra Señora del Carmen, fue jurada patrona de las armas de Chile, primero por el voto general del pueblo, por haber experimentado su protección en el restablecimiento del estado que yacía bajo la opresión de los tiranos, mediante el esfuerzo del Ejército Restaurador de Los Andes y después del 14 de marzo último por el acto solemne en que concurrieron las corporaciones, y un inmenso pueblo en la Santa Iglesia Catedral, al objeto de ratificar, como ratificaron expresamente aquel juramento ofreciendo erigirle un templo en el lugar donde se diese la batalla, a que nos provoco el General enemigo Osorio: no debe tardarse un momento el cumplimiento de esta sagrada promesa. O'Higgins – Irisarri*

> *The Immaculate Queen of the Angels, in her invocation of Our Lady of Carmen, was sworn in as patron saint of the arms of Chile, first by the general vote of the people, for having experienced her protection in the restoration of the state that lay under the oppression*

of the tyrants, through the effort of the Army of the Andes and after March 14 last for the solemn ceremony attended by the corporations, and an immense people in the Holy Cathedral Church, in order to ratify, as they expressly ratified that oath offering to erect to her a temple in the place where the battle took place, to which the enemy General Osorio provoked us: the fulfilment of this sacred promise should not be delayed for a moment
O'Higgins – Irisarri[1]

During the war between Chile, and the Peru-Bolivian Confederation (War of the Pacific), between 1836 and 1839,all Chilean soldiers, both army officers and soldiers, were entrusted to the Virgen del Carmen.[1] The troops that participated in the various phases of the war, as well as the civilian population, carried with them the scapular of Carmel, From the beginning of the war, the Catholic Church provided health and spiritual relief to the combatants. It was recorded that 'the possession of the scapular, medallions and images gave the soldiers the courage to go out to battle; these material elements meant a greater closeness to the maternal and protective figure that they needed[1]'. One story is that of the naval hero of Arturo Prat, who before the naval battle of Iquique, wrote to his aunt that the night the sailors boarded the corvette Esmeralda they received the scapular of Carmen for protection in battle. He was killed in the battle, and the Peruvian sailors found him wearing his scapular among his garments, according to the inventory they gave to Miguel Grau, captain of the monitor Huáscar.[1]

At the end of the War of the Pacific, with Chilean victory, General Manuel Baquedano gave his sword into the hands of the image of the Virgin of Carmen with great acclamation from the people. He is said to have thanked the Virgen del Carmen for the victory in the war, saying to the dean of the Cathedral of Concepción, 'No, monseñor, yo no fui quien ganó esa batalla, sino mi señora del Carmen, quien me inspiró súbitamente una acción y un movimiento, que por mí mismo no habría ejecutado', 'No, monseigneur, I was not the one who won that battle, but my Lady Carmen, who suddenly inspired me an action and a movement, which I would not have executed myself'[1]

Although the Virgin of Carmel was designated as patron or general of the armies of Chile, this title was not canonically granted by the Holy See, so she was only seen as the protector of the armies of Chile and Argentina. However, at the Marian Congress of 1918 it was decided to declare Her as 'Patron of Chile" this was achieved, on October 24, 1923, through a Vatican decree issued by Pope Pius XI, Chileans were authorised to name the Virgin of Mount Carmel this advocation as 'Patron of Chile'. The oath of canonical patronage was carried out on December 8, 1923 in the Plaza de Armas de Santiago, feast of the Immaculate Conception.[1]

The coronation of the Virgen del Carmen took place three years later and the image venerated in the Basilica of the Savior was crowned.[1] In 1987, during the visit of Juan Pablo II to Chile, the coronation of the image of the Virgin of the Carmen was realised in the Votive Temple of Maipú.[1] In 2007, the feast of the 16th July was established as a National Holiday as the 'day of the Virgin of Carmen'.[1]

In Santiago de-Chile, the Confraternity of Our Lady of Mount

Carmel is very important in organising the feast of Our Lady of Mount Carmel.

In Argentina, the Virgin of Carmen de Cuyo is the Argentine counterpart of the Virgen del Carmen de Maipú.[2] The origin of the devotion is the same. In the 18th century, the image that is venerated today existed in the Jesuit church in the capital of the Province of Mendoza. A confraternity of Our Lady of Mount Carmel existed in this church. Don Pedro de Núñez was the donor of the image. In 1776, the image was transferred to the Church of San Francisco. There was great devotion in the Governorate to Our Lady of Mount Carmel.[2] General San Martin opted for the dedication of Our Lady of Mount Carmel for his troops[2] to respect the most common devotion in the Mendoza area, after consulting his comrades-in-arms. In the year 1814 San Martin had to lead the peaceful inhabitants of Cuyo in the war of liberation. The troops needed a Mother to protect them and make sense of the sacrifice of war. So Martin named Our Lady of Mount Carmel Generala of his Army. This was a decision he made with his General Staff. 'The devotion to the Virgin of Carmen was deeply rooted in Cuyo and almost all the soldiers wore her scapular, which is why it was his preference.'[2] In a ceremony on January 5, 1817, during which San Martin gives her his baton, names her Generala, and also blesses the Flag of the Andes. She was greeted by targets and the band with boxes and bugles, and a twenty-one gun salute, before the army in a great gala and all the people of Mendoza.

After the victories of Chacabuco and Maipú, Martin wrote in a Letter, which is displayed, next to the baton of command, in the same Basilica of San Francisco de Mendoza. 'La decidida protección y ayuda que ha prestado al Ejército de los Andes su Patrona y Generala, Nuestra Madre y Señora del Carmen, son demasiado visibles.Un cristiano reconocimiento me estimula a presentar a dicha Señora, que se venera en el Convento que rige Vuestra Paternidad, el adjunto bastón como propiedad suya y como distintivo del mando supremo que Ella tiene sobre dicho Ejército'. José de San Martín 1818.[2]

'The determined protection and help that the Army of the Andes has given its Patroness and Generala, Our Mother and Lady of Carmen, are too visible. A Christian recognition encourages me to present to the said Lady, who is venerated in the Convent that governs Your Paternity, the attached staff as her property and as a hallmark of the supreme command that She has over the said Army. 'José de San Martín 1818.

A decree of 1994 recognises with the degree of Generala of the Argentine Army: the Most Holy, under the invocation of Our Lady of Carmen.

Being General of the Argentine Army, as well as the sash, she is accompanied by the Argentine flag and those of Peru and Chile, as she is the Patron Saint of the two neighbouring countries. She holds in her right arm the baton that San Martin gave her as general of the Army of the Andes In her left arm is the Child Jesus, who holds the scapular.

The third Country which was liberated was Peru. In Peru, there is also great devotion to Nuestra Senora del Carmen, being important in Lima, where she is considered the patroness of the Barrios Altos and Creole music.[3] Our Lady of Mount Carmel is the Patroness of Lima, the festivity of the 16th July happens in the old zone of the city adjoining the Historical Center of Lima, and dates back to the 16th century. On that day, her image comes out in procession from her Church in Barrios Altos and brings together the people of Lima, who honour her with traditional instruments (jarana). Creole music singers sing to honour the Virgin. The crowds eat traditional food. The Virgin of Carmen of Lima is the depository of the Keys of the City of Lima and was twice decorated with the Civic Medal of the City has the Order of the Sun of Peru in degree of Grand Cross with Brilliant. She is Canonically Crowned. The Virgin of Carmen of Lima is also the Perpetual Mayor of the City of Kings and can freely leave the Lima Center and go to other districts. During the procession, transport workers and the police salute her. The Brotherhood of the Blessed Virgin of Carmen of Lima provides several groups of persons to carry the statue.[3] Outside Lima, in El Callao is the shrine of Virgen del Carmen de la Legua, which is canonically crowned.[3] It was brought from Spain in 1556. There are also many other shrines of Our Lady of Mount Carmel in Peru, and many local customs, with much folklore and tradition is linked with the 16th July feast, Such shrines are Paucartambo, in Cusco[3] , which was crowned by Pope John Paul II, in 1985, in Chavín, Huancavelica, in the District of Lircay; in Ancash, District of Llipa; in Huancabamba, capital of the province of the same name and in Llata (Huánuco) with its sanctuary in the Chapel of the Virgen del Carmen, Patroness of the city of Llata.[3]

Spanish missionaries brought the devotion to Our Lady of Mount Carmel to Bolivia. The devotion to her is intimately linked with the history of the country. She was seen as a protector by the patriots during the struggles for independence in 1809. On July 16, 1809 during the procession at the feast of the Virgen del Carmen there was a revolution in the city of La Paz, led by Don Pedro Domingo Murillo[4], which led to independence from Spain. Some days later, the patriots repeated the procession of the Virgin of Carmen, in thanksgiving for the triumph of the uprising, with the statue wearing the Phrygian cap of freedom instead of the crown and with a sword in her hand.[4], Pope Pius IX proclaimed her 'Patron of Bolivia' by a Papal Bull in 1851 which was ratified by the government of Bolivia in 1852.[4] ,A Law of October 11, 1948 proclaimed Our Lady of Mount Carmel 'General and Patron of the Armed Forces of the Nation'. The Feast Our Lady of Mount Carmel is celebrated with great devotion in many towns and cities of the country, with the participation of the Armed Forces of the Nation[4], who accord Her the rank of Generala. The statue at La Paz is more than 206 years old. It is the image used in 1809 and is referred to as the Virgin of Carmen the 'Revolutionary' or also the 'Beautiful'[4],. It is venerated in the Church of Carmen in the heart of the City, at the, former Monastery of the Discalced Carmelites.[4],

In Colombia, truck drivers have made Our Lady of Mount Carmel their Patroness.[5], In many areas of the Caribbean Region of Colombia; in almost all the municipalities of the seven departments of that region of the north of the country they escort the procession of Our Lady of Mount Carmel with decorated trucks, blowing their horns, while in riverside towns of the Great Magdalena River, processions of boats are organised. In Puerto Colombia, Department of the Atlantic[5], there is a story that some sailors left a box forgotten in the port and when it was opened, an image of Our Lady of Mount Carmel was found, which became the Patroness of that municipality and the Department of the Atlantic. In the historic centre of the capital, Bogota, Barrio La Candelaria, is the National Shrine of the Virgen del Carmen,[5] and there, every July 16 the drivers of the city, especially taxi drivers of the city, lead the celebrations.Other places where the Feast of Our Lady of Mount Carmel is celebrated are Salento (Quindio), Cúcuta Norte de Santander, San Estanislao de Kostka, among many others, The Virgen del Carmen is Patroness and Queen of the Armed Forces of Colombia, the National Police, Marine Corps and Air Force and the Fire Department.[5]

Guatemala is another important country of South America where the devotion to Our Lady of Mount Carmel was imported from Spain, and the story of this is linked with Saint Teresa of Avila.[6]

Around the year 1566, she had a vision in which she saw the glorious Virgin sheltering the nuns and friars of her order under her white mantle. She ordered the sculpting of a small image of the vision. Then she wished that this statue be taken to the Americas. Hence it arrived in Guatemala, and is now in La Ermita del Cerro, in Guatemala City.[6] It is still processed through the city on 16th July. Apart from this there are several other churches dedicated to Her in the Capital City. The Brotherhood of the Holy Scapular and the Third Order of Carmen were established in Santiago de Guatemala in 1634. Another church belonging to the Carmelites is that of Santa Teresa, which was founded in 1816.

In Venezuela, too, one of the most popular devotions is that of the Virgen del Carmen. Boconó del Estado Trujillo, is one important centre of the devotion, among many others.[7]

In many of the Central American countries, including Costa Rica, Nicaragua, Panama, Puerto Rico, the fishermen and the sea are the focus of the celebrations of Our Lady of Mount Carmel. This is also the case in Mexico, where the most important centre of the devotion is Ciudad del Carmen, in Campeche,[8] where she is also referred to as Stella Maris. At the beginning of 1900, the fishermen of the city gave the Virgin and child a golden crown. In 1956, the image was pontifically crowned by order of Pope Pius XII. There is also a basilica in Her honour in the city of Catemaco, in the state of Veracruz. She is said to have she appeared in 1664 to the fisherman Juan Catemaxca. She is also venerated in Playa del Carmen, Quintana Roo, a tourist city, in the Municipality of Solidaridad, Quintana Roo, according to tradition,[8] the Virgin of Carmen, appeared to fishermen who were lost on the high seas and thanks to this they were rescued. Another place where she is celebrated is Perote (Veracruz) and its proximity in Teziutlan (Puebla).[8] There it is said that she arrived by boat, that is why in her journey they always take her in a simulated 'ship', her honour guard always accompanies her. She had been appointed as General of the Teziuteca forces in her fight against the Austrian invaders.

Finally, In the city of Celaya[8] in the state of Guanajuato, one of the most important religious festivities is that of the Virgen del Carmen on July 16, during which the image of the Virgin is taken down from her altar and receives the visit of thousands of faithful among religious celebrations and popular festivals.

Thus, across the south of America, Our Lady of Mount Carmel has been a refuge for the People and a defender of the rights of the citizens, even to the extent of her being recognised as a general and defender of the people.

References:

1 *Virgin of Carmel of Chile https://es.wikipedia.org/wiki/Virgen_del_Carmen_de_Chile*
2 *Virgin of Carmen de Cuyo https://es.wikipedia.org/wiki/Virgen_del_Carmen_de_Cuyo*
3 *https://es.wikipedia.org/wiki/Virgen_del_Carmen# Peru*
4 *https://es.wikipedia.org/wiki/Virgen_del_Carmen# Bolivia*
5 *https://es.wikipedia.org/wiki/Virgen_del_Carmen# Colombia*
6 *https://es.wikipedia.org/wiki/Virgen_del_Carmen# Guatemala*
7 *https://es.wikipedia.org/wiki/Virgen_del_Carmen# Venezuela*
8 *https://es.wikipedia.org/wiki/Virgen_del_Carmen# Mexico*

TWENTY THREE

OUR LADY OF MOUNT CARMEL IN SPAIN - IN THE FOOTSTEPS OF SAINT TERESA

SPAIN IS ONE OF THE COUNTRIES WHERE DEVOTION TO OUR LADY OF Mount Carmel is most deeply established. We have already discussed the link between sailors and fishermen and Our Lady of Mount Carmel, and the fishermen have named the Virgin of Carmel their faithful protector while the Spanish Navy has granted her the title of Admiral.[1,2] For this reason, the Virgen del Carmen is also referred to as 'the star of the seas' *(Stella Maris).*

The first Carmelite convent of the Iberian Peninsula was in Perpignan, which is now in France, but at that time was a city which belonged to the Crown of Aragon. The date of its foundation was between 1265 and 1269. After this, the order spread rapidly throughout the Iberian peninsula , and reached Seville in 1358. From this city developed the first Carmelite Bética Province, in 1499.[1] At the same time, the first communities of Carmelite nuns began to develop in Spain. During the XVI century, Santa Teresa de Jesús and San Juan de la Cruz , introduced important reforms within the Order which gave giving rise to the 'Discalced Carmelites'[1], a new austere congregation that is separated from the parent order, which was renamed 'Carmelitas Calzados' or 'Antigua Observancia'[1], Both orders have continued their development over successive centuries.

Almost all the towns and cities on the Spanish coast express local devotion to Our Lady of Mount Carmel, known here as the Virgin of the Carmen. Therefore they all organise processions and colourful maritime pilgrimages with the image of Our Lady every 16 of July.[3] Wikipedia lists the following celebrations of this type; Almeria, Roquetas de Mar (Almeria), Adra (Almeria), Garrucha (Almería), Águilas (Murcia), Algeciras (Cádiz), La Alfoquía (Almería), Arminza (Vizcaya), Amorebieta-Echano (Vizcaya), Barbate (Cádiz), (Isla Mayor (Seville), Cádiz , Camariñas (La Coruña), Cariño (La Coruña), Cee (La Coruña), Chiclana de la Frontera (Cádiz), Corralejo (Las Palmas de Gran Canaria), Corcubión (La Coruña), El Perelló - Sueca (Valencia), El Puerto de Santa María (Cádiz), Estepona (Malaga), Isla Cristina (Huelva), Rincon de la Victoria (Malaga), La Cala del Moral (Rincon de la Victoria , Malaga), La Isleta - Las Palmas de Gran Canaria , La Linea de la Concepción (Cádiz), La Orotava (Santa Cruz de Tenerife), Los Realejos (Santa Cruz de Tenerife), Los Urrutias (Murcia), Málaga, Marbella (Malaga), Marín (Pontevedra), Mazagón - Palos de la Frontera (Huelva), Molina de Aragón (Guadalajara), Puente Mayorga - San Roque (Cádiz), Puerto de la Cruz (Santa Cruz de Tenerife), Puerto del Son (La Coruña), Punta Umbría (Huelva), Revilla de Camargo - Camargo (Cantabria), Rota (Cádiz), San Fernando (Cádiz), San Pedro del Pinatar (Murcia), Suances (Cantabria), Santander (Cantabria), Santurce (Vizcaya), Santa Cruz de Tenerife (Santa Cruz de Tenerife), Torrevieja (Alicante), Santa Pola (Alicante), Vigo, Zahara de los Atunes (Cádiz).[1]

It is also of significance that the advocation of and devotion to Our Lady of Mount Carmel is also present in certain locations in the interior of the Iberian Peninsula, and therefore not linked to the sea, but historically have been consecrated to the Virgen del Carmen.

Wikipedia lists the following places, among others, where this is true ; La Cistérniga (Valladolid), Asturianos (Zamora), Baeza (Jaén), Beniaján (Murcia), Cáceres , Córdoba, Cox (Alicante), Dúrcal (Granada), Guadix (Granada), Hinojosa del Duque (Córdoba), Jerez de la Frontera (Cádiz), Las Fraguas (Cantabria), Peleas de Abajo (Zamora), Peñausende (Zamora), Rute (Córdoba), San Marcos Caves (Málaga), San Fulgencio (Alicante) and Setenil de las Bodegas (Cádiz).[1]

Furthermore, in the big cities, particularly Andalucia, there are many confradias - Confraternities - of Our Lady of Mount Carmel; In Seville, There are six Confradias or Hermandades de Gloria dedicated to the Virgen del Carmen, all of which organise processions in July; they are those of the churches of Calatrava, Salvador, Santa Catalina, San Gil, Santa Ana, and Puente Triana.[4] Many of the members of the San Gil confraternity are also members of the Cofradia Macarena. There is also a Cofradia del Virgen del Carmen Dolorosa,[5] which processes in Holy Week, and which is particularly linked with the Spanish Navy, which sings the Salve Marinera before it during the procession. Equally, in the area of Granada, the fiesta of the 16th July is greatly celebrated, as also in Malaga[7] and Marbella, In Cordoba, the Virgen del Carmen of the church of San Cayetano[6] was canonically crowned in 2012.

References:

1 *https://es.wikipedia.org/wiki/Virgen_del_Carmen# Espana*

2 *https://hermandaddelcarmencoronada.org/*

3 *https://www.surinenglish.com/lifestyle/201707/11/seaside-devotion-20170711124033.html*

---

4 *Hermandades de Gloria de Sevilla Juan Martinez Alcalde Boletin de Las Cofradias de Sevilla 1988*

5 *https://es.wikipedia.org/wiki/Hermandad_del_Carmen_(Sevilla)*

6 *https://www.facebook.com/pages/category/Religiousorganization/Carmen -de-San-Cayetano-236768546370935/*

7 *https://m.facebook.com/Carmen-del-Perchel-1970285569905105/*

TWENTY FOUR

A Land of Miracles and Apparitions of Our Lady of Mount Carmel

Italy has very many important churches dedicated to Our Lady of Mount Carmel.

The Most important in Italy, which are in the hands of the Order include the Carmine Maggiore of Naples, home of the Madonna Bruna, San Martino in Bologna, Santa Maria in Traspontina in Rome, San Martino ai Monti in Rome, the Basilica of Our Lady of Mount Carmel in Florence, home of the Icon of the Madonna del Popolo, the Sanctuary of the Madonna of Trapani, Santa Maria Della Vittoria in Rome, Santa Maria Della Scala in Rome, The Carmine Maggiore of Palermo and Catania, and churches in Messina, Venice, Milan, Cagliari and many others.[24-34]

There are Numerous Sanctuaries dedicated to Our Lady of Mount Carmel.[1-23] Because of the times when the order was dispossessed of their churches, some are in the hands of the order, some are in the hands of Secular Clergy, and some are in the hands of the Confraternities of Our Lady of Mount Carmel.

Wikipedia lists the following sanctuaries:
Places where there are Sanctuaries dedicated to the Blessed Virgin of Mount Carmel (Italy):

Avigliano (PZ) - Feast of Santa Maria del Carmine - Site – Facebook Basilica

Accadia (FG) - Sanctuary of the Madonna del Carmine (Accadia)
Acquafondata (FR) [7] small sanctuary near the 'Serre' pass at 1000 Mt above sea level

Alberobello (BA) - Small church located in Via Garibaldi with the Saints Medici and the Madonna del Pozzo

Anghiari, locality Combarbio (AR) - Sanctuary of the Madonna del Carmine at Combarbio

Ariano Irpino (AV)

Bagnara Calabra (crowned)

Catania (CT) - Sanctuary of the Madonna del Carmine (Catania) Sassari

Ceprano (FR)

Chianni (PI) - Sanctuary of the Madonna del Carmine (Chianni)

Chianni, locality Rivalto (PI) - Sanctuary of the Madonna del Carmine (Rivalto)

Imperia, location Costa d'Oneglia (IM) - Sanctuary of Nostra Signora del Carmine (Imperia)

Laurenzana (PZ) (Crowned)

Lavagna (GE) - Sanctuary of Nostra Signora del Carmine (Lavagna)

La Spezia, district of Rebocco

Luino (Varese Lombardy)

Mesagne (BR) Basilica (Crowned)

Miane, locality Visnà (TV)

Montefalcone di Val Fortore (BN) - Sanctuary of the del Carmine

Crowned(Montefalcone di Val Fortore)

Montefusco (AV)

Montevecchia (LC) (Crowned)

Monza (MB)

Naples (NA) - Basilica sanctuary of Santa Maria del Carmine Maggiore

Nuoro (NU)

Ostuni (BR)

Pagani (SA) - Sanctuary of the Madonna delle Galline

Pagliarelle (KR)

Palmi (RC) - Sanctuary of Maria Santissima del Carmelo (Crowned)

Pesaro (PU) - Sanctuary of the Beata Vergine del Carmine

Prunetto (CN)

Ragusa (RG)

Reana del Rojale, Ribis (UD)

Riccia (Crowned)

Rovello Porro, (Province of Como) - Sanctuary of the Beata Vergine del Carmine

San Cataldo (CL)

San Felice del Benaco (BS)

San Mango sul Calore (AV)

Santa Margherita Ligure, locality Nozarego (GE) - Sanctuary of Nostra Signora del Carmine (Santa Margherita Ligure)

Santa Teresa di Riva (ME) - Sanctuary of Santa Maria del Carmelo (Santa Teresa di Riva)

Santu Lussurgiu (OR)

Sorrento (NA) - Sanctuary of the Madonna del Carmine (Sorrento)
Teulada (CA)

Tornareccio (CH) - Sanctuary of the Madonna del Carmine (Tornareccio)

Trapani Sanctuary Madonna di Trapani

Many of these Sanctuaries[35-61] are linked with stories of Apparitions of Our Lady of Mount Carmel. Here we give the stories of these Apparitions:

Sanctuary of Madonna del Carmine, Aquafondata.
The Sanctuary of the Madonna del Carmine, Aquafondata is in the province of Frosinone in Lazio. The oral tradition and some written testimonies trace the foundation of the sanctuary following the apparition of the Madonna del Carmine to the peasant Nicolina Carcillo (1783-1862).

On July 16, 1841, the day of the Feast of Our Lady of Mount Carmel, Nicolina Carcillo, and other farmers of Acquafondata were working in the fields as a common working day, ignoring the fact that it was a Marian feast. The Virgin Mary appeared to her and asked her to promote the construction of a chapel that would become a place of devotion of the people, and asked that the day of 16 July should be respected with religious practice and with rest from work. Nicolina was troubled and felt that she could not deal with the situation, because her husband, Benedetto Simeone (1781-1861), is an atheist who would never believe her words, and certainly would not help her in the construction of the chapel. So the Madonna, before disappearing, leaves her a mark, by overturning a huge stone that will convince Benedict and the other peasants.

The sanctuary of the Madonna del Carmine Accadia

The sanctuary of the Madonna del Carmine is located near Mount Crispiniano, in the municipal territory of Accadia in the Abruzzo region. According to tradition, the Madonna del Carmine appeared to a shepherd boy between 1200 and 1300. She appeared in a slit of the rock on the summit of Mt Crispiniano, From the fourteenth century, an important sanctuary dedicated to Our Lady was built on the site of the apparition.

The Sanctuary of the Madonna del Carmine at Combarbio

The sanctuary of the Madonna del Carmine at Combarbio is a sacred building located in Combarbio in Anghiari. It consists of the church and the ancient Carmelite convent, and was erected between 1536 and 1552 to the design of the grand-ducal engineer Giovanni Alberto Camerini da Bibbiena, in the place where the Madonna appeared on July 16, 1535 to a shepherdess.

Madonna del Carmine Campomaggiore (PZ)

In Campomaggiore, Our lady of Mount Carmel appeared to two farmers to save all the inhabitants from a landslide in 1885.

Madonna del Carmine Laurenzana (Potenza).

The beautiful face of the Virgin of the Statue of Our Lady of Mount Carmel is such that the Holy Virgin appeared to the artist and asked him: 'How did you make me so beautiful, did you see me in heaven?' The image is crowned by the Vatican Chapter on July 16, 1930.

Madonna del Carmine Miane (TV)

The church of the Madonna del Carmine is mentioned in a Venetian map of 1683 and in the acts of the pastoral visit of the Bishop Agazzi (1696) in which it speaks of the hermitage of the Carmine, consisting perhaps of a small church and the home of the hermit who kept it. It is said that the image of the Madonna and Child appeared to some shepherds, and that one of them had carved a statuette in a cave. Others say that this was a gift from a pilgrim in the Holy Land. There had been an intention to transfer the Statue of Our Lady to the village, but because it was too heavy it was decided to build a sanctuary along the way and so the Madonna del Carmine Church was born.

Madonna del Carmine Mottola (Puglia)

The devotion began in 1506, when Our Lady appeared to a shepherd in an area on the slopes outside the town. In the seventeenth century, the fervent devotion of the city caused another church to rise within the city walls.

Madonna del Carmine Montevecchia (LC)

The imposing sixteenth century Sanctuary of the Madonna del Carmine of Montevecchia was built after the Virgin Mary appeared to a shepherdess on July 11, 1536. The church was designed by the architect Giovan Battista Camerini from Bibbiena. Built between 1536 and 1552, it was first occupied by the Observant Franciscans and then by the Carmelites until the end of the eighteenth century. Finally, it was entrusted for a short period to the Camaldolese monks.

Madonna del Carmine Racconigi (Cuneo):
On July 16, 1493 the Blessed Virgin appeared to a deaf-mute, giving him back his word and hearing. A votive pillar recently erected in memory of the Marian apparition where a Carmelite convent existed until 1802.

Madonna del Carmine Terravecchia (Cosenza)
In the sanctuary of Terravecchia there is an image of the Virgin Mary with a monster snake ('The Madonna of the Carmine that kills the dragon'): It is said that in an unhealthy marsh, near today's church, lived a monster (a snake-shaped dragon), which terrorized the population by periodically killing the children of the village; the population's great faith in the Virgin of Carmel saved them: on Tuesday after Easter, the Madonna with Baby Jesus in her arms appeared in the sky and with a spear pierced the belly of the snake to free the last victim.

Madonna del Carmine Tornareccio (CH)
In Tornareccio, the building of the church was due to an apparition of the Madonna to two young girls who grazed pigs in the 'Colle della Porcareccia'. Local tradition said that Our Lady appeared on August 30, and according to tradition, Our Lady guaranteed the

eradication of the cholera epidemic that had hit the country if a church was dedicated to her. Inside the maple trunk is preserved where the Madonna appeared.The year of appearance is likely, according to documents, to be in the first half of the sixteenth century, and the church is documented as early as in 1568, the year of the first pastoral visit to Tornareccio.

Our Lady of Mount Carmel is also linked with several Major Miracles. Here we list some:

Our Lady of Mount Carmel of Palmi

There has long been a devotion to Our Lady of Mount Carmel in the town of Palmi, in Calabria.The miracle of the Madonna del Carmine of Palmi, occurred between October 31, 1894 and November 16, 1894 in this city: the statue of Our Lady of Mount Carmel was seen by the faithful to move her eyes and change in colour of her face for 17 days. In the evening of November 16, the faithful organised a procession of the statue through the city streets. When the procession reached the end of the city, a violent earthquake hit the entire district of Palmi, ruining most of the houses but bearing only nine victims out of about 15,000 inhabitants, because practically all the population was on the street following the procession. The consequence of the procession was therefore that all the people were out of doors and survived the earthquake. The Catholic Church officially recognised the miracle, by ordering the Crowning of the statue, by a decree of the Holy See on September 22, 1895, the statue was crowned on November 16, 1896.

Our Lady of Mount Carmel Avigliano (PZ)

In Avigliano, the year 1694 was characterised by disastrous events: first there was a famine and then an earthquake devastated the entire region, however the damage was slight in Avigliano and there were no victims. This event, which is celebrated on the 8 September, was considered a miracle of the Blessed Virgin del Carmine (Of Mount Carmel).

Our Lady of Mount Carmel Rutigliano (Bari)

In Rutigliano (Bari), the intercession of Our Lady of Mount Carmel caused a continuous earthquake to cease in 1764.

Our Lady of Mount Carmel Campomaggiore (PZ)

In Campomaggiore, Our Lady of Mount Carmel is the patroness of the town, because she saved all the inhabitants from the landslide that destroyed the town in 1885 by revealing to two peasants the imminent catastrophe.

Our Lady of Mount Carmel Laurenzana (PZ)

The sanctuary of the Madonna del Carmine developed in the first half of the seventeenth century. This came about because of the liberation of the town from the contagion of the plague, which was seen to have occurred by the intercession of the Madonna. Therefore, the University of Laurenzana, with an act dated 7 August 1656, declared the Virgin of the Carmine protector of the country together with the Madonna delle Grazie, in Sant'Antonio da Padova and to the Beati Egidio da Laurenzana and Gaetano.

Our Lady of Mount Carmel Leonforte (Enna)

Our Lady of Mount Carmel saved the town from a plague epidemic.

Our Lady of Mount Carmel Villa Bartolomea (Verona)

In 1855 Our Lady's intercession led to the end of cholera that had killed many people.

Our Lady of Mount Carmel Luino (Varese Lombardy)

In the sanctuary of Our Lady of Mount Carmel in Luino, numerous votive offerings, including some crutches now useless to those who had begun to walk miraculously are to be found. At the foot of the image of the Madonna lies a scapular and the pistol balls fired against it, and stopped by it, leaving a devout Ticinese, miraculously unharmed. Most of all, pious traditions attributed to Our Lady the protection of the inhabitants of places near Lake Maggiore, who had been repeatedly hit by serious epidemics, the scourge of the plague and other serious adversities. In this sanctuary, the Confraternita del Carmine was founded in 1585 to work with the friars in their apostolic work.

Our Lady of Mount Carmel Montefalco (AV)

The Montefuscani, attribute to Our Lady of Mount Carmel the role of liberator of the pestilence that afflicted the country back in 1855. Since then the faith has grown day by day making sure that the church represented, over time, a privileged place for the presence of the faithful who go on pilgrimage several times during the year. These are the main reasons that led to the signing of the decree that now transformed the church into a sanctuary.

Our Lady of Mount Carmel San Mango sul Calore (AV)
In 1630, this sanctuary was restored by 16 families in thanksgiving for the end of plague.

Madonna delle Galline, Pagani.
The sanctuary of the Madonna delle Galline is a Marian sanctuary located in Pagani, Campania, home to the Archconfraternity of the Madonna delle Galline.

There is a popular tradition that in the sixteenth century, during the Easter octave, some hens, scratching about for food, dug up a small wooden table on which was painted the Madonna del Carmine (or Madonna del Carmelo) - Our Lady of Mount Carmel. This image is said to have performed eight miracles. In 1609, a cripple, who had fallen asleep in a room belonging to the ancient parish of San Felice, where the table found by the hens was kept, saw the Madonna in his sleep. She invited him to get up and throw away his crutches because he was healed. The miracle attracted much attention, so that a small oratory was constructed and soon there were several new healings. Thus, between 1609 and 1610 there were seven other miracles which led to great devotion to the Madonna del Carmine, which became renamed Madonna delle Galline. Thus to this day, a great feast is held, and, in the procession, birds are allowed to perch on the statue of Our Lady of Mount Carmel and on the people.

Furthermore, images of Our Lady of Mount Carmel have also been pontifically crowned in Anoia (RC) in 2012.

Thus, in Italy, there are numerous stories of apparitions, liberation from pestilence and famine, preservation from earthquakes, the finding of paintings miraculously, all related to Our Lady of Mount Carmel.

References:

1 *https://it.wikipedia.org/wiki/Nostra_Signora_del_Monte_Carmelo*
2 *https://it.wikipedia.org/wiki/Santuario_della_Madonna_del_Carmine_(Accadia)*
3 *https://it.wikipedia.org/wiki/Santuario_della_Madonna_del_Carmine_(Acquafondata)*
4 *https://it.wikipedia.org/wiki/Santuario_della_Madonna_del_Carmine_(Avigliano)*
5 *https://it.wikipedia.org/wiki/Santuario_della_Madonna_del_Carmine_(Catania)*
6 *https://it.wikipedia.org/wiki/Santuario_della_Madonna_del_Carmine_(Chianni)*
7 *https://it.wikipedia.org/wiki/Santuario_della_Madonna_del_Carmine_al_Combarbio*
8 *https://it.wikipedia.org/wiki/Chiesa_del_Carmine_(Messina)*
9 *https://it.wikipedia.org/wiki/Santuario_della_Madonna_del_Carmine_(Montefalcone_di_Val_Fortore)*
10 *https://it.wikipedia.org/wiki/Basilica_santuario_di_Santa_Maria_del_Carmine_Maggiore*
11 *https://it.wikipedia.org/wiki/Santuario_della_Madonna_del_Carmine_(Rivalto)*
12 *https://it.wikipedia.org/wiki/Santuario_di_Santa_Maria_del_Carmelo_(Santa_Teresa_di_Riva)*

---

13 *https://it.wikipedia.org/wiki/Santuario_della_Madonna_del_Carmine_(Sorrento)*

14 *https://it.wikipedia.org/wiki/Santuario_della_Madonna_del_Carmine_(Tornolo)*

15 *https://it.wikipedia.org/wiki/Santuario_della_Madonna_del_Carmine_(Tornareccio)*

16 *https://it.wikipedia.org/wiki/Santuario_di_Maria_Santissima_del_Carmelo*

17 *https://it.wikipedia.org/wiki/Santuario_di_Nostra_Signora_del_Carmine_(Imperia)*

18 *https://it.wikipedia.org/wiki/Santuario_di_Nostra_Signora_del_Carmine_(Lavagna)*

19 *https://it.wikipedia.org/wiki/Santuario_di_Nostra_Signora_del_Carmine_(Santa_Margherita_Ligure)*

20 *https://it.wikipedia.org/wiki/Santuario_della_Madonna_delle_Galline*

21 *https://it.wikipedia.org/wiki/Chiesa_della_Beata_Vergine_del_Carmine_(Ribis)*

22 *https://it.wikipedia.org/wiki/Chiesa_di_Santa_Maria_del_Carmine_(Morrocco)*

23 *https://it.wikipedia.org/wiki/Ispica#Chiesa_Madonna_del_monte_Carmelo*

24 *https://en.wikipedia.org/wiki/San_Martino,_Bologna*

25 *https://en.wikipedia.org/wiki/Santa_Maria_in_Traspontina*

26 *https://en.wikipedia.org/wiki/San_Martino_ai_Monti*

27 *https://en.wikipedia.org/wiki/Santa_Maria_del_Carmine,_Florence*

28 *https://en.wikipedia.org/wiki/Madonna_of_Trapani#:~:text=The%20Basilica%2DSanctuary%20of%20Maria,Carmel%20in%20Trapani%2C%20in%20Sicily.*

29 *https://en.wikipedia.org/wiki/Santa_Maria_della_Vittoria, _Rome*

30 *https://en.wikipedia.org/wiki/Santa_Maria_della_Scala*

31 *https://it.wikipedia.org/wiki/Chiesa_del_Carmine_Maggiore*
32 *https://en.wikipedia.org/wiki/Carmini*
33 *https://it.wikipedia.org/wiki/Chiesa_di_Santa_Maria_del_Carmine_(Milano)*
34 *https://it.wikipedia.org/wiki/Chiesa_di_Nostra_Signora_del_Carmine_(Cagliari)*
35 *https://www.itrullidialberobello.it/chiese/chiesa-madonna-del-carmine*
36 *https://www.beweb.chiesacattolica.it/edificidiculto/edificio/28420/Chiesa+della+Madonna+del+Carmine*
37 *https://turismo.reggiocal.it/en/culture/churches-and-monasteries-reggio-calabria/madonna-del-carmine-sanctuary-bagnara-calabra*
38 *https://www.carmelitanicentroitalia.it/dove-siamo/conventi-della-provincia/b-vergine-maria-del-carmelo-ceprano/*
39 *http://www.comune.laurenzana.pz.it/laurenzana/detail.jsp?otype=100068&id=103330*
40 *https://bvdelcarminereboccosp.wordpress.com/*
41 *https://madonnadelcarmineluino.com/*
42 *http://www.basilicacarminemesagne.it/default.asp?sec=154*
43 *https://www.facebook.com/pages/category/Community/Santuario-del-Carmine-Miane-807725189296301/*
44 *http://www.prolocomontefusco.it/santuario%20carmine.html*
45 *https://santuario.parrocchiamontevecchia.it/*
46 *https://www.carmelomonza.it/*
47 *http://www.diocesidinuoro.it/festa-al-carmelo/madonna-del-carmelo/*
48 *https://www.confraternitadelcarmineostuni.it/*
49 *https://www.facebook.com/calabria.meravigliosa/photos/ oggi-le-celebrazioni-per-la-madonna-del-carmine-o-beata-vergine-maria-del-monte-/1159161487444992/*
50 *https://www.arcidiocesipesaro.it/santuario-beata-vergine-del-carmine-pesaro/*

---

51 *https://www.cittaecattedrali.it/it/bces/411-santuario-della-madonna-del-carmine*

52 *https://www.santuariocarmineragusa.it/*

53 *https://en.wikipedia.org/wiki/Sanctuary_of_the_Madonna_del_Carm ine,_Riccia*

54 *http://www.comune.rovelloporro.co.it/zf/index.php/musei-monumenti /index/dettaglio-museo/museo/1*

55 *http://santuariodelcarmine-sanfelice.it/*

56 *https://www.italia-italy.org/loc12300-chiese-san-mango-sul-calore/chiesa-madonna-del-carmelo-san-mango-sul-calore*

57 *wikipedia.org/wiki/Santuario_di_Nostra_Signora_del_Carmine_(Santa_Margherita_Ligure)*

58 *https://it.wikipedia.org/wiki/Santuario_di_Santa_Maria_del_Carmelo _(Santa_Teresa_di_Riva)*

59 *https://sardegna.beniculturali.it/it/466/beni-dichiarati-di-interesse-culturale/15040/santu-lussurgiu*

60 *https://it.wikipedia.org/wiki/Santuario_della_Madonna_del_Carmine _(Sorrento)*

61 *https://it.wikipedia.org/wiki/Santuario_della_Madonna_del_Carmine _(Tornareccio)*

TWENTY FIVE

THE PARDON OF NOTRE DAME DE CARMES NEULLIAC BRITTANY

AS A RESULT OF THE FRENCH REVOLUTION , THE CARMELITE FRIARS disappeared from France. One church in Brittany which was left to us by the Carmelites is that of Notre Dame de Carmes in Neulliac. This fifteenth century church used to be supported by the Lords of Rohan, a local family of Breton Dukes.[1,2,3]

One very interesting painting in the church is that of King Louis XIII dedicating France to the Virgin of the Rosary, and receiving the Scapular from Her. In fact King Louis XIII dedicated France to the Virgin of the Rosary in the hope that his wife, Queen Anne of Austria, would conceive a son, which she did, and the Son grew up to become King Louis XIV.

In this church, three confraternities are erected, those of the Rosary, of the Scapular, and of the Souls in Purgatory.

There is a processional statue of Our Lady of Mount Carmel which, in the past, used to be carried in procession by young men about to go to do their military service.

In this church, every 15th of August, the feast of Our Lady of Mount Carmel is celebrated, which in French is called The Pardon of Notre Dame de Carmes de Neulliac. On the 15th of August, after a Marian vigil, a torchlight procession is held. On Sunday August 16, mass is held in the morning. A procession is then held to the fountain and this is followed by a bonfire and this is accompanied by feasting and dancing.

It is beautiful that these confraternity celebrations are still held as a vestige of past times.

References:

1 *https://www.brittanytourism.com/matching-what-i-want/ideas/exploring-brittanys-chapels/*

2 *https://www.tripadvisor.co.uk/Attraction_Review-g13345425-d13344592 -Reviews-Chapelle_Notre_Dame_de_Carmes-Neulliac_Morbihan_Brittany.html*

3 *https://actu.fr/bretagne/neulliac_56146/neulliac-le-pardon-de-notre-dame-de-carmes-samedi-15-et-dimanche-16-aout_35442639.html*

TWENTY SIX

IRELAND, PENAL TIMES, AND A MISSION TO AFRICA

WHEN DISCUSSING CARMEL WITHIN DIFFERENT EUROPEAN Cultures, one must not forget Ireland.

The present Irish Culture is very influenced by the fact that the Irish for the most part remained faithful to the Catholic Church in Rome during the protestant Reformation and the penal times which followed. In parallel with this was the constant struggle with the English Overlords and the establishment of a National Identity. The Irish suffered greatly from Famine and from wars such as the intervention of Cromwell's army.

In Penal times, Mass rocks were rocks used as an altar in mid-17th century Ireland as a location forsaying Mass. Isolated locations wereused because saying the Catholic Mass was as a result of both Cromwell's campaign and the Penal Law of 1695[4]. One such Mass Rock is in the until recently Carmelite Parish of Knocktopher Co Kilkenny.

The consequence is that the Irish character was marked with the disappearance for centuries of outward celebrations of the Faith but a dogged determination to maintain the Essentials of it whatever the circumstances.

The Carmelite Order in Ireland reflected this situation. It had had a great number of Monasteries in the Middle Ages, but lost them all during the reformation Period. Whitefriars in Central Dublin is important as the Shrine of Our Lady of Dublin[1]. Originally this black oak statue had been venerated in St Mary's Abbey[1]. This image is not one of the scapular vision, but is a statue of Our Lady with the Christ child , which is of sixteenth century origin and, after the sacking of the Abbey in 1539, was hidden and preserved. It was found by Fr John Spratt in 1824[1] and brought to Whitefriar Street Church. It is said that during the reformation period it was partially burnt, rescued, buried and then, as it was hollowed out at its back, it was used as a hog-trough.[2]

Apart from Whitefriars, there are Carmelite Churches at Knocklyon, Kinsale, Kildare, Moate, Terenure College and Gort Muire.[3] In Kinsale, there are other remnants of Penal Times , such as the Old Mass House, where Mass used to be said, and 'ye olde masshouse on ye rocke' and Abbey Well, where people used to gather to recite the Rosary to spite the law[5].

The Discalced Carmelites of Dublin Contributed greatly to The Emancipation of Catholics. Saint Teresa's Church in Dublin, founded in 1797[6] was the spiritual Home of Daniel O'Connell, the architect of Catholic Emancipation[6].

So the Irish Carmelites have a history of gradual development through several centuries of gradual development while the modern Irish state gradually emerged from the difficulties of Penal Times, but the Carmelites always had a large following; witness the huge devotion to the Holy Child of Prague which is so evident in Ireland[7].

Ultimately, in the 1950s, three Irish Carmelite Brothers; Elias[8], Kilian[9] and Malachy Lynch were responsible for the reestablishment of the Carmelite Presence in England. Fr. Malachy became the First Prior of the re-established Aylesford. Kilian Became Prior General, and, apart from Aylesford, Founded the Carmelite House in Fatima and laid the Foundation Stone of the Basilica of Valletta.

The Irish Carmelites established a mission in Zimbabwe in 1946, which has grown into a thriving community[3].

References:

1 *https://en.wikipedia.org/wiki/Our_Lady_of_Dublin*

2 *https://www.interfaithmary.net/black-madonna-index/dublin*

3 *https://carmelites.ie/*

4 *https://en.wikipedia.org/wiki/Mass_rock*

5 *A Short History of the Carmelite Friary, Kinsale, Co Cork.S.M. Hession, O.Carm. May 2010. http://carmeliteskinsale.ie/*

6 *'It's probably Ireland's busiest church' - St Teresa's Church in Dublin city centre Nora-Ide McAuliffe https://www.irishtimes.com/news/social-affairs/religion-and-beliefs/it-s-probably-ireland-s-busiest-church-st-teresa-s-church-in-dublin-city-centre-1.2454677*

7 *https://www.nmni.com/blogs/the-child-of-prague#:~:text=The%20Child%20of%20Prague%20is,became%20a%20very%20common%20item.*

8 *https://www.carmelite.org/past-present/heritage-archive/obituaries/elias-lynch*

9 *http://thecarmelitelibrary.blogspot.com/2019/10/*

10 *A Stumbling Pilgrim Guided by Indirections: A Biography of Carmelite Friar Fr Malachy Lynch 1899-1972 Fr Wilfrid McGreal. Saint Albert's Press*

TWENTY SEVEN

ICONS OF OUR LADY OF MOUNT CARMEL

IN THE EASTERN PART OF EUROPE, IN SLAV COUNTRIES SUCH AS Poland, Belarus, Ukraine, and Rumania, as well as in Middle Eastern Countries such as Lebanon, the Carmelites and Discalced Carmelites are the custodians of many Icons, often painted according to the Byzantine Iconographic Canons. Sometimes the populations who venerate these icons are of Latin Rite, sometimes of Byzantine Rite. The churches which host these icons reflect the folklore and culture of the local populations. The Icons are often ancient, sometimes they are very modern. These icons all have their own stories and are another way of venerating Our Lady of Mount Carmel. Here we describe some of them.

KRAKOW[1]

Our Lady of the Sand or 'the Lady of Krakow' was painted over the side entrance to the church, thus on entering the interior, one had to bow to the Mother of God. Our Lady of the Sand is depicted in a torso, holding the Baby in her arms and tilting her head in his direction. The painting is crowned by the Vatican Chapter.

Within the church in Krakow (the church of the Visitation) is the Bracka Chapel, the seat of the Confraternity of the scapular, containing a very regal 'Mother of God of the Scapular' a Hodegetria virgin who carries a sceptre and who, with the Child Jesus wears a crown.

The Mother of God Wola Gułowska[2]

In the oldest document about Wola Gułowska from 1548, we can read about the revelation of the Virgin Mary to a pious woman named Barbara, that a temple dedicated to her, founded by the heir of Wola Gułowska, would be built in this place. The first Carmelites came to this place in 1633. Carmelite monastery served as a refuge for Catholicism and Polishness, but also for the followers of the Greek rite (Uniates), whose tsarist authorities persecuted. In the mid-nineteenth century, the partitioners intended to create an Orthodox monastery here. Hence the Carmelites left in 1864, but returned in 1924. Wola Gułowska is today a large Marian shrine. Her real ornament is the image of the Mother of God, today honoured in the title of the Patron of the Soldiers of September. This is in honour of the Polish soldiers who fought the last battle against the Germans in 1939 nearby. The church contains both the image of the Mother of God Wola Gułowska and a copy of the Virgin Mary of Gulow, crowned by Cardinal Glemp.

The Bołszowiecka Mother of God[3,11]

The image of the Bołszowiecka Mother of God, worshiped for four hundred years in the Bołszowce Sanctuary, is currently in the church of St. Catherine in Gdansk. It is of unknown author, but the creation of the image is estimated at around 1620.The image was crowned in 1777. The miraculous image was brought to Gdansk on July 21, 1968. The Carmelite fathers, fleeing the Bolshevik army, brought a picture, which had enjoyed great veneration in Kresy, to Krakow, and then gave it to the church of St. Catherine in Gdansk.

THE SANCTUARY OF THE MOTHER OF GOD IN BILSHIVTSI[12]

The sanctuary was founded in 1624. It has a long and interesting story. For many years, the miraculous image of the Mother of God was kept here. During the wars, the church was destroyed and closed during the Soviet Union era. After the proclamation of independence of Ukraine, the newest history of Sanctuary began and in 2001, the church resumed its activities, however the icon remains in Gdansk. There are several versions about the finding of the icon. According to one of them, Hetman of the Polish Army Martyn Kazanovsky found it when he fought with the Turkish-Tatar invaders. At a time when it seemed that there was no hope for salvation and victory, the Hetman began to pray sincerely. His dog rolled into the water and brought to the master a scroll, in which there was a miraculous image of the Virgin Mary with a baby. The troops saw this as a real miracle and after this discovery, the troops successfully defeated the attackers. On his return to home, Martin Kazanovsky placed the icon in the chapel of his palace, but then decided to expose it to the veneration of the people. So, he built a wooden church and gave the icon to the Carmelite Order.

OUR LADY OF TREMBOWELSKA[3]

The Carmelite Order is famous for spreading the cult of the Scapular Virgin and devotion of the Holy Scapular. Where the Carmelites settle, the image of the Blessed Virgin of the Scapular appears. This happened in Gdańsk. On their return to Gdansk, the nuns brought a picture that was saved from the Bolsheviks in Trembowla. As a work of art, it dates from the turn of the 16th and 17th centuries. Its prototype is the wonderful image of the Madonna Bruna from the Neapolitan Carmelite Church of Santa Maria del Carmine. The

Madonna holds the Baby in her arms, the Scapular hangs from her right hand, and her right arm is decorated with a star - in accordance with the title 'Sea Star.' At the bottom of the picture there are figures with Scapulars on their necks, in the cleansing fire, awaiting salvation – reminding us of the promise related to the scapular.

Our Lady of Consolation
(Matki Bożej Pocieszenia) Pilzno/Pilsen[4]

The first Carmelites came to Pilzen in 1841, substituting the Augustinians. In the church in Pilzno there is a famous image of Our Lady of Consolation. The history of this image of the Madonna deserves attention. According to one legend, the picture was brought to Pilzno by Sierosław, a student of St. Methodius. Others believed that the history of the painting began in the eleventh century, when it was hung in the castle tower. Probably the Benedictines, to whom the settlement belonged, were the first promoters of the cult of the Mother of God. A special moment of the cult's increase was the year 1241 after the Tartar invasion. It was the Mother of God who was credited with miraculous rescue from enemies. At that time, the painting was transferred in a solemn procession to the parish church. At the end of the 13th century, the Pilsen NM Brotherhood was founded, which was founded to pay tribute for the subsequent saving of the stronghold from the Tartar invasion in 1287. During the Pilsen fire in 1474. the image of the Pilsen Lady was destroyed. Around 1500, one of the Augustians had visions of the Mother of God to convince his brothers to paint her new image. The new painting was by Lazarus Gertner. A second tragic event for the city and the image was March 18, 1657. This was the - assault of Hungarian troops commanded by Rakoczy.

The city was plundered and finally burned. The residents placed the surviving fragment of the painting on the wall of the monastery church damaged by fire. The painting was renewed after the Swedish invasion in 1663. During the Galician uprising, the Austrian army wanted to burn the picture. Thanks to the determination and the ruse of two women: Miss Bozańska and Miss Bobrowiecka, the image of the Mother of God survived. Today, many pilgrims come to the image of the Madonna of Consolation to ask for favors for themselves and their loved ones.

Our Lady of the Scapular of Mount Carmel Monastery of Discalced Carmelites, Czerna, Poland[13]

This Icon is crowned by the Vatican Chapter. In this Monastery of the Discalced Carmelites, Pope John II had considered becoming a Carmelite but was prevented by the Second World War.

The convent was founded in 1629 as the Hermitage by Agnieszka Firlejowa née Tęczyński. Religious life began in 1633. In fact, the monastery fulfilled its function until 1797. In 1875-1911 it belonged to the Austrian Province. After a period of weakening of religious observation, the work of renewing religious life was undertaken in 1880 by the Discalced Carmelites of Austria, France and Belgium. Since then, the monastery has had a novitiate. The church has a grace-famous image of Our Lady of the Scapular, crowned with papal crowns by Cardinal Franciszek Macharski, July 17, 1988.

Our Lady Of The Good Death

The Carmelite Convent in Warsaw is nowadays in the hands of the Archdiocese of Warsaw, and is used for state occasions. In it is an

Icon called 'Our Lady Of The Good Death'[9], a clear reference to the Sabbatine Promise.

Mother of God of Hudagai Belarus[7]

The icon of the Mother of God of Hudagai is one of the Christian shrines in Belarus. Located in the parish church of. Hudagai (Astraviec county). The icon is painted, probably, in XVI - the beginning. XVII century on a board of the small sizes using tempera. The icon belongs to the iconographic type 'Our Lady of Tenderness'. It belongs to the Byzantine-Orthodox tradition, repeating the iconographically famous Byzantine icon 'Mother of God of Vladimir'.The origin of the icon and the time of its appearance in Hudagai are unknown. According to church tradition, the icon came here through Russian merchants, later belonging to the owner Hudagai Rozwadowski, from 1735 - Ludwica Voina. In 1764 Polotsk coach Joseph Voina and his wife Ludwika (from Sulistrowski) founded a Discalced Carmelite monastery near the church. At this time the icon became famous as being miraculous. After the church was closed by the Russians (1866), the icon was moved to the church in Ašmiany . In 1906 she was returned to the revived Hudagai parish. On July 15, 2007, the icon of the Mother of God was crowned with papal crowns.

Mother of God Berdyczowska (Mother of God of the Holy Scapular) Ukraine[8]

The church and monastery of the Discalced Carmelites in Berdyczów, which has been the central Marian sanctuary in Ukraine since the 18th century, was founded by J. Tyszkiewicz, the governor of Kiev. In the years 1630-1642. This was because of a vow he made when captured by the Tartars. The icon is a copy of the Salus Populi Romani Icon in Rome (Santa Maria Maggiore), The monastery was dissolved by the Russians in 1866. The people insisted on the return of the Carmelites in 1991. The most important event in the sanctuary, in recent times, was the coronation with papal crowns of a copy of the image of Our Lady of Berdyczów. The coronation occurred on July 19, 1998. The crowns with which the Child Jesus and the Mother of God were adorned were consecrated by John Paul II in Krakow on June 9, 1997. The Episcopate of Ukraine announced this place on October 27, 2011, the National Shrine of Ukraine

Our Lady of Mount Carmel of Luncani, Romania[6]

The new Carmelite Monastery in Luncani, Romania has a newly designed icon of Our Lady. This icon, which is unique, presents a Carmelite Marian spirituality in the religious and cultural context of the location which is largely Orthodox. It combines both Byzantine and Carmelite traditions and evokes immediately the images of Carmel and of the Lady of the Place. There are a few particular characteristics. One such is the 'mantle', which is a typically oriental sign of protection.

Mary's right hand holds her mantle which welcomes rather than covers her faithful servants. These are men and women, members of the Carmelite Family of the 20th century, representatives of a new humanity emerging from her Tent, visibly happy and praying. They include Blessed Titus Brandsma, witness to the struggle for freedom from all forms of absolutism; Blessed Isidore Bakanja, a humble witness of the faith; Saint Teresa Benedicta of the Cross (Edith Stein), who is a symbol of the encounter between Christianity and Judaism; Anicka Zelikova, Third Order Carmelite, who was particularly interested in bioethics. They all stood up to evil, and they banished the desperation brought about by the horrors of human violence, because they found refuge in their Mother and with her in her Son the Saviour.

From Mount Carmel the prophet Elijah's voice also rises in a scroll with the motto zelo zelatus sum pro Domino Deo exercituum. This connects the two inspirational figures of the Carmelite charism. The Carmelite shield recalls the great undertaking of the Carmelite Family in spreading the Marian message.

This new icon is particularly important in promoting the Carmelite message in this part of Romania.

We should also explain that in Romania there are two Discalced Carmelite Monasteries which are in the Byzantine Style[5] and the Byzantine rite, these are the Holy Cross Skite at Stânceni and the Monachal Complex at Snagov. In Sofia, Bulgaria, too, there is a Discalced Carmelite Monastery which follows the Byzantine Rite. Many beautiful Marian icons are also scattered across the Teresian nuns' monasteries all over Eastern Europe, which are too many to mention.

Finally, in Lebanon[10], the Carmelite Nuns of Harissa have produced a beautiful Virgo Orans as a Mother of Carmel. She is dressed in the Carmelite nun's Habit, and this icon has become very popular in Carmelite Monasteries all over the world. Mary's hands are lifted in prayer, and she bears Christ, whose hands are also raised, in a medallion on her breast. This type of icon is also referred to as 'Our Lady of the Sign', and recalls the famous Our Lady of Blancharne, the most famous and miraculous of the Icons of Constantinople.

There are many other modern Icons of Our Lady of Mount Carmel. What we have described illustrates how Our Lady of Mount Carmel is celebrated in Eastern Europe by Icons, some old, some new.

References:

1 *https://en.wikipedia.org/wiki/Church_of_the_Visitation_of_the_Blessed_Virgin_Mary,_Krak%C3%B3w*
2 *https://en.wikipedia.org/wiki/Wola_Gu%C5%82owska*
3 *https://en.wikipedia.org/wiki/St._Catherine%27s_Church,_Gda%C5%84sk*
4 *http://interfaithmary.net/blog/black-madonna-pilzno*
5 *http://www.monasteresaintelie.com/skete_foundation.html*
6 *http://carmelites.info/citoc/citoc/julyaug2002/citoc_magazine_julyaug2002_1.htm*
7 *https://commons.wikimedia.org/wiki/Category:Church_of_the_Visitation_of_the_Blessed_Virgin_Mary_in_Hudahaj*
8 *https://ukrainetrek.com/blog/architecture/monastery-of-the-discalced-carmelites-in-berdychiv/*
9 *https://en.wikipedia.org/wiki/Carmelite_Church,_Warsaw*
10 *http://www.carmelitehermitage.org/DC/Saints/Olmc.htm*
11 *http://www.dobrewakacje.eu/en/Bolsheviks/ New Add*
12 *https://www.rkc.lviv.ua/category_2.php?cat_1=10&cat_2=115&lang=4 13 https://karmelczerna.pl/*

TWENTY EIGHT

THE FEAST OF OUR LADY OF MOUNT CARMEL IN HAIFA, ISRAEL

WHILE OUR READERS WILL WELL UNDERSTAND HOW WE celebrate the feast of Our Lady of Mount Carmel in Malta and Europe on the sixteenth of July, they may not know that the feast is celebrated at Haifa and on Mount Carmel itself, on Stella Maris Monastery on the second (or sometimes on the third) Sunday after Easter - Domenica in Albis. Here I would like to explain why.

Mount Carmel is a coastal mountain range in northern Israel stretching from the Mediterranean Sea towards the southeast. There are a number of towns there, especially the city of Haifa, Israel's third largest city, which is located on the northern slope.

The settlement of the Carmelites on Mount Carmel has changed a great deal over the centuries. The first hermits who settled on Mount Carmel in 1150 made their centre a chapel consecrated to Our Lady and called themselves the *'Brothers of Our Lady of Mount Carmel'. They rebuilt their monastery* at Wadi es Siah around the year 1200, and the ruins of this can still be seen. In 1291 the armies of Egypt conquered Acre and Haifa, burned the monastery and church on Mount Carmel and killed the friars who still remained, while they sang the Salve Regina[11]. Most of the friars had already left for Europe.

In 1631 the Discalced Carmelites returned to the Holy Land, led by the Venerable Father Prosper. He constructed a small monastery on the promontory at Mount Carmel, close to the lighthouse, and the friars lived there until 1761, when Dhaher al-Omar, the then effectively independent ruler of Galilee, ordered them to vacate the site and demolish the monastery.

The Order then moved to the present location, which is directly above the grotto where the prophet Elias is said to have lived. Here they built a large church and monastery, first clearing the site of the ruins of a medieval Greek church, known as 'the Abbey of St. Margaret' as well as a chapel, thought to date back to the time of the Byzantine Empire.

Between 1827 and 1836 the current monastery and church of Stella Maris were built on the north point of Mount Carmel, above a cave that recalls the presence of the prophet Elias. Maltese lay brothers were involved in the building of the monastery and the decoration of the church.In Particular, the dome of the church was decorated by the Maltese Carmelite Luigi **Poggi** (1924-1928).[10]

During the Napoleonic invasion of 1799, the Stella Maris monastery of Carmelite Friars was badly damaged, because the French used the monastery as a hospital for wounded soldiers, and the mamelukes slaughtered all the soldiers, forcing the friars to again temporarily abandon the monastery.[1]

In 1816 Italian brother Giovanni Battista Casini went to oversee its restoration. While he visited Genoa in 1820, he commissioned a statue of Our Lady of Mount Carmel from sculptor Giovanni

Battista Garaventa. It is said that when Giovanni Battista ordered the statue, he had not enough money for gold crowns, so he ordered a silver one for the Virgin and a copper gilt one for the child, saying 'You will know how to procure yourself a better one', which happened sometime later in Naples, when a rich nobleman presented two crowns as a result of a miraculous cure which he had experienced.[1] The cedarwood image was solemnly crowned at the Vatican in 1823 and remained in Rome until 1835, when it finally reached Mount Carmel. On June 10, 1836, the restored church was blessed, Our Lady's statue enthroned, and regular monastic life resumed at Stella Maris. Garaventa's work was made to be vested in fabric, so only the head and hands were finely carved. Therefore, in 1933, the Roman sculptor Emanuele Rieda refashioned the body with carved robes.

In the first world war, the Carmelites were again expelled from the monastery. On 14th November 1914, the monastery was searched for arms. Then on the 17th December, the friars were given three hours to leave the monastery. On 17th December 1914, the inhabitants of Haifa watched as a sorry procession of monks, clad in their brown habits and shod with sandals, moved slowly from the monastery to the town. They had been given three hours to evacuate their monastery. They took with them what they could of their sacred objects. Their archives were entrusted to the Spanish consular representative, Scopenik, who looked after them faithfully until the end of the war. The Turks, in order to justify their expulsion, claimed that the monks had been signalling to enemy ships. The Carmelites denied the charge, blaming the Germans for the calumny, and especially Dr. Loytved Hardegg, the German

Consul, 'who had incited the army against them so as to despoil them of their property.' The two Carmelites who protested were seized and brought to Damascus, where they were condemned to death on the charge of spying. They were saved from Execution thanks to the intervention of the Pope and the King of Spain, whose subjects they were.[2]

Then in May 1915, 'Turkish soldiers destroyed the little pyramidal monument in front of the Monastery on the pretext of a search for arms and scattered the bones of Napoleon's soldiers interred under it. Again the Carmelites blamed the Germans for the outrage.'[2] ... The soldiers removed the cross from the monument, and took it to Jerusalem, when it was returned after the war and replace.[2]

When the Carmelites were being expelled, the Haifa inhabitants asked the Superior to allow them to take the statue of Our Lady of Mount Carmel from Stella Maris to Saint Joseph parish, the Latin Catholic Parish in Haifa City, because, facing the continuous bombardments of the French and English ships, they hope to have refuge and protection from Our Lady of Mount Carmel. So they moved the statue of the Virgin to the Latin Church of St. Joseph in the city centre, where the statue remained until the end of the war.The parishioners also wanted to protect the statue from the Turks, and they hid the statue, moving it from one family to the other through the duration of the war.

After the war, after Easter 1919, when the Carmelites returned to the Monastery, the Haifa population, spontaneously and as thanksgiving, brought back the statue in Procession to its sanctuary in Stella Maris Monastery.

Since 1919, fifteen days after Easter, this procession has been repeated every year. On the second or occasionally the third Sunday after Easter, the statue of Our Lady of Mount Carmel traverses Haifa from the Roman Catholic parish to the Stella Maris monastery in a solemn procession with the patriarch, bishops, friars and sisters, musicians, scouts, seminarians, and a crowd of people from many faiths. At first it was a small local procession in Haifa, sometime after, it became a regional procession with people coming from the whole of *Galilee*[4], but now persons come from all around the Holy Land, and is considered the second most important procession, after the Jerusalem Procession of Palm Sunday. This traditional procession in honour of Our Lady of Mount Carmel, popularly called Talaat al-Adra, the 'Ascent of the Virgin', believers make a vow to help carry the statue up the slope of Mount Carmel.[5] The procession departs from the Chapel of the Holy Family, and proceeds to climb up Mount Carmel to the Stella Maris Church. Participants include the Patriarch of Jerusalem, bishops, priests and other religious, as well as the local Arab communities and the procession is led by Scouts with their bands. Along the route which runs from the Latin parish of Haifa to the Stella Maris Carmelite monastery, located on Mount Carmel, the faithful of all the rites walked reciting prayers and singing hymns to the Virgin.

In 2019, it was the centenary of this procession.

> This year we celebrate the centenary of the procession of Our Lady of Carmel in Haifa. The first procession was held on April 27, 1919, Sunday in albis, and was organised to solemnly bring back to the sanctuary of Stella Maris the statue of Our Lady of Carmel, that in 1914 at the beginning of the First

> World War, had been transferred to the parish church in the city. The Vicar Father of Mount Carmel at that time, the Englishman P. Francis Lamb (1867-1950), writes in his memoirs that there was an extraordinary participation of the people and that the English authorities were struck by this manifestation of faith and devotion for the Mother of God in the Latin Catholic community of Haifa. It was linked to the end of the Great War and the desire to thank the Lord and Our Lady for the return of peace. The procession was repeated in the following years until it became the most important in the Holy Land after that of Palm Sunday in Jerusalem.'[3]

Over the past hundred years, the procession also experienced critical moments especially in the years 1948-49. In 1948, the year of the proclamation of the State of Israel, the procession fell on April 18, less than a month before the proclamation of the State and the beginning of hostilities that led to the first Israeli-Arab war. The following year, because of the very small numbers of Christians, there was concern about organizing the procession because of the small number of the faithful and the fear of repercussions. It was the then new Israeli mayor of Haifa who favoured the procession by guaranteeing public order.[6]

In the centenary year, the limits to freedom of movement make it impossible for those who once came from Lebanon to participate.[7,8] On the other hand, hundreds of Filipino, Indian and other African and Asian immigrant workers took part in the public act of devotion to the Virgin Mary, along with pilgrims from Europe, while many Jews and Muslims also gathered at the procession.[7,8]

During the procession, the statue of the Blessed Virgin Mary of Mount Carmel is placed on a cart carrying children dressed as cherubs; the cart is pulled by ropes by a group of faithful believers, and prayers and chants to Mary are sung throughout the journey. The faithful, during the procession, threw flowers and sweets inside the cart as a sign of devotion.[6] Many young girls were dressed in the colours and dress of the Virgin Mary as part of a vow. The scouts led the procession and girls wore the traditional Palestinian dress to honour the statue of Our Lady of Mount Carmel, a faithful replica of the precious original statue in the Monastery church.[9]

This procession has been an expression of deep commitment of the Christians of the Middle East to their faith. The fact it has survived over a hundred years, through many difficulties suggests that the Virgin, in some way, has always providentially watched over her faithfulness and the continuation of her procession.

References

1 *Haifa by Laurence Oliphant 2018 page 67*

2 *Ottoman Haifa: A History of Four Centuries under Turkish Rule 2010 Alex Carmel page 161-162.*

3 *Message for the centenary of the procession of Our Lady of Carmel (Haifa, 5 May 2019) Fr. Saverio Cannistrà, General Superior, dco*

4 *http://www.carmelholylanddco.org/historical-procession-with-our-lady-of-mount-carmel-heading-to-stella-maris-haifa/*

5 *https://www.holyland-pilgrimage.org/our-lady-of-mount-carmel-procession-c*

6 *https://www.lpj.org/posts/centenary-of-the-procession-of-the-blessed-virgin-mary-of-mount-carmel-in-haifa.html*

7 *http://www.fides.org/en/news/65980- ASIA_HOLY_LAND_Haifa _more_than_5_thousand_Christians_took_part_in_the_traditional_ procession_in_honour_of_Our_Lady_of_Mount_Carmel*
8 *https://www.indcatholicnews.com/news/37049*
9 *http://en.lpj.org/2016/04/12/traditional-procession-of-our-lady-of-mount-carmel/*
10 *http://www.carmelholylanddco.org/stella-maris-church/*
11 *Journey to Carith: The Sources and Story of the Discalced Carmelites Peter-Thomas Rohrbach - 1966 Page 53.*

TWENTY NINE

THE CELEBRATION OF OUR LADY OF MOUNT CARMEL IN THE PHILIPPINES

THE IMAGE OF NUESTRA SEÑORA DEL CARMEN ENSHRINED AT THE Minor Basilica of San Sebastian is the first ever image of Our Lady of Mount Carmel in the Philippines. The venerated image of Our Lady of Mount Carmel De San Sebastian - otherwise known as the Queen of Quiapo - arrived in the Philippines on May 4, 1618 with the third group of Augustinian Recollect missionaries, The Augustinian Recollect missionaries, the first Catholic missionaries who came to the island, brought it with them from Mexico.[1,2,3] The image had been donated by the Discalced Carmelites Nuns of the Monastery of San José Acapulco Messico as a symbol of brotherhood. It was originally venerated in the makeshift Church of San Juan Bautista de Bagumbayan. The church was damaged seriously by two consecutive earthquakes — one in 1863 and another in 1880. In 1621 it was moved to the church of San Sebastián. The Carmelite Prior General in Rome granted the Augustinian Recollects permission to promote the brown scapular of Our Lady of Mt. Carmel in San Sebastian Church. This church was made of steel and from 1887-1891, a four-year project was launched to build an all-steel church of San Sebastian. While the project was ongoing, the church was raised to a status of Minor Basilica, attached to St. Peter's Basilica in Rome. The San Sebastian Basilica is at Quiapo, Manila, Philippines. The Basilica was made a National Historical Landmark in the Philippines on August 1, 1973. Since then, the devotion to Our Lady of Mount Carmel has continued growing, so that now, hundreds of people wear the 'brown scapular' of the Virgin.

During the Second World War, the image and the San Sebastian Church were spared from the attacks of the Japanese.

The head and hands of the Virgin and the entire image of the child is made of precious ivory. The face has this pristine beauty that inspires much awe and devotion while the Child, with its unusual stance of his arms, is also a beauty to behold that inspired millions of devotees through the centuries.

The head and hands of the Virgin and the Child Jesus are of ivory, and both wear heavily embroidered vestments in traditional gold and brown colours. Unfortunately, the heads of the Virgin and Jesus were stolen in July 1975. Fortunately, the image of the Child was retrieved but the head of the Virgin is still missing as of this writing. The head of the sacristans, Felipe Dy, head of the sacristan mayores, offered to restore the statue from the generous donations of parishioners. The well-known religious sculptor of Maximo Vicente re-created the missing parts of the original images.[6,7]

In December 1989, during the bloody coup against the President Corazon Aquino, San Sebastian and the Carmel image remained unscathed despite the fighting in the streets.

In 1990, thousands of people flocked to San Sebastian to ask for prayers to the image of Our Lady of Mt. Carmel, after the deadly earthquake, which hit northern Luzon on the Feast Day of the image.

The devotion to Our Lady of Mount Carmel is still evidently strong and miracles have continued to happen so that in 1991, under the Papal Decree issued by Pope Blessed John Paul II, the image was canonically crowned with much rejoicing. The coronation coincided with the church's Centennial Celebration in 1991. In the decree she was referred to as 'Queen of Heaven'.

There are two fiesta celebrations dedicated to Manila's beautiful flower of Carmel, the Liturgical feast of July 16 and the unique Traditional fiesta every January 29. Because of the rainy season in the country that occurs from June until the later parts of the year, July 16th. Carmelite fiesta cannot be celebrated with much pomp. For this reason the Recollect Fathers petitioned the Holy Father in Rome to have a special feast for the Virgin nearest to the feast of St. Sebastian, the titular feast of the Basilica, to celebrate her fiesta with as much pomp and solemnity that she deserved. The noble petition was granted in 1691 when a Papal Bull granted this indult in perpetuity. The January fiesta was first celebrated a day after the feast of St. Sebastian then later moved to January 23, three days after the titular patron's feast until it was formally celebrated every January 29 with the celebrations between January 21 to 28. Due to the reforms of the Second Vatican Council, the January fiesta was halted during the late 1970's or early 1980's. In line with the 400th anniversary of the arrival of the image in the country, the January fiesta was revived in 2018, a chance for the new generation of devotees and a joy to those who knew the celebrations during their youth to celebrate her fiesta as their forefathers did.

In 2018, the long-forgotten Tradition of 'Dungaw' was revived. The

'Dungaw' is where the image of the Black Nazarene (also brought the Augustinian Recollects in the Philippines) and the Del Carmen meet from the balcony of San Sebastian Church. The 'Dungaw' marks the silence of the noise of the iconic Procession of the Black Nazarene for the meeting of the two Great Patrons of Quiapo, the King and Queen of Quiapo.

The 'Dungaw'[4,5] scene replays the fourth station of the Via Crucis; the traditional meeting of Mary with Jesus. It is a very brief scene, only 3 minutes within a procession that this year lasted for 18 hours. However, for all those present, it is a most touching moment.

The Augustinian Recollects have been for centuries the guardians of these two images that are so much loved by the Filipinos. Both images are of Mexican origin, and from Mexico they sailed in the Manila Galleon early in the 17th century. The Nazarene arrived together with the first Recollects, in 1606, and settled with them in their first Manila convent of San Juan de Bagumbayan. Already in 1621, the archbishop of Manila attested to the existence of a confraternity of Nuestro Padre Jesús Nazareno in the Recollect convent.

At present, the image of Nuestro Padre Jesús Nazareno is venerated in the church of Quiapo, the very barrio in old Manila where San Sebastian belongs. It is known as the 'Black Nazarene', because of its dark colour, which is attributed to a fire that almost destroyed the ship that transported it. An image of the Lord carrying the cross, it inspires such a strong devotion among the faithful. On its feast day, 9th of January, the devotees flock in the hundred thousand, many of them barefoot and penitent. The massive crowds and the intensity of the devotees have, in not a few occasions, resulted in deaths by suffocation or crushing, a sad occurrence in events of popular religiosity.

The highlight of the *traslacion* was the *dungaw or salubong* at the Quiapo Church, where the image of the Black Nazarene was brought to meet the image of Our Lady of Mt. Carmel. Traditionally the *salubong* is a part of the annual *traslacion* of the Black Nazarene held outside the San Sebastian Church. Many devotees come before dawn to get a glimpse of the historic meeting while offering prayers of devotion. It used to be that both images meet for the traditional dungaw during the Feast of the Black Nazarene, but 2018 will be the first time that the Black Nazarene looked out to the image during the Our Lady's *traslacion*. From that year on, the dungaw will be repeated on the 16th July feast of Our Lady of Mount Carmel.[4,5]

In 2018, the image of Our Lady of Mt. Carmel of San Sebastian celebrated its 400th anniversary of the arrival to the Philippines. This was celebrated in a procession on the river (fluvial procession) when the arrival of the Augustinian Recollects was re-enacted. Because she is patroness of the sea, Our Lady of Mount Carmel will travel the waters of the islands from San Sebastian Church, where she is venerated, to Quirino Grandstand, and there Holy Mass was celebrated. After the mass, Our Lady of Mount Carmel will be returned to San Sebastian Church in a great pilgrimage through Manila from Quirino Grandstand. It was during this that the dungaw was celebrated.[4,5]

While celebrations of Christ Meeting his Mother are quite common in Europe - particularly Italy, in Holy Week, it is unique that a celebration like the dungaw happens during the feast of Our Lady of Mount Carmel.

References:

1 *http://sansebastianchurch.org/about-us/our-lady-of-mount-carmel/*
2 *http://sansebastianchurch.org/about-us/parish/*
3 *http://cbcpnews.net/cbcpnews/church-hopes-for-return-of-stolen-head-hands-of-our-lady-of-mount-carmel-statue/*
4 *https://www.agustinosrecoletos.com/2014/02/the-augustinian-recollects-revive-the-meeting-between-our-lady-of-mount-carmel-and-the-black-nazarene-of-quiapo/?lang=en*
5 *https://www.agustinosrecoletos.com/2018/05/cuarto-centenario-virgen-del-carmen-filipinas/?lang=en*
6 *http://www.quiapochurch.com/400-years-of-our-lady-of-mt-carmel-of-san-sebastian-basilica/*
7 *https://recoletosfilipinas.org/2018/05/05/our-lady-of-mount-carmel-and-the-brown-scapular/*

THIRTY

TWO CELEBRATIONS OF OUR LADY OF MOUNT CARMEL IN THE ANDES

THE FEAST OF OUR LADY OF MOUNT CARMEL IN PAUCARTAMBO, Peru is probably the most impressive example of how an Indigenous Population in South America celebrates the feast of Our Lady of Mount Carmel, with a particular blend of Folklore - especially dance - and Catholic religiosity,

This festival is held every year, between July 15 and July 18, in the town of Paucartambo, at an altitude of 3,017m and 110km from the city of Cusco.[1]

The devotion of the Virgen del Carmen is intimately linked to the identity of Paucartambo as a town. The primary form of the expression of this identity is the protagonist of the dance, since it is mainly through the dance that the Virgin is worshiped. The dance is organized in gangs and is the ritual means through which the Paucartambinos strengthen their identity, and constitutes in itself a prayer, an offering to the Virgin. Paucartambo is considered the folkloric capital of the region and the Paucartambo Festival is one of the best opportunities for outsiders to experience Andean customs and celebrations. Visitors will have the chance to enjoy performances of an astounding variety of traditional dances, including the qollas, the qhapac negros, the chuncho, the saqra, the tarpuy and more. Many of these dances also incorporate elaborate costumes and storylines – a series of beautiful spectacles that never fail to captivate all in attendance.

The traditional dances in tribute to the Virgen del Carmen de Paucartambo, performed every year in mid-July, summarise the colonial, republican and contemporary history of the province. The culture and geography of Paucartambo includes the high Andean areas and the Amazonian plain, and so represent different ways of understanding the world. This has led to a combination of pre-Christian and Catholic elements in expressing the sacred. This led to a particular combination of music and ritual dances in order to celebrate important moments of social experience, such as the celebration of the Virgen del Carmen de Paucartambo.

This convergence of indigenous, European and mestizo traditions in the memory of the people of Paucartambo is renewed every year by the passage of the dancers, with their bright costumes and their interactions during the feast of the Virgen del Carmen in Paucartambo making it one of the best known events of popular Catholicism in Cusco.

La Virgen del Carmen, called by its devotees Mamacha Carmen, is represented by a sculpture of the Virgin Mary with the Child, preciously carved in wood during the colonial era, and whose pedestal, built by the Carpenters Guild of the Society of Craftsmen, dates from 1886.[6,7]

Thousands of believers participate in the festival in order to venerate the Virgin of Carmen (Our Lady of Mount Carmel), locally called 'Mamacha Carmen', and who is patroness of the mestizos. (persons of combined European and Indigenous American descent).[6,7]

THE FOLLOWING IS THE USUAL SCHEDULE OF THE PAUCARTAMBO FESTIVAL OF THE VIRGIN OF CARMEN:

JULY 15TH

The Virgen del Carmen Festival begins with the blasting of a rocket and the ringing of bells.[1,4,5,8]

People visit the church, pray and leave flowers for the virgin.

During the day, dance troupes and bands swirl among the crowds. The gathering that starts this festival is done in the main square where bands of musicians play their instruments while richly dressed choirs sing in Quechua, giving rise to ingenious choreographies that represent passages of Peruvian history.

During the day walking troupes dancing in the narrow cobbled streets of the town, preceded by bands and orchestras go down the streets. Everything is transformed into colourful costumes and musical chords. Parades take place throughout the day, with rows of costumed and masked dancers making their way down narrow, cobblestone streets and across the town's historic Charles III Bridge. The dances represent the combat between the highlands' Q'olqas and the Chunchus from the west that compete for the love of the *Mamacha del Carmen*.[1,4,5,8]

The first night of the festival starts with a fireworks display and a bonfire. A group of locals act out scenes of purgatory as they leap through the flames and perform acrobatic feats; Performers jump through fires to 'cleanse' themselves; they stage battles and perform acrobatics. Musical serenades to the Virgin are played through the night until dawn.[1,4,5]

July 16th

The formal celebration opens with the firing of twelve rockets, and ringing of bells while the authorities, dance groups and people gather. Candles and flowers are presented to the sanctuary of the Virgen del Carmen, where her Statue is located (the cerapaykuy or greeting of the Virgin).[1,2,4,5,8]

There is a dawn mass. At 10:00 a.m. the main mass is celebrated with beautiful chants from the *Qollas* and *Qhapac negros*. After mass, the celebration continues with music bands and dance groups that go out to the streets and squares joyfully throwing dolls and miniature pieces of furniture from the balconies. At 3:00 p.m., the procession starts with Our Lady on the processional platform being followed by devotees and dancers.[1,2,4,5,8]

This is the festival's main day, in which the Procession of the Virgen del Carmen takes place in the afternoon. The Virgin Carmen is showered with rose petals and flowers as she is paraded through town. This procession is especially relevant, as it is a symbolic display of the locals' devotion to Christianity. During the procession, groups of dancers dressed as demons climb on the roofs of the houses, and are chased away. With the blessing of the faithful and warding off demons, the virgin's presence signifies good triumphing over evil. On the main day the Virgin is led in procession to bless those present in Paucartambo and scare off demons.[1,2,4,5,8] The dancers 'Sajras' perform gymnastic and risky tests on the roofs of houses, showing their Inca attire and colonial style. At the end of the procession a war is waged against the demons, from which the faithful emerge triumphant.

As the afternoon continues, dancing and singing take over the streets and last into the night.[1,2,4,5,8]

July 17th

The *'bendición y guerrilla'* (blessing and guerrilla) is celebrated on July 17th. After the blessing of the mass, the troupes head towards the cemetery chanting to remember deceased dancers and they sing, dance and honour the souls of the deceased. This is a moving celebration of life and remembrance of death. There is another procession in the afternoon that crosses the famous Carlos III bridge.Once the procession is over, the celebration continues in the square with music and dances.

July 18th

On the final day, the sacred image of the Virgin is taken to the temple and blessed by the priest as festivities begin to wind down.Our Lady of Mount Carmel is placed in the baptistry to carry out the traditional *'ocarikuy'* where kids and teenagers get a blessing. Finally everything concludes with 'kacharpari', or farewell party.[1,2,4,5,8]

July 19th

There is a farewell Mass as the final formal event of the festival. The image of Our Lady returns to its altar and is dressed in her everyday clothes. The ceremony takes place with the presence of devotees, dance groups and musicians.[1,2,4,5,8]

The Dances and Groups of Dancers who Accompany the Virgin del Carmen

Over the course of the festival each of the dozen or so dance groups in full regalia enacts the story of the existence of the town – one group represents the wealthy Spanish-blooded landowners with massive noses who strut side-to-side with jugs of beer and spurs on their boots. Other masked characters parody colonial and religious figures, including matadors, demons, lawyers, merchants and warriors. There are also malaria victims, nurses with hypodermic needles and big-nosed, drunken Spanish conquistadors, and Capaq Negro, a black-masked character representing the African slaves who worked at the nearby silver mines. A group of devils, masked in Chinese dragon-style headdresses, scale the roofs of the town and entice the onlookers, tempting them to sin.[9]

Danzaq

The 'Danzaq' or 'Tusuq' is a dance where those to whom seductive abilities are attributed towards quinceañeras (fifteen year old) girls. They conquer the married and console the widows. They make up one of the best-dressed groups, due to their colour and elegance when dancing. They cover their heads with chucos, they wear short ponchos interwoven with ornaments, and blue pants divided in fringes, in the colours of the rainbow. This is one of the most representative dances of the province of Paucartambo.[2]

Chunchachas

This dance represents the women of the Kosñipata jungle, but it has a clear mestizo influence, because of the clothing worn and the music that accompanies it. Its costumes consist of a crown of

Amazons, complete with hair, a breastplate that represents the Virgin, two 'ch´uspas' (pouch that is used to carry coca and cocoa leaves) that serve to carry her wayruros, a suitable dress in which she carries a chonta (a sort of palm tree) and the sinehon.[2]

Qhapaq Negro

This dance in Spanish means 'Rich Black Man' and recalls the slave age of the black population, so they carry chains as a sign of submission. At present, the Negros of Paucartambo are considered the slaves of the Virgen del Carmen, to whom they offer their beautiful and amazing dance and sentimental songs.[2]

Qhapaq Qolla

It is a representative dance of the inhabitants of the Qollasuyu, its origin dates from colonial times, when the Qollavino merchants arrived in Paucartambo. The dance draws its essence from the faith in 'Mamacha del Carmen' and this is to whom, during the party, they sing, they dance and cheer in the guerilla. The dancers wear beautiful and ornate monteras, the waq´ollo and lliclla made of vicuña; the q´epi contains a dissected vicuna.[2]

Qhapaq Ch´uncho

This dance represents the warriors of the jungle of Qosñipata (district of the province of Paucartambo). In their clothing they use multi-coloured feathers called 'ch´ucu', long hair, mesh mask, and carry a spear of 'chonta'. The Band is typical (two whistles, drum and bass drum).[2]

The Origin of the Festival of Our Lady of Carmen in Paucartambo

There are numerous legends regarding the origin of the Festival of Our Lady of Carmen in Paucartambo. Devotion to the Virgin Mary in colonial Peru is an extension of the same devotion in Spain, where the images of the Virgin had become very popular since the twelfth century. The veneration of the image in Paucartambo seems to date back to 1665.[3]

One legend regarding the origin of the devotion in Paucartambo is as follows; When the Viceroy of Peru Pedro Fernandez de Castro Andrade, Count of Lemos, travelled to Upper Peru, between Puno and Cuzco, he was told that in Pucara, a miracle had happened when the likeness of the Virgin appeared on a rock. When he personally saw it, he admired it for its perfection. He sent a painter to Pucara to copy it on canvas, which could not be done. So, the Viceroy Count of Lemos himself ordered that identical effigies be carved, and they were intended to be sent to Pucara and Puni, to be worshiped in the church. Several years passed, but one of the images was not collected by people from Puno and stayed in Pucara. So, Doña Maria Campos, a rich lady, who used to travel from Puno to Paucartambo arranged to bring the image to Paucartambo, from which date the feast is celebrated with all the solemnity possible.[9]

Another legend is that the roots of this festival lie in the 17th century when llama herders of the high Andean plateau frequently travelled to Paucartambo with their animals in order to trade with the locals. During one of these trips, the face of the Virgin Mary appeared to both visitors and locals in a clay pot[3,4,5]. Inspired by this apparition, the people of Paucartambo created an image of the Virgin as well as a church to house it[3,4]. Since that time, citizens of the town have held a festival every year to honour and pay tribute to this sacred image. Another legend goes back to the 13th century, before the discovery of America. According to folklore, a wealthy young woman was going heading to Paucartambo to trade a silver dish and she came across a beautiful, bodiless head. She placed it on a dish, and the head spoke to her, saying her name was Carmen and that she was not to be feared, but trusted. The locals of Paucartambo soon began asking Carmen for help with their needs. It is said that they witnessed rays of light shining from her head and that she performed many miracles among the community.[9]

Another story is that the Virgin of Carmen was made patron of the chapel of the Assumption, located at a distance from the town of Paucartambo. Paucartambo then had, as its patron, the Virgen del Rosario. The statue of Virgin del Carmen used to be taken to the main town, like other local saints, for the feast of Corpus Christi. The chunchos, as the Amazonian communities of the neighboring lowlands are called, destroyed the area's farms in one of their incursions, killing Spanish residents and setting fire to the Assumption chapel. The image of the Virgen del Carmen was thrown into the Amaru Mayu River by the attackers, but it was saved because it came to land on one of the islands in the river, which since then bears the name of Mother of God. The image was taken to Paucartambo where it still showed the marks of the arrows that the Amazonians had shot at it. This story gives a legitimate reason why this religious image belongs to the people of

Paucartambo and its relationship and how it interacts with them.[9] The cult of the Virgin became one of the essential elements of the connection of the natives of Peru with Catholicism and the Virgin del Carmen was one of the religious images which was one of the earliest and most widespread in the Cusco towns. As well as images, musical pieces were composed in her honour. There is a four-voice carol to give thanks to Our Lady of Carmel in the archive of the San Antonio Abad Seminary of Cusco. There is also an oral tradition hymn of Cusco Queen of Carmen; 'Quechua Queen of Carmen Qasqaykirayku nucñu Maria qawarimuwayku - Because you are Queen of Carmen, look at us, sweet Mary'.[9]

La Virgen Del Carmen was declared patron of folk dances in 1972 and it was crowned by Pope John Paul II in February 1985 at a ceremony in the city of Cuzco.[9]

Fiesta de la Tirana

The Fiesta de la Tirana is an annual festival held in the locality of La Tirana in the Tarapacá Region of northern Chile, about 70km inland from the coastal city of Iquique.[11] The celebration takes place on July 16 in honour of the Virgen del Carmen, the patron saint of Chile.[11] La Tirana is the biggest religious festivity in Chile and attracts between 200, 000 and 250, 000 visitors during the week of celebrations, while the village's permanent population normally numbers 1,200 inhabitants. Music and Dancing, as well as fireworks[11], is a big part of the celebrations of Fiesta de La Tirana, and dance groups and pilgrims dance before the virgin. 'The doors of the 'temple,' or sanctuary, at La Tirana are formally opened on July 10, and bailes, or dance groups, arrive to make their entrada or entrance between July 11-14. Over 207 religious brotherhoods or bailes, from Arica to Copiapó, participate in this event.[12]

The *bailes*, or groups, provide the festival's main component, which is the dances they, who come to dance before the statue of the Virgen del Carmen in the sanctuary.[11] In the days leading up to 16 July, members of the *bailes* hold performances to greet the Virgin, or 'La Chinita', as the locals call her. As the dancers make their way through the streets of the town to the sanctuary, thousands of visitors gather to watch the different dances that emerge around the Virgin.[11] The groups dress in colourful traditional clothing and the events are an incredible combination of European, Mestizos, Creoles and Indian culture.[12]

The Origin of the feast

The story of the origin of The Festival of La Tirana dates back to 1540, when an expedition led by the discoverer of Chile – Diego de Almagro, arrived in the area[12]. It is part history, part legend and concerns Ñusta Huillac, an Incan princess who rebelled against the European conquerors in the 1540s. Taking refuge in an oasis near Iquique, she was known for ruthlessly executing or enslaving any Europeans or Christians who encroached on her territory – which is how she got the name La Tirana, meaning 'the tyrant'[11]. However,Ñusta Huillac eventually fell in love with one of her prisoners, Vasco de Almeida, and converted to Christianity in order to marry him (and, later, to join him in the afterlife).[11] Betrayed and furious, her subjects killed her and her lover.[11] Around 1650 Antonio Rondon built a hermitage next to the cross of her grave. In the 18th century a little town and church was created in that location. Today there is a Museum – Museo de La Tirana - located in front of the church. The lovers remain buried in the place where the festival is celebrated.[12]

The present church, Santuario de Nuestra Señora del Carmen de La Tirana[11], was erected at their burial site in the 18th century and dedicated to the Virgen del Carmen. This church is now a place of pilgrimage and devotion for thousands of faithful believers, and has become the central point of the Fiesta de la Tirana.[11]

Today La Tirana Festival is a celebration that is done in the name of the Virgen del Carmen, but it still has many traditions that stretch back centuries to the indigenous Andean people.[11] The masks, costumes, music and dance all have historical significance.[12] Descendants of these indigenous persons still travel to the festival to make vows to the Virgin and to receive blessings.[12]

Entering the Village

Each baile is assigned a specific time for entry to the village, and the same order applies for departure at the end of the week. The baile dances first at a plaza at the entrance to the town, in front of the statue of the Cruz del Calvario, or Calvary Cross.[10,12,13] Normally there is a priest there to formally welcome and bless the group at the Cruz Calvario.[10,12,13] This is the first dance performed by each baile during the celebrations.[12] It is a sensory mosaic filled with lots of color, sound, energy and movement. The atmosphere and energy are electric and the central plaza is filled with thousands of dancers.[12]

The bailes then proceed on to the Sanctuary. Each baile has allocated times and places for dancing in the street[13]. They do so to and in front of that group's image of Our Lady of Mount Carmel.[13] No dancing takes place when Masses are being held in the temple.[13] Onlookers know not to walk between the image and the dancers.[13]

Dancing for the Virgin of Carmel

The Dance groups known as bailes come to dance before the Virgen del Carmen, in the sanctuary at La Tirana.[12] Their entrance to the sanctuary is called the Entrada[4]. When dancers enter the sanctuary, they first bow at the main altar, then to an image of Nazarene, Jesus carrying the cross, before turning to the Virgen del Carmen.[13] Dancing before the Virgin is a very emotional experience.[12] There are over 200 official dance groups from all over the country, who all come to announce they have returned to fulfil their promise to her. Because there are so many dance groups, the performances run for days, and are scheduled around the clock.[12] Thus, every different dance group is assigned a specific entry time to see the Virgin, and they have 20 minutes to dance before her. The temple doors officially open on July 10th, and the bailes and pilgrims dance before the Virgin from July 11th until July 14th.[13]

The dancers are dressed in the most beautiful costumes with lots of glitter and colour.[12] They enter the temple accompanied by their band and banner. Romantic melodies of vintage ballads, boleros and waltzes fill the air and where the songs of one dance group ends, another begins. The dancers offer their blood, sweat and tears to the Virgin.[12]

When dancing, they sing to the virgin.[13] Their songs typically announce who they are and that they are back with joy after much sacrifice and distant travel, to come before their mother.[13] The principal themes of these hymns are: joy to be at the feast and to return to encounter the Virgin; thanksgiving and homage; the abnegation of the pilgrim; the confession of sins; prayer for pardon, blessing life and health; the pain and sadness of saying goodbye. One encounters cosmic themes as well: sun, moon and stars; sky and rivers; life and death.[13]

When leaving the entrada before the Virgin, the dancers do so on their knees, shuffling out backward, and the next group follows in immediately.[14] Later, when they dance in the square, they do not sing.[13]

After ***bailes*** have made their entries and become eligible to dance, the square and streets begin to fill with rows and rows of dancers and their bands, all lined up in front of their statue of the Virgin and the cloth standard of their society all night and day.[13] Only during morning Masses in the sanctuary does the dancing in the square ever totally stop.[13] At some point during the feast, each association celebrates a special Mass particularly for its members, with first communion for children.[13] In a small chapel nearby, and at a larger chapel recently rebuilt on the site of the original church, weddings and baptisms are often celebrated for those who have prepared for these sacraments at home but waited to celebrate them here.[13]

At some point between the entrada and the *despedida,* the parallel goodbye, each baile hosts a formal visit from another baile.[13] The two bailes ar matched by drawing lots[13], A visit entails the dance group coming in its *trajes* (special dance costumes) and dancing outside the compound or camp of the host baile.[13] Then there are speeches of welcome and introduction and the host group serves a meal, which is the only time dancers can eat in their trajes, while the visiting group presents a gift of thanks to the hosts[13]

Throughout the feast — including during Masses and while bailes are dancing before the Virgin — pilgrims wait in lines outside to enter the sanctuary at a special door that allows them to walk up and touch the Virgin's dress.[13] They ask that religious objects, and even children, be passed up the stairs by volunteers to be blessed by touching them to the Virgin's clothes in the sign of the cross.[13]

Dancing against the Devils

One of the most important parts of the festival is the Danza de los Diablos, which in English means the Dance of the Devils.[12] This was brought to Chile by Bolivian salt miners.[12] For this dance, and throughout the festival, many people wearing fearsome costumes and masks.[12] The demon masks have bulging eyes, curling horns and bright colours.[12] These costumes hark back to indigenous customs, adapted by Christianity to chase the demons away.[12] All costumes and dances must be approved by the federation.[13] The costumes are considered sacred, but a surprising proportion of costumes have no explicitly Christian images.[13] Some, on the surface, seem quite the opposite.[13]

The Eve of the feast day of the Virgen del Carmen

On the eve of the feast, in the morning, the bishop celebrates Mass for the representatives of the armed forces[13], since Our Lady of Mount Carmel is the Patroness of Chile's Armed Forces.[12]

On July 15, families dedicate time to cleaning and visiting the graves of loved ones who had been brought to La Tirana to be buried.[13]

By 9pm at night, the square has filled up with large crowds who eagerly await midnight and the official start of the feast of the Virgen del Carmen.[12] At 10 p.m., though it cannot come close to accommodating everyone in town, the square is packed for a 'solemn' Eucharist and vespers.[12]

At midnight the celebrations begin with people waving balloons and lights, orange lanterns float into the sky, the band plays music and firework displays surround the city.[12] The dance groups take turns dancing and singing, and everywhere you look people are socializing and in good spirits. People stay up all night and dance groups continue performing in the square well after sunrise.[12]

The feast day of the Virgen del Carmen

At 9a.m. a major event takes place in the square.[12] The statue of the Virgin, a smaller one from the temple, is lowered into the square. Hundreds of coloured ribbons are attached to the base of her pedestal which are thrown to the audience, who hold them and sing while she is lowered.[12] This is then followed by Mass.[12] At 2:30p.m., a procession of the image of the Virgin parades its way through the streets, followed by statues of St Joseph and of Jesus.[12] At each block, dance groups have the opportunity to sing to the Virgin, walking backwards, in front of her, so that they don't turn their back to her.[12] Big crowds line the streets and follow the procession throwing confetti and shouting 'Viva La Virgen'. The procession lasts for about seven hours, before it returns back to the temple. Inside the sanctuary some associations have been given the honour to sing before the larger statue of the Virgin.[12]

Saying Goodbye to the Virgin of Carmel

The final part of the feast is saying Goodbye to the Virgin of Carmel. There are so many groups that the last dance groups do not leave La Tirana until July 19th, but the groups start singing their farewell song and dance to the Virgin, on midnight after the 16th July.[12] This dance is called the despedida.[13] Again the bailes enter the temple, with music, bows at the main altar and to the Nazareno, dancing and singing.[13] The goodbye dances can be even more emotional than the entrance dances; often the dancers will cry.[12] The final dances are done in the same order as the entry dance and continue for 24 hours a day until the 19th July, except during Mass.[12] Those in the group who have completed their *manda,* or promise, and don't expect to dance next year, go up to the altar and remove part of their trajes.[13] The bailes leave the church shuffling backwards on their knees, so as not to turn their backs on the Virgin.[13] They leave the church and proceed to the Calvary Cross, where they dance again. Then some dance back at their camp briefly, a celebratory dance, they say, to take their minds off their grief. After this, they cannot dance for the rest of the feast.[13]

One week after the groups have departed La Tirana, the bailes gather together in their home cities for a fiesta chica.[12] This follow-up dance is to bring the devotion and joy of La Tirana, back to their own streets.[12]

References:

1 *https://colourfulperu.com/virgen-del-carmen-festival-paucartambo/*
2 *https://www.livinginperu.com/the-paucartambo-festival/*
3 *https://www.cusconative.com/paucartambo-festival/*
4 *https://www.perurail.com/blog/paucartambo-festival/*
5 *https://pie-experiences.com/virgen-del-carmen-festival-paucartambo/*
6 *https://louismontrosephotography.com/peru-la-festividad-de-la-virgen-del-carmen-in-paucartambo*
7 *https://www.cuscoperu.com/en/festivities-events/july-august/virgin-of-carmen-paucartambo*
8 *https://www.tourinperu.com/blog/paucartambo-festival-cusco-worship*
9 *https://everywhereplease.com/virgen-del-carmen-festival-in-peru/*
10 *https://en.wikipedia.org/wiki/Fiesta_de_La_Tirana*
11 *https://www.amexessentials.com/about-fiesta-de-la-tirana-chile/*
12 *https://www.carnivaland.net/festival-tirana/*
13 *https://www.catholicsandcultures.org/chile-day-day-feast-la-tirana*

THIRTY ONE

The Italian Migrants Take Our Lady of Mount Carmel to New York

In the nineteenth century, large numbers of Italian Migrant workers went to the United States. With them they took their customs, and their love for Our Lady of Mount Carmel.

It is impossible to describe all the Churches dedicated to Our Lady of Mount Carmel in the USA, so we will talk about three churches, founded by the Italians, whose Italian Character remains till this day, which are all in different parts of New York.

The Church of Our Lady of Mount Carmel is a parish church in the Archdiocese of New York. It is located in East Harlem[1,2], Manhattan, New York City. The statue venerated in the church is a vested statue of the Blessed Virgin Mary under the title of Our Lady of Mount Carmel. Pope Leo XIII granted the image a Canonical Coronation on 12 May 1903, and Pope Pius X implemented the Pontifical decree and donated a gemstone for the crown. The coronation ceremony occurred on 10 July 1904. It is one of the four canonically crowned images in the United States of America.

Around 1880, East Harlem was the centre of immigration from southern Italy. These poor people left family, language and culture behind them. But they did carry their religious fervour with them. They longed for some comfort from home. A group of men, formed themselves into the Mount Carmel Society, to hold a religious 'Festa' or Feast to Our Lady. We would call this Society a 'Fratellanza'. The Festa was to be similar to the many festivals of Italy. In the beginning, In a very humble setting, the men and their families venerated a painting of Our Lady, prayed a Rosary in Her honour as no priests were available for Mass, and celebrated the Lady. Gradually word of the devotion began to attract pilgrims.

The church itself was constructed in 1884 by Reverend Emil Koerner of the Congregation of Priests of Saint Mary of Tinchebray. The church was built at night throughout 1884 by Italian men, after they had finished a hard day's work. The women prepared food, carried bricks and helped push the wheelbarrows. Until its completion in 1885, the parishioners held mass at East 111th street, but the formal opening of the church was not until 7 August 1887. The congre-gation was mostly made up of incoming Italians and Bohemians, and Our Lady of Mount Carmel became the second Italian parish in New York City and the first Southern Italian parish. Since the first feast of Our Lady of Mt. Carmel on 16 July 1881, its annual feast has been a major event in East Harlem, it is recorded that at one time attended by more than 100, 000. The image of the Blessed Virgin Mary venerated under the title of Our Lady of Mount Carmel,was brought by an Italian immigrant and saloon owner, Antonio Petrucci from Polla, near Salerno, Italy. Its statue replaced the poster image used by the Italian immigrants devotees who first settled in the area. The Statue of Our Lady, affectionately known as 'the original Mount Carmel', 'the real Mount Carmel', 'A Madonn du Carm' (in the Italian dialects of southern Italy), 'Ma Mere du Mont Carmel' (in French/Creole) or just 'Momma', is now venerated by all Catholics. Thousands of Haitian pilgrims, Latino devotees, and Asian ethnics join in the Great Feast of Our Lady of Mount Carmel on July 16th.

The parish was placed under the care of the Polish Pallottine fathers in 2013.

It is worth recording three published miracles attributed to this image of Our Lady of Mount Carmel, as in the Parish Register:

June 1929: Maria Carelli, a child of nine years, daughter of Donato and Anna Bonito, residing in Union City, N.J., had cerebral meningitis and was declared incurable by the doctors. The mother, greatly disturbed, made a vow to the Lady of Mt. Carmel, asking for the recovery of her child. The night between May 5th and 6th she looked like a corpse and the mother was convinced that death was near at hand. Early in the morning, however, Maria from her bed called her mother and said: 'Mother, I saw the Blessed Lady and She has given me medicine to cure me.' Maria Carelli now is fully recovered and, to fulfil their vow, she and her mother obligated themselves to visit the Madonna once a year for the rest of their lives.

The first of July 1923, Pasquale Marella was hit by a car and brought to the hospital with cerebral disturbances. The end was in sight. His mother made a vow to the Lady of Mt. Carmel and, miraculously, after a few days every complication disappeared, and Pasquale came to our sanctuary to render thanks to the Heavenly Mother.

ANGELA MUCCI of 239 Nelson St., Brooklyn, badly burned her legs which necessitated painful methods for relief and immediate healing. In desperation, she finally decided to entreat the Madonna and after 29 days of torture the complications suddenly ceased and where there was a serious burn there remained not even a scar. (August 1929)

OUR LADY OF MOUNT CARMEL CHURCH - BELMONT - BRONX, NEW YORK

At the end of the 19th Century and the beginning of the 20th Century a great number of Italian immigrants entered America through the Port of New York.[3,4] Many came and settled in the Bronx, especially in the Belmont section. What kept them together was their common language and faith.

The faithful from the Belmont section had to make a long journey to church of St. Philip Neri to attend Mass, receive the sacraments and to bury their dead.

So a committee was formed and a mission was opened in Belmont. The first mass was held on June 13, 1906 in a store front at 659 E. 187 St. Hence, a basement Church was built on 187 St. and Belmont Ave. in 1907, and the upper Church was built in 1917, dedicated to Our Lady of Mt. Carmel. In the 40's and 50's, more than 40,000 Italians made Our Lady of Mt. Carmel on E. 187 St. their parish. The parish celebrated its 100th Anniversary in 2006 The parish continues to serve the Italian community of the Bronx and welcomes the new immigrants from Latin America and serves them with the same devotion and love with which the Italians were received and served by the parish.

Shrine Church of Our Lady of Mount Carmel
Williamsburg Brooklyn

Another Italian shrine church in New York is the one at Williamsburg[5]. Italians in Williamsburg hold three major feasts especially close to their hearts — Easter, Christmas and the annual Giglio Festival at Our Lady of Mount Carmel parish.[6]

The Feast of San Paolino Di Nola and Our Lady of Mount Carmel, which opens on Wednesday, July 8, celebrates both the return of a fourth-century Italian bishop from captivity and the Blessed Virgin Mary's patronage of Mount Carmel. The Feast of Our Lady of Mount Carmel itself falls on July 16, so the festival runs on until Sunday, July 19, with closing benediction that night. When St. Paulinus (San Paolino) was liberated and could return to Italy following captivity there was great jubilation among the townspeople of Nola as they greeted their bishop, carrying lilies (giglio). Thus, the Italian festival of the Giglio developed into the huge structures that are danced with in the street today.

This festival is a major fundraiser for Our Lady of Mount Carmel parish, however, despite other attractions, such as the specialty foods and games, the festival remains religious in nature.

The same celebration has been celebrated and re-enacted here in Brooklyn for the past 128 years at the Shrine Church of Our Lady of Mount Carmel. The Moorish Galleon is reproduced and built in the streets of Brooklyn. The Lily, or Giglio as it is called in Italian, has developed into a huge, 72-foot, four-ton tower decorated with flowers and angels and topped with a statue of San Paolino. Both structures are staffed with full orchestra and singers providing entertainment, and over three hundred men lift the structures through the streets of the parish directed by a single man, called in Italian the 'Capo Paranza,' or 'Capo.'

The 12-day festival will offer a continuous celebration of religious activities in the church (daily Masses, novenas and processions) and secular activities in the streets (social events, food concessions and games of chance).

The first night, Wednesday July 8, starts with a coronation Mass in honour of Our Lady of Mount Carmel. A candlelight procession follows this. The Sunday of the week of festivities is Giglio Sunday when the dancing of the Giglio and boat happens. There is also the children's Giglio. Another tradition of the week of celebrations is the Questua — the tradition of distribution of blessed bread throughout the parish neighborhood. People customarily give donations in return to the church. This takes place on Questua takes place on the Feast of St. Benedict, July 11, who is considered to be the father of monasticism and hospitality.

We have also found, in the Archdiocese of Chicago, the Our Lady of Mount Carmel Festival, organised by the Our Lady of Mount Carmel Society (fratellanza) in the Church of Saint Joseph Hammonton.[7] This is another celebration of Italian Tradition, but we need, for reasons of space, to return to New York. Other congregations of priests might minister to the Italian Population of this city, but it is worth mentioning that The Carmelite Friars of the North American Province of St. Elias runs The National Shrine of

---

Our Lady of Mount Carmel, which was founded to encourage and perpetuate devotion to Mary and her scapular under the special title of Our Lady of Mount Carmel. It is situated on 60 beautiful acres in the mid-Hudson region of New York State.

Our Lady of Mount Carmel continues to be part of the life of the Italians in the great city of New York.

References:

1 *https://en.wikipedia.org/wiki/Church_of_Our_Lady_of_Mount_Carmel _(Manhattan)*

2 *http://www.mountcarmelshrine.com/*

3 *https://ourladymtcarmelbx.org/*

4 *https://en.wikipedia.org/wiki/Our_Lady_of_Mount_Carmel _Church-(Bronx)*

5 *https://mountcarmel-annunciation.com/*

6 *https://www.olmcfeast.com/about/about-the-feast*

7 *https://www.smmcp.net/*

THIRTY TWO

Images of Our Lady of Mount Carmel Crowned by the Pope or the Vatican Chapter

One Important way of honouring Images of Our Lady which have become important objects of pilgrimage, veneration, and sources of graces is by crowning them canonically, originally by the 'Vatican Chapter' and more recently by the Pope, when he is visiting the appropriate country. Many Images of Our Lady of Mount Carmel have been Canonically Crowned, some as early as in the 17th century, many quite recently, The list given by wikipedia is incomplete, because it does not list the Image in Valletta, Malta, discussed elsewhere in this book, and crowned in 1881.[1]

Furthermore we know of the Nuestra Señora del Carmen Coronada of Málaga[2] and the Nuestra Señora del Carmen Coronada of Cordoba[3], neither of which are mentioned in the list. The Image of the Virgin of Carmel in Rute[4] (Cordoba, Spain) has also been recently crowned. However we below give the list published in wikipedia of Crowned Images of Our Lady of Mount Carmel.

We will briefly attempt to say something about those images we have not yet mentioned.

The story of Nuestra Senora del Carmen de Apicala, Colombia[5], is simple. The townspeople were greatly devoted to Our Lady of Mount Carmel. An unknown pilgrim presented himself to sculpt the statue from wood. When the sculpture was unveiled, all fell on their knees in prayer, but the sculptor had disappeared before they could ask his name.

Nuestra Señora de la Virgen del Carmen at La Ceja Colombia[6] has been celebrated as patroness of the parish since 1790. This is in honour of the memory of the devotion of José Pablo de Villa, a founder of the Ceja, towards this Marian advocation and because the first name of the place given by Spanish conquerors was 'Valle de Santa María'. The church is a Minor Basilica.

Nuestra Señora del Carmen del Azuay in Cuenca, Ecuador[7], is also known as 'Parroquia **Nuestra Señora del Carmen 'Virgen** de Bronce'[8], because on a special platform, above the public roads, a sculpture in bronze sits on a marble pedestal. It is known as the Bronze Virgin, because it has been sculpted with this material. It belongs to the Quito school and was erected in the month of Dec-ember of 1904, in honour of the 50th anniversary of the declaration of the dogma of the Immaculate Conception.

Nuestra Señora del Carmen de Paucartambo in Cusco, Peru[9] is linked with the Spaniard colonists' relationship with the local native tribes. Local craftsmen carved the body with *maguey, plaster and half-candelabra cloth.* According to specialists, the head and hands were carved by Cusco artists. It is said that every year, an image of the Virgin of Carmen was taken from the Hacienda Asunción to Paucartambo for the feast of Corpus. One year, the natives (chunchos) rebelled, their arrows wounded the body of the Virgin in the eye and chest. Finally they threw her into the river *Amaru*

Mayu (Serpent River), which since then is called *Madre de Dios* because it caused the image of the Virgin to be beached on an islet, from where it was recovered and moved afterwards to Paucartambo. The dance of the chunchos in today's celebrations is an offering to the Virgin, who, in spite of her faults, has a special predilection for the native tribes.

Nuestra Señora del Carmen de San Sebastián arrived in the Philippines[10] in 1617, from Mexico, accompanying the Augustinian Recollect Sisters. Later, in the American period, it was given to the Discalced Carmelites. It is known as the 'Queen of Quiapo'. The Minor Basilica which houses the image is made of steel. The head and hands of the images are made of Ivory, and the heads of Mother and Child were stolen in mid 1970s. That of the Mother is still missing. This first ever image of Our Lady of Mount Carmel in the Philippines.

Pope John Paul II, when he was a young adult, thought seriously of becoming a Discalced Carmelite. The only reason he did not join the novitiate in Czerna, Poland[11] was because the Carmelites were not accepting novices because of the war. Later in November 1987, he ordered the crowning of the Image of Our Lady of Mount Carmel in this monastery.The original painting of Our Lady of the Scapular in Czerna was a painting painted with oil technique on canvas in the first half of the 17th century by an unknown painter. It was a gift from the monastery of the Discalced Carmelites of Krakow. Due to the humidity of the unheated church, the painting began to disintegrate, so it was moved to a more dry place, and a new painting painted on a copper sheet by the Krakow artist Paweł

Gołębiewski was ordered, Many pilgrimages to this image by the people of the area and from all over Silesia, with the experiencing of many graces began to occur, and the resulting offerings led to the creation of a decorative dress and crowns from these offerings in 1974.

The Carmelite Order was the first order to be established within the walls of Jerez after the reconquest. It was first established in 1587 in a former convent of Benedictines, outside the city walls. In 1600, the Carmelites moved to their current location, first building a chapel and then to the current church, which then became a Basilica. This Basilica is part of the only monastery that was created within the walls, because of the great devotion that then existed in Jerez to Our Lady of Mount Carmel. The Church is known as La Basílica Menor de Nuestra Señora del *Carmen* ***Coronada de*** *Jerez de la Frontera.*[12]

Our Lady of Carmen Coronada de San Fernando[13] is a polychrome wooden image representing the Blessed Virgin of Mount Carmel, which is venerated in the Conventual Church of Our Lady of Mount Carmel in San Fernando near Cadiz, Since 1901 She is the Patron of the Spanish Navy, and since 1955 she wears the sash of Captain General that was delivered in person by HM the King of Spain Juan Carlos I. She is the Patron of the City of San Fernando since 1921 and holds the title of Mayor of Perpetual Honour of San Fernando since 1955.

Our Lady of Carmen Coronado is a polychrome wooden image of the Blessed Virgin of Mount Carmel , which is venerated in the Parish of San Juan Bautista del Farrobo of La Villa de La Orotava[14]

(Tenerife). She is the Lady of the Village and is the *Honorary and Perpetual Mayor*. The devotion dates back to the beginning of the 17th century, supported by the Franchy Family, one of the most important and influential families of the Village. The old image was replaced by the current one at an unknown date, because it was lost or left in a very bad state after the fire in the Franciscan monastery in 1801. Due to the confiscation of 1835, the image was moved to the neighboring Parish of San Juan Bautista. Presently the Venerable Brotherhood and Brotherhood of Our Lady of Carmen Coronado, with canonical headquarters in the Parish Church is currently formed by almost 4000 members.

Virgen del Carmen of Burgo de Osma-Ciudad de Osma Spain[15] is the Image of Our Lady of Mount Carmel conserved in the Discalced Carmelites Church of Osma. The convent was founded in 1589 by Saint John of the Cross. The devotion to our Virgin of Carmen and the Order of Saint Teresa and Saint John of the Cross, led to the founding of the Brotherhood of the Carmen in 1614 and is still thriving, and still celebrates the feast in July. This brotherhood enabled the survival of Carmelite traditions after the suppression of the monasteries.

Our Lady of Mt. Carmel was proclaimed patron of the town of Rute in southern Spain on February 13, 1924. Her image goes back to the late 1600s, when Luisa Roldán (La Roldana) of Seville carved the head and hands. It was meant to be dressed, so the statue did not have a proper body until the 1960s. It occupies a neo-baroque setting over the main altar, also of the 1960s. Celebrations in her honour are held both on February 13th and on July 16th.

In Rome, the Basilica of Santa Maria in Montesanto[16] is so called because it once was a small church belonging to the Carmelites of the Province of Montesanto in Sicily. Monte Santo of course refers to Mount Carmel. The titular painting is crowned by the Vatican Chapter. The composer Handel wrote music for vespers for the 16th July Feast here.

The other images have been referred to elsewhere. This group of images give great witness to the widespread nature of devotion to Our Lady of Mount Carmel.

Nuestra Señora del Carmen de Santiago[17], 19 December 1926 Santiago, Chile
Nuestra Senora del Carmen del Maipú[17], 3 April 1987 Maipú, Chile
Nuestra Señora del Carmen de Apicala, 16 July 1942, Tolima, Colombia
Nuestra Señora de la Virgen del Carmen, 25 July 1971,La Ceja, Colombia
Nuestra Señora del Carmen del Azuay, 16 July 2002, Cuenca, Ecuador
Vergine di Montesanto, 3 December 1659, Rome, Pope Alexander VII
Madonna of Trapani[18], 14 March 1734, Trapani, Pope Clement XII
La Madonna delle Galline[19], 15 August 1787, Pagani, Pope Pius VI
Madonna del Carmine, 11 July 1875, Naples[20]
Nuestra Señora del Carmen de Paucartambo, 13 February 1985, Cusco, Peru
Nuestra Señora del Carmen de San Sebastián (1617 arrival), 18 August 1991, Quiapo, Manila, Philippines

Our Lady of the Scapular of Mount Carmel, 7 November 1987, Monastery of Discalced Carmelites, Czerna Poland
Virgen del Carmen, 23 April 1925, Jerez de la Frontera Spain
Nuestra Señora del Carmen de San Fernando, 12 October 1951, San Fernando, Cadiz Spain
Nuestra Señora del Carmen, 17 July 1988, La Orotava Spain
Virgen del Carmen, 29 July 2018, Burgo de Osma-Ciudad de Osma Spain
Our Lady of Mount Carmel of New York[21], 10 July 1904, Manhattan, New York

The Image of the Virgin of Carmel in Rute (Cordoba) has also been recently crowned. Also, the painting Madonna del Carmine in Sanctuary Basilica of Mesagne[22], near Brindisi Italia was Crowned by the Vatican Chapter. It is said that the image at Mesagne miraculously became very heavy and could not be moved from the chosen spot.

References:

1 *Is-Santuarju tal-Karmnu Sammut L. 1952*
2 *https://www.gloriasdemalaga.org/archicofradia-de-ntra-sra-del-carmen-coronada/*
3 *https://es-es.facebook.com/pages/category/Religious-Organization/Carmen-de-San-Cayetano-236768546370935/*
4 *https://anastpaul.com/2021/07/16/our-lady-of-mount-carmel-nuestra-senora-del-carmen-rute-cordoba-andalucia-spain-17th-century-and-memorials-of-the-saints-16-july/*

---

5 *http://www.elnuevodia.com.co/nuevodia/especiales/generales/470750-carmen-de-apicala-la-ciudad-milagrosa-del-tolima*

6 *https://es.wikipedia.org/wiki/Bas%C3%ADlica_Menor_de_Nuestra_Se%C3%B1ora_del_Carmen*

7 *https://ec.viajandox.com/cuenca/iglesia-del-carmen-de-la-asuncion-A3487*

8 *https://www.ubica.ec/info/virgendebronce*

9 *https://www.cuscoperu.com/en/festivities-events/july-august/virgin-of-carmen-paucartambo*

10 *https://pintakasi1521.blogspot.com/2016/09/nuestra-senora-del-carmen-de-san.html*

11 *https://karmelczerna.pl/*

12 *https://basilicadelcarmen.com/*

13 *https://hermandaddelcarmencoronada.org/*

14 *https://www.laorotava.es/en/lugares/17-san-juan-bautista-church*

15 *https://www.burgodeosma.com/virgen-del-carmen-2017.html*

16 *https://en.wikipedia.org/wiki/Santa_Maria_in_Montesanto_(Rome)*

17 *https://es.wikipedia.org/wiki/Virgen_del_Carmen_de_Chile*

18 *https://en.wikipedia.org/wiki/Madonna_of_Trapani*

19 *https://it.wikipedia.org/wiki/Festa_della_Madonna_delle_Galline*

20 *https://en.wikipedia.org/wiki/Santa_Maria_del_Carmine,_Naples*

21 *https://en.wikipedia.org/wiki/Church_of_Our_Lady_of_Mount_Carmel_(Manhattan)*

22 *http://www.basilicacarminemesagne.it/default.asp?sec=1*

THIRTY THREE

CATHEDRALS DEDICATED TO OUR LADY OF MOUNT CARMEL

THERE ARE SEVERAL CATHEDRALS ACROSS THE WORLD WHICH ARE dedicated to Our Lady of Mount Carmel. Several such cathedrals are in the Far East.

The **Cathedral of Our Lady of Mount Carmel** is in Malang, East Java, Indonesia[7], and is the seat of the Roman Catholic Diocese of Malang. It was built in 1934 in the neo-gothic style and was originally named for St Teresa but was renamed in 1961.

The **Apostolic Vicariate of Jolo**[1,2,3,4,5,6] is a Latin Catholic missionary pre-diocesan jurisdiction in the Sulu province on Mindanao island, Philippines. Its cathedral episcopal see is the Marian Cathedral of Our Lady of Mount Carmel, in Jolo, Sulu, Autonomous Region in Muslim Mindanao (ARMM).It is exempt, i.e. directly dependent of the Holy See not part of any ecclesiastical province, yet for the purpose of apostolic cooperation usually grouped with the Archdiocese of Zamboanga. Tragically, it has on three occasions been bombed.

On January 10, 2010, a grenade exploded in front of the cathedral, shattering the windows. The grenade was thrown at the tombs of Francis Joseph McSorley and Benjamin de Jesus, two former bishops. On May 20, 2010 a grenade exploded in front of the cathedral at 9:30 in the evening. The cathedral suffered minor damages.

Much more seriously, on January 27, 2019, the cathedral was bombed during a mass, killing at least 18 people and injuring 82 others. The Islamic State claimed responsibility for the attack. The church building was repaired following the attacks. It was reconsecrated in July 2019

In India, Kerala, is the Mount Carmel Cathedral[8]. It is in Alappuzha, Alappuzha District, and is also called St Mary's Forane Church. It is one of the oldest churches in India.

Also in India is the **Roman Catholic Diocese of Alleppey** , which is a diocese centred on the city of Alleppey in the Ecclesiastical province of Trivandrum in India. It lies along the Arabian Sea between the dioceses of Cochin and Quilon, covering an area of 333 square kilometres was established in 1952, and its Cathedral is dedicated to Our Lady of Mount Carmel.

Many Cathedrals of Our Lady of Mount Carmel are in South America.

The **Cathedral of Our Lady of Mount Carmel** or **Cathedral of Maturín**[9] It is a Catholic temple located in Maturín, Monagas state, in Venezuela. It is one of the largest churches in the country. Its construction began on July 16, 1959, on the day of Our Lady of Mount Carmel, and it was inaugurated 22 years later, on May 23, 1981. Also in Venezuela is the **Cathedral of Our Lady of Mount Carmel** or **Cathedral of San Fernando de Apure**[10] in the city of San Fernando de Apure, The temple is the seat of the diocese of San Fernando de Apure. Its construction took about 10 years beginning in 1959. It was consecrated in February 1969. **Our Lady of Mount**

Carmel Cathedral, also **Guasdualito Cathedral**[11], is in the city of Guasdualito, Venezuela. The church acquired cathedral status in 2015 with the separation of the jurisdiction of the Diocese of San Fernando de Apure .It functions as the headquarters of the Roman Catholic Diocese of Guasdualito which is a suffragan of the Metropolitan Archdiocese of Mérida and was created by decision of Pope Francis[4] on December 3, 2015.

The **Our Lady of Mount Carmel Cathedral**, also **La Dorada Cathedral**[12] Is the main Catholic temple of the Diocese of La Dorada-Guaduas. Located opposite the Simón Bolívar Park or Las Iguanas Park, in La Dorada, Caldas, Colombia. This religious building dates back to the middle of the 20th century. Stylistically it has Romanesque and neo classical features, The **Our Lady of Mount Carmel Cathedral** or **Villavicencio Cathedral**[13] Is located in the Colombian city of Villavicencio, capital of the department of Meta. It is the mother church of the archdiocese of Villavicencio and was elevated to cathedral on February 11, 1964.A fire destroyed the cathedral in 1890. The current building was rebuilt in 1894.

The **Our Lady of Carmel Cathedral** also called **Formosa Cathedral**[14] is a Catholic cathedral in Formosa, Argentina. It is the seat of the Diocese of Formosa. In 1896, construction began for the new cathedral. In November 1954 the new Sanctuary of the Virgen del Carmen was opened.

The **Our Lady of Mount Carmel Cathedral** or **Puntarenas Cathedral**[15] is a temple of the Roman Catholic church located in the city of Puntarenas canton of Puntarenas, in Costa Rica. It was built in 1902. It is the seat of the Roman Catholic Diocese of Puntarenas. It was elevated to cathedral on April 27, 1998.

The **Our Lady of Mount Carmel Cathedral** is located in the Plaza de Armas of Puerto Montt[16], and is the seat of the archbishop of the Archdiocese of Puerto Montt in Chile. With the creation of the Diocese of Puerto Montt in 1939 By Pope Pius XII it was elevated to cathedral. It was repaired in 1941 and then in the 1960s due to damage caused by the 1960 earthquake. Also in Chile is the **Military Cathedral of Our Lady of Mount Carmel**, also **Military Cathedral of Santiago**[17] is a Catholic temple that functions as the episcopal seat of the military bishopric of Chile. It is located in the commune of Providencia, in Santiago the capital of Chile.

One Cathedral is in the USA

St. Mary, Our Lady of Mount Carmel Cathedral, also known simply as **St. Mary's Cathedral**, is a Catholic cathedral and parish church located in Gaylord, Michigan[18], United States of America. It is the seat of the Diocese of Gaylord. The first bishop of Gaylord, Edmund Szoka, had the present cathedral built. The cornerstone was laid on July 25, 1975. The new cathedral was dedicated to Our Lady of Mount Carmel on June 25, 1976.

References:

1 *'Police investigate grenade attack on cathedral in S. Philippines'. Catholic News Agency. January 12, 2010. Retrieved January 27, 2019.*
2 *Digal, Santosh (January 11, 2010). 'Mindanao: a grenade explodes in*

front of Jolo Cathedral, no injuries'. AsiaNews. Retrieved January 27, 2019.

3 *Garcia, Bong (May 21, 2010). 'Grenade explodes outside Jolo church'. SunStar Philippines. Retrieved January 27, 2019.*

4 *Pareño, Roel (May 22, 2010). 'Grenade explodes near Jolo cathedral'. PhilStar Global. Retrieved January 27, 2019.*

5 *'Death toll in Jolo blasts lowered to 18'. CNN Philippines. January 27, 2019. Retrieved January 27, 2019.*

6 *'Jolo church attack: Many killed in the Philippines'. BBC News. January 27, 2019. Retrieved January 27, 2019.*

7 *https://en.wikipedia.org/wiki/Cathedral_of_Our_Lady_of_Mount_Carmel,_Malang*

8 *http://www.dioceseofalleppey.com/vg/index.php*

9 *https://en.wikipedia.org/wiki/Cathedral_of_Our_Lady_of_Mount_Carmel,_Matur%C3%ADn*

10 *https://en.wikipedia.org/wiki/Cathedral_of_Our_Lady_of_Mount_Carmel,_San_Fernando_de_Apure#:~:text=The%20Cathedral%20of%20Our%20Lady,the%20plains%20of%20South%20American*

11 *https://en.wikipedia.org/wiki/Our_Lady_of_Mount_Carmel_Cathedral,_Guasdualito*

12 *https://en.wikipedia.org/wiki/Our_Lady_of_Mount_Carmel_Cathedral,_La_Dorada*

13 *https://en.wikipedia.org/wiki/Our_Lady_of_Mount_Carmel_Cathedral,_Villavicencio*

14 *https://en.wikipedia.org/wiki/Our_Lady_of_Carmel_Cathedral,_Formosa*

15 *https://en.wikipedia.org/wiki/Puntarenas_Cathedral*

16 *https://en.wikipedia.org/wiki/Our_Lady_of_Mount_Carmel_Cathedral,_Puerto_Montt*

---

17 *https://en.wikipedia.org/wiki/Military_Cathedral_of_Our_Lady_of_ Mount_Carmel,_Santiago*
18 *https://en.wikipedia.org/wiki/St._Mary,_Our_Lady_of_Mount_Carmel_Cathedral_(Gaylord,_Michigan)*

THIRTY FOUR

CARMELITE DEVOTION TO OUR LADY OF SORROWS

EMANUELE BOAGA WRITES THAT FROM THE FOURTEENTH CENTURY, the Carmelites had an important devotion to Our Lady of Sorrows.

We know that today, there continues to be this devotion. There exists a relatively recently founded a 'Confraternity of Our Lady of Mount Carmel of Sorrows' which participates in the Holy Week of Seville, and that it is the Confraternity of Our Lady of Mount Carmel which organises the Holy Week procession in Taranto and in other Italian cities. In The East, the Carmelites and Discalced Carmelites have many Outdoor ways of the Cross up a hill, or Calvarias on which Pilgrims celebrate the Passion of the Lord, but to illustrate this devotion, we choose the Polish shrine of Obory, a shrine of Our Lady of Sorrows dating to the fourteenth century, and which is an important pilgrimage site.

The Shrine of Our Lady of Sorrows with a church with 400 years of history which is surrounded by beautiful gardens. The interior of the church is in a Baroque-Rococo style and it houses an organ that was played by Frederic Chopin in his lifetime. Obory is only a short distance from the town of Golub-Dobrzyn and it is known for its ancient Carmelite monastery dating from the 17th century and its Marian shrine. The church and monastery were funded by Luke and Anna Rudzowski who also donated a hill in Grodzisko and half their estates to the Order. The patron of the shrine is the Mother of

God. The statue represents the figure of Our Lady, carved from the wood of the lime tree, which is shown bent over the body of Jesus Christ who is laid on her knees after he had been taken down from the cross. The statue is most likely the work of an artist from Pomerania from the end of the 14th century.

In 1605 this small figure was brought by the founders of the monastery from a monastery in Bydgoszcz by the founders to the church in Obory. After the first wooden temple burnt down in 1627, the statue was housed in the new, also wooden, church and finally prominently placed in a niche on the main altar in 1696. In the church in Obory there are numerous votive offerings as evidence of miracles experienced by pilgrims.

The monastery and the church, originally made of wood, were replaced in the mid-18th century for structures of brick, built in the Baroque style, with a tower over its west wing. Stations of the Cross, that is a Calvaria, have recently been added to the shrine.

Today, the church and monastery are a well-known Sanctuary of Our Lady of Sorrows, popularly known as Our Lady of Oborsa.

On Sunday, July 18, 1976, the Primate of the Millennium, Stefan Cardinal Wyszyński, surrounded by over 20, 000 faithful, crowned Pieta Oborski with papal crowns and on May 3, 1982, Holy Father John Paul II gave the Apostolic Blessing: 'I bless the pilgrims to the Mother of God in Obory.'

Reference:
https://www.poland.travel/en/monu

PART 4

THE WEDNESDAYS OF OUR LADY

(L-Erbgħat Tal-Udienza)
Valentin Borg Guzman O.Carm.S.Th. D.
First Published Malta 1979

Translation and Additions by
Dr. Mark Agius M.D.
Rector of the Archconfraternity
of Our Lady of Mount Carmel, Valletta

TRANSLATOR'S PREFACE

In my younger years, living beside the great Basilica Sanctuary of Our Lady of Mount Carmel, then being built in Valletta, Malta, I frequently wondered why the Carmelites and the people celebrated the Wednesdays of Our Lady with such great devotion.

I never had the opportunity of actually participating in these evening devotions, as it was judged that my duty at my age was to do my schoolwork in the evenings.

However my curiosity persisted and was rewarded last year (1981) when during my honeymoon, I revisited the now complete Basilica to participate in the festivities which marked the Hundredth anniversary of the Crowning of the Miraculous Picture of Our Lady of Mount Carmel which is venerated there. It was on this occasion that I picked up a copy of Fr Borg Gusman's book. Its importance as a piece of original research was at once obvious. Here was a link between Mount Carmel, Aylesford and Canterbury, and the Carmels of Italy and Malta, which still survives as a major popular devotion in Malta, thus demonstrating the essential unity of the Carmelite Tradition.

What was, however, more important was the series of Sermons on the Scapular by Fr. Tonna. I was, for a while, dubious about the wisdom of publishing a book in England which teaches so much about Mary's power as a Mediatrix. My doubts have been dispelled by an account I have recently read about Mother Mary of Jesus, the saintly prioress of Notting Hill Carmel, who was God's instrument in the spread of the Second Order (Primitive Observance) throughout England in the early part of the twentieth century.

Mother Mary's life and work are such an inspiring sign of God's will that England should turn again to Mary, the Mother of Carmel. When Our Lady appeared to Mother Mary, she said but one thing; 'I grant all'. This is her message, through Carmel, to England.

Our Lady is Queen of Heaven by virtue of her Union with God. It is because she is Queen that she can give help to her devotees, who wear her own badge, the scapular, to strive to follow her in achieving that prayerful union with God of which she is, herself, the most perfect example. This, in essence, is the message of the fourth part of this book.

I come from a country where devotion to Our Lady of Mount Carmel is so widespread that it has been called 'Malta Karmelitana'. If this book will help in spreading this devotion in England, Her Dowry, it will have been worth translating.
Mark Agius 6/2/1982

I wrote the above in 1982, and then I left my manuscript aside until today, 31/12/2016, New Year's Eve. Since then, I had revised my translation and again had determined to publish it. However much time had gone by and it was evident that the manuscript of Fathers Borg-Guzman and Tonna required a revision.

Father Borg Guzman had produced a very persuasive theory about how the Carmelites had developed the devotion of the Seven Joys of Our Lady, from the custom of Saint Bertold to Genuflect seven times to the sea in honour of Our Lady, seen in the cloud by Elijah, and had related this to the Seven Joys of Our Lady in heaven which had been revealed to Saint Thomas of Canterbury by Our Lady, which was particularly important to the Carmelites since their Mother House, Aylesford, was quite close to the shrine of Saint Thomas, and the Carmelites entertained pilgrims on their way to this shrine. Father Borg Guzman also produces a good argument as to why the name 'Tal-Udienza'- 'Of the Audience', by relating the name to the local Carmelite Devotion to Our Lady 'Dell'udienza' in Sambuca in Sicily and its relation to freedom from epidemics in Sicily and in Malta, however a full account of the devotion of Madonna tal-Udienza needs to address several issues as follows:

- *Why should the day Wednesday be chosen?*
- *How does the devotion to the Joys of Our Lady relate to the broader devotion and relationship of the Carmelite Order to Our Lady?*
- *How in fact does the devotion of the Wednesdays tal-Udienza relate to the scapular Devotion of Our Lady of Mount Carmel?*
- *Does the devotion to the Joys of Our Lady continue today within the Carmelite Order? Is so, Where?*
- *Does the devotion to the Joys of Our Lady relate to the general devotion to Our Lady in the Catholic Church and to other manifestations of Marian Devotion such as the Rosary?*
- *How is the devotion to the Joys of Our Lady celebrated in the Carmelite Order today apart from in Malta?*
- *How is the devotion of the Wednesdays tal-Udienza celebrated in Malta today?*

Attempting to answer these questions open up a wide vista of sometimes unexpected relationships which demonstrates how devotions develop over centuries across time and space, so that what appears a local devotion may in fact be a local manifestation of a general trend.

It is now possible, by doing internet searches using the Google search engine, to find much new information; thus, whereas Father Borg Guzman could only point to one leaflet from Sicily as a recent example of devotion to the Joys of Our Lady, our search showed numerous such examples, throughout Italy, especially in the south. Furthermore, our search provided evidence of devotion to the Joys of Our Lady throughout Europe during the Middle Ages and indeed up to Baroque times, as evidenced by popular songs, art, and old books. Furthermore, our research provided further evidence of the link between the Joys of Our Lady and devotion in England to Thomas Becket of Canterbury, and also that the Joys of Our Lady became a central point from which devotion to Our Lady developed into such important modern devotions such as the Rosary, and in fact fulfilled an important, indeed a core aspect, of the functioning of the Church, which is the necessity, in each individual person's prayer life, of meditation on the life and death of Jesus Christ our Saviour and His Mother, in order that each person is aware on a daily basis of the reality of Christ and the salvation which he offers us.

While I saw it necessary to publish all the new information which I have discovered, I wished that Father Borg Gusman and Father Tonna's work be untouched, hence I publish their work in full in ordinary script, while my comments will be in italics. I have, however, had to rearrange Father Borg Guzman's book into chapters for clarity.

I hope this study of the Wednesdays of Our Lady will help the reader understand the importance of devotion to Our Lady, the Theotokos, Mother of God for our lives and for the Human Race.

Mark Agius

INTRODUCTION

The devotion of the Wednesdays of Our Lady is both popular and widespread in Malta. People expect it to be organised, they love it and attend the ceremonies, but they know very little about its origins.

Professor P. Anastasju Cuschieri O.Carm, , who wrote about this devotion, felt that he had to be honest with his readers and tell them that, despite his having researched diligently, he could not say when these Wednesdays had first been organised. Furthermore he could not say definitively what they meant, and he stated that we know nothing about their history. (See Ir-Regina tal-Carmelu, 9[1917] 264).

We were not discouraged by this statement. Every created thing must have its beginning, and everything has a meaning, even if, over time, this has been forgotten or has undergone change. Everything has a history behind it.Therefore, if we search systematically, rather than simply enthusiastically, we should certainly find some information about these Wednesdays.

O n the other hand, Cuschieri's statement was very encouraging to us, since it implied that the outcomes of our research would be useful and original, which any researcher would wish for. We will overcome the passage of time in order to shed light on this devotion.

Hence we researched widely, not just in Malta but also abroad. We spent much of the summer of 1977 in the Carmelite Library of Our International College of Saint Albert in Rome, reading books and taking notes. In June and July of last year (1978), we were able to visit libraries in Sicily, in Catania, Agrigento, Sciacca and Sambuca. We were lucky enough to find information, not all we needed, but enough. We discovered much information. We were able to demonstrate that this devotion, although it does not originate within the Order, has become a devotion which is particular to the Carmelite Order, which is in some way related to the Marian devotion of Our Lady of Mount Carmel. We came to understand its original meaning and the changes which this has undergone among the Carmelites since the sixteenth century. Finally, we were able to discover why these Wednesdays are known as 'Tal-Udienza '(of the Audience) and how and when the devotion entered Malta, as well as other details related to this devotion.

However, during the seven Wednesdays 'Tal-Udjenza' the preacher should, not merely teach the devotees the history of the devotion but should also give his listeners useful teaching about faith and morals. Therefore, it happens that, when the preacher is not a Carmelite, his teaching is usually about the Joys of Our Lady or some other Marian aspects.

This is what we do not wish to happen. Not only the flavour but the whole structure of these sermons should be not only Marian but specifically Carmelite. It is clear from History that very quickly, this devotion became a Carmelite one, indeed, a particular devotion of the Carmelite Order.

There is much Carmelite literature which can be used on these Wednesdays, including literature in Maltese. However, it needs to be brought up to date and to reflect the Magisterium of the Church. The Vatican II Council warns preachers 'to pay attention to avoid every false exaggeration 'when they speak of Our Lady. They must carefully avoid anything which may lead our separated brethren or any other person into error about the true Doctrine of the Church'. (Dogmatic Constitution on the Church 'Lumen Gentium', n.67)

Therefore, in this book, as well as the history of the Wednesdays of Our Lady (of the Audience), we thought it best to present some sermons which are up to date and appropriate to be preached. Thus preachers will have at their disposition material which is reliable and useful.

We present only six sermons, one for each of the last six Wednesdays. On the first Wednesday, one could briefly narrate the history of this devotion with some moral applications. Thus this book is divided into two; the first part is historical, the second is doctrinal.

In the doctrinal part, consisting of six talks, the Author, P. Ewgenju Tonna O.Carm. depends greatly on the 'Novena del Carmine' by P. Ludovico Saggi O.Carm.This Novena has been liked very much, and so has been printed in the 'Antologia dello Scapolare' (Rome,[s.d.], sez.4, fasc.1, pp.1-30), edited by P.Sebastiano Marras and P. Emanuele Boaga, both Carmelites.

May this book encourage in its readers a burning devotion to the seven Wednesdays of Our Lady.

P.Valentin Borg Gusman, O.Carm.
Carmelite Convent,
Valletta
Candlemas 2nd February 1979

References:

Prof. P. Anastasju Cuschieri O.Carm l-Erbgħat Tal-Udienza Ir-Regina tal-Carmelu, 9 [1917] 264
Kostituzzjoni Dogmatika fuq il-Knisja 'Lumen Gentium', nru.67
P.Ludovico Saggi O.Carm, Novena del Carmine Antologia dello Scapolare' (Ruma, [sd], sez.4, fasc, 1, pp.1-30)
P.Sebastiano Marras O.Carm., P. Emanuele Boaga O.Carm. Antologia dello Scapolare' (Ruma, [sd], sez.4, fasc, 1, pp.1-30)

THIRTY FIVE

The Joys of Our Lady

Every year, during Lent, the Church becomes sad as it considers the sufferings and death of its Bridegroom Jesus Christ. When Easter comes, that is on the day he rises again, she removes every sign of mourning and expresses great joy with the singing of Alleluia.

However, since Mary, the Mother of Jesus, co-operated in a special way with the action of her Son the Saviour (LG, n.61), most of all because she had stood at Calvary beside his cross (John 19, 25) and suffered with Her while He died (LG, n.61), the Church does not forget Her in her joy. The Church turns to Mary and invites her to rejoice, because He who She had born has risen from the dead.

From the beginning of time, children have rejoiced in the happiness of their parents. Therefore, the first Christians felt that they should rejoice with Our Lady, their Mother in the order of Grace (LG, n.61), and that they should commemorate some of Her joys. Thus it came about that some of these Joys, commemorated by some holy Fathers of the Church, began to become the object of devotion.[1]

It was in the middle of the eleventh century when this Marian devotion first appeared in the Liturgy. In an antiphon, found in a manuscript of that time, five joys are mentioned.[2] But two more were soon added in the celebrated hymn of the twelfth century Gaude Virgo Mater Christi.[3] Over the years, they not only doubled in number and increased three times, but increased in number to twenty-five.[4] The reason was this; some authors give two series each of seven – those which Mary experienced on earth and those which Mary experienced in Heaven. Also not all authors agree in the circumstances of Joy which they mention. Sometimes they do not agree on the circumstances of joy which they mention, often they include more than one circumstance within each Joy.[5]

A. The Number of Joys

However, we can say for certain that, from the twelfth century till now, the usual number of joys was always seven. Many believe that it was Our Lady Herself who chose to reveal this number, apparently to more than one man. Indeed, John Heroilt O.P. (+1468) says that She gave the names of the Joys to a shepherd, without giving his name.[6] We do not know whether he was speaking of Saint Arnold of Cornobonet O.S.B. (+1228). However it is true that in the life of this saint, (printed in 1660) we find it written that the Virgin Mary appeared to him and encouraged him to have devotion to the main seven joys which she experienced in heaven. She mentioned them to him one by one.[7]

The same is said about Saint Matilda,[8] but the oldest apparition, and the one which is most well-known is that to Saint Thomas Becket, Archbishop of Canterbury (+1170). Before our Lady appeared to him, he used to honour her by praying in honour of the seven joys which she had experienced on earth. These are the joys in the hymn we have mentioned as Gaude Virgo Mater Christi.[9]

Almost everyone agrees that it is the other series of joys, that which

Mary experiences in Heaven, which She revealed to Saint Thomas. She wished to encourage him to also be devoted to these,[10] or, by other accounts, to show him that she was more pleased if he honoured these than those she enjoyed on earth.[11] Others have said that Saint Thomas did not properly recognise the joys, so Our Lady appeared to him, to teach him to add one of Her heavenly joys to the six main joys she had experienced on earth. This heavenly Joy includes a number of privileges and occasions of Joy for Mary.[12]

Notes

1 Gabriele Roschini. O.S.M. La Madonna second la fede e la teologia.v.4, Roma. 1954, p.412: 'I suoi ineffabili gaudi ricordati occasionalmente da alcuni Sancti Padri,...incominciarono a diventare oggetto di culto'.

2 Roschini., La Madonna, ... v.4, Roma. 1954, p.412: 'I suoi ineffabili gaudi.....solo verso la metà del secolo XI incominciarono a diventare oggetto di culto. Si trovano infatti (però in numero di cinque, e non gia di sette) in un' antifona liturgica conservata in un manoscritto di quel tempo.'

3 Roschini. Mariologia, t.2, pars 3, edRomae, 1948, p.182: 'Transitus vero a numero quinque ad numerum septem facilis fuit et cito factus est. In celebri hymno saec. XII 'Gaude Virgo Mater Christi'..., cum additione gaudi dierum Epiphaniae et Pentecostes, numerous septem gaudiorum obtinetur. Cfr. La Madonna, p.143.

4 Roschini., La Madonna, p.413: '......i Gaudi di Maria (prima in numero di cinque, poi in numero di sette, ed anche a volte, di nove, di dieci......di venti e di venticinque)'

5 See further on in this study under h) List of the Joys.

6 See Roschini., Mariologia, t.2, pars 3, p.183 La Madonna, p.413

---

7 See GIORGIUS COLVENERIUS, Kalendarium Marianum, in J.J. BOURASSE', Summa aurea de laudibus BVM Dei Genetris sine labe concept, Parisiis, 1866, III, p.946; Roschini., Mariologia, p.183 La Madonna, p.413

8 Roschini., Mariologia, p.183:' Etiam in op.'Liber gratiae specialis' S. Mectildis quid simle legitur'; La Madonna, p.413-414: 'Un che di simile si legge anche nel 'gratiae specialis' di S. Metilde.'

9 See PIETRO MARIA ALBERTO DAL BUONO, O.Carm.,Divozione de' sette mercoledì del Carmine in ossequio di Maria Vergine Madre di Dio riverita sotto il titolo delle Sette Allegrezze, Bolognia 1724, pp.7-8; PIERLUIGI BAGNARI, O.Carm., Divozioni che si praticano nella Chiesa della Traspontina in onore di Nostra Signora del Carmine, Roma, 1728, p.24; Modo da recitare le sette Allegrezze della B. Vergine Maria di Monte Santo, Catania, 1849, p.130; Roschini., Mariologia, p.183 La Madonna, p.413

10 This is the view of PELBART (according to Roschini) and the author of the book 'Modo da recitare le sette Allegrezze (Catania, 1849), He writes 'La Vergine Santissima li disse che al pari delle sette Allegrezze che senti mentre era nel mondo, alter tante ora ne goda spiritualmente nell'Empireo: onde con ugual divozione le venerasse ancora'(p.5)

11 This is the view of DAL BUONO, Divozione...,p.9: @ Sappipero, che molto più sarai da me gradito, se prenderai a fare memoria di quelle Sette principali Allegrezze, che gode fra l'altre il mio cuore nel cielo'; BAGNARI, Divozioni, ...pp.23-24:'gli comparve la Vergine gloriosa, e gli disse: E perche, figliuol mio, solamente con me ti rallegri di quelle Allegrezze, che gia sono passate, e non piu tosto ti rallegri di quelle Allegrezze, che ora io godo nel cielo, e che in perpetuo dureranno: In avvenire dunque rallegrati meco con queste sette Allegrezze'; TARINO, Nostra Signora, ..., p.131: 'gli comparve personalmente la Vergine, ...(e) gli soggiuse che le sarebbe tornado più gradito, se facesse menzione delle principali Allegrezze che gode il suo cuore lassù in cielo....'.

12 Vincenz Vella, Id-devot tal Madonna tal Carmnu, Malta 1898, p.288: 'Darba wahda deritlu Maria, u kaltlu: Inti o iben mahbub tighi, dejjem ittini gost u piacir, mita inti tghidli d-devozioni tal-ferh tighi. Imma sabiex actar icun collox seuua, jiena irrid nghalmec chif ghandec tkasamhom u daun huma l'isbah granet ta' ferh li chelli mita cont ninsab f'din l-art, u il Gloria li biha ninsab onorata fis-Sema'.

THIRTY SIX

THE JOYS OF OUR LADY IN EUROPE

EVIDENCE THAT THE JOYS OF OUR LADY WERE A WIDESPREAD DEVOTION IN EUROPE DURING THE MIDDLE AGES AND BEYOND

It is clear from a Google search that throughout the Middle Ages, and later, the Joys of Our Lady were a widespread devotion in Europe. The main aim of this chapter is to demonstrate that the Joys of Our Lady were known all over Europe at least from the fourteenth century, and were an important expression of Marian Devotion, especially in popular culture, as in popular songs, but also in genteel settings, such as books of hours. There are even suggestions that from this devotion, a psaltar began to develop which eventurally developed into the rosary.

THE JOYS OF OUR LADY IN MEDIEVAL ENGLAND

It would seem that devotion to the Joys of Mary was widespread in Medieval England and that one manifestation of this was that the Joys of Mary were frequently sung in popular verse. One poem 'The Five Joys of Mary' dated late 13th or earlier 14th century is quoted by R.T. Davies in Medieval English Lyrics no 20 p 78 Faber London 1963. In a note to the poem, Davies says (op.cit. p316) 'The five joys of Mary made a common medieval theme though the number of joys was sometimes greater.' [1]

It should be noted that the mother house of the Carmelites in Aylesford was a well known stop for pilgrims on their way to Canterbury, thus Adair in 'The Pilgrims Way' (Book Club Associates1978) p.58, says 'The medieval bridge at Aylesford felt the tread of many pilgrims over its narrow humped back. They could find sustenance nearby at the door of the Carmelites or White Friars'.[2] He goes on to point out that the present friars 'have also restored the ancient guest house, the Pilgrim's Hall. The same author mentions (op. cit. p68) that pilgrims to Canterbury could visit several stations in the Cathedral, one of which was the shrine of St. Mary Undercroft. There was therefore a Marian element in the Canterbury Pilgrimage, which one might expect the Carmelites at Aylesford to encourage among their pilgrim guests.[2] Thus, Bagniari may be nearer the mark than previously thought by Fr. Borg Gusman, as St. Thomas a Becket's devotion to the Joys of Mary was obviously an easily available vehicle for the Aylesford Carmelites to spread Marian devotion among their Canterbury Pilgrim Guests. One important piece of evidence for this is that the Carmelite Church at Verona, where the seven Joys are celebrated up until today, is unusually named for Saint Thomas Becket.

As to whether devotion to the Joys of Mary was associated with devotion to Our Lady of Mount Carmel in Medieval England, I can only quote the Will of John of Gaunt, Duke of Lancaster, as quoted by McCafferty (the white Friars Dublin 1926) p168,[41] who in turn quotes Royal Wills, Nichol p145,[3] and also is quoted by Sheppard 'The English Carmelites' p. 43 (London, Burns Oates 1943).[4] He left to the altar of Our Lady of Mount Carmel (in the priory of London) his old white vestment of cloth of Gold called Rakamas, with all belonging to it, and fifteen marks of silver in honour of the fifteen Joys of Our Lady. This was more money than he left for other orders. Both McCafferty and Sheppard point out that he was a friend to the Carmelites, a member of the Scapular Confraternity, that he had founded the Carmelite Monastery at Doncaster and had given presents to many Carmelite convents. He had written to the Pope after the Chester Miracle to ask that the Carmelites be known as the Bretheren of the Mother of God. (Sheppard op. Cit. p24 quoting Bodlian Library, MS Badley 73, Fi85a) and protected them during the peasant's revolt. He had many Carmelite confessors, including William de Reynham, John Bulby, Walter Dysse and Stephen Paryington. (See Sheppard op. cit. p24, 28, 42, 43, and McCaffery op.cit.p168, 192, 216, 217, 225, 226, 287). If he associated the Joys of Mary with Our Lady of Mount Carmel, it seems reasonable to suppose that others did so too, and that he did so under the influence of his Carmelite Confessors.[3,4,41]

Another medieval poem on the joys of Mary presently in print is a carol 'The Seven Joys of Mary', published in 'A Meditation on Christ's Nativity', a recording of Christmas Music and readings by the Choir of St. John's College, Cambridge, published by Argo Records 1968.[42]

THE JOYS OF MARY; CAROL

A Google Search shows 13 songs about the Joys of Mary in the English Language. All date from medieval times. All are in the form of carols for singing at Christmas.[43,44,45,46]

Five refer to the five Joys of Mary. Seven refer to seven Joys of Mary, one of which is extended to 14 Joys, and another, collected in North Carolina lists three alternative joys. One lists ten Joys. We know that One dates circa 1471-1485, one is a fifteenth century manuscript in the British Museum, and one, in very old English, is a manuscript in Trinity College Cambridge. Another is dated between 1400 and 1700. They were all collected and published between 1833 and 1933. When, during the

Commonwealth, Christmas was abolished, these disappeared from all but very remote parts of England, and also from the British American colonies, and they were then re-discovered, so that one was rediscovered as a folk song in the Appalachian mountains in Cherokee County North Carolina.

What is interesting is to see the development of theology in a folk context about the Joys which Mary is said to have enjoyed.

Let us start with the versions with five Joys; Most list the following Joys;Annunciation, Nativity, Resurrection, Ascension of Our Lord into Heaven, Crowning of Mary in Heaven, so that, if we go by the Borg Gusman classification, four are Joys Mary experienced on Earth, and one is a joy Mary experienced in Heaven. However two versions refer to the Crucifixion and Resurrection, suggesting that Mary, despite her suffering at seeing her son crucified, was Joyous at seeing him accept the suffering for mankind's redemption, and then seeing the culmination of this redemption in his Resurrection. In one version, the final Joy is the Last Judgement, which is to come, when the Redemption of Mankind will have come to its final fulfilment, while all the other versions refer to Mary being Crowned in Heaven.[43,44,45,46]

The versions with seven Joys are presumably of later Date, as suggested by Borg Gusman. Here, however, there is a mixture of theological mysteries and Joys that any Mother may experience watching the development of her child, also there are joys which imply watching her son Jesus being a 'Good Man', by using good deeds to benefit his fellow men by curing their ills...but, of course, these miracles also gradually show that He is also God. Thus there is a gradual revelation in the folk verses of Jesus truly both God and Man.-the mystery of the incarnation. Even the mystery of the Nativity

---

is referred to as a mother sees her child - 'when he was first her son'...The theme of ordinary things which would cause any mother to rejoice in her human child is continued in the extra verses which are added to make 10 or 14 Joys. Other ordinary causes of Joy which are listed are, in various versions, the child suckling at her breast-in 2 versions, reading the Bible – in 2 versions, going to school- 1 version. Joys caused by His miracles by which he benefits man are curing lame-6 versions, healing the blind- 8 versions, Bring dead to life – 8 versions, make crooked straight [which could also mean convert to a better life] 2 versions, change water into wine- 2 versions, bring up ten gentlemen (lepers) -2 versions, help the poor -1 version, write without a pen -1 version. Joys caused by theological concepts are described in an interesting way, thus the redemption is described as the Crucifixion, with implications as with the versions with five joys in 3 versions, while the concept of carrying the cross [remember the idea that Mary met Jesus carrying the cross on his way to calvary] occurs in 3 versions. In one version only, He Rises from the Crucifix - Resurrection. In four versions, Jesus Wears the Crown of Heaven, and in 2 versions He ascends into heaven (and in one case-the North Carolina one- is safe in Heaven), as a cause of Mary's Joy. The cause of Mary's Joy is that Jesus opens (for us) the Gates of Heaven in two versions, and in one version the cause of joy is that he has shut the gates of hell. In two cases, in the North Carolina Version, the cause of Joy is inverted, as if to suggest that Jesus, as God can also punish- thus 'make the well sick or make the rich poor'...perhaps conditions in the Appalachians were so difficult that a God who might punish was more 'credible'. In no case in the versions with seven or more Joys is the crowning of Our Lady in Heaven ever mentioned. Nor, in the versions with seven joys is the Annunciation ever mentioned.[43,44,45,46]

It seems that, while the versions with five joys were meant to remember the main theological mysteries which show Mary's part in the redemption of Mankind, in the versions with seven joys, the gradual revelation of Jesus as both God and Man, and then his redemption of Mankind is seen through the eyes of Mary.[43,44,45,46]

While talking about music, it can also be noted that the great English Composer Thomas Tallis (c. 1505 1585) wrote an eight verse motet entitled' Gaude gloriosa Dei mater (Rejoice, glorious mother of God)', which is in fact the seven heavenly joys. It was probably written in the latter part of Queen Mary's reign. (saturday chorale.com/2013/07/03/feature-thomas-tallis-1505-1585-gaude-gloriosa/) The Joys listed are; Mary is raised above the heavens. She rejoices to see the King whom all serve (God),She is fit to be called the mother of God, she is model of virtues, she is glorified as mother of the church, she is helper and intercessor of sinners, She is saviour of the damned, People are saved from the Devil's power by her, In her name all enter the kingdom of heaven.[5]

The Joys of Mary and Painting Art

A number of paintings exist about the Seven Joys of Mary; They provide evidence of the existence of this devotion in the areas where the paintings were made.

One painting is by Hans Memling (ca.1435-1494): Seven Joys of the Virgin or Advent and Triumph of Christ (1480) in the Alte Pinakothek-Munich,[6,7,8] *quoted in (www.theartofpainting.be/AOM- Seven_Joys_and _seven_Sorrows.html) and (http://idlespeculations-terryprest.blogspot.co.uk/2011/12/seven-joys-of-mary.html) (https://twitter.com/medievalpoc /status/627162284595539969)*

Hans Memling was the most prolific painter of religious pictures in Bruge in the late fifteenth century. He originated around 1433 in the German town of Nordlingen, near Mainz. He moved to Brabant and worked in the workshop of Rogier Van Der Weyden, and then moved to Bruges. He entered the Painter's Guild of Bruge in 1466 and continued to be a member till his death in 1494. Memling was popular among the Florentine Merchants of Bruges. He was a 'Flemish Primitive' in terms of his style of art.[6,7,8]

The donors of the painting of the 'Seven Joys' were Peter Bulyync and his wife Catherine van Riebeke. It was to be placed in the chapel of the Guild of Tanners in the Church of the Ladies of Bruges. It is a combination of scenes in a vast landscape which could be used to educate the faithful about the New Testament,which illustrate twenty-five scenes of the life of the Virgin, including the seven Joys. The landscape includes towns, castles, meadows, and roads. The 'Nativity' is the central scene, and other smaller scenes include 'the Annunciation', the 'Resurrection', the 'Visitation', and the 'Entry of Christ into Jerusalem'[6,7,8]*. ('René Dewil - The Art of Painting - Copyright')*

Also painted are the Epiphany (Visit of the wise men), the escape from the massacre of the Innocents, The resurrection and appearances of Christ after the Resurrection, Pentecost and the Death and Assumption of Mary [6,7,8] *(http://idlespeculations-terryprest.blogspot.co.uk/2011/12/seven-joys-of-mary.html)*

It is to be noted that the traditional 'Seven Joys of Mary' are the Annunciation, The Visitation', The Birth of Christ, The Adoration of the Magi, the Meeting with Simeon in the Temple, the Finding in the Temple and the Coronation of the Virgin. All these scenes were painted by Memling.[6,7,8]

Thus, this painting shows that there was knowledge of the Seven Joys of Our Lady among the Flemish people in Bruges during the fifteenth century.[6,7,8] *('René Dewil - The Art of Painting - Copyright')*

Another painting is The Seven Joys of the Virgin, attributed to Bernard van Orley (ca. 1492-1541/1542), which is at the Galleria Colonna.[9,10] *Rome (www.theartofpainting.be/AOM-**Seven_Joys**_and_ **seven_Sorrows**.htm) Bernard van Orley (who lived between 1487 and 1491 – 6 January 1541), is also referred to as Barend or Barent van Orley, Bernaert van Orley or Barend van Brussel. He was a leading artist in Dutch and Flemish Renaissance painting, and he also worked asa designer of Brussels tapestry and of stained glass. He never visited Italy, but belongs to the group of Italianizing Flemish painters called the Romanists, who were influenced by Italian Renaissance painting. In particular he was especially influenced by Raphael.*[8] *('René Dewil - The Art of Painting - Copyright')*

He was born and died in Brussels, and was the court artist of the Habsburg rulers, and 'served as a sort of commissioner of the arts for the Brussels town council'[10] *(wikivisually.com/wiki /**Bernard_van_Orley**). The paintings of the Seven Joys and Seven Sorrows of the Virgin are generally believed to be late works by the artist, from the 1520's.*[10,11] *http://www.sothebys.com/de/auctions/ecatalogue/lot.141.html/2011/old-master-british -paintings-day-sale-l11034) (wikivisually.com/wiki/Bernard_van_ Orley) The painting is an Italianate Madonna and Child with seven roundals with smaller paintings of each of the seven Joys, including the Annunciation, The Nativity, The Adoration of the Magi, The appearance of the*

Resurrected Christ to the Virgin, the Ascension, Pentecost, The Coronation of Our Lady in Heaven. It is reminiscent of many paintings of Our Lady of the Rosary which include the mysteries of the Rosary in roundels around the main paintings.[10,11] *Again, this painting bears witness to the knowledge of the devotion to the Joys of Our Lady in Brussels, and therefore among the Habsburgs in the early sixteenth century.*

A print exists also of The Seven Joys of Mary by Lucas Cranach, the elder, 1472-1553.It too represents the Joys of Mary in Roundals surrounding a central picture of Our Lady reading, with a book - presumably the bible, in her hand.[12] *Here the Joys are the Annunciation, Nativity, Epiphany, Finding in the temple, Appearance to Mary after Resurrection, Pentecost, and Crowning of Mary in Heaven.*[12] *(http://www.artic.edu/aic/collections /artwork/4049).* ***Lucas Cranach the Elder*** *(Lucas Cranach der Ältere) was a German Renaissance painter and printmaker in woodcut and engraving. He was court painter to the Electors of Saxony for most of his career. He is known for his portraits, both of German princes and those of the leaders of the Protestant Reformation, whose cause he embraced with enthusiasm, becoming a close friend of Martin Luther. He also painted religious subjects, first in the Catholic tradition, and later trying to find new ways of conveying Lutheran religious concerns in art.*[12] *This shows that the seven Joys of Our Lady were known in Northern Germany in the fifteenth to sixteenth century, including among Protestant Reformers.*

A third painting is the 'Altarpiece of the Seven Joys of the Virgin, depicting the Adoration of the Magi, The Presentation in the Temple and Christ Appearing to Mary', c.1480 (oil on panel), by the Master of the Holy Family, (fl.1470-1515) in the / Louvre, Paris, France.[13,14,15,48] *(http://www .art.com/products/p11723137-sa-i1348641/master-of-the-holy-family-altar piece-of-the-seven-joys-of-the-virgin-of-the-adoration-of-the-magi.htm), (http://www.bridgeman-berlin.de/fr/asset/215399//), (http://www. pbs learning media.org/ resource/ xir215399/altarpiece-of-the-seven-joys-of-the-virg-ger-xir215399/)*

The Master of the Holy Family was a German Northern Renaissance Painter, active ca.1470-1515.[13,14,15,48] *The painting in the Louvre is circa 1480, Again it points to knowledge of the devotion to the joys of Our Lady in Germany in Frankfurt in the fifteenth century. Another German painting of the fifteenth century is the Altarpiece of the Dominicans in the Unterlinden museum at Colmar, Alsace, France, which is an Oil on Wood Altar-piece attributed to Martin Schongauer and his entourage, painted circa 1480*[47] *(http://www.pbslearningmedia.org/resource/xir215399 /altar piece-of-the-seven-joys-of-the-virg-ger-xir215399/). Today this altarpiece is disassembled, but until the French Revolution it had been held intact in the chapel of Colmar's other Dominican convent,which now houses the city's municipal library. It was a tryptych which, when open, depicted the Passion of Christ, from the Entry into Jerusalem to Pentacost, including a Noli me tangere, depicting the scene when the risen Jesus meets Mary Magdalene. When its wings are closed, the altarpiece presented to the faithful eight paintings depicting the Seven Joys of Our Lady, to which the altar was dedicated.*[47] *This clearly suggests that the faithful in Alsace knew about the Seven Joys of Mary in the late 15th century.*

The Joys of Mary and Books of Hours

(http://www.gla.ac.uk/services/specialcollections/collectionsaz/ manuscript sunnamedcollections/) Books of Hours originated in France.[49] *They were collections of prayers for the use of the laity to use in private prayer. Their main content were a series of prayers and psalms called 'The Hours of the*

Virgin', which are similar to the Little Office of Our Lady recited by Carmelite Tertiaries today . The prayers were directed to Mary, the Mother of God, and were to be recited daily at set 'hours' during the day. Books of Hours were extremely popular throughout the Middle Ages. Indeed, from the mid-thirteenth century to the mid-sixteenth century, more were produced, both in print and manuscript, than any other type of book. They were often very lavishly illustrated with richly coloured painted illuminations. Although they usually comprised a basic set of standard texts, Books of Hours could be designed and decorated according to the requirements and budget of the purchaser. Typically, Books of Hours would contain the following elements; a full Calendar in French in red and black; the Hours of the Cross; the Hours of the Holy Spirit; the sequentiae of the Gospels, the Hours of the Virgin; the prayers to the Virgin 'Obsecro te' and 'O intemerata'; the 'Salve regina'; the Penitential psalms and litany of the saints; the Office of the dead ; two prayers in French, (the rest of the text was usually in Latin) the 'Joys of the Virgin' and the 'Seven requests of our Lord'. This description is based on the ' Glasgow Hours', an example in the University of Glasgow library. Other Books of Hours which are definitely described as including the Joys of Our Lady are the Rothschild Prayer book c1505- 1510 in the Kerry Stokes Collection, Perth, National Library of Australia,[16,17] where the Seven Joys are prefaced by an Illumination of the Virgin and Child on a Crescent Moon.[16,17] (http://www.abc.net.au/ radionational/programs/booksandarts/rothschild /6670130) (http: //www.medievalists.net/2015/05/28/rothschild-prayer-book comes-to-australia/),The Walters Book of Hours (http://www.thedigitalwalters.org/Data/WaltersManuscripts/html/W202/ description .html). The Walters Hours is dated ca. 1460-70, and was completed in the circle of Willem Vrelant, -1481 in Bruges, Flanders according to the use of Sarum.[18] It is an example of the prayer books made in the third quarter of the thirteenth century in Bruges for English owners. It contains the Seven Joys of the Virgin, attributed in heading to Pope Clement, granting Indulgence of 100 days for regular daily recitation: 'Quicumque hec septem gaudia in honore beate marie virginis semel in die dixerit.C.dies indulgenciarum optinebit a domino papa clemente qui ea proprio stilo composuit. Virgo templum trinitatis. deus summe bonitatis... Per hoc gaudium precamur. quod hunc regem mereamur. habere propicium. Et ab eo protegamur. protecti recipiamur. in terra vivencium...De secundo gratulans. cum tu solem...O maria tota munda. a peccatis nos emunda. per hec septem gaudia. Et secunda nos secunda. et domine tecum ad iocunda paradysi gaudia. Amen. Oratio. O domina glorie. O regina leticie. o fons pietatis...' [18] *This means that the Joys of Our Lady must have been known about in Flanders and in England by the mid fifteenth century.*

The Prayerbook of Alphonso V of Aragon' is written in the Dominican use. (http://www.bl.uk/manuscripts/FullDisplay.aspx? ref=Add_MS_ 28962) It contains not only the the Seven Joys of the Virgin Mary but also 'The Seven Joys of the Virgin Mary,[19] *'Septem gaudia beate virginis Marie' and a description of the vision of St Thomas Beck relating to the Seven Joys of the Virgin Mary, incipit: 'Legitur quod beatus Thomas martir' or The Seven Spiritual Joys of Mary according to St Thomas Becket,*[19] *'Septem gaudia spiritualia beate virginis'.'The origin of this Book is Spain,Valencia, and its date is 1436-1443,*[19] *so the Joys of Our Lady must have been known about in Spain in the early fifteenth century. The University of Reading's Book of Hours (https://www.reading.ac.uk /GCMS/ Book-of-Hours/gcms-resources-book-of-hours- home. aspx) is one of many that were produced in Paris*[20] *c.1410-25, for patrons who wished to follow the use of Paris. All these Books of Hours follow the same French prayer cycle which had become standard as early as the 1350s, and which included The Fifteen*

Joys of the Virgin seven penitential prayers referred to as the Seven Requests, as well as a short prayer to the True Cross. Thus the Joys of Mary in a fifteen Joy format had already become commonplace in France by the mid fourteenth century.

THE SEVEN JOYS OF THE VIRGIN IN ANCIENT LITERATURE, AND NORSE, GAELIC AND FRENCH AND IBERIAN LITERATURE.

When, in around 1462, (that is Fifteenth century) the French writer Antoine de la Sale wrote his satire called 'Les Quinze Joies de Mariage', that is ,'The Fifteen Joys of Marriage', it parodied in form the popular litany ''Les Quinze Joies de Notre Dame", or 'The Fifteen Joys of Our Lady', thus demonstrating its popularity in France at that time. The original poem 'le XV. Joyes nostre Dame' by Christine Pizan dates around the years 1402-1405. It has been commented on by Jean-François Kosta-Théfaine[21,22] (Les XV. Joyes nostre Dame rimes de Christine de Pizan 2008 p.255-277 http:// crm .revues.org/ Jean-François Kosta-Théfaine).

He points out that 'this religious piece is inscribed in a characteristic movement of the fourteenth and fifteenth centuries that sees the birth of Marian poetry'. She says that the poem 'comprises sixteen quatrains of octosyllabic rhymes, with the addition of the Ave Maria after each of the stanzas', and points out that from the twelfth century onwards, there is a tendency to associate the repeating of the 'Ave Maria' with the meditation on the 'Five Joys of the Virgin'.[22] Kosta-Théfaine quotes Hélène Millet as suggesting that these 'Ave Marias' embellished the text in the same way as decorations in Books of Hours, thus 'making it possible to compensate for 'the poverty of the participation of the intellect in spiritual exercises'...this is of great importance in suggesting how 'Ave Marias' said like an eastern 'mantra' helped develop the Modern Rosary as a form of religious meditation.[22] *On the other hand, Maureen Boulton suggests that the 'Ave Marias' act as 'an imitation of the treatment of the invitatory (Psalm 94), where pairs of psalm verses are punctuated with the beginning of the Ave Maria'.*[22] *Boulton suggests that this is similar to another prose prayer, also common in Books of Hours called the Doulce Dame de misericorde, in which each paragraph , is also punctuated by an 'Ave Maria gratia plena.'*[22] *Thus, Maureen Boulton says that, 'in versifying the prayer, Christine produced a poem of extraordinary conciseness and stylistic variation, and gives the intrusive Latin prayer a formal function in her poem by using it as a refrain for each stanza'.*[22]

Gérard Gros has rightly called this prayer an 'eminently feminine prayer'. He points out that the Fifteen Joys are presented as an exaltation of motherhood. The Fifteen Joys celebrate the Virgin as a woman in her own right. The Virgin, like the author of these Joys, 'has experienced the same pains: that of childbirth but also and above all, that of the loss of the fruit of her entrails'. Gérard Gros points out that In the Fifteen Joys, while Mary definitely appears as the guarantor of the salvation of the human being, according to Christine de Pizan, men count much more than women on the Virgin to save them . The reason for this is simple according to Gros: 'it is for women, the earthly reflection of the Virgin, to save the world.'[22]

Christine de Pizan shows originality, in that although the fifteen joys of Mary in verse or prose existed for a long time, these texts were in Latin. Furthermore, while one frequently encounters five, seven, nine or twelve 'joys' in the twelfth and thirteenth centuries, Gérard Gros points out that there are only two examples in the late Middle Ages of 'Fifteen Joys'.[22]

It has however also been pointed out that the Fifteen Joys of the Virgin use many of the same incidents as occur in another prayer, called 'The Oroyson of our Lord' These incidents are: The Annunciation, The Nativity, The Visit of the shepherds, The Epiphany,of the Kings, the Presentation in the Temple, The Resurrection, The Ascension and Pentecost.[22]

In Middle English, there is a reference to 'The Five Joys of the Virgin in the fourteenth Century Poem (1375) Sir Gawain and the Green Knight. This is a a late 14th-century Middle English chivalric romance. Gawain's Shield has a pentacle 'endless knot' inscribed on it. The five points of the pentacle represent Gawain's virtues, for he is 'faithful five ways and five times each' as a source of Gawain's strength. Sir Gawain and the Green Knight (Middle English: Sir Gawayn and þe Grene Knyȝt)[50] *is a late 14th-century Middle English chivalric romance. The five points of the pentangle, the poet adds, represent Gawain's virtues, for he is 'faithful five ways and five times each'. The poet goes on to list the ways in which Gawain is virtuous: all five of his senses are without fault; his five fingers never fail him, and he always remembers the five wounds of Christ on the cross (often said to correspond to the five senses). He derives his courage and strength from thinking on the five joys of the Virgin Mary. Cliffs notes (https://www.cliffsnotes.com/literature/) point out*[50] *that 'Medieval lists of the joys (joyful events) in the life of Mary varied in number — five, seven, and fifteen being most common), but these five are probably the Annunciation, the Nativity, the Resurrection, the Ascension, and the Assumption'. The fifth five is Gawain himself, who embodies the five moral virtues of the code of chivalry: 'fraunchyse' (generosity), 'felawschyp' (fellowship, fellow-feeling), 'clannes' (purity, chastity), 'cortaysye' (courtesy), and 'pité(Piety, or Love as in Corinthians 13:13).' Thus, the poet makes Gawain the epitome of perfection in knighthood through number symbolism.*[50,23] *Furthermore, A picture of the Virgin holding the infant Christ appears on the inside of Gawain's shield, reminding readers again of his chastity, his Christian devotion, and his status as Mary's knight.*[50,23] *(https://www.cliffsnotes.com/ literature/).*

Thus the Joys of Our Lady contributed through this Arthurian Poem /Legend to the Medieval Concept of the Ideal, Virtuous, Chivalrous Knight who was an Ideal Christian Man, who in particular has a devotion to Our Lady.

There are other Middle English texts about the Joys of Our Lady. Some Meditations on the Joys of Mary (http://d.lib.rochester.edu/teams/ text/saupe-middle-english-marian-lyrics-introduction) are reported in the article Middle English Marian Lyrics by Karen Saupe.[24] *She says that Meditation on Mary's 'joys' describe the events of Mary's life in terms of their spiritual significance for mankind, because it is suggested that her experiences describe the redemption of all humankind, from faithfulness on earth to reward in heaven*[24] *(http://d.lib.rochester.edu/teams/text /saupe-middle-english-marian-lyrics-introduction). There is a tendency to structure these meditations in fives, and Saupe explains this in terms of the five letters in the name 'Maria' and the five wounds Christ received on the cross, which is also a popular focus for meditation. This tendency produced variations*[24] *(http://d.lib.rochester.edu/teams/ text/ saupe-middle-english-marian-lyrics-introduction). In practice the Franciscan tradition of the five joys included the Annunciation, the Nativity, the Resurrection of Christ, the Ascension of Christ into heaven, and the Assumption of Mary into heaven, however sometimes the Epiphany (the visit of the Magi) is included and the Ascension omitted*[24] *(http://d.lib.rochester.edu/teams /text/saupe-middle-english-marian-lyrics-introduction). One version combined both traditions to describe six joys. It has been pointed out that the number five was 'neither peculiar to England nor absolute there'. A related tradition of describing the heavenly joys - often seven or even fifteen. Poems about the Joys of Mary tend to be quite formal rather than personal, but they recognise a complete sense of Mary's significance in the world*[24] *(http://d.lib.rochester.edu/ teams/text /saupe-middle-english-marian-lyrics-introduction).*

From 1300, there are 'chansons d'aventure' (a term suggested by E. K. Chambers) in English Literature which are poems which imitate a variety of secular, chivalric French songs. These 'chansons d'aventure' reached their peak in England in the late fourteenth and early fifteenth centuries[24] *(http://d.lib.rochester.edu/teams/text/saupe-middle-english-marian-lyrics-introduction). While in the secular, amorous form, the song usually tells of a despondent dreamer/speaker who goes out into the country, where he meets a woman and speaks with her, in the religious adaptations of the form, the dreamer usually discovers Mary or sometimes Christ, and by speaking with her or observing her, comes to a fuller understanding of his own circumstance*[24] *(http://d.lib.rochester.edu /teams /text/saupe-middle-english-marian-lyrics-introduction). In one case, the speaker thinks upon Mary's five joys as he rides, and his mind turns to the possibility eternal bliss. Thus the five joys of Mary were discussed in the fourteenth century in England.*

There are approximately fifty extant marian texts in the Norse language[25]*. (http://nordicwomens literature.net /article/rejoice-mary). These include poems on the Joys of Mary (Gaude Maria). Norse Marian poems could have been written in Norwegian monasteries.*[25] *In Sweden, poems to the Virgin Mother were written in both Latin and Swedish. Swedish-language Marian poetry influenced on its Danish counterpart through the Birgittine order.*[25] *The Swedish poems included, a long poem about 'Marias sju* *fröjder' (The Seven Joys of the Virgin Mary), one version of which is included in the devotional book Siælinna thröst (Solace for the Soul).*[25] *Approximately thirty Danish prayer books have survived from the Late Middle Ages. The Danish Marian songs in the prayer books are of three types: praise of the Virgin Mary, descriptions of Mary's sorrows, and descriptions of Mary's joys.*[25] *The Danish prayer book contains poems about the Virgin Mary's joys.*[25] *'Gaude virgo mater Christi' (Rejoice, Virgin Mother of Christ) is a lyric Latin tradition that can be traced far back in time and which has many variants. The 'Rejoice, Mary' poems were presumably originally written (and sung) for the Marian festivals. (http://nordic womens literature .net/article/rejoice-mary) 'Glæd dig Maria Guds moder, og fryd dig' (Rejoice, Mary, Mother of God, and Be Gladdened) is the longest and most discussed of the Danish joy-poems. There are four similar extant Swedish and one extant German poem. It is clear from the text that the first-person narrator is a woman.*[25] *This is nonetheless apparent in three of the poem's petitions: 'og hans tro tjenestekvinde dø' (fourth joy; and die His faithful servant woman), 'alsomhelst vil jeg din tjenestekvinde være' (sixth joy; most of all I want to be your servant woman), and 'giv mig min jomfrudom således at leve / at jeg må være uden din vrede' (seventh joy; give me my virginity thus to live / that I may be without your wrath). This last petition suggests that the woman who is speaking is young, and that an effort on her part is necessary to live in a state of virginity.*[25] *(http://nordicwomens literature.net /article/rejoice-mary). The seven joys discussed in the poem are: the Annunciation, the Visitation, the Nativity of Jesus, the Adoration of the Magi, the Passover pilgrimage to Jerusalem, the Finding in the Temple, the Assumption of Mary. Ernst Frandsen has suggested that the fifth and sixth joys should have been the Resurrection of Christ and the Ascension of Christ to Heaven.*[25] *(http://nordicwomens literature.net/article/rejoice-*

mary). A second poem is 'Rejoice, Mary, Mother of Christ', which consists of seven stanzas. It describes the usual Mary joys. The third Danish joy-poem, 'Glæd dig, Guds moder, jom¬fru Maria, fuld med ære' (Rejoice, Mother of God, Virgin Mary, full of glory), is not about joys which came to Mary, but about the joy she represents, so that the first-person voice asks to share in this 'eternal joy'.[25] (http://nordicwomens literature. net/article/rejoice-mary).

The website on Celtic Irish folklore[26] http://terreceltiche. altervista .org/seven-joys-mary/ quotes Irish versions of the Carol of 'The Seven Joys of Mary, which we have described. It quoted them as 'The seven consolations of the Virgin Mary', quoted in'Traditional Songs of the North of Ireland'[27] (Derek Bell & Liam Ó Conchubhair, Dublino: Wolfhound Press,1999), quoting popular tradition from Liam Ó Conchubhair (Rann na Feirste, Donegal) , while another version of the carol is quoted by Aoife Ní Fhearraigh. The songs of 'The seven Joys of Mary' were sang when poor women and widows went 'a-gooding' before Christmas.They would go from house to house begging charity to ask for money to buy good things to eat. They would carry with them a cup of wassail for drinking and 'two dolls, dressed the one to represent the Saviour, and the other the Virgin Mary', wearing garlands of evergreen,'and during the week before Christmas they are carried about the country by poor women, who, in return for their exhibition, expect a halfpenny, which it is considered as insuring the height of ill-luck to deny'. These Dolls are called Advent Images.[26,27]

In Spain, (http://deipraesidiofultus.blogspot.co.uk/2016/06/singing-gozos.html) the Gozos are sung.[28] In Spanish, gozos literally mean joys, expressions of gladness The singular of this word traces its origin to the

Latin gaudium.The Septem Gaudia Beatæ Mariæ Virginis in Latin, which are the Seven Joys of Mary in English, are called the Siete Gozos de María in Spanish. The gozos in Castilian are called goigs in Catalan or gojos in Valencian.[28]

The Llibre Vermell originated[51] *from the Marian Shrine and Benedictine Monastery of Montserrat. In it is the following poem on the Joys of Our Lady; Ballada dels goytxs de Nostre Dona en vulgar cathallan a ball redon.*

Los set goytxs recomptarem et devotament xantant
humilment saludarem la dolça verge Maria.
(We tell you of the seven joys and sing with devotion,
humbly greeting the sweet Virgin Mary.)

R: Ave Maria gracia plena - Hail Mary, full of grace,
Dominus tecum Virgo serena - The Lord may be with you, serene Virgin

Verge fos abans del part
pura e sens falliment
en lo part e prés lo part
sens negun corrumpiment.
Lo Fill de Déus Verge pia
de vós nasque verament.

Verge tres reys d'Orient
cavalcant amb gran coratge
al l'estrella precedent
vengren al vostré abitatge.
Offerint vos de gradatge Aur
et mirr' et encenç.

Verg'estant dolorosa
per la mort del Fill molt car
romangues tota joyosa
can lo vis resuscitar.
A vos maire piadosa
prima se volch demostrar.

Verge lo quint alegratge
que'n agues del fill molt car
estant al munt d'olivatge
al cel l'on vèès pujar.
On aurem tots alegratge
si per nos vos plau pregar.

Verge quan foren complitz
los dies de pentecosta amb vos
eren aunits los apostols et de costa.
Sobre tots sens nula costa
devallà l'espirit sant.

Verge'l derrer alegratge
que'n agues en aquest mon
vostre Fill amb coratge
vos munta al cel pregon.
On sots tots temps coronada
Regina perpetual.

The Joys listed are Annunciation, Nativity, Epiphany, Resurrection, Ascension, Pentecost, Assumption and Crowning in Heaven.[51]

Regarding Spain, we would add that the Joys of Our Lady are Commemorated in the LLuc sanctuary of Our Lady[51] *in Maiorca.At the end of the 14th century seven stone crosses presenting the seven Joys of the Virgin Mary were erected along the pilgrim's trail.There is also a Joys of the Virgin Stained Glass Window in the Cathedral of Maiorca. There are websites which document that the devotion of the Joys of Our Lady exists in the Philippines and Singapore.*

The Joys of Mary in Middle Europe - Czech Republic and Switzerland

Svatoňovice sedmipramenná 'Fountain' in the Czech Republic has been known since time immemorial[29] *(http://www.msvatonovicekostel.cz /informace) .People were being buried there during the Thirty Years War. On it on Sunday, October 27, 1715 peasant Vaclav Šrejber hung wooden box with a statue of the Virgin Mary. This grew into a shrine with a miraculous statue because of numerous healings and cherry trees which miraculously blossomed. The Statuette of the Virgin Mary of Seven Joys normally is venerated after the pilgrimage mass.*[29]

A chapel of Our Lady of the Seven Joys was founded in 1445 in the Swiss village of Sembrancher[30] *(http://www.wherewewalked.info/feasts/ 11-November/11-13.htm). The Virgin of Seven Joys was especially loved in this area of southern Switzerland after the Battle on the Planta when a large army of invading Savoiards was defeated on November 13, 1475.*[30] *As a result, Bishop Walter Supersaxo ordered 'that in the future the anniversary of this triumph will be a holiday, that the feast of the seven joys of the Holy Virgin will be celebrated throughout the diocese, and on that day the penitential psalms and collects for the dead will be read, after having read the names of those who took part in combat.' As a consequence, the feast of Our Lady of the Seven Joys was celebrated in November in the Diocese of Sion until 1915.*[30]

Le Sette Allegrezze Della Vergine in Old Italian Books

Le Sette Allegrezze Della Vergine are mentioned in several old books. Often the writers were not Carmelites, and yet they recommended devotion to the devotees of Our Lady of Mount Carmel, including confraternity members.

Giuseppe Maria Fornari and Francesco Vecchi, published in 1690[31] *'Anno memorabile de Carmelitani, nel quale a giorno per giorno si rappresentano le vite, l'opere, & i miracoli di S. Elia profeta loro patriarca, e di tutti li santi, e sante, beati, e venerabili eroi del suo sacro ordine della beatissima madre di Dio Maria Vergine del Monte Carmelo, ... ordinato, e disposto dal padre maestro Giuseppe Maria Fornari ... Tomo primo [-secondo]: Tomo secondo, che contiene li mesi di luglio, agosto, settembre, ottobre, nouembre, e decembre' In Volume 2 of this book, which translated is called 'Memorable year of the Carmelites, where day by day we describe the lives, works, and miracles of St. Elijah the Prophet their patriarch, and all the saints, and the holy, blessed, and venerable heroes of the sacred order of Blessed mother of God Virgin Mary of Mount Carmel, ... ordered, and discussed by the novice master Giuseppe Maria Fornari ....: second Volume, which contains the months of July there, August, September, October, nouembre and december', in this book Fornari refers to a 'Messa all* Altare della nostra Signora, con recitare le sue Litanie, e sette allegrezze' , that is, a mass said at the altar of Our Lady, with the recitation of her litanies and the seven Joys. They also refer repeatedly to the forty days indulgence to those of the scapular confraternity who daily say seven paters and aves in honour of the seven Joys of Our Lady.*

In 1698, Carlo Bartolomeo Piazza[32]*, Guillaume Vallet and Josè Maria Fonseca de Evora in ' Della pietà romana' describe the members of the confraternity of Our Lady of Mount Carmel as reciting every day as their custom seven Paters and Aves in honour of the Seven Joys of Our Lady which the Queen of Angels enjoys in Heaven and say that Pope Paul the fifth had given them 40 days indulgence whenever they said these.*

Giuseppe Navarra, an Oratorian, in 1746 published[33] *'Meditazioni per tutti i giorni dell'anno sopra gli Evangelj delle domeniche, e feste, con molte novene, settenarj, tridui, ed altri divoti esercizj. Proposte alla pietà de' fedeli dal padre Giuseppe Navarra sacerdote della congregazione dell'Oratorio di S. Filippo Neri. Divise in cinque tomi: Tomo terzo che contiene le meditazioni sulle feste ancor novissime de' santi, dal mese di gennaio fino all'ultimo di luglio' , in it he recommends 'Settenario per la Festa della Santissima Vergine Maria del`Carmine. Ne' sette giorni antecedenti la detta Solen~ nità mediterai le sette Allegrezze , le quali la ... di la sua Chiesa , 0 almeno l' Imma inedella Madonna Santissima del Carmelo' .Thus he recommends that in the seven days preceeding the feast of Our Lady of Mount Carmel one should meditate on the Seven Joys of Our Lady in church or at least in fromt of an image of Our Lady.*

In 1750, Sante Pascucci of the Order of Preachers, or Dominicans,[34] *in 'Esercizj di divozione per celebrare le feste della SS. Vergine Maria dati in luce del p.l.f. Sante Pascucci ... a beneficio de' principianti nella servitù di sì gran Signora' advised that in some part of the morning the devotees of Our Lady of Mount Carmel should say seven Pater and seven Ave in honour of the Seven Joys that the Blessed Virgin enjoys in Heaven.*

In 1761, Alessandro Diotallevi of the Company of Jesus,[35] *wrote in 'Trattenimenti spirituali per chi desidera d'avanzarsi nella servitù e* *nell'amore della Santissima Vergine. Dove si ragiona sopra le sue feste' wrote about her Sette Allegrezze`- Seven Joys enjoyed by her in Heaven showing her greatness and power, and linked these with Our Lady of Mount Carmel.*

The 'Istruzione per le sorelle strettamente aggregate alla venerabile Confraternita della Beata Vergine Maria del Monte Carmelo della città di Fermo' [36]*, dated 1826 is a book of instruction for the ladies enrolled in the confraternity. They are enjoyned to recite the Chaplet of the Joys, in the principle feasts of Our Lady.... 'e nelle sette Festività principali della Madonna recitare le Sette Allegrezze di MARIA SS'. Indulgence of 40 days is also mentioned to those members of the confraternity who recite seven paters and aves in honour of the seven joys of Our Lady.*

In 1838, Saint Alfonso Maria De Liguori[37]*, in '****Sacro Novenario per apparecchio alle Sette Iestività di Maria Santissima****' recommends reciting seven Pater ed Ave in honour of the Seven Joys of Our Lady 'delle sette Allegrezze di Maria' (as do devotees of Our Lady of Mount Carmel) and comments 'Sia benedetta la Santa, ed Immacolata Concezione della B. Vergine', that is, 'May the Blessed immaculate Conception of the Blessed Virgin be blessed'.*

'Le chiese d'Italia: dalla loro origine sino ai nostri giorni : opera, Volume 3' [38] *by G. Antonelli, 1845 deals with - Church buildings. It says 'nel 1605 vi fu istituita una confraternita sotto il titolo della Madonna delCarmine, e nel 1610 cominciò a nominarsi delle sette allegrezze'. Therfore it reports that a confraternity in honor of Our Lady of Mount Carmel founded in 1605 was later in 1610 renamed 'Of the Seven Joys'.*

In 1870, Gio. Battista Guidicini wrote[39] *in 'Cose notabili della Città di*

Bologna ossia Storia cronologica de'suoi stabili pubblici e privati' about a house with a dyer's workshop which belonged in 1715 to Giuseppe Nerti , and said that a portion of the duty [from using the canal] belonged to the Compagnia della Sette Allegrezze-Confrateriniy of the seven Joys of Our Lady which was based at the nearby Church of Our Lady, near which was the house where the Confraternità di S. Maria del Carmelo, which was later in 1640 called delle Sette Allegrezze (Of the Seven Joys) used to meet. This same Church was also mentioned[40] in 'Origine delle porte, strade, borghi, contrade, vie, vicoli, piazzuole, seliciate, piazze, e trebbi dell'inclita citta di Bologna con i loro nomi, pronomi, luoghi, confini, comercio, e cose notabili, che in detta città si ritrovano colla distinta narrazione di tutti i sotteranei, acquedotti de fiumi, o torrenti, Reno, Savena, Avesa, e luoghi dove cominciano ... opera non meno serie, che dilettevole di Ciro Lasarolla' by Carlo Salaroli, Carlo Pisarri, Gaetano Ferratini in 1743. They mention that this church , which is not far from San Martino Maggiore, is also called 'Degli Annegati'- of the Drowned ones.

It is clear from all these old books in the Italian Language that in the seventeenth, eighteenth and nineteenth centuries, the devotion of the Seven Joys and the attached indulgencies were well known in Carmelite Confraternities in Italy.

It is also clear from all the evidence we have found that the devotion of the Seven Joys of Our Lady was very common across Europe from medieval times.

References:

1 *R.T. Davies in Medieval English Lyrics nru 20 p 78 Faber London 1963*
2 *J. Adair''The Pilgrims Way' (Book Club Associates1978) p.58*
McCafferty (Whitefriars Dublin 1926) p168

---

3 *Royal Wills, Nichol p145*

4 *Sheppard 'The English Carmelites' p. 43 (Londra, Burns Oates 1943) 'A Meditation on the Nativity of Christ' , Choir of Saint John's College, Cambridge Argo Records 1968*

5 *saturdaychorale.com/2013/07/03/feature-thomas-tallis-1505-1585-gaude-gloriosa/*

6 *www.theartofpainting.be/AOM- Seven_Joys_and_seven_Sorrows.html*

7 *http://idlespeculations-terryprest.blogspot.co.uk/2011/12/seven-joys-of-mary.html*

8 *https://twitter.com/medievalpoc/status/627162284595539969René Dewil - L-Art tat-Tpinġija*

9 *www.theartofpainting.be/AOM-Seven_Joys_and_seven_Sorrows.htm*

10 *wikivisually.com/wiki/Bernard_van_Orley*

11 *http://www.sothebys.com/de/auctions/ecatalogue/lot.141.html/2011/ old-master-british-paintings-day-sale-l11034*

12 *http://www.artic.edu/aic/collections/artwork/4049*

13 *http://www.art.com/products/p11723137-sa-i1348641/master-of-the-holy-family-altarpiece-of-the-seven-joys-of-the-virgin-of-the-aturation -of-the-magi.htm*

14 *http://www.bridgeman-berlin.de/fr/asset/215399//*

15 *http://www.pbslearningmedia.org/resource/xir215399/altarpiece-of- is-seba 'joys-of-the-virg-ger-xir215399 /*

16 *http://www.abc.net.au/radionational/programs/booksandarts/rothschild/ 6670130*

17 *http://www.medievalists.net/2015/05/28/rothschild-prayer-book -come-to-australia /*

18 *http://www.thedigitalwalters.org/Data/WaltersManuscripts/html/W 202/description.html*

19 *Http://www.bl.uk/manuscripts/FullDisplay.aspx?ref=Add_MS_28962*

---

20 *https://www.reading.ac.uk/GCMS/Book-of-Hours/gcms-resources-book-of-hours.home.aspx*
21 *Les XV. Joyes Notre Dame rims de Christine de Pizan 2008 p.255-277*
22 *http://crm.revues.org/ Jean-François Kosta-Théfaine*
23 *https://www.cliffsnotes.com/literature/*
24 *http://d.lib.rochester.edu/teams/text/saupe-middle-english-marian-lYrics-introduzzjoni*
25 *http://nordicwomensliterature.net/article/rejoice-mary*
26 *http://terreceltiche.altervista.org/seven-joys-mary/*
27 *'Traditional Songs of the North of Ireland' (Derek Bell & Liam Ó Conchubhair, Dublino: Wolfhound Press, 1999*
28 *http://deipraesidiofultus.blogspot.co.uk/2016/06/singing-gozos.html*
29 *http://www.msvatonovicekostel.cz/informace*
30 *http://www.wherewewalked.info/feasts/11-November/11-13.htm*
31 *Giuseppe Maria Fornari , Francesco Vecchi, 'Anno memorabile de Carmelitani, nel quale a giorno per giorno si représentano le vite, l'opere, & i miracoli di S. Elia profeta loro patriarca, u ta 'tutti li santi, e sante , beati, e venerabili eroi del suo sacro ordine della beatissima madre di Dio Maria Vergine del Monte Carmelo" 1690*
32 *Carlo Bartolomeo Piazza, Guillaume Vallet u Josè Maria Fonseca de Evora f''Della pietà romana' 1698*
33 *Giuseppe Navarra, 'Meditazioni per tutti i giorni dell'anno sopra gli Evangelj delle domeniche, e feste, con molte novene, settenarj, tridui, ed altri divoti esercizj. Proposte alla pietà de 'fedeli dal padre Giuseppe Navarra sacerdote della congregazione dell'Oratorio di S. Filippo Neri. Divise in cinque tomi: Tomo terzo che contiene le meditazioni sulle feste ancor novissime de' santi, dal mese di gennaio fino all'ultimo di luglio" 1746*
34 *Sante Pascucci of he Order of Preachers or the Dominicans 'Esercizjdi*

---

di Divozione per celebrare le Feste della SS'. Vergine Maria dati in luce del p.l.f. Sante Pascucci a beneficio de' principianti nella servitù di sì gran Signora''1750

35 *Alessandro Diotallevi SJ , 'Trattenimenti spirituali per chi desidera d'avanzarsi nella servitù e nell'amore della Santissima Vergine'. Dove si ragiona sopra le sue feste'1761*

36 *'Istruzione per le sorelle strettamente aggregata alla venerabile Confraternita della Beata Vergine Maria del Monte Carmelo della città di Fermo', 1826*

37 *San Alfonso Maria De Liguori, ''Sacro Novenario per apparecchio alle Sette Iestività di Maria Santissima' 1838*

38 *G. Antonelli, 'Le chiese d'Italia: dalla loro origine sino ai nostri giorni: opera, Volume 3' , 1845*

39 *Gio. Battista Guidicini 'Cose notabili della Città di Bologna ossia Storia cronologica de'suoi stabili pubblici e privati' 1870*

40 *Carlo Salaroli, Carlo Pisarri, Gaetano Ferratini 'Origini tad-delle porte, strade, borghi, contrade, vie, vicoli, piazzuole, seliciate, piazze, e trebbi dell'inclita citta di Bologna b'maromi nomi, pronomi, luoghi, confini, comercio, e cose notabili, che in detta città si ritrovano colla distinta narrazione di tutti i sotteranei, acquedotti de fiumi, o torrenti, Reno, Savena, Avesa, e luoghi dove cominciano ... opera non meno serie, che dilettevole di Ciro Lasarolla 1743.*

41 *McCaffery (Whitefriars Dublin 1926) p168.*

42 *'A Meditation on Christ's Nativity' Choir of St. John's College, Cambridge, Argo Records 1968.*

43 *Waltz B. Remembering the Old Songs: The Joys of Mary Inside Bluegrass, March 1999 https://www/lizlyle.Iofgrens.org/RmOISngs/RTOS-JoysMary.html.*

44 *https//mainlynorfolk.info/wyndham-read/songs/thesevenjoysofmary.html*
45 *THE SEVEN JOYS OF MARY Alternate Title:The Very First Joy That Mary Had For Christmas. Version 1 Words and Music: Traditional Source: Henry Ramsden Bramley and John Stainer, Christmas Carols New and Old, First Series (London: Novello, Ewer & Co., 1871), Carol No. 12 https://www.hymnsandcarolsofchristmas.com/Hymns_and_Carols/seven_joys_of_mary.htm*
46 *https://en.wikipedia.org/wiki/the_Seven_Joys_of_Mary(carol)*
47 *https://musee-unterlinden.com/en/oeuvres/alterpiece-of-the-dominicans/*
48 *//www.bridgemanimages.com/en-US/master-of-the-holy-family/altar piece-of-the-seven-joy-of-the-virgin-depicting-the-adoration-of-the-magi-the-presentation-in/oil-on-panel/asset/215399*
49 *http://www.gla. ac. uk/services/specialcollections/collectionsaz/manu scriptsunnamedcollections/*
50 *Middle English: Sir Gawayn and be Grene Knyzt https://quod.lib.umich.edu/c/cmme/Gawain?rgn=main;view=fulltext*
51 *Llibre Vermell de Montserratt https://en.wikipedia.org/wiki/Libre _Vermell_de_Montserrat*
52 *https://www.lluc.net/es/?utm_source=google&utm_medium=organic &utm_campaign=GMB&utm_content=HospederiadeLluc*

THIRTY SEVEN

Is This a Devotion Proper to the Carmelites?

A) A Devotion proper to the Carmelites?

From what we have said it is clear that it was not, nor could it be, the Carmelites who began this devotion to the seven Joys of Our Lady, since it had begun in the eleventh century, before the Carmelite Order had even been founded. It is true that at that time there were only five joys, but it is also true that by the twelfth century these had already increased by two Joys, to seven.

If it is true that Saint Thomas spread this devotion as much as he could, then we must state that this particular devotion had already been spreading its roots among the faithful by the year 1170. It was in this year that he died a martyr, after he had spent six years in exile in France.[13]

Therefore, we cannot agree with the view of Bagnari that the devotion of the seven joys of Our Lady is a devotion proper to the Carmelites as if they themselves had invented it.[14] Perhaps Vella is closer to the truth when he says that 'Saint Thomas had thought this devotion to everyone, but in a particular way it became a devotion proper to the Carmelites.'[15]

Nor were the Carmelites the only ones who embraced this devotion. The seven Holy Founders of the order of the Servants of Mary had the habit of, every Saturday, after the singing of the Salve

Regina, making a remembrance of the seven joys of Our Lady. This devotion began among them in 1241 and was then prescribed to their novices.[16]

One should also mention the Franciscan Friars Minor. Because of their devotion to the Joys of Our Lady, Pope John XXII and Pope Pius X gave them some indulgences.[17]

However, it was the name of the Carmelites which remained most well-known and linked with this particular devotion to the Blessed Virgin Mary. So now, let us discuss when they first began to practice this devotion.

B) The Antiquity of the Devotion of the Joys of Our Lady in Carmel

In 1711, Andrea Mastelloni wrote that he had often asked himself why the Carmelites celebrate the Seven Joys of Our Lady. Since he was never able to establish when this devotion entered the Carmelite Order, he decided that it must be very ancient.[18]

More than a hundred years earlier, Egidio Leoindelicato had come to the same conclusion. In 1600 he gives a list of the seven Joys by which the Carmelites honour Our Lady on the Wednesdays between Easter and Pentecost, and he calls it 'an ancient and holy devotion' in Carmel.[19]

We have many witnesses that in the sixteenth century this devotion was widespread in Carmel. In 1597, Camillo Di Ausilio published in Naples a summary of the antiquities of the Carmelite Order.

Among other things, he mentioned the seven Joys of Our Lady, to which the Carmelite Friars had devotion.[20] The evidence of Nikola Aurifico Bonfigli is earlier. In 1591, he published in Florence a book about the indulgences, privileges and graces given by the Popes to the Order. He adds the obligations and good works which one must carry out to receive them. He recommends to the devotees of the Scapular who wish to enjoy the Sabbatine Privilege but are unable to fulfil the obligations required, he advises to say Seven Our Fathers and Seven Hail Marys in honour of the Seven Joys of Our Lady; a change which, he writes, had been suggested by the General Chapter of Piacenza (1575).[21]

Lastly, one must mention the Constitution of the Carmelite Congregation of Mantua. This was written in 1540, and it orders the members of this Congregation that, during the Liturgy of the Hours, after the Office of Readings (Matins), the hymn 'Gaude Virgo Mater Christi' should be sung, which, as we have seen, contains the seven main Joys of Our Lady. Furthermore, it orders that on feasts of double class the whole antiphon 'Gaude flore virginalis' should be sung.[22]

However, did the Devotion to the Joys exist in Carmel before the sixteenth century? In a manuscript codex of the fourteenth century we find a Carmelite breviary which clearly mentions the seven Joys of Our Lady. It includes 211 pages and is divided into two. According to antiquarians, the first part, up to page 153, is of the first half of the fourteenth century. The second part, page 153-211, is of the last twenty-five years of the fourteenth century. The codex was written in France.[23]

We have an older example of this devotion from the Carmelites of the Province of Lombardy. They had a convent in Verona which according to Mariano Ventimiglia was founded in 1300.[24] John Baptist Lezana is more precise. He writes that, from a report on the Convents of Italy, which had been produced on the orders of Innocent X, that this convent was already in existence in 1300, although it is unknown exactly when it was founded.[25] In a manuscript about the antiquities of the Carmelites in Verona, kept in the Municipal Archives of this Town, we find that in 1230, these religious people had a church there. After many years, someone gave them a house, where they then began to build a church dedicated to the Annunciation, which was consecrated in 1316 by Fr, Tebalto, the bishop of Verona.[26]

The manuscript dates from 1786, and it appears that the author did not know the history of this church well. From a careful study by Alfonso Rossi, we learn that, in 1316, the Carmelites, who had not been long in Verona, dedicated their church to Saint Thomas Becket. Later, in 1351, bishop Pietro della Scala gave them some houses, which had been left by Fieramonte Gazzeri, and they built, beside the other church, one in honour to the Annunciation, Finally, in the fifteenth century, the two churches were united into one, which exists till today, and, in 1504, they consecrated its main altar to Our Lady under the title of the Annunciation. Nonetheless, the people continued to use the old title of Saint Thomas.[27]

Therefore, in the first years of the fourteenth century, the Carmelites were in Verona, and they dedicated their first convent and first church to Saint Thomas Becket. Why did they do this? What relationship did they have with this English Saint? Indeed, it is well known that Carmelites usually dedicate their churches to Our Lady, and not to Saints.

It appears that the reason is to be found in the devotion to the seven Joys of Our Lady, for which this saint was famous, and they could justify their break with usual custom because this devotion had a strong relationship to the other devotion to Our Lady of Mount Carmel. With this devotion the Carmelites usually honoured Mary, the Lady of and Mother of Carmel.

According to Lezana, in this church there was a very revered image of Our Lady.[28] If it were not that he adds that it was an image of which Christofero Silvestrani (Berenzone) often spoke, one would assume that this image was one of Our Lady of Joy or of the Annunciation. However, the image which Silvestrani mentions, and even shows a picture of, is one of Our Lady of Sorrows, known as 'La Madonna dello Spasimo.' However, no one can suggest that the Carmelites of Verona did not have a great devotion to the seven Joys of Our Lady, since this was very strong- to the extent that it still is alive today. Although the convent and church is now in the hands of the Diocesian Clergy, every Wednesday, a service is still held in honour of the Joys of Our Lady, and linked with the devotion to Our Lady of Mount Carmel.

We will quote Silvano Brunelli, once the Parish Priest of this Church. In 1937, he issued a book called 'The devotion of the seven joys of the Blessed (Virgin) Mary which are said every Wednesday in the church of Saint Thomas of Canterbury, Verona'.[30] He begins the book with a brief historical sketch about the devotion to Our Lady of Mount Carmel and the spiritual advantages of those who are enrolled in the Scapular. He then mentions the Marian Mysteries or seven occasions of Joy for Mary which are commemorated every Wednesday in his Church. He ends with a description of what happens on Wednesdays, and where the function in honour of the Joys takes place. It takes place on the altar of Our Lady of Mount Carmel. The prayer (kurunella) of the seven Joys of Our Lady is recited, with a Pater, Ave and Gloria after each verse (which commemorates one Joy) and finally, the celebrant says the 'oremus' of Our Lady of Mount Carmel.[31]

Here we give the view of Bagnari as to whether the devotion to the seven Joys of Mary existed in Carmel before the fourteenth century. In 1728, he wrote on the origins of this devotion [32] and he proposed the theory that it has existed among the Carmelites from the time they first migrated to Europe, and more specifically when they began to live in England.[33]

According to Vincent of Beauvais (+1264), the Carmelites migrated to Europe in 1238.[34] Joachim Smet, the historian of the Order clarifies that this is only an approximate date,[35] Gava and Coan specify that this date refers to a general and official migration and does not refer to other private migrations.[36] Hence they argue that before 1238 there had been some other private migrations.[37]

It is possible that Lezana was referring to a private migration when he says that the Carmelite Hermits migrated to England in 1212.[38] Otherwise, he has made a mistake, and caused others to make the same mistake, including Bagniari. Bagniari, on the authority of Lezana, wrote that the Carmelites migrated to England in 1212, that is 41 years after the death of Saint Thomas Becket.[39] Today the date of the Carmelites' official migration to England is historically certain: it is the year 1242. They were brought to Hulme by Sir William Vescy and to Aylesford by Sir Richard Grey of Condor.[40]

Finally, Bagniari argues by sophistry that since this devotion has some relation with the Carmelite tradition before the migration[41] and, since Carmel belongs entirely to Mary, therefore, when the Carmelites arrived in England and found the devotion which Saint Thomas Becket had, they inevitably imitated this Saint by promoting the devotion to the Seven Joys of Our Lady.[42]

C) Why Carmel embraced the Devotion of the Joys of Our Lady

Whenever it was that this devotion entered Carmel, the main reason why it was promoted by the Carmelites is linked with the Carmelite Tradition of the small cloud seen by the Prophet Saint Elias. (3 Kings 18, 42-45)

In 1627, Pier Thomas Saraceni recounts that he used to often hear some Carmelite Religious say that Saint Bertold, standing on Mount Carmel, used to salute seven times a day, with his face to the ground, the Mediterranean Sea. He would use the salutation of the Angel to Mary 'Hail Mary'. When he made this salutation, he was understood to be remembering that little cloud which Elias saw rising from the sea, after for seven times he had sent his servant to look and find out if there was anything to see. In that cloud, the prophet foresaw the future incarnation of Christ. Because of this, the Carmelites of Saraceni's time used, at every hour of the divine Office, to kneel down and sing the angel's salutation with the greatest devotion.[43]

About thirty years later, (1656) we find Lezana quoting Saraceni in order to explain the development of this custom of the 'Hail Mary' among the Carmelites. He notes that in the rubrics of the Roman Breviary it is not required that the Hail Mary' should always be said after every canonical hour. However, it is the practice of the Carmelites to say this antiphon, usually on their knees, both before and after each canonical hour, together with the 'Hail Holy Queen'. This suggests that in this repetition of these seven 'Hail Marys' we have a remembrance within the Carmelite Order of Mary, who Elias saw within that cloud after he had sent his servant up the mountain seven times.[44]

Daniel of the Virgin Mary is more resolute. In his view, it is certain that it was both because of the Cloud seen by Elias and because of the custom of Saint Bertold that within Carmel there is the custom of saying both the 'Hail Mary ' and the 'Salve Regina' in each of the canonical hours.[45]

Mastelloni is equally certain, although he speaks of only one antiphon: the 'Salve Regina'. However, we are particularly interested here in his conclusion that even the devotion of the seven Joys of Mary was related, for the Carmelites, to the custom of Saint Bertold and thence to the cloud seen by Saint Elias.[46] As far as we know, this Neapolitan author was the first to suggest this theory. [47]

He was followed by Bagniari, who added another custom of the early Carmelites; because Elias saw the cloud after seven attempts, the early Carmelites used to gather together seven times a day in order to Honour the Virgin Mary, of whom the cloud was a type or figure.[48]

This last assertion is quite arbitrary, lacking any document or proof. Therefore it is not surprising that it was never repeated, and had no impact on Carmelite Tradition or on the writers of the Order. On the other hand, although Mastelloni does not give any proof of what he says, it is well known that many other Carmelite writers, both before and after him, have insisted that the devotion of the Seven Joys of Our Lady is part of the ordinary cult with which Carmel honours Mary. Among others, we can mention Leoindelicato, Maruggi, Dal Buono, Bagniari, and Di Giovanni.[49] They all agree that the devotion of the Joys is the Devotion with which the Carmelites honour Our Lady of Mount Carmel. Therefore, Valerio Hoppenbrouwers, an author of our time, is right to observe that a characteristic of the devotion of the Joys of Our Lady is that it is often linked with the other devotion to Our Lady of Mount Carmel.[50]

Notes

13 *See Il-liturgija tas-Sigħat skond ir-rit Ruman Kummissjoni Liturgika għall-Provinċja Ekklesiastika Maltija, Malta, 1976, p.1990.*

14 *BAGNARI, Divozioni: 'Come poi questa divozione ritrovasi fra Carmelitani, che come propria si sostiene' (p.26); 'Quindi e, che per queste, ed alter ragioni si sostiene quasi come propria, ed originate da Carmelitani una tale divozione' (p.28).*

15 *Vella id-devot, ... pp.288-289.*

---

16 *See Roschini., La Madonna, p.414: PHILIP SGAMAITA Chronica, in Mon. Ord. Serv. B.V.M., t.XVI, p.153s.:Liber Officiorum Ordinis ServorumB.V.M.1629, p.164*

17 *See Roschini., La Madonna, p.414*

18 *ANDREA MASTELLONI, O.Carm., Trattamenti Spirituali, part.4, Napoli, 1711, p.232:'Piu volte ho fatto riflessione fra me medesimo, perché noi Carmelitani celebriamo l'Allegrezze della Madonna. Non ritrovando memoria da che tempo sia stata introdotta questa divotione nell'Ordine Nostro, io la stimo antica'.cfr.ib., part.1, Napoli, 1709, p.80.*

19 *EGIDIO LEOINDELICATO, O.Carm.,Giardino Carmelitano,Palermo, 1600, p.218: 'Modo da dirsi le seguenti orationi, quali per antica consuetudine e per pia divotione dir si sogliono alla sacratissima Madre del Signore Maria Vergine del Monte Carmelo nei sette Mercordi dopo Pasqua di Resurretione'.*

20 *See CAMILLO DI AUSILIO, O.Carm., Sommario dell'antichissima origine della Religione Carmelitana (Napoli, 1597; Verona, 1601; Venetia, 1603). In this final edition, which is the one we used, 'Le Sette Allegrezze della Gloriosa Vergine Maria Madre d'Iddio' are in pp.306-308.*

21 *See NICOLO AURIFICO BONFIGLI, O. Carm., Sommario delle grazie, privilegii et indulgenze concesse da molti Sommi Pontefici, ..alla religion carmelitana, Firenze, 1591, p.28.*

22 *Costitutiones, et statute ord.ac obs.Carmelitarum Mantuan. Congregationis, Bononiae, 1540, cap.III, p.6, n.7:'Cantetur laus illa....post Matutinas, Gaude Virgo Mater Christi. In totis duplicibus, 'Gaude flore virginalis' usq.in finem, decantetur'.*

23 *See AUGUSTINUS FORCADELL, O.Carm, Commemoratio solemnis beatae Mariae Virginis de Monte Carmelo, Romae, 1951, pp.202-207. mainly p.204.*

24 *See MARIANO VENTIMIGLIA, O.Carm., Il sacro Carmelo italiano*

(Napoli 1779), quoted by GIOVANNI GAVA-ANGELO COAN, O. Carm., Carmelo: profile, storia, uomini e cose, Roma, 1951, p.278, n.19.This convent is listed as part of the Carmelite Province of Venice because, although originally in the province of Lombardy, it had already come under the jurisdiction of the province of Venice.

25 *JOHN BAPTIST DE LEZANA, O.Carm., Annales sacri prophetici et eliani ordinis beatissimae Virginis Mariae de monte Carmeli, tom.4, Romae, 1656, p.478: 'Veronense etiam Coenobium in ea nobilissima civitatesitum, hoc anno 1300 existitisse, etsi a quo tempore sui exordia desumpserit, haud certum sit, ex quibusdam Instrumentis, quae in eo conservantr, habetur. Sic enim ex relatione Conventuum Italiae iussu Innocentij Decimi facta, elicimus'.*

26 *ALFONSO MARIA ROSSI, O.Carm., I Carmelitani a Verona. In Rivista Storica Carmelitana, Aprile-Settembre 1931, p.54: 'Alcuni fascicoli manoscritti che si trovano nell'Archivio municipal Veronese, I piu interessanti sono i seguenti, ...2. Libro contenente le copie spedite all'Ecc.mo Mag.to-1786, Priore F. Gerol.Fracastor –In questo libro, cartaceo e assai chiaro, si leggono queste parole che alludono all'antichità dei Carmelitani in Verona. '......e detti Padri furono posti in possesso di quella (chiesa) circa l'anno 1230, e dopo alquanti anni ebbero in dono alcun casa, ...nel qual luogo detti Padri diedero principio ad una chiesa dedicate alla B.V. Annunziata, come si vede dalla confermazione di Pietro Vescovo di Verona, ...così nel 1316 fu questa chiesa de Carmelitani consacrata dal Vescovo di Verona Fr. Thebaldo'.*

27 *ROSSI, O.Carm., I Carmelitani a Verona pp.51-52: 'Nel 1316 i PP. Carmelitani, che da poco avevano preso stanza in Verona, dedicarono una chiesa in onore di S. Tommaso Arciv. E martire di Cantorbery, Nel 1351, avuta dal Vescovo Pietro della Scala l'investitura di certe case lasciate da Fieramonte Gazzeri, eressero presso alla prima una seconda chiesa dell'An-*

---

nunziata, Nel secolo XV le due chiese vennero sostituite con l'attuale e nel 1449 si era messo mano alla facciata.....Nel 1504 si consacrò l'altar maggiore all'Annunziata, ma il popolo conserve il titolo vecchio di S.Tommaso'.

28 *LEZANA. Annales sacri, tom.4, p.478: 'Titulus Ecclesiae est S. Thomae Cantuariensis; et in ea devotissima Imago Sanctissimae Deiparae, quam saepius commemorate Christophorus Silvestranus, vir doctissimus, eius Conventus Alumnus'.*

29 *The picture of this image of Our Lady of Sorrows is in the last page of his book: Lettioni sopra il* Magnificat *(Verona 1593), For comments about this pictures see ROSSI, I Carmelitani a Verona pp.53; VALERIUS HOPPENBROUWERS, O.Carm.,Devotio mariana in ordine fratrum b.m.v.de monte Carmelo a medio saeculo XVI usque ad finem saeculi XIX, Romae, 1960, p.282.*

30 *SILVANO BRUNELLI, Devozione delle Sette Allegrezze di Maria Santissima che si recitano ogni Mercoledì alla sera nella Chiesa di S.Tommaso Cantuariense in Verona, Verona, 1937.*

31 *BRUNELLI, Devozione......, pp.9-27.*

32 *BAGNARI, Divozioni, p.21: 'Per commune sodisfazione de'devoti di Maria Vergine, ho giudicato ancora essere mio preciso debito significar loro d'onde abbia avuto origine la divozione delle di Lei sette Allegrezze, che si dicono unite alli sette Pater e Ave in tutte le chiese de'Carmelitani'.*

33 *BAGNARI, ib.,p.27s,: 'Viene poi in oggi sempre piu coltivata questa divozione colle sette Allegrezze, che in tutte le chiese de'Carmelitani si recitano, attesoche essendosi portati in Inghilterra dal Monte Carmelo i nostri Religiosi, ...si può dire per indubitato, che in quel tempo si stabilise ancora lo ossequiare Maria, come si fa ora colle sue sette Allegrezze.'*

34 *See Biliotheca mundi (4v.,Doui, 1624),IV, 1275, quoted by JOACHIM SMET, O.Carm.,The Carmelites:a history of the brothers of Our Lady of Mount Carmel, ca.1200 until the Council of Trent,(s.1.),Private Printing, 1975, p.12.*

---

35 *SMET, The Carmelites..., p.12:'This date need not be regarded as anything more than approximate'.*
36 *GAVA-COAN, Carmelo, pp.99-100:'Senza dubbio, secondo il parere degli storici dell'Ordine e di scrittori estranei, l'anno delle emigrazioni generali, o per così dire ufficiali, fu il 1238: questo non esclude altre emigrazioni, piu o meno private, anteriori a questa data.'*
37 *GAVA-COAN, ib.....,pp.100:'altre emigrazioni, piu o meno private, anteriori a questa data.....dobbiamo supporle se vogliamo spiegare la controversia sorta in Europa sulla legittimita canonica dell'ordine prima del famoso Concilio Lateranense.....Seguendo queste supposizioni, percio, potremmo già delimitare gli estremi della prima emigrazione; cioe tra il 1215-anno del Concilio Later-anense IV-e il 1238'.*
38 *LEZANA. Annales sacri, tom.4, p.196: 'Ann Christi 1212, ...Eoenim tempore, cum aliqui ex Carmeli Eremitis in Angliam venissent'. He quotes in favour of this date John Bale and Thomas Bradley (Scropus).*
39 *BAGNARI, Divozioni, p.27:'....essendosi portati in Ingilterra dal Monte Carmelo li nostri Religiosi l'anno 1212 (Lezana Annal.), che vale a dire 41 anni dopo la morte di S.Tommaso Cantoariense, che l'anno 1171 fu martirizato(lec.6 brev.)'.*
40 *SMET, The Carmelites..., p.1213:'The Carmelites were brought to Hulne by Sir William Vescy and to Aylesford by Sir Richard Grey of Condor in 1242...... 'The Carmelites were brought into the Royal presence by their noble patrons around Christmas and were granted permission to remain in England.'*
41 *For this Carmelite Tradition, see notes 43-47.*
42 *BAGNARI, Divozioni, p.27: 'Essendosi portati in Inghilterra dal Monte Carmelo li nostril Religiosi, ..., ben si può concludere, che non mancassero loro d'imitare un'anima così grande, e di molto infer-vorita nello ossequiare la Vergine, tanto piu che loro erano d'una Religione*

specialmente a Maria dedicate. E siccome il S. Martire onorava la Madre di Dio....cosi Loro, e per alludere alli sette sopra accennati saluti fatti a Maria Vergine dal Santo Padre Elia, e praticati da San Bertoldo, come pure posti in perfetta osservanza da tutti que' Religiosi del Monte Carmelo, che sette volte al giorno adduvansi in chiesa ad ossequiare Maria Santissima, si puo dire per indubitato, che in quel tempo si stabilisse ancora lo ossequiare Maria, come si fa' ora, colle sue sette Allegrezze.'

43 *PETRUS THOMAS SARACENI.O.Carm., Menologium Carmelitarum, Bononiae, 1627, p.233: 'Quosdam ex nostris saepius audivimus referents, hunc sanctum virum (Bertoldum) in praerputis Carmeli montis, septies quotidie reclinatus. Mediterraneum Mare Angelico Ave, religioso usu consalutare, in illius Nubeculae memoriam, quam Dux noster Elias, e marinis fluctibus ascendentem septima vice conspexit, future Incarnationis sacrum prognosticon. Imo his quoque temporibus, usu publice venit ut universi Ordinis nostri fratres in sing(ulis) Canon(cis) horis flexis genibus Canticum illud mellifluum, maximo devotionis ardore recitare consuescant'.*

44 *LEZANA. Annales sacri, tom.4, p.31, n.4: 'Pariter circa illud quod praedictus Petrus Saracenus relato loco dixit de Salutatione Angelica septies quotidie a B. Bertoldo replicate ad homorem Virginis, cuius nubecula illa prognosticon fuit, illud animad-vertendum, quod cum iuxta rubricas Breviarij Romani in fine Canonicarum horarum Angelica salutatio non simper repetatur, usu tamen nostrae Religionis, ne dum in ipsarum principio, sed in fine quoque singularum repetitur, et saepius flexis genibus, cum Antiphona Salve Regina. Quo inni videtur septiplici hac Angelicea salutationis reiteratione, septem illius vincibus a puero Eliae quasi interpellatae Virginis memoriam voluisse recolere'.*

45 *DANIEL A VIRGINE MARIA, O.Carm., Vinea Carmeli, Antuerpiae, 1662. P.762, n.1311:'S. Bertholdus....eo loco Carmeli, ubi S.Elias*

Nubeculam typo Virginis Deiparae insignem conspexit, quotidie septies Angelicam salutationem replicabat, Deinde mos ille per totum Ordinem inolevit, ut in septem horis Canonicis cum salutatione Angelica reiteretur quoque Salve Regina'.

46 *MASTELLONI, Trattenimenti Spirituali, part, 1 (Napoli 1709),p.80: Una tale divotione riconosce il principio da questo nostro Santo Padre Generale (Bertoldi di Malefaida), quale ogni giorno sette volte saliva nell'alto del Monte Carmelo, in quel luogo, in cui il Profeta nostro Patriarca (Elia) adorato haveva la Virgine Madre in figura, e prostrato per terra profondamente adoravalo. Io sono di parere, che dalla sua si originasse la nostra divotione, che dura fin'al presente......: la memoria delle sue sette Allegrezze'. In part.4 (Napoli 1711),p.232, he again writes: '......questa divotione nell'Ordine nostro, io la stimo antica, ed originaria per un' imitatione delle Sette Adorationi fatte da Elia Profeta, quando vide sorger dal Mare la Nuvoletta che figuravala, e dalla gran pioggia che da lei derivossi, non solo indicato il Parto Vergineo, ma anco le sue principali Allegrezze.'*

47 *See HOPPENBROUWERS, Devotio mariana, p.280.*

48 *BAGNARI, Divozioni, p.26s:'Come poi questa divotione ritrovasi fra Carmelitani...., ve ne sono moltissime ragioni, e fra le altre una si e, che colla divozione delle sette Allegrezze, si viene ad alludere alle sette adorazioni, che il Padre S. Elia offri a Maria Vergine raffigurata in quella Nuvola, che sortiva dal Mare; per il di cui motive, li primi Religiosi del Monte Carmelo si radunavano anch'essi sette volte al giorno ad ossequiare Maria Vergine'.*

49 *LEOINDELICATO, Giardino Carmelitano, p.218:'Modo da dirsi le seguenti orationi, quail per antica consuetudine, e pia devotione dir si sogliono alla sacratissima Madre del Signore Maria Vergine del Monte Carmelo....Le quail sono le seuenti, cioe: 'Prima Allegrezza...'*

ELIA MARUGGI O.Carm.,Tesoro spiritual della religion della gloriosa Vergine del Carmelo, Catania 1624, p.150:'....soglino li devote della B. Vergine del Carmine visitor le sue chiese, e contenplar le sette Allegrezze della B. Vergine'.
DAL BUONO, Divozione, 'Divozione de' sette mercoledì del Carmine in ossequio di Maria Vergine Madre di Dio riverita sotto il titolo delle sette Allegrezze ' (the entire title of the book), ...see also p.5.
BAGNARI, Divozioni, 'Divozioni che si praticano....in onore di Nostra Signora del Carmine(book title), ...Sette Allegrezze di Maria Vergine, che si recitano tutti li Mercoledi da divoti del Carmine...'
CIRILLO DI GIOVANNI, O.Carm., Vita di Sant'Elia Profeta, Palermo, 1743, p.56:'Le Sette Allegrezze che si recitano in onore di Maria Vergine del Carmine'.
50 *HOPPENBROUWERS, Devotio mariana, p.280: 'Peculiare huius devotionis est, quod saepe connectitur cum cultu beatae Mariae Virginis de monte Carmelo, imo iuxta plures auctores, praesertim italos pertinent ad cultum ordinarium, quo Mater Carmeli honourari solet'.*

THIRTY EIGHT

The Golden Age of the Devotion of the Joys of Our Lady in Carmel (XVII and XVIII centuries)

FROM THE DOCUMENTS WHICH WE HAVE MENTIONED IT IS CLEAR that the devotion of the Seven Joys of Our Lady has been in use among the Carmelites from at least the beginning of the fourteenth century. We cannot be certain if it existed in Carmel earlier, from the time that the Carmelites first came to England. As far as we know, only Bagnari is of this view, but his argument is not certain, as it is based on a supposition which is not certain.[51]

It seems that, throughout the fourteenth and fifteenth centuries, this devotion had begun to take firm root within Carmel, to the extent that, by the middle of the sixteenth century it was definitely being practiced by the 38 convents of the Mantuan Congregation- 31 convents of friars and 7 of nuns.[52] By the Constitution of 1540, they were obliged to sing the Hymn 'Gaude Virgo Mater Christi' every day, and in certain feasts, also the antiphon 'Gaude flore virginalis'[53]

Later (1575) we find that the General Chapter recommended this devotion[54], while Bonfigli (1591) and Di Ausilio (1597) witnessed its practice within the Carmelite Order.[55]

Let us now discuss the Golden Age of this devotion in Carmel, that is when it was at its peak, particularly within the Italian Provinces. This period includes the seventeenth century as well as a large part of the eighteenth century. We will simply discuss facts which were either interesting or important.

(i)Provinces and Convents

Leoindelicato opens the seventeenth century with a list of Joys of Our Lady which are celebrated in his province of Sant'Angelo in Sicily, on the first seven Wednesdays after Easter[56]. If these were being celebrated by all the churches of the Province, then we can say that about 50 convents were celebrating this devotion.[57]

Two years afterwards (1602), the Congregation of Mantua renewed the Constitution of 1540, which ordered the Carmelites to sing the hymn 'Gaude Virgo Mater Christi', which includes the seven main Joys of Our Lady.[58] From the catalogue of the General of the Carmelite Order, Henry Silvio, it appears that in 1613, this Congregation had 54 convents spread all over Italy to the north of Rome.[59]

From a manuscript of 1603, we know that the Carmelite novices of the convent of Genoa had the duty to say the antiphon 'Gaude flore virginalis' every day.[60] This convent was of the province of Lombardy.[61] Therefore, this province also, at least in the convent of Genoa, used to honour Mary by celebrating her Joys.

If we study the Carmel of Venice, we find devotion to the Joys of Our Lady not only in Venice but in many other parts of the Carmelite Order. Indeed, in 1675, Francis Mondini wrote that both in Venice and in many convents of the Order, there was the Holy Custom of saying seven Our Fathers and seven Hail Marys every

Wednesday in remembrance of the seven Joys of Our Lady. He expresses the wish and hope that this devotion should be the common patrimony of all Carmelite Churches.[62]

This was not a vain hope or futile wish. About 50 years later (1728), Bagnari repeats that this devotion took place in all the Churches of the Order.[63]

Finally, we will mention the Carmelite Province of Santa Maria della Vita, In Naples, in the convent which has the same name as the province, there was the novitiate. In 1706, both the novitiate and its chapel were dedicated to Our Lady of Joy: 'Nostra Signora dell'Allegrezza'.[4] This was not for the reason suggested by Hoppenbrouwers, that there is a relationship between the devotion of the Joys of Our Lady and that to Our Lady of Mount Carmel[65], but for another reason which we will mention below.[66]

(ii) The indulgences given by Paul V

To recognise and encourage this particular devotion, Paul V, in 1606, gave forty days indulgence to all men and women enrolled in the Scapular every day that they say seven Our Fathers and seven Hail Marys in honour of the seven joys of the Blessed Virgin Mary.[67]

The giving of these indulgences led to a huge increase in the popularity of the devotion of the Joys, which further spread throughout the Carmelite Order, as can be witnessed by the vast literature about it in the seventeenth and eighteenth centuries. Before this point we only find three authors (Bonfigli, Di Ausilio, and Leoindelicato) who give us information about it, but after this point, the authors multiply at a rate of seven to one.

(iii) A Profuse literature

Many nations can boast of having contributed to the rich literature on the Joys of Our Lady, but none more than Italy. The Italian Carmel exceeds all others and takes first place in the number of authors who in one way or another contributed to the golden age of this devotion.To show this, here we give a list of authors from seven nations who advocated this devotion, with the year in which they published:

Italy: Giovanni Battista Madalena Da Brembo (1611), Elija Maruggi (1624), Francesco Mondini (1675), Giuseppe Maria Fornari (1690), Andrea Mastelloni (1709, 1711), Pietro Marija Alberto Dal Buono (1724), Piero Luigi Bagnari (1728), Giuseppe di Gesu (1739), Cirillo di Giovanni (1743), and the unknown author of the booklet about the miraculous healing which happened in Florence on the 21st January 1755, through the intercession of Our Lady of Mount Carmel (1755).[68]

Spain: Juan Bonet (1664), Gabriel Serrada (ed.3, 1755), Rocco Albert Faci (1767) and the author of the Rule of the Third Order of Our Lady of Mount Carmel (1797).[69]

France: Toussaints Foucher (1619), Mark of the Birth of the Virgin Mary (1681).[70]

Germany: John (of the Cross) Weiss-Charles (of Saint Anastasius) Freywillinger (1643), Pacificus of the Cross (1727).[71]

Portugal: Ludovicus of the Presentation (1621).[72]

Belgium: Daniel (of the Virgin Mary) Audenaerde (1662).[73]

Poland: Constantine Stanislaus Stralkowski (1764).[74]

(iv) Office of the Joys of Our Lady: While we only know two French authors who wrote about the Joys of Our Lady, we owe the Office of the Joys of Our Lady to one of them; Mark of the Birth of the Virgin Mary. He created a way in which the Carmelite Tertiaries could reflect on the Joys of Our Lady while saying the Little Office of Our Lady. Since he includes the prayer for the close of the day with the canonical hours, he considers eight Joys rather than seven. He suggests using this method on the days of a feast of Our Lady, on their Octaves, and on Saturdays.

On these days, the Tertiaries can make the intention to honour Mary for the Joy she experienced:
-At Matins: when she was addressed by the angel, and the Holy Ghost descended on Her to make Her the Mother of God;
-At Lauds: When she went to visit Elisabeth and, in ecstasy, sang the song of the 'Magnificat';
-At Prime: When she miraculously gave birth to her Divine Son but stayed a virgin, as a ray of sunlight passes through a crystal without doing damage to it, and as how Jesus, after he rose from the dead, entered the room where the apostles were without opening the door;
-At Terce:When the three Kings (Magi) came to visit and adore her Son after he was born;
-At Sext: When she found her Son Jesus in the temple after she had spent three days anxiously searching for him;
-At None: When she saw him raised from the dead and full of glory;
-At Vespers: When she was assumed into heaven;
At Compline: When she was raised above all the choirs of angels and crowned Queen of all the Saints by her Son, Our Lord.[75.]

After each of these canonical hours, a short prayer was to be said to God by the merits of Jesus Christ, in order to atone for the distractions that the person may have experienced when reciting that hour.[76]

(v) Tertiaries, members of Scapular Confraternities, and the Sabbatine Privilege

In order to further spread the devotion of the Seven Joys of Our Lady, the Carmelites were keen to recommend it in writing to the tertiaries and all the members of the Confraternities of Our Lady of Mount Carmel. Therefore, in France, Mark of the Birth of the Virgin Mary inserted the Office that we have described into the manual of the Third Order, and in Spain, the Seven Joys of Our Lady were also inserted into the manual of the Third Order.[77] However we do not know whether the Office of the Joys was said in meetings of the Third Order in the seventeenth and eighteenth century. By the middle of the nineteenth century, however, at least in Italy, the office was being said in the monthly meetings of the Third Order.[78]

Dal Buono and Bagnari aimed to reach even more people. They aimed to influence all the male and female members of the Confraternities of Our Lady of Mount Carmel[79] and all the devotees of the Scapular.[80]

In order that all those who could not fulfil the obligations required of them by the Sabbatine Privilege should not be deprived of its great benefit, that is, that on the first Saturday after their death (or shortly afterwards) they would be freed from purgatory and go to enjoy God forever, many Carmelite Priests used to change these obligations into the recital every day of seven Our Fathers and seven Hail Marys in honour of the Blessed Virgin Mary. This change had been recommended by the General Chapter of Piacenza.[81]

Among such Carmelites we could mention Daniel of the Virgin Mary. He says openly that he used to give people the choice, either to say these seven Our Fathers and seven Hail Marys in honour of the Blessed Virgin Mary or the little Rosary, otherwise known as the Stellarium.[82]

(vi) Statue, Image, feast(?)

According to Fornari, in the church of the Carmelite Friars of Milan (in that of the province of Lombardy and not that of the Congregation of Mantua) , there was a statue of Our Lady of Joys: 'Della nostra Signora di gioie' and an image of the five honours of Mary: 'di cinque honouri di Maria Vergine'.[83]

We do not know what these five honours are. Could they be the five original Joys of Our Lady which first were the objects of devotion? We cannot exclude this possibility because Roschini mentions that a feast in their honour was held in a number of places, such as Cologne. Later then another feast of the Seven Joys was held.[84]

We have no evidence at all in terms of documents or writers as to whether in the church of Milan, which we have mentioned, a feast used to be held either in honour of the five or the seven Joys of Our Lady.

One could say that, according to Andrea Gargiulo, such a feast used to be held in Naples, in the Church of Santa Maria della Vita. This is true, but this was only a private feast in the Novitiate, since this, as well as the altar of its chapel was dedicated to 'Our Blessed Mary of Joy: 'a nostra Signora dell'Allegrezza'.[85] This feast was, in fact, the feast of the birth of Our Lady (8th September).

The same writer explains why these religious people had chosen this name for their novitiate and for the altar of its chapel, and why they celebrated the feast of the 8 of September in this particular way. The reason why, if the birth of Our Lady was a cause of celebration for the whole world[86], it was particularly so for this group of Carmelite Religious was that on the eve of this feast in 1705 they had received news that had given them great joy: This was that they could cloth twelve novices who had a priestly vocation and six more who wished to become brothers. This permission had not been given to them for several years. Again the next year, on the 31st August 1706, they again received permission to admit the same number of novices, twelve who wished to become priests and six who wished to become brothers.

It was because of these two occasions of joy that they dedicated the novitiate, as well as the altar of its chapel to 'Our Blessed Mary of Joy: 'a nostra Signora dell'Allegrezza', and they began to celebrate a private feast of nine days. This would start on the feast of the dedication of the churches of the Carmelite Order: the 31st of August, the day in which they had been given the permission which we have mentioned in 1706, and also the first day of the novena of the Birth of Our Lady, and would last until the 8th September.[87]

NOTES

51 *See the previous notes 33 and 42.*

52 *For these convents, see LUDOVICO SAGGI, O.Carm.,La Congregatione Mantovana dei Carmelitani sino alla morte del B. Battista Spagnoli (1516), Roma, 1954, pp.153-225.*

53 *See the previous note, n.22.*

54 *Referred to by Bonfigli, the General Chapter was held in Piacenza. See the previous note n.21: HOPPENBROUWERS, Devotio mariana, p. 280, n.9. The General Chapter was held in Piacenza on two occasions: in 1503 and in 1575. It seems to us that Bonfigli is referring to the latter date, in which he is mentioned as a preacher and as the president of a board before which some theses were defended. (See Acta Capitulorum Generalium, v.1, Romae, 1912, pp.489-491).*

55 *See what we have said before, in nn.20 and 21.*

56 *LEOINDELICATO, Giardino Carmelitano, p.218: 'Modo da dirsi le seguenti orationi (delle sette allegrezze alla sacratissima Madre del Signore Maria Vergine del Monte Carmelo nei sette Mercoledì dopo Pasqua di Resurrezione'.*

57 *See the statistics of the number of convents of the Carmelite Order in 1600, according to the catalogue of the General of the Order: Enrico Silvio (Asti 1613), published in Analecta Ordinis Carmelitarum, II (1911) 313. It is also in GAVA-COAN, Carmelo, p.272-273.*

58 *Regula et Constitutiones Sacre Congreg. Mantuanae Ordinis Carmelitarum, Bononiae, 1602, 2, 16:'...cantetur Laus ille....post Matutinas:Gaude Virgo Mater Christi'.*

59 *See Analecta O.Carm.,II(1919) 313; GAVA-COAN, Carmelo, p.273.*

60 *See Scritture relative ai PP.Carmelitani: Ordini osservati dai novizi del Carmine di Genova, a. 1603, Genova, Bibl.Univ., E.VIII, 13; HOPPENBROUWERS, Devotio mariana, p.103, n.41.*

---

61 *SAGGI, La Congregazione Mantovana, p.197: 'Il Convento di Genova: da non confondere con l'altro convent appartenuto alla provincial di Lombardia'; See also HOPPENBROUWERS, ib.; GAVA-COAN, Carmelo, p.278, n.20.*

62 *FRANCESCO MONDINI.O.Carm., Carmelo il favorito, Venetia, 1675, p.123: 'La devotione all'anime giocondissima e alla Vergine Maria Madre gratissima costumata qui' nel Veneto Carmelo, e in molte parti della mia Religione (bramo, e spero in tutte le Chiese), di venerare L'Immacolata Regina il Mercoledì, recitando sette volte il Pater Noster, e l'Ave Maria in memoria delle sette Allegrezze'.*

63 *BAGNARI, divozioni:'....la divozione delle di Lei sette Allegrezze, che si dicono unite alli sette Pater e Ave in tutte le Chiese de' Carmelitani ' (p.22); 'Viene poi in oggi sempre piu coltivata questa divozione colle sette Allegrezze, che in tutte le Chiese de' Carmelitani si recitano' (p.27); See also p.17.*

64 *Regarding the novitiate, see LORENZO MARIA BRAN-CACCIO, O.Carm., Il fascetto di mirra, Napoli. 1708, in the dedication: 'A nostra Signora dell'Allegrezza'; regarding the altar of the chapel of the novitiate, we have the statements of ANDREA GARGIULO, O.Carm. In his booklet Registro del novitiate de' Carmelitani osservanti di Santa Maria della Vita e pratiche degl'esercitii spirituali de' novitii, Napoli, 1708, p.59, we find written: 'Il titolo dell'Altare del novitiate e di Nostra Signora dell'Allegrezza'.*

65 *HOPPENBROUWERS, Devotio mariana, pp.280-281: 'Itaque relationem quamdam statuebant inter gaudia Virginis et cultum Matris Carmeli et haec forte fuit causa, quare patres reformationis Sanctae Mariae de Vita novitiatum Matri guadiorum dedicaverunt.'*

66 *See further n.87.*

67 *Bull of 30th October 1606, 'Cum Certas': 'Omnibus utriusque sexus*

Christifidelibus, qui dictam Confraternitatem (Beatae Mariae de Monte Carmelo), ..ingredientur et habitum receperint, .. Qui autem qualibet die septies orationem Dominicam et toties salutationem Angelicam ad honourem septem gaudiorum ejusdem Beatae Mariae Virginis recitaverint, quadraginta dies (conceduntur)' (Bullarium carmelitanum, pars2, 1718, p.31, n.7). See also THEODORUS STRATIUS, O.Carm.,Instructio fratribus Carmelitis Antiquae Observantiae regularis, Romae, 1640, pp.19-20; GIUSEPPE MARIA FORNARI, O.Carm., Anno memorabile dei Carmelitani, v.2, Milano, 1690, p.122.

68 *See GIOVANNI BATTISTA MADDALENA DA BREMBO, racconta d'alcune gratie fatte dalla sacratissima Vergine Maria del monte Carmelo a'suoi divoti co'l celeste Tesoro delle indulgenze consedute da diversi Sommi Pontefici, Pavia-Modena, 1611, pp.*
70-71; GIUSEPPE DI GESU', Istruzione intorno al sacro abitino di Maria Vergine del Carmine, Torino, 1739, p.324; Relazione dell'instantaneo miracoloso guarimento accaduto in Firenze per intercessione di Maria Santissima del Carmine il di' 21 gennaio 1755, Firenze, 1755, p.6. We have already mentioned the other authors and their books.

69 *See JUAN BONET, O.Carm., Espeio de vida y exercicios de virtud para los amantissimos hijos de la siempre Virgen Maria, de su tercera orden del Carmen, Barcelona, 1664, p.111; GABRIEL SERRADA, O.Carm., Escudo triumfante de el Carmelo, su santo escapulario...., ed.3, Madrid, 1755, p.333.*

FACI translated into Spanish the book that we have mentioned of GIUSEPPE DI GESU'. See Instrucción necesaria para saber el valor y preciosidad del santo escapulario.....resumida y traducida del idioma toscano al español por el M.R.P.M. Fr. Roque Alberto Faci, Zaragoza, 1767. See Regla de la tercera Orden de penitencia de la Madre de Dios del Carmen, sita en el Real Convento de observancia de RR.PP. Carmelitas

Calzados de esta Corte, para el uso de los Hermanos Terceros, dispuesta por el Rmo. General Fr. Theodoro Estracio, (s.l.), 1797, pp.63-82.

70 *See TOUSSAINTS FOUCHIER, O. Carm., La fontaine d'Helie, errousant le parterre de l'Eglise et des ames devotes, divisee en quatre canaux...., ed.4 reveue et augmentee par l'auteur, Paris, 1624, p.240. (the first edition came out in Lyons 1619: see Bibliotheca Carmelitana, t. 2, coll. 849-850); MARC DE LA NATIVITÉ' DE LA VIERGE, O.Carm., Manuale di terz'ordine della beatissima Vergine del Carmine, tr. dal francese di Girolamo Aymo, Venezia, 1686, pp.39-40.*

71 *See IONNES WEISS-CAROLUS FREYWILLIGER, O. Carm., Maria carmelitana, das ist, Kurtze Summa der geistlichen Gnaden, Privilegen, Indulgentz, Abasz und Statuten, Collen, 1643, pp.153-158; PACIFICUS A CRUCE, O. CARM., Sylva spiritualis florum, oder Geistlicher Blumen-Wald, da ist, Hundert sechs und vierzig moral und sittliche Feyertags-Predigen, Augspurg und Graetz, 1727, p.518.*

72 *See LUIS D'APRESENTACAO, O. Carm., Vida e morte do padre fr. Estevao da Purificacao, religioso da ordem de N. Senhora do Carmo da provincia de Portugal, Lisboa. 1621, p.59.*

73 *For Daniel of the Virgin Mary, see notes 45 and 82 of this study.*

74 *See COSTANTINUS STANISLAUS STRZALKOWKSI, O. Carm., Accessus ad paradisum caelestem per varias orationes et actus iaculatorios, Cracoviae, 1764, pp. 101-102.*

75 *'Si puo anco aggiungere una delle sette allegrezze principali della B. Vergine, particolarmente nei suoi giorni festivi, nelle loro ottave, e nei sabati.*

Al Mattutino, habbiate intentione d'onorare il misteriodell'Annunziazione, e l'allegrezza, che la B. V. Ne senti, con la discesa dello Spirito Santo in essa, per renderla Madre di Dio.

Alle Laudi, onorate l'allegrezza, che ella hebbe, visitando Santa Elisabetta, quando tutta estatica pronunzio quell divino cantico Magnificat.

A Prima, quella che hebbe nella nascita del suo divinissimo figlio, che usci miracolosamente, e senza lesione del suo ventre verginale, come il raggio del sole passa un bel cristallo, e come l'istesso Salvatore dopo la sua resurrezione, entro nel luogo, ove erano gli Apostoli radunati, senza prevalersi d' aperture di porte.
A Terza, l'allegrezza che hebbe, quando li tre Re vennero ad adorare il suo figlio nuovamente nato.
A Sesta, quella che hebbe, quando lo ritrovo nel Tempio, dopo haverlo cercato con gran passione tre giorni.
A Nona, quella che hebbe, quando lo vide risuscitato, e colmo di Gloria.
A Vespro, quella nella quale fu trasportata, nel suo proprio passaggio da questo mondo, che fu in'un atto de piu puri ed ardenti d'amore, de quali una pura creatura possa essere capace.
A Compieta, che e il fine e compimento di tutto l'ofizio del giorno, potrete contemplare, ed onorare la sua esaltazione nella gloria, sopra tutti i cori degli Angioli; e come fu coronata Regina di tutti li Santi dal suo figlio nostro Signore' (pp.39-40).

76 *'Alla fine di ciascun'ora, dite per riparare li mancamenti, che potetehaver commessi, ancorche non li consociate: 'Mio Dio! Gradite quest' ofizio, che ho recitato a vostra eternal lode. Io vi prego di ricevere tutte le orazioni, che nostro Signore Gesù Cristo ha sempre fatte, per supplier, e soddisfare a difetti da me commessi, e che il tutto sia a vostra maggior Gloria, e salute della mia anima'(p.40).*

77 *See Regla de la tercera Orden, (s.1), 1797, pp.63-82.*

78 *See further forward notes 92, 106, 109, 114, 167.*

79 *The title of DAL BUONO'S book is: 'Divozione de' sette mercoledì del Carmine in Ossequio di Maria....riverita sotto il titolo delle sette Allegrezze, proposta, ..a 'Confratelli e Consorelle del Carmine'.*

80 *BAGNARI, Divozioni, p.5:, 'Per commune sodisfazione de' devote di Maria Vergine....';p.28: 'Io per tanto avendo voluto fare una nuova* *composizione delle medesime sette Allegrezze di Maria Vergine....,ad ogni una di esse pure ho aggiunta la preghiera di farsi alla medesima Vergine dalli divoti del suo Sacro Scapolare del Carmine in beneficio della loro anima corrispondente all'Allegrezza con cui si onora'.*

81 HOPPENBROUWERS, *Devotio mariana, pp.279-280: 'Praesertim in confraternitate sacri scapularis devotionem propagabant; gestatio quidem habitus nullam obligationem huiusmodi imponebat, sed multi patres opera ad privilegium sabatinum lucrandum praeserpta commutantes septem Pater noster et Ave Maria ad honorem gaudiorum dicenda confratribus iniungebant...Bonfigli (Sommario, 28) asseverat quod capitulum generale Placentinum hanc commutationem superioribus suasit'.*

82 DANIEL A VIRGINE MARIA, *Vinea Carmeli, p.476: 'Caeterum ego (practicant et alii) eiusmodi impotentibus vel legitime impeditis soleo inungere, ut quotidie, ...recitent ad honorem septem gaudiorum beatae Virginis Mariae septies orationem dominicam et salutationem angelicam...aut coronam parvam, stellarium dictam'. This small rosary, also known as the 'Stellarium', or the rosary of the twelve stars', used to consist of saying for three times an Our Father and four Hail Marys (in all, three Our Fathers and 12 Hail Marys), in honour of the twelve privileges or main virtues of the Virgin Mary. See ROSCHINI, La Madonna, pp.329-332.*

83 FORNARI, *Cronaca del Carmine di Milano, Milano 1685, pp.248, 401.*

84 ROSCHINI, *La Madonna, v.4, p. 414: 'Si può in fine aggiungere che in vari luogi e stata celebrata anche la festa dei Sette Gaudi, preceduta dalla festa dei Cinque gaudi (a Colonia ecc.)'.*

85 HOPPENBROUWERS, *Devotio mariana, p.281: '.... patres reformationis Sanctae Mariae de Vita novitiatum Matri gaudiorum dedicaverunt'. See also BRANCACCIO, Il fascetto di mirra, on the dedication A nostra Signora dell'Allegrezza. GARGIULO, Registro del* *novitiato..., p.59: 'Il titolo dell'Altare del novitiato e di Nostra Signora dell'Allegrezza.'*

86 *See the antiphon of the 'Magnificat' for the second Vespers of the feast.*

87 GARGIULO, *Registro del novitiato..., p.59: 'Il titolo dell'Altare del novitiato e di Nostra Signora dell'Allegrezza: Causa nostrae letitiae.' La sua festa e quella che principia nella festa della Dedicatione delle chiese dell'Ordine nostro, e si continua fin, al giorno della Natività della Beata Vergine, e ciò si perche la* nascita sua gaudium annunciavit universe mundo, *si perché doppo l'afflittioni di molti anni di sospensione di vestire, la vigilia della sua Natività l'anno 1705 comparve e si riceve la prima licenza di vestire 12 novitii chierici e 6 laici, con tenerezza e giubilo commune, e nell'anno seguente, che fu il 1706, nell'ultimo di Agosto, primo giorno della novena, festa della Dedicatione delle chiese dell'Ordine, si e ricevuta nuova licenza per altri 12 chierici e 6 laici, raddoppiandosici l'allegrezza.'*

THIRTY NINE

A Serious Crisis in the Devotion of the Joys of Our Lady in Carmel

Towards the end of the eighteenth century, Carmel could boast of 54 provinces spread all over the world. However, soon a time of scarcity, in which it almost died entirely, was about to befall it. By less than a century later, only 8 of these provinces survived. It was the French Revolution which was the cause of the beginning of this destruction, followed by the Empire of Napoleon and the liberal governments which succeeded it.

(i) The bad state of Carmel

The Carmelite Order suffered everywhere. It was destroyed in France by the Laws for the Suppression of Convents (1790) – with the loss of 8 provinces including 130 convents and 900 religious. The same occurred in Belgium and Holland. In Holland, there only remained the convent of Boxmeer in the Catholic Duchy of Van der Bergh, but by 1840, it only contained two religious.

Carmel in Germany fared no better. In 1802, 20 convents of the province of southern Germany and all those of Northern Germany were confiscated. In Bavaria, only the convent of Straubing survived, but only on condition that it would not admit any new members.

Also destroyed were the two provinces of Poland, the Russian Province of Saint Joseph, and those of Lithuania and Bohemia.

Because of similar laws of suppression of Convents, in Iberia, Carmel lost the Portuguese Province with its mission in Brazil and 78 Spanish Convents.

Finally, in Italy, because of laws in 1810, 1866, 1887 and 1890, all of which related to suppression of convents and / or confiscation of ecclesiastical property, the Italian Carmel was almost totally destroyed, with the loss of 18 provinces and two famous congregations - that of Mantua and the Discalced one of Saint Elias - in total about 350 convents. Even the General and the Officials of the Order were driven out of the Curia Generalizja.

The situation was so serious and frightening that many expected that this was the end of the life of the Order of the Blessed Virgin Mary of Mount Carmel.[88]

(ii) Decadence of the Devotion of the Joys of Our Lady

Given the serious crisis which was dominating Carmel, it is not surprising that the devotion of the Joys of Our Lady also suffered serious loss. In these severe circumstances, during the first half of the nineteenth century, practically no Carmelite wrote further about it. The one exception was Italy.

In 1846, two small devotional books were published, one in Naples and one in Rome. Both publish some prayers which are to be said during the novena of Our Lady of Mount Carmel, but both also add the Devotion of the Joys of Our Lady. The authors chose not to give their names.[89]

Three years later (1849), two more church books were published in two other cities of Italy: Florence and Catania. The first discusses in brief the rule of the Carmelite Third Order, and the privileges, indulgences and other things with regards to this Order.[90] Among other things, there are published a reproduction (with some minor alterations) of the Office of the Joys of Our Lady of Mark of the Birth of the Virgin Mary,[91] the prayers in honour of the seven joys which was said during the monthly meetings of the tertiaries,[92] and the prayers which were said every Wednesday, after the first mass, in the Basilica of Our Lady of Mount Carmel in Florence, in honour of the Joys of Our Lady.[93]

The subject of the other book was the seven Joys of Our Lady as they were celebrated in the Carmelite Churches of the Sicilian Reform of Monte Santo.[94] It describes the ceremonies which are held during the first seven Wednesdays after Easter Sunday[95] and also those which are held every Wednesday.[96] These latter are the same as those which are held in Florence during the Wednesdays throughout the year.

Only four years later, a new edition was published of the famous posthumous work of Simone Grassi about the indulgences, privileges and graces given to the Carmelite Order and to its confraternities and churches, with some useful teaching for the members of the confraternity of the scapular and for all Christians who visit Carmelite churches.[97] Among this teaching, there is one item which relates to the Devotion of the Seven Joys of Our Lady.

Most of the male and female members of the Confraternity of the scapular of Our Lady of Mount Carmel believed that the reciting of the seven Our Fathers and seven Hail Marys in honour of the Seven Joys of Our Lady was an obligation for all those who wore the scapular, so that they would not gain the indulgences and privileges of the scapular, and all the spiritual benefits of the scapular unless they said these prayers. Indeed everyone used to refer to these prayers as the Our Fathers and Hail Marys of the Scapular. Many people, when they did not say these prayers, used to state this omission in confession, as if they had sinned against the obligation required of them by the Confraternity of the Scapular of Carmel. On the other hand, they thought that, when they said these prayers, they had done everything required of them by this confraternity.[98] This belief is wrong, because these prayers are only devotional and not obligatory. Those who say them simply gain the forty days indulgence given by Paul V.[99]

When pointing this out, the author is not against the devotion of the Joys of Our Lady, as one might think. Indeed he is so much in favour of it that he does not only encourage the members of the confraternity not to neglect it,[100] but he even suggests two series of seven Joys each to them - the main Joys which Mary enjoyed on earth and the Joys of Mary in Heaven - they could choose whichever series they wished. He even recommends this devotion to the heads of families, so that they say this devotion with their families together every evening.[101]

Once more there is a total stop in publication of literature on the devotion in honour of the Joys of Our Lady. Fortunately, this hiatus only lasted sixteen years. In 1869, a new edition appeared of the little Office of Our Lady according to the ancient rite of the Carmelite Order.[102] Here we draw attention to the fact that to author or editor of this version of the little Office is not Angelo Savini, as Hoppenbrouwers states,[103] Savini, who at that time was Apostolic Vicar General of the Carmelite Order, merely gave his permission for it to be printed.[104]

As with Mark of the Birth and the Rule of the Third Order of 1849, in this Office we find a method by which the Tertiaries can honour the Joys of Our Lady while they say the Liturgy of the Hours.[105] It repeats word for word the advice of the Rule. It suggests to them prayers in honour of the Joys taken from the Rule of 1849 which are to be said during the monthly meetings of the Third Order. In these Monthly meetings the series of Joys to be meditated on is to be those which Mary is enjoying in Heaven.[106]

Notes

88 *We have taken all the information about the poor state of Carmel during the French Revolution, the Empire of Napoleon and the Liberal Governments which followed from GAVA-COAN, Carmelo, pp.165-172;SMET, I Carmelitani, in Lo Scapolare (a cura del comitato italiano VII centenario dello Scapolare), fasc.2, Roma, 1951, p.96.*

89 *Divoto esercizio da praticarsi per nove giorni precedenti la festa di Maria SS. Del Carmine coll' aggiunta delle Sette Allegrezze di Maria SS. I sette mercoledi dedicati alla Vergine, Napoli, 1846; Novena di Maria Santissima del Carmine coll'aggiunta del Settenario ed Allegrezze della stessa Beata Vergine, Roma, 1846.*

90 *Compendio e Dichiarazione della Regola del Terz'Ordine della Beatissima Genitrice di Dio V.M.del Monte Carmelo con la narrazione dei* *privilegi, e indulgenze concesse a detto Ordine, e con l'aggiunta di altre cose riguardanti il medesimo, Firenze, 1849.*

91 *See Compendio e Dichiarazione..., pp.62-63.*

92 *See ib., Modo di fare le adunanze o tornate mensuali, pp.165-169.*

93 *See ib., Formula di Orazione per le sette Allegrezze di Maria Vergine solita usarsi in Firenze tutti i Mercoledì dell'anno dopo la prima messa, pp.180-188.*

94 *Modo di recitare le sette Allegrezze della B. Vergine Maria di Monte Santo, Catania, 1849.*

95 *See Modo di recitare......: Divozione per li sette Mercoledì dopo Pasqua, pp.19-22.*

96 *See ib., pp.7-13.*

97 *Compendiosa Narrazione delle indulgenze, privilegii e grazie concesse all'Ordine, Confraternite e Chiese della Gloriosa Madre di Dio Maria Vergine del Carmine con l'istruzione distinta per i Confratelli del Sacro Scapolare e per tutti i fedeli che visitano le Chiese dello stesso Ordine del P. Simone Grassi Carmelitano, coll'aggiunta in fine della novena in preparazione alla festa, Roma, 1853. We have said that this work is posthumous, because P. Simone Grassi died on the 29th of January 1723 and it was printed for the first time four years later (1727), in Florence, See what the editor himself says, in the edition of 1853, Al Divoto Lettore, p.6. We have also said that this book is famous, because by 1807, there had already been sixteen editions. See HOPPENBROUWERS, Devotio mariana, pp.30, 329.*

98 *Compendiosa Narrazione, ..., Roma, 1853, p.66 s.: 'Molti sono gli atti di divozione, colli quali professano i Confratelli, e Consorelle del Carmine onorare e riverire Maria Vergine loro Madre, e Signora; fra questi hanno in costume recitar divotamente sette Pater noster, e sette Ave Maria in memoria di sette principalissime prerogative, colie quali l'anima beata della* *gran Regina degli Angeli viene onorata....Da che prese motive la maggior parte dei Confratelli di credere, che il recitare questi Pater noster sia obbligo unito a quelli che portano l'Abitino Carmelitano, in tal maniera, che se vogliono godere delle Indulgenze e Privilegi, e participazione dei beni spirituali, debbono per obbligo recitare ogni giorno questi sette Pater noster ed Ave Maria, quali percio da molti, per non dire assolutamente da tutti, sono detti e chiamati: I Pater noster dell'Abito; e tanta forza appreso alcuni ha acquistata questa opinione, che sogliono molti nella Confessione accusarsi talvolta d'aver trasgredito l'obbligo della Compagnia del Carmine col non aver recitato i soliti Pater noster dell'Abito, e recitandoli credon d'aver soddisfatto interamente a tutte le obbligazioni loro'.*

99 *Compendiosa Narrazione, ..., p.67: 'Questa opinione e un manifesto errore, perché non si deve tenere per obbligazione cio, che e solamente di semplice divozione, non essendo tenuto per obbligo chi porta l'Abito del Carmine a recitare ogni giorno questi sette Pater noster, perché come s'è detto e una semplice e mera divozione, mediante la quale i Confratelli acquistano ogni volta 40 giorni d'Indulgenza conceduta dal Sommo Pontefice Paolo V'.*

100 *Compendiosa Narrazione, ..., p.68: 'Non si deve con tutto ciò trascurare la recitazione di queste sette Pater...; ma con devota attenzione immaginandosi il Confratello di essere a lei (Maria) presente, li reciti ad onore, e in memoria delle di lei Allegrezze'.*

101 *Ib.: 'Ma chi avendo maggior divozione, volesse con alcune pie congratulazioni far più lungo e divoto questo spiritual esercizio, potra a'detti sette Pater Noster ed Ave Maria, tramezzare le seguenti orazioni, dicendo affettuosamente in questo modo' (p.68). 'Altra formula d'orazione per le sette Allegrezze di Maria Vergine ' (p. 70). 'Questa breve, e così ordinata Orazione d'una delle due predette formule, potrebbe praticarsi da'capi di famiglia, insieme co'loro subordinati, ogni sera nelle case loro....'(p.74).*

---

102 *Offizio parvo della B. Vergine Maria per tutti i tempi dell'anno secondo il rito ed antica consuetudine del Sagro Ordine Carmel-itano, Roma, 1869.*

103 *See HOPPENBROUWERS, Devotio mariana, pp. 50, 279 n.7.*

104 *See the actual title of the book: Offizio parvo......con licenza del Rev.mo P. Maestro Fr. Angelo Savini, Vicario Generale Apostolico di tutto l'Ordine Carmelitano.*

105 *See Offizio parvo, p.229.*

106 *See Offizio parvo, Le Sette Allegrezze della Santissima Vergine Maria, p. 202.*

FORTY

THE DEVOTION OF THE JOYS OF OUR LADY OF MOUNT CARMEL IN THE 19TH AND 20TH CENTURIES

TOWARDS THE CLOSE OF THE NINETEENTH CENTURY CARMEL BEGAN to recover from the misfortune which it had suffered. The storm was over and in October 1889, the General of the Order was able to call a General Chapter of the Order in Rome. A new Prior General was chosen to lead, or rather to restore Carmel. He was Luigi Maria Galli. It was a good choice, because this General did all he could to re-establish Carmel on a sound footing.[107]

In the same way as how the poor state of Carmel had reduced the prominence of the devotion of the Joys of Our Lady, its restoration helped encourage the dissemination of this devotion. Thus, four years before the end of the century (1896), two books were published by order of General Galli,[108] One book was meant for the members of the Third Order, and the other was for the devotees of Our Lady of Mount Carmel.

The book written for the Tertiaries was a new edition of the Rule of 1849, but without the Office of the Joys. It limits itself to mentioning only one series of Joys, those of Our Lady in Heaven, which were to be recited during the monthly meetings of the tertiaries.[109]

The book written for the Devotees of Our Lady of Mount Carmel was a new edition of the famous Novena of Our Lady of Mount Carmel by Simone Grassi, together with some other prayers.

Among these prayers were the Seven Joys of Our Lady - those of the Rule of 1849, which used to be said every Wednesday in the Basilica of Our Lady of Mount Carmel in Florence, after the first Mass. Therefore they are one series of Joys, composed from the main Joys of Our Lady in this world and in Heaven.[110]

The Nineteenth Century contributed further to the development of this devotion. During the last years of the century, two more books were published which, despite the fact that their main subject was the Devotion to Our Lady of Mount Carmel, also discussed the devotion of the Seven Joys because of the relation of this devotion to that of Our Lady of Mount Carmel. The author of the first book is Pietro Tarino. The book is called 'Nostra Signora del Carmelo', and it was published in 1897.[111] In it we find two series of Joys, those enjoyed by Mary on this earth, to which Saint Thomas Becket had devotion before Our Lady appeared to him,[112] and another series of Joys which She enjoys in Heaven which she chose to tell him about. These are said to be more pleasing to her and dearer to her.[113] Six of these are the very ones which we find in the Rule of 1849 to be used in the monthly tertiary meetings, except for 'The complete union of Our Lady with the will of God.' Instead of this he includes the special protection of Mary for Her devotees.[114]

The author of the second book is the Maltese Father Vincent Vella, chaplain of Santo Spirito Hospital (Rabat, Malta), which is now closed. In 1894 he had preached the novena of Our Lady of Mount Carmel in the Carmelite Church of Mdina, where, the following year (1895) he had preached the sermons for the Wednesdays 'Tal-Udienza'. Because people liked his sermons, he was then asked to preach during the same Wednesdays in the Basilica Sanctuary of Our Lady of Mount Carmel in Valletta. He did this in 1897. Because of many peoples' requests, and on the advice of several Carmelite Religious, he decided to print the sermons he had given in both churches, as well as more information regarding the Carmelite Order. The following year (1898), his book was published with the name 'Id-Devot tal-Madonna tal Karmnu' ('The devotee of Our Lady of Mount Carmel').[115] It consists of three parts: The beginnings of the order and its progress until the time of the author; the obligations, ceremonies, indulgences and privileges of those who are enrolled in the Carmelite Scapular; the novena of Our Lady of Mount Carmel, The Wednesdays of Our Lady 'Tal-Udienza', and prayers during the Mass of Our Lady of Mount Carmel and to some Carmelite Saints.[116]

Here we are interested in the Wednesdays of Our Lady 'Tal-Udienza', where the writer mentions the seven Joys of Our Lady. After mentioning how devotion to these Joys had developed, he gives a list of them and makes a long meditation or short sermon on each one of them. Finally he gives their chaplet (kurunella), where there are some changes and differences from earlier versions. [117]

We now come to the twentieth century. In this century, the devotion of the Joys of Our Lady has not grown at the same rapid rate as that to Our Lady of Mount Carmel. While devotion to Our Lady of Mount Carmel has become strong, devotion to the Joys of Our Lady is not so well established. It may be that this is because of the two world wars of 1914 and 1939. The fact is that only six books which we know of have been published within this century which refer to the devotion to the Joys of Our Lady.

The first of these was published during the first year of the First World War (1915). It is a new, corrected edition of the Rule of the Third Order of 1849. It was published on the order of Giovanni Maria Lorenzoni who was acting as Prior General[118] instead of Pio Maria Mayer.[119] Like the previous issue of 1889, only lists the series of Joys which relate to the life of Mary in the Kingdom of Heaven.[120]

We again find the same occasions or circumstances of Joy ten years later (1925), in the Manuale del Terz' Ordine della B.V. Maria del Monte Carmelo,[121] It is in Italian, and printed in Rome, but in the same year and in the same place an English version or translation was published called 'Carmelite devotional handbook'. This was not reserved to tertiaries but could be used by all devotees of Our Lady of Mount Carmel.[122] In it, the Joys are referred to as 'Seven prayers of joy in honour of the B.V.M. of Mount Carmel'.[123]

Two years before the start of the second world war, Silvano Brunelli published his booklet about the devotion of the Joys of Our Lady in Verona, in the church of Saint Thomas of Canterbury.[124] This church, which we have already mentioned, had been founded by the Carmelites.[125] Although it is no longer served by the Carmelites, the devotion to the Joys of Our Lady is still alive there, having been initiated there by the order in the first years of the fourteenth century, and it is still linked there with the devotion to Our Lady of Mount Carmel. Indeed the book first gives historical information about the devotion of Our Lady of Mount Carmel and the spiritual advantages (indulgences and privileges etc.) that are received by those who are enrolled in the Carmelite Confraternity.[126] It then describes the Joys which are commemorated every Wednesday evening on the altar of Our Lady of Mount Carmel. Finally at the end of the last 'Joy' it quotes the final 'Oremus', It is the short version of that of Our Lady of Mount Carmel.[127]

Regarding the content of the Joys celebrated in Verona, they are those that Our Lady enjoyed on earth, that is the series of seven to which Saint Thomas Becket had devotion before Our Lady appeared to him.[128]

Almost at the same time, in Malta the prayer manual 'Il-Ħajja Nisranija' [The Christian Life], by Father P.P. Grima and Francis Sciortino was published. Its stated aim was to increase and strengthen further 'among all Christians devotion to the Holy Sacrifice of the Mass and towards the Great Virgin Mary of Mount Carmel'. (128 bis) In pages 221-224 it includes a 'Novena to Our Lady Mary Virgin of Carmel,' where we find the seven Joys of Our Lady.

The final book that we know of is that by the Dutch Valerius Hoppenbrouwers, It is named 'Devotio mariana in ordine fratrum b.m.v.de monte Carmelo a medio saeculo XVI usque ad finem saeculi XIX'[129] (Marian Devotion among the Order of the Brothers of the Blessed Virgin Mother of Mount Carmel from the middle of the fourteenth century till the end of the nineteenth century). In the first article of the fifth chapter he discusses particular devotions to Our Lady which have been embraced and encouraged by the

Carmelite Order. One of these, the first one he mentions, is that of the Seven Joys. He gives a historical synthesis of the period which we have mentioned.[130]

It is certain that this study by Hoppenbrouwers is the most serious and critical review which has ever been written about this devotion among the Carmelites. However it is unfortunately very dry and somewhat limited. Also it does contain some mistakes.[131] We are however very happy with the conclusion that he comes to, which is that the special character of this devotion is that it is often linked with that to Our Lady of Mount Carmel. Indeed that many Carmelite writers, especially Italian ones, consider that this devotion is part of the ordinary cult with which the Mother of Carmel is usually honoured.[132] We have already had occasion to evidence this conclusion with some writings of the twentieth century,[133] but we can now quote a source which is even more recent. Last July, we acquired a leaflet which was being distributed by the Carmelite friars of Catania during the novena of Our Lady of Mount Carmel. Its title is 'The seven Joys of Our Lady of Mount Carmel (Le sette allegrezze della Madonna del Carmine), In it is the chaplet of the Joys, with an Our Father, Hail Mary and Glory Be after each one. At the end of the last Joy is a poem (of eight quatrains) in honour of Our Lady of Mount Carmel.[134]

Notes

107 *See Acta Capitulorum Generalium, v.2.Romae, 1934, pp.487, 489; GAVA-COAN, Carmelo, p.176.*

108 *Compendio e dichiarazione della Regola del Terz' Ordine della beatissima Genitrice di Dio V.M. del Monte Carmelo con la narrazione dei* *privilegi e indulgenze concesse a detto ordine e con l'aggiunta di altre cose riguardanti il medesimo, ristampato per ordine del Rmo P. M. Luigi Maria Galli, Generale dell'Ordine Carmelitano, Firenze, 1896; Novena in apparecchio alla solenne festività di Maria Vergine del Carmine, composta dal Padre Simone Grassi, carmelitano, con aggiunta di altre preghiere, ristampate per ingunzione del Rmo P. Mo. Luigi Maria Galli, Generale dei Carmelitani, Firenze, 1896.*

109 *See Compendio e dichiarazione, 1896, pp.92-94.*

110 *See Novena in apparecchio, pp.38-41. We have called it famous, because by 1853 there had already been 21 editions published. See HOPPENBROUWERS, Devotio mariana, p. 31.*

111 *PIETRO TARINO, Nostra Signora del Carmelo, Mondovi, 1897.*

112 *See TARINO, Nostra Signora..., pp.130-131.*

113 *TARINO, Nostra Signora...,p. 131: 'Mentre un giorno egli (S.Tommaso) stava occupando in questo pio esercizio, gli comparve personalmente la Vergine benedetta; e dopo di avergli mostrato la sua soddisfazione per questo suo divoto ossequio, gli soggunse, che le sarebbe tornato più gradito, se facesse menzione delle sette principali allegrezze che gode il suo cuore lassù in cielo, colla recita appunto di questi sette pater ed ave'.*

114 *See TARINO, ib., p.131-132.*

115 *VINCEZ VELLA, Id-devot tal Madonna tal Carmnu, Malta (Valletta) 1898. For the information we have given, see what the author himself says in the same book.pp.5-6.*

116 *See VELLA, Id-devot...., pp.16-210 (first part), pp.210-251 (second part), pp.252-368 (third part).*

117 *See VELLA, ib., pp.287-312, and notes 12 of this study, 149-151.*

118 *Compendio e dichiarazione della Regola della Terz Ordine della Beatissima Vergine Maria del Monte Carmelo, con la narrazione dei* *privilegi e indulgenze concesse a detto Ordine e con l'aggiunta di altre cose riguardanti il medesimo, edizione corretta e ristampata, per ordine del Rev.mo Giovanni M. Lorenzoni, Generale dell'Ordine Carmelitano, Roma, 1915. In the review of this book in Analecta Ordinis Carmelitarum (III, 1916, p.321), it is said that this compendium was published in 1916. Could this be a mistake?*

119 *In 1912, because of his health, Mayer retired early to the convent of Englewood (U.S.A.), but he continued to hold the title and some jurisdiction of Prior General of the Carmelite Order (see GAVA-COAN, Carmelo, p.249).*

120 *See Compendio e dichiarazione (1915): Sette Allegrezze in onore della B.V. Maria del Carmine, pp.155-160.*

121 *See Manuale del Terz' Ordine della B.V. Maria del Monte Carmelo, Roma 1925, pp.183-184.*

122 *Carmelite Devotional Handbook (adapted from the Italian) for the use of Tertians and other clients of Our Lady of Mount Carmel, Rome, 1925.*

123 *Carmelite Devotional Handbook, p.140 'Seven prayers of joy in honour of the B.V.M. of Mount Carmel'.*

124 *Devozione delle Sette Allegrezze di Maria Santissima che si recitano ogni Mercoledì alla sera nella Chiesa di S.Tommaso Cantuariense in Verona, Verona, 1937.*

125 *See notes 24-31 of this study.*

126 BRUNELLI, *o.c., 'Brevi cenni storici della devotione della Madonna del Carmine e vantaggi spirituali concessi dai Sommi Pontefici agli iscritti alla Confraternita'.*

127 *Ib., p.19: 'Devozione delle Sette Allegrezze di Maria Santissima che si recitano ogni Mercoledì alla sera nella Chiesa di S.Tommaso Cantuariense..'*

128 *See ib., pp.19-21.(128 bis) In the introduction 'a word to the reader'* *we used the third edition of this manual (1950). The second edition was in 1939, but we do not know the date of the first edition.*

129 *HOPPENBROUWERS, O.Carm.,Devotio mariana in ordine fratrum b.m.v.de monte Carmelo a medio saeculo XVI usque ad finem saeculi XIX, Romae, 1960.*

130 *See o.c., cap.5, art.1: Devotiones particulares: -1.Devotio erga Virginem gaudiorum, pp.278-281.*

131 *Mainly when he writes about Bettini and Savini.See pp.18, 50, 279, (n.8),281(n.17).*

132 *O.c., p.280: 'Peculiare huius devotionis est, quod saepe connectur cum cultu beatae Mariae Virginis de monte Carmelo imo iuxta plures auctores, praesertim italos, pertinet ad cultum ordinarium, quo Mater Carmeli honourari solet.'*

133 *See what we said in the previous pages and notes 120-121, 123, 126-127.*

134 *For more information or to acquire this leaflet, write to the Director of the Third Order, or another Carmelite Friar, 'Santuario del Carmine' Via G. Verdi, 20-Catania.*

FORTY ONE

THE CARMELITE CHAPLET OF THE SEVEN JOYS OF MARY AT THE PRESENT DAY

THE IMPRESSION GIVEN BY FATHER BORG GUSMAN AT THE END OF the last chapter is that it is unusual to find leaflets similar to the one from Catania or to find modern evidence that the Celebration of the Joys of our Lady is common in Italy. A recent internet search shows an entirely different story. It appears that in fact the Joys of Our Lady are celebrated throughout Sicily and Italy, particularly in churches owned or once owned by the Carmelites.

A Google search on Le Sette Allegrezze Della Madonna drew no references of relevance, but one on Le Sette Allegrezze Della Madonna del Carmelo drew several references. What these entries show is a chaplet, which is more or less uniform and can be seen on 'official' websites of the Carmelite Order in Italy, and many reports that this chaplet of the joys of Our Lady is recited during the feast of Our Lady of Mount Carmel among other prayers, such as the rosary and the Flos Carmeli, on the eve or on the feast of Our Lady of Mount Carmel, in the church or during a procession or pilgrimage, in many small towns and villages in Italy and Sicily. In many of these places, because of the suppression of monasteries in the 18th century, these celebrations are organised by secular clergy and a lay confraternity. Such Towns and Villages are; Cerami (EN), Montefalcone Valfortore (BN),Giuliana (PA) at the sanctuary of the Madonna dell' Udienza, Mistretta, Mussomeli, Bovalino Superiore (Calabria), Vetralla, Trapani, Terracina.[1,2,3,4,5,6,7,8,9]

In some places, such as the sanctuary of Montefalcone, Valfortore (FG), Gerace (RC)[10] and Bovalino Superiore[9], the seven Joys are recited during the seven Wednesdays preceding the feast of Our Lady Of Mount Carmel.In Bovalino Superiore, there is a specific text for the Seven Joys, which is kept in a manuscript written in dialect in the Church of Saint Catherine. In this text the Joys are described in seven addresses in verse in which she is described as 'Clear Star', 'Loving Mother', 'Great Virgin and Mother', 'Great Lady', 'Queen of Paradise', 'Hope of the Just and refuge of Sinners', 'Mother, Daughter and Bride of the Holy Trinity'. In the verses Her great merits are remembered, because of which She assists from her 'sublime throne' and enjoys in Heaven 'An ineffable eternal Joy' and is exalted above all the choirs of angels. The verses emphasize that 'no grace is given on earth' which does not come through her hands. In the verses the Virgin is asked to 'turn an ear of mercy to the prayers of her faithful to purify their hearts of all that causes unhappiness to her pure eyes and to defend them from all the temptations and dangers of the world.'

In Mistretta[4], the seven joys are recited on the eve of the feast, and, after the pilgrimage to the shrine, at noon, after babies are presented to Our Lady, they are enrolled in the scapular and given a leaflet containing the seven Joys. In Vetralla, because of the grace of the town being protected in an earthquake, the inhabitants vowed to fast on the eve of the subsequent seven feasts of Our Lady of Mount Carmel in honour of her seven joys.

In Trapani[11] the people celebrate fifteen days in honour of Our Lady of Trapani 'à quinnicina a Maronna', These are the days between the first and fifteenth of August. The shrine of Our Lady of Trapani is looked after by the Carmelites. People go on foot or in groups to visit the shrine, and devotion to Our Lady is particularly intense. This is based on the

---

Indulgence for the feast of the Assumption given to Carmelite Churches by Pope Gregory XIII in the Bull Cum Sicut of 17 th. february 1579. On the thirteenth day of this Quindicina, the people say: 14 Pater, an Ave, and nine Salve Reginas are recited in honour of the seven Joys which Mary ever Virgin enjoyed on Earth and the Seven Joys which she presently enjoys in Heaven, so that the nine Salve Reginas represent our wish to praise, thank and bless her in union with the nine choirs of Angels.

In Terracina, the[14] feast of the Our Lady of Mount Carmel is preceded by seven days in honour of the seven Joys of Our Lady.

In San Giovanni Gemini[12], in the province of Agrigento, the feast is preceded by a solemn Novena in which the whole population recites the rosary, and the Seven traditional Joys of Our Lady, and attends Mass. The feast is now celebrated in July in the days between the sixteenth July and the preceding Sunday, but in the past, it used to be solemnised on the Sunday of Pentecost, preceded by seven Wednesdays. On the feast day and the preceding seven Wednesdays the Blessed Sacrament used to be exposed for veneration.

In Maiori[13], the seven Joys are recited together with the rosary on the days between the fifteenth of July and the fourteenth of August.

In S.Ilario, Diocese of Casale Monferrato[16], Piedmont, the seven Joys of Our Lady used to be recited every Wednesday.

In Barcellona Pozzo di Gotto[14] (Messina), where the Carmelites have had a convent since 1583, Every year between Easter and Pentecost, seven Wednesdays in honour of Our Lady are held. Each Wednesday includes a pilgrimage to the sanctuary, participation in mass, and recitation of the seven joys of Our Lady.

In Pisciotta, a report was published on the internet describing a week's spiritual exercises in the presence of a copy of the Madonna Bruna from the Carmine Maggiore of Naples. It is reported that on the last day, a visit was made to the Carmelite nuns of the Carmel of Roccagloriosa[7]*, near Pisciotta. The congregation prayed the seven Joys of Our Lady together with the nuns.*

In Trastevere, Rome, the Statute of the Venerable Archconfraternity of the Blessed Sacrament and of Blessed Mother of Mount Carmel in Trastevere[17] *states in its first article that members should, apart from wearing the scapular, abstain from meat on Wednesdays, or recite every day seven Paters and Aves in honour of the Seven Joys of the Blessed Virgin Mary.*

Thus, the conclusion of this Google Search is that the devotion to the seven joys of Mary, linked with the devotion to Our Lady of Mount Carmel is indeed present in many small towns and villages in Italy, especially in the South and Sicily. This devotion is linked with the feast of Our Lady of Mount Carmel, and with several local customs linked with this feast, and may consist of the recitation of the Joys on days before the feast or during the feast, but also, in some places, the Joys may be recited on a series of Wednesdays before the feast or at other times, for instance before the feast of the Assumption or on the Wednesdays between Easter and Pentecost - which is similar to the situation in Malta, but is not linked with the name 'dell'Udienza'.

References:

1 *https://www.madonnadelcarminecerami.com/devozioni-carmelitane/le-sette-allegrezze/*
2 *http://www.santuariomontefalcone.it/centenario.html*

---

3 *https://www.parrocchiasantarosalia.it/?page_id=667*
4 *http://nellaseminara.altervista.org/la-storia-della-devozione-alla-ssvergine-maria-del-monte-carmelo-la-sua-chiesa-e-la-sua-festa-a-mistretta/*
5 *https://www.ilfattonisseno.it/2017/07/mussomeli-ottavario-in-onore-della-madonna-del-monte-carmelo-dall8-al-15-luglio/*
6 *http://www.sbti.it/Bov-storia-forme%20devozionali.htm*
7 *https://www.monastericarmelitani.org/monasteri-federati*
8 *http://www.processionemisteritp.it/Trapani/madonna%20trapani/*
9 *piccione%20alberto/quindicina.htm*
10 *https://www.eventiesagre.it/Eventi_Feste/21057301_Festa+Della+Madonna+Del+Carmelo.html*
11 *https://www.youtube.com/watch?v=5sCLWePTeVo*
12 *http://www.madonnaditrapani.it/it/40/preghiere-quotidiane-durante-la-quindicina*
13 *https://www.unamontagnadieccellenze.com/festa-maria-santissima-del-carmelo?lang=en*
14 *https://www.santamariaamaremaiori.it/rosario-popolare/*
https://www.europamediterraneo.it/la-devozione-alla-regina-del-carmelo-a-barcellona-pozzo-di-gotto/
15 *https://www.gazzettinodelgolfo.it/terracina-festeggia-la-madonna-del-carmine-e-san-rocco/*
16 *https://www.cittaecattedrali.it/en/bces/398-chiesa-di-s-ilario-casale-monferrato*
17 *http://www.arciconfraternitadelcarmine.it/laconfraternita/*

FORTY TWO

Listing the Joys in the Carmelite Tradition

It is difficult to be certain which the Seven Main Joys of Our Lady are. The famous hymn of the twelfth century 'Gaude Virgo Mater Christi 'mentions the following mysteries or circumstances of Great Joy for Mary's Heart:[135]

The Annunciation
The Birth of Christ
The Adoration of the Kings
The Resurrection of Christ
The Ascension of Christ
The Descent of the Holy Ghost on the Apostles
The Assumption of Our Lady into Heaven

We know that the same mysteries are listed in the codex of Ratisbon of 1351.[136] These are the Joys which Mary had in this world. However in other codexes, other Joys are mentioned,[137] because different authors do not agree. When we searched carefully we found more than twenty authors, practically all Carmelites, who list these Joys. We can divide them into three groups, based on the number of series of Joys which they propose:

(i) A single series of Joys

One group, which is the largest, mentions only one series of Joys, but not all follow the same system. Some choose one simple series of Joys, which includes either the Seven Main Joys of Our Lady on this earth or in Heaven others propose one composite set of Joys, including both Joys on Earth and Joys in Heaven.

A. Among those who follow the first system, that of a single simple series of Joys, there are two tendencies. The first is of those who prefer to speak only about the Joys of Our Lady in this World, perhaps because they are more biblical; and the other is those who favour the Joys which Our Lady enjoys in Heaven, because, they believe, Our Lady herself chose to reveal them to Saint Thomas Becket.

1. The Seven Joys of Our Lady on Earth: If one studies carefully the mysteries or circumstances of joy which those who use the Seven Joys of Our Lady on Earth quote, one finds the following differences:

a) Di Ausilio, Leoindelicato, Maruggi and Strzalkowski agree entirely with the list given by the Hymn 'Gaude Virgo Mater Christi' and the codex of Ratisbon of 1351. (138)

b) Mark of the Birth includes the Visitation and the Finding in the Temple; the first after the Annunciation and the second after the Birth of Christ and the Epiphany of the Magi. He counts the Resurrection of Christ as the sixth Joy, He excludes the Ascension and Pentecost and counts the Assumption of Our Lady into Heaven as the last Joy. (139)

c) The Author of the 'Regla de la tercera Orden, ...del Carmen', follows Mark of the Birth with a single difference.Although, like Mark of the Birth, he mentions the Resurrection as the sixth Joy, but the reason he gives why Mary enjoyed great Joy at the Resurrection is not biblical: 'Because Jesus appeared to her and spoke to her'.[140]

d) Brunelli includes the Presentation in the Temple instead of the Visitation. Like Mark of the Birth, he includes among the Joys the Finding in the Temple and excludes Pentecost, but then disagrees with Mark by preferring the Ascension instead of the Assumption of Our Lady into Heaven.[141]

2. The Seven Joys Enjoyed by Our Lady in Heaven: From Mondini we know that some Carmelite Convents used to celebrate not the Joys enjoyed by Mary on Earth, but those enjoyed by Mary in Heaven.[142]

a) Di Giovanni gives us the following seven:

1. The Assumption of Mary together with her exaltation above all the choirs of the angels;
2. The accidental happiness of the souls in Heaven because of her presence;
3. The honour and obedience offered to Her by the angels and the Blessed Souls;
4. Her omnipotent power of supplication and her universal mediation of all Graces to us;.
5. Her merits which raise her to the right of her Son Jesus, very close to the throne of God;
6. Her special patronage towards those who show her true devotion, in that she grants them graces in this life and eternal glory in the next;
7. All the graces and privileges with which she is adorned as well as the happiness and glory she is experiencing in Heaven, which will never lessen or end (143).

b) Another slightly different view of these Heavenly Joys is that of those who, instead of ' Our Lady's special patronage towards those who show her true devotion' insert 'that Her will is completely in Union with the Will of God'. The authors who state this include the authors of the ' Compendio e dichiarazione' of 1896 and 1915, the 'Novena in apparecchio' (1896), the 'Manuale del Terz'Ordine (1925) and the 'Carmelite devotional handbook'(1925).

B. In 1728, Bagnari began a new method. He linked together the Seven Joys of Our Lady on this Earth with the Seven others of Our Lady in Heaven, so that in each meditation of Joy he includes one Earthly Joy and one Heavenly Joy.[144] Thus, if one separated the Joys from each other, one would find that he celebrated fourteen occasions of Joy. It seems that some people liked this method of having one composite series of Joys, but we find three tendencies among the authors who took this idea up.

1. The anonymous author of the booklet 'Divoto esercizio' unites the seven Earthly Joys which we quoted in A1(a)[145] with the Heavenly Joys which we put in A2(a),[146] except for one case: He does not include Mary's exaltation above all the choirs of the angels. Instead he repeats in other words (perhaps by mistake?) the accidental blessedness which the souls in Heaven enjoy because of the beautiful presence of Mary.[147]

2. On the other hand, the author of the 'Novena di Maria Santissima del Carmine', does like the idea of one composite series of Joys, but, perhaps because of the length of the method, he is certainly not in favour of uniting two occasions of Joy for Mary into each meditation, Therefore he prefers to write about four of Her Joys in Heaven and in-between them, include an Earthly Joy.

The Heavenly Joys are:

The exaltation of Mary above all the choirs of the angels,

The honour offered to Mary by the angels and the Blessed Souls in Heaven as their Queen.

Mary's special patronage towards those who show her true devotion,

Mary's happiness and glory which she is experiencing in Heaven, which will never lessen or end.

The three Earthly Joys include

The Joy Mary experienced at the Annunciation.

Mary's Joy in the Finding in the Temple

and

Mary's Joy when she saw Her Son Raised from the Dead and Ascending to Heaven.[148]

3. Finally, we discuss the composite series of two Maltese, Father Vincent Vella and Mr. Francis Sciortino. Vella's series includes six Joys of Mary in this World and one Joy in Heaven. However he is unclear because he says one thing in the meditations and another in the chaplet. He appears to be influenced by two separate sources: Mark of the Birth and Fornari.

Indeed, in the meditations or short sermons, about the Joys, he exactly copies Fornari: Annunciation, Christmas, Epiphany, Presentation in the temple, and Finding in the temple. For the sixth Joy, he links together two circumstances of the Resurrection of Jesus and his Ascension.On the other hand, he gives a different list in the chaplet. Like Mark of the Birth, after the Annunciation, he lists the Visitation, but then he agrees with neither Mark nor Fornari, since after Christmas and Epiphany, he neither includes the Presentation nor the Finding in the Temple, but instead chooses the Resurrection and the Assumption.[149]

According to this author, it was Our Lady Herself who explained to Saint Thomas how he was to properly celebrate Her Joys: six from her Life on Earth (those of the meditations or those of the chaplet?) and one from Her Life in Heaven.[150] In the meditations, this latter includes three Marian privileges: the Assumption, Her Regality and her Mediation of Grace (being an advocate of mankind before the throne of Her Son Jesus, called 'ascending mediation'). In the chaplet, because he had made the Assumption a separate (sixth) joy, in the seventh Joy he includes the Exaltation of Mary over all the blessed souls in Heaven, as well as her Regality and Her Mediation as an advocate before the throne of Her Son.[151]

Sciortino is more clear in his thinking. He presents the same circumstances of Joy which Vella mentions in the Chaplet, however, in the seventh Joy, he only mentions the exaltation of Mary over all the choirs of angels.[152]

(ii) Two series

The first time we meet two series of Joys of Our Lady, one of Joys on Earth and one of Joys in Heaven is in Mondini (1675). Therefore, in terms of Timeline, the Composite series (method of Bagnari) is posterior to that of Mondini. In other words, first there were two series, and then developed a composite one.

A. The series of earthly Joys which we find in Mondini includes the

---

Joys which we noted in (i)A1.d., in other words the series which includes the Presentation and the finding of Jesus in the Temple instead of Pentecost and the Assumption. The series of Heavenly Joys agrees substantially with the list we gave in (i) A2.a., as well as the following one, since it includes in the Joys both the Patronage of Mary and Her agreement and union of her will with the Will of God.[152 bis]

B. Fifteen years later (1690) Fornari brought together in brief the two series of Joys suggested by Mondini. A great improvement by Fornari is that he removed many extra words from the description of the Heavenly Joys, simplifying the language and making the drafting of one Joy similar to another, Thus, in the Third Joy, so that it does not appear similar to the sixth or seventh one, he removes from it any reference to 'ascending and descending' Mediation of Mary and simply quoted Her total conformity with the will of God. Also, because the special patronage of Mary for her devotees is included in her univertial mediation of Graces, he leaves out this special patronage and simply speaks about Mary's exaltation above all the choirs of Angels, which is a Glory which is only indirectly written into the first Joy quoted by Mondini.[153] Dal-Buono follows Fornari both with regards to the Earthly Joys and the Heavenly Joys.

C. The writer of the 'Offizio Parvo' does not entirely follow Fornari. Although he agrees with Fornari regarding the Heavenly Joys he differs somewhat from Fornari regarding the Earthly Joys. Indeed he includes the Visitation instead of the Presentation. Like Farnari, he separates the Resurrection of Jesus from his Ascension to Heaven and counts them as the sixth and seventh Joys respectively.[155]

D. In Sicily, neither Mondini nor Fornari exerted much influence. In the Carmelite Reform of Monte Santo, during the first seven Wednesdays after Easter, the friars used to celebrate the seven Joys mentioned in the hymn 'Gaude Virgo Mater Christi' and in the codex of Ratisbon of 1351.[156] On the other Wednesdays of the year, they would recite a composite series of Joys made up of seven Joys of Mary on this earth and seven Joys of Mary in Heaven. In each 'Joy' are united two circumstances - each of Great Joy to Mary:

1. The Annunciation and the exaltation of Her above the Serafin;
2. Christmas and the filling of all Heaven with the dazzling Beauty of Mary;
3. Epiphany and the honour given to Mary by all the creatures and souls of Heaven;
4. The Resurrection of Jesus and Mary's mediation (ascending and descending) of Grace to her devotees;
5. The Ascension of Jesus and Mary's Queenhood;
6. Pentecost, where she received the Holy Ghost in a deeper way than the Apostles, and her patronage, in particular towards those who wear her scapular on their breast;
7. Mary's Assumption into Heaven and the eternal nature of her favours, privileges and pre-eminence which can never be decreased,[157]

Thus, there are two series which we find venerated among the Carmelites of Monte Santo; one regarding Earthly Joys and one of which is composite of Earthly and Heavenly Joys. This composite series occurs in the same year (1849) in the 'Compendio e Dichiarazione'. We do not know which author copied from which, however the two composite series are identical - word for word.

E. Finally we come to Tarino. Regarding the series of Earthly Joys, he, like Mondini and Fornari, includes the Presentation of Jesus and the Finding in the Temple instead of Pentecost and the Assumption of Mary. Regarding the Heavenly Joys, he follows the system of those who include the patronage of Mary towards her devotees without mentioning at all the conformity and union of Her will with the Will of God (in a similar way to Di Giovanni),[158] Otherwise Tarino takes both the content and the very words of the other Joys from the Series of Heavenly Joys given by the 'Compendio e Dichiarazione' of 1849.[159]

(iii) THREE SERIES

At least two authors give three series of Joys, one being Joys in this World, another Joys in Heaven, and a third being a composite one including Joys from both one set and the other. These Authors are Bagnari and the anonymous author of the 'Compendio e Dichiarazione'(1849).

A. Let us start with Bagnari. We have already discussed the new method which he uses in composing his series of Joys of Mary.[160] However, before he describes this method and covering himself against the criticism which might be levelled against him because of its length,[161] he presents two series, one of Joys on Earth and one of Heavenly Joys. Regarding the Joys on Earth, he is slightly different from all others which we have quoted so far. He agrees most with the Joys of the hymn 'Gaude Virgo Mater Christi', found also in the codex of Ratisbon which we have often mentioned.[162] The one difference regards Pentecost. Instead of the Joy which Mary enjoyed because of this mystery, he prefers her joy when she presents Jesus in the Temple and she hears Simon declare him to be the Messiah.[163]

In the series of heavenly Joys, he agrees substantially with those who, like Di Giovanni, choose the patronage of Mary towards her Devotees and excludes entirely the union of Her will with the will of God.[164]

Out of these two series, he then produces another series to be said by the devotees of Our Lady of Mount Carmel in the Church of Traspontina (Rome) every Wednesday after the mass known as that of Devotion.[165] It is the composite series. In each Joy is mentioned two circumstances of Great Joy to Mary's Heart, one an earthly Joy and one a heavenly Joy. To every Joy, is attached a brief prayer to Our Lady of Mount Carmel.[166]

B. The 'Compendio e Dichiarazione' (1849) also gives three series of Joys, one to be said during the Liturgy of the Hours on Saturdays, and especially during feasts of Our Lady, and another to be said by the Carmelite Tertiaries of Florence during their monthly meeting, and a third series which was usually said in the Carmelite Basilica in Florence every Wednesday, after the first mass.[167] This latter is a composite series, while the one used in the Tertiary meetings is the series of Heavenly Joys. The series to be said in the divine office includes the main Joys which Mary experienced in this world.

Let us be honest. Although this compendium was very popular, it was not at all original. For the main Joys which Mary experienced in this world, he depends entirely on Mark of the Birth, according to the Italian translation of Geloramo Aymo O.Carm.[168] The only difference is in the Joy to be contemplated at Vespers. Mark mentions the Assumption of Our Lady into Heaven, while the compendium prefers the Ascension of Jesus into Heaven.[169]

If we then consider the series of Heavenly Joys, we find that this substantially agrees with Mondini, with the modifications made by Fornari. In fact the compendium does not mention the patronage of Mary towards her devotees, but, (like Fornari) only speaks about Her will being united with the will of God(fifth Joy).[170]

Furthermore, the composite series is identical with that which used to be said in the Wednesdays of the year, except for the seven Wednesdays after Easter in the Carmelite churches of the Sicilian reform of Monte Santo.[171] However we cannot say for sure whether the compendium copied this series from that of Monte Santo or vice versa. Both were published in the same year (1849).

However it is clear that many authors who later wrote about the Joys of Our Lady used the Compendium. These include the authors of the 'Offizio Parvo, the 'Novena in apparecchio', the 'Manuale del Terz'Ordine', the 'Carmelite devotional handbook', and the editors of the compendium in its editions of 1896 and 1915.

From what we have said so far, it should be evident how true is the statement which we made at the beginning of our attempt to list the Joys of Our Lady. We said that it is not easy to determine which are in fact the seven main joys of Our Lady. The biggest difficulty is determining which the series of Joys in this World is, because although everyone agrees about four mysteries: Annunciation, Birth of Christ, Epiphany and Resurrection, there is disagreement about the others.There are at least eight different possibilities:

1. Ascension, Pentecost, Assumption (Di Ausilio, Leoindelicato, Maruggi, Strzalkowski, 'Divoto esercizio', 'Compendio e Dichiarazione' of 1849 [the composite series], 'Modo di recitare');
2. Presentation, Ascension, Assumption (Bagnari).
3. Presentation,Finding in Temple, Ascension, (Mondini, Fornari, Dal Buono, Tarino, Brunelli);
4. Presentation,Finding in Temple, Assumption (Vella [in the meditations on the Joys]);
5. Visitation, Finding in Temple, Assumption (Mark of the Birth, 'Regla de la tercera orden');
6. Visitation, Finding in Temple, Assumption ('Compendio e Dichiarazione' of 1849 [(in the Liturgy of the Hours], Offizio Parvo');
7. Visitation, Ascension, Assumption(Vella [in the chaplet of the Joys];Sciortino);
8. Finally, the 'Novena di Maria Santissima del Carmine' only mentions three Earthly Joys: Annunciation, Finding in Temple, Resurrection and Ascension as a single Joy.

The seven Heavenly Joys are clearer. They all agree on six which we have already mentioned. They only differ in one respect, of which there are three tendencies:

1. Both the special patronage of Our Lady to her devotees and the union and conformity of her will with the Will of God (Mondini);
2. The will of Mary as we have just said with no mention of Her Patronage (Fornari, Dal Buono, 'Compendio e Dichiarazione [1849,

1896, 1915], 'Offizio Parvo', 'Novena in apparecchio', 'Manuale del Terz'Ordine', 'Carmelite Devotional Handbook');

3. Her special patronage to her devotees, without any direct mention of the union and conformity of her will with the Will of God (Bagnari, Di Giovanni, 'Novena di Maria S. Del Carmine', 'Modo di Recitare....di Monte Santo, 'Compendio e Dichiarazione' of 1849 [composite series], Tarino).

Regarding the composite series of Joys, one must note that, while most writers link two circumstances in each Joy: one in this world and one in heaven, three authors have different systems. Two of them are the Maltese Vella and Sciortino; their series is made out of six Joys in this world (the first six Joys) and one heavenly Joy which includes several privileges (the seventh Joy). Finally, the author of the Novena of Our Lady of Mount Carmel alternates four heavenly joys with three Joys on Earth.

NOTES:

135 *There are various versions of this hymn: see BLUME-DREVES, Analecta hymnica medii aevi (51t., Leipzig 1890-1921): t. 31, pp.197-198; t. 32, p.103; t. 36, pp.57-60; t. 40, p.115; t.42, pp.82-84. We do not know which version was used by the Mantuan Congration. Furthermore, the two Carmelite Authors who quote this Hymn, Camillo di Ausilio and Constantine Stanislaus Stralkowski do not agree entirely between themselves, however the mysteries are those which we have mentioned. See also ROSCHINI, La Madonna, p.413.*

---

136 *ROSCHINI, o.c.,p.414: 'Un codice di Ratisbona del 1351, cosi recenice i sette Gaudi: (1) Godi per la Concezione deifica; (2) Godi* per il sacro *parto;(3) Godi per la venuta dei Magi; (4) Godi per il resucitado; (5) Godi per Gesù asceso; (6) Godi per il Fuoco mirifico; (7) Godi per l'assunzione al cielo'.*
137 *ROSCHINI, ib.: 'In altri codici vengono nominate altri Gaudi'.*
138 *So, according to these authors, Mary enjoyed Her Greatest Joys in 1. The Annunciation; 2. The Birth of Christ;3.The Adoration of the Magi;4. The Resurrection; 5. The Ascension of Christ to Heaven; 6. Pentecost; 7; the Assumption of Our Lady into Heaven, According to Leoindelicato (Giardino Carmelitano, p.218) and Maruggi (Tesoro Spirituale, p.150), the Carmelites used to celebrate these Joys on the first seven Wednesdays after Easter Sunday.*
139 *So, according to Mark of the Birth, the following is the series of Joys: 1. The Annunciation, 2. The Visitation, 3.Christmas, 4. Epiphany, 5. The Finding in the Temple, 6. The Resurrection, 7. The Assumption of Our Lady into Heaven.*
He also lists as an eighth Joy the exaltation of Mary over all the choirs of angels and her Crowning as Queen of all the Saints, but this is just used as a conclusion because this author, in the Office of the Hours, also includes the prayer at the end of the day (Compline).
140 *Regla, p.72: '.... en memoria del gozo que tuviste, cuando Jesu-Christo nuestro Señor te saludo', y visito' después de su gloriosaresurrección'.*
141 *So, according to Brunelli, the seven Joys of Mary are these Mysteries or Occasions of Joy: 1. The Annunciation; 2 The Birth of Christ; 3. The Adoration of the Magi; 4. The Presentation in the Temple; 5.The Finding in the Temple; 6. The Resurrection; 7. The Ascension of Christ to Heaven. This position of Brunelli is not original. It is also present in Fornari in 1690; he himself depends on Mondini (1675).*
142 *See MONDINI, Carmelo il favorito, p.123.*

143 *See DI GIOVANNI, Vita di Sant'Elia, pp.56-59.*

144 *BAGNARI, Divizioni, p.28: 'Io per tanto avendo voluto fare una nuova composizione delle medesime seta Allegrezze di Maria Vergine...., mi sono impegnato per quanto ho Saputo e potuto di tenere una specie di nuovo metodo col restringere in ogn'una delle sette Allegrezze uno dei giubilei che Maria Vergine ebbe in Terra, con uno di quelli, che ora, secondo la rivelazione, gode in Cielo'.*

145 *See n.138.*

146 *See n.143.*

147 *The composite series of this Author is:*

1. *Annunciation and the beatitude of the Blessed Souls in Heaven, because the presence of Mary lights Heaven with Her Presence ('illumina il Paradiso')*
2. *Christmas and the beatitude of the Blessed Souls in Heaven, because of her beautiful presence ('La Vostra chiarezza illumine tutto l'Orbe Celeste')*
3. *Epiphany and the honour and obedience of the Blessed Souls towards Her.*
4. *The Resurrection of Jesus and the omnipotent power of Her Supplication.*
5. *The Ascension of Jesus and Mary's special patronage towards those who show her true devotion.*
6. *Pentecost and the High Place she enjoys in Heaven because she is very close to the Holy Trinity.*
7. *The Assumption of Mary to Heaven and the eternity of her Joy which will never lessen or end.*

148 *See Novena di Maria Santissima del Carmine coll'aggiunta del Settenario ed Allegrezze della stessa Beata Vergine, Roma, 1946, pp. 46-47. He unites the two mysteries of the Resurrection of Jesus from the* *dead and his Ascension into Heaven as the sixth Joy: ' Rallegratevi, o Maria, per quell content, che godeste qui in terra, in rimirar risorto immortale, ed ascender con li suoi redenti Israeliti nel suo Regno il ripromesso Salvatore dei secoli' (p.47).*

149 *See VELLA Id-devot, pp.288s., 310-311.*

150 *O.c., p.288: 'Jena (Marija) irrid nghallmec chif ghandec tkassamhom u daun huma l'isbah granet ta'ferh li chelli mita cont ninsab f'din l'art, u il Gloria li biha ninsab onorata fis-Sema.....Is-seba' ferh: mita jena geit mgholliha fis-Sema bir-ruh u bil gisem, fein geit incurunata Regina tas-Sema u ta'l'art, maghmula Avucata tal bnedmin kuddiem it-tron t'Ibni Gesu'.*

151 *See ib., p.312.*

152 *See Il-Ħajja Nisranija, it-tielet ħarġa, Valletta, 1950, pp.221-224. Therefore, according to this author, the seven Joys of Our Lady are: Annunciation, Visitation, Christmas, Epiphany, Resurrection, Ascension, Exultation of Mary above all the choirs of angels.We have said that the author of these Joys is Mister Francis Sciortino, because at the end of the introduction of this book, there was a P.S. note which said:'the Spiritual Reading and the prayers before and after Communion are written by Father Peter Paul Grima, now deceased, and all the rest of the book is the work of Francis Sciortino.*

152 bis) Since Mondini's work was, as far as we know, the first list of Heavenly Joys, we show them here so that one can compare them to other sets which came later to see what changes were made later.

1. Despite being a Human Person, Mary was raised close to God's throne in Heaven;

2. Her body and soul are so full of beauty that they continue to make heaven beautiful and fill the Blessed souls with Joy;

3. Her wishes are so united with the will of God, that she receives from

Him all that she asks for Her devotees;

4. Since she is the Mother of God, she is honoured as such by the blessed souls in Heaven;

5. The Glory which she enjoys will never end or diminish;

6. All the graces which she asks for mankind are inevitably granted and no grace is granted by God except by Her;

7. She gives all help on earth and eternal glory after their death to her true devotees who honour her.

153 *See FORNARI, Anno memorabile, pp.148-149.*

154 *See DAL BUONO, Divozione, pp.8 (joys on this Earth), 10-11 (Heavenly Joys that Mary informed Saint Thomas about), 14-17 (Heavenly Joys which are said every Wednesday and on Feast Days in the Church of S. Martin Maggiore, Bolognia), 25-137 (meditations on these Heavenly Joys).*

155 *See Offizio Parvo, Roma, 1869, p.202 (Heavenly Joys), p.229(Joys in this World).*

156 *See what we said in the beginning of the section: h) Listing the Joys.....*

157 *Modo di recitare le sette Allegrezze della B. Vergine Maria di Monte Santo, Catania, 1849, pp.19-22 (Joys in this World), 7-13 (composite series). One should note the sixth Joy of the Composite Series. Although many mention the patronage of Mary towards her devotees, it is the Carmelites of Monte Santo or the Author of the Compendio e Dichiarazione (1849) who include the Scapular of Our Lady of Mount Carmel. Naturally they are referring to the traditional belief in the promise of Our Lady to Saint Simon Stock, that the Scapular is a sign of protection from danger and from eternal fire, and traditional belief in the Sabbatine Privilege – the quick acquisition of eternal glory.*

158 *Compare the sixth Joy of Tarino with that of Di Giovanni (sixth Joy). Although Mondini, much before Di Giovanni, also speaks about the* *patronage of Mary towards Her devotees (seventh Joy), he does not exclude the union of her will with that of God. Mondini quotes this in the third Joy.*

***159** Compare Tarino, Nostra Signora del Carmelo, pp.131-133 with Compendio e dichiarazione (1849), pp.167-169.*

***160** See note 144.*

***161** BAGNARI, Divozioni, p.28: 'Questo e tutto quello che mi e riuscito di fare in una così breve orazione, se bene mi persusado, che non mancherà d'avere la taccia di troppolunga da qualche spirit mal consigliato, e non avvezzo alla divozione'.*

***162** According to HOPPENBROUWERS, Devotio mariana, p.281, n.17, this is the usual series of Joys: Series ordinaria comprhendebat mysteria Annuniationis, Nativitatis, Epiphaniae, Resurrectionis, Ascensionis, Pentecostes et Assumptionis'.*

***163** See BAGNIARI, Divozioni, p.22. In his opinion, these are the Joys to which Saint Thomas Becket had devotion before Our Lady appeared to him.*

***164** See ib., pp.24-25. According to Bagnari, this is the series of seven Heavenly Joys which Our Lady notified Saint Thomas about and asked him to be devoted to: 'In avvenire dunque rallegrati meco con queste sette Allegrezze (e sono le seguenti) ...'*

***165** Ib., p.13: 'Sette Allegrezze di Maria Vergine, che si recitano tutti li Mercoledi da Divoti del Carmine nella Chiesa della Traspontina terminate la messa, detta della Divozione'.*

***166** See ib., pp.13-17. The two circumstances of joy of which the meditations are composed: 1. Annunciation and exaltation of Mary in Heaven above all the blessed souls in heaven; 2. Christmas and the huge brightness of Mary's purity, which enlightens even the wisdom of the blessed souls; 3. Epiphany and the honour given Mary by these souls as Queen of Heaven; 4. The Presentation of Jesus in the temple and her*

---

universal mediation (ascending and descending) of all Graces; 5. The Resurrection of Jesus and Mary's patronage towards her true devotees; 6. The Ascension of Jesus and Mary's participation in his Infinite Greatness seated on the right of God the Father; 7. Mary's Assumption to heaven and her eternal Glory which cannot be diminished.

167 *See Compendio e Dichiarazione (1849), pp.62, 165, 180.*

168 *See MARC DE LA NATIVITE, Manuale di terz'ordine, pp.39-40.*

169 *MARC, p.40: 'A Vespro, quella, nella quale fu trasportata nel suo proprio passaggio da questo mondo': Compendio, p.63: 'A Vespro, l'allegrezza che provo quando vide risuscitato a vita immortale'.*

170 *See Compendio e Dichiarazione (1849), p.168.*

171 *See this series in (ii)D. Of our study.*

FORTY THREE

THE CHAPLET OF THE JOYS OF OUR LADY IN THE ITALIAN POPULAR CARMELITE TRADITION

In Italy, the Joys of Our Lady continue to be celebrated by the Scapular Confraternities and the Carmelite order as a chaplet. The following is the result of a Google Search regarding the content of this chaplet. Here we describe the content of the Italian Chaplet on Le Sette Allegrezze Della Madonna del Carmelo.

A google search on Le Sette Allegrezze Della Madonna del Carmelo provides a number of different versions of a prayer or chaplet containing these 'Joys'. It is clear that the way in which this chaplet is to be used is either, in certain main Carmelite churches for public recitation after morning mass on Wednesdays, or in other, smaller locations, to be recited during the feast celebrations of Our Lady of Mount Carmel or during the days leading up to the feast. It may also be used privately. It is clear that in many locations this chaplet is used regularly at appropriate times. In some places, especially in Sicily, the chaplet is in the local dialect. However, there is one version which is very common, and is found on 'Official' Carmelite websites run by the order. Perhaps the most useful of these websites is http://www.materdecorcarmeli.it/preghiere-carmelitane.html , organised by P.Luco Maria Zappatore, O.Carm.,[1] Parish Priest of S.Maria Regina Mundi, Rome. He describes the 'Allegrezze' or Joys of Mary as one of the most ancient prayers to Our Lady of Mount Carmel. He explains that these are the Joys which Our Lady enjoyed on Earth, thus emphasising the 'positive' aspect, in contrast with the 'seven sorrows'.

He lists eight including the conclusion; because of the eight times Elias sent his servant up mount Carmel to look for a sign - the cloud. His servant went once, returned, and then was told to return seven times, so he went eight times in all. In the cloud he saw, Carmelite Tradition has always seen a representation of the Immaculate Conception and Mary's role as Dispenser of Graces, writes Father Zappatore.

Father Zappatore points out that the old texts of the 'Allegrezze' exist in Latin, and that there are many versions in Italian, sometimes including verses. He quotes the oldest known version, that of the 'Laudario dei battuti di Modena', that is of the confraternity of flagellants of Modena, whose church was officiated by the Carmelites. This text dates to 1300. As quoted by Father Zappatore it has been modernised to make it more understandable, but the rhythms and cadences of the original have been maintained. In common with other Italian versions, which are probably based on it, each verse or 'Joy' charmingly calls on the Virgin Mary to be Joyful for a particular reason.

Rallegrati, Vergine Maria, Madre di Gesù Cristo!
Che all'annuncio di Gabriele, di Dio ministro,
concepisti il Figlio.

Rallegrati, Vergine Maria, che senza pena alcuna,
partoristi il tuo figlio, nella cuna,
restando vergine.

Rallegrati, Vergine Maria, che vedesti la stella
che guidò i Magi presso la capanna,
per offrirti oro, incenso e mirra.

Rallegrati, Vergine Maria, che quando il giusto Simeone,
prese nelle sue mani il Cristo, disse senza esitazione,
che era luce e salvezza al mondo intero.

Rallegrati, Vergine Maria, per il gran dolore
che ti colpì nel vedere il Cristo che muore,
ma che poi risorge il terzo giorno, secondo la promessa.

Rallegrati, Vergine Maria, che vedesti salire al cielo, in festa,
il tuo figlio Gesù e tornare al Padre,
dove regna in eterno alla sua destra.

Rallegrati, Vergine Maria, per la discesa
dello Spirito Santo, che nel cenacolo, in attesa,
con gli apostoli in preghiera hai ricevuto.

Rallegrati, Vergine Maria, che salisti al cielo con tanto onore,
circondata dagli angeli e dai santi,
ove regni per sempre con amore.

Al qual regno ci conduca il frutto benedetto
del tuo seno, Gesù, nostro Signore,
dove troveremo per sempre gioia e onore.
AMEN.

Thus, in this version of the 'battuti di Modena', the Joys are Annunciation, Nativity (without Pain), Epiphany, and Presentation in Temple, Death and Resurrection of Jesus, Ascension of Jesus, Pentecost, Assumption of Our Lady to the Kingdom of her son.

Another website, http://www.preghiereperlafamiglia.it/devozione-all sette-allegrezze-di-maria.htm, aims at encouraging private family prayer.[2] *It describes how the Blessed Virgin had, in apparitions to S. Arnolfo of Cornoboult and San Tommaso of Canterbury stated her pleasure at the honour which they gave to her Joys enjoyed on Earth, and invited them to also honour Her joys in Heaven, which she listed for them. A great devotee and apostle of the Joys of Our Lady, (allegrezze) was Saint Bernardino (and other Franciscan saints), who is said to have claimed that all the graces that he had received were due to this devotion. This website gives the following version of the Joys, both the Joys on Earth and those in Heaven, with an Ave after each Joy. The format is similar to the version of the Battuti, calling on Our Lady to be happy for various reasons.*

Le sette allegrezze di Maria SS. in terra

I. *Rallegratevi, o Maria piena di grazie, che, salutata dall'Angelo, concepiste il Divin Verbo nel Vostro seno verginale con una gioia infinita dell'anima vostra Santissima. Ave*

II. *Rallegratevi, o Maria che ripiena di Spirito Santo, e trasportata da un vivo desiderio di santificare il Divin Precursore, intraprenderete un viaggio sì disastroso, superando le alte montagne della Giudea, per visitare la vostra parente Elisabetta, dalla quale foste ricolmata di magnifiche lodi, ed alla cui presenza, levata in ispirito pubblicaste colle parole più energiche la gloria del vostro Dio. Ave*

III. *Rallegratevi, o Maria sempre vergine, che senza alcun dolore deste alla luce, annunziato dagli spiriti beati, adorato dai pastori e ossequiato dai re, quel divino Messia che tanto desiderate per la comune salute. Ave*

IV. *Rallegratevi, o Maria, che, essendo venuti dall'Oriente i Re Magi scortati da una stella miracolosa per adorare il vostro Figlio, li vedeste, prostrati ai suoi piedi tributargli i debiti omaggi e riconoscerlo per vero Dio, Creatore, Monarca e Salvatore del mondo. Qual gioia provaste mai, o Madre beata, nel vedere sì presto riconosciuta la sua grandezza e presagita la futura conversione dei Gentili! Ave*

V. Rallegratevi, o Maria, che dopo aver per tre giorni con estremo dolore cercato il Vostro Figlio amabilissimo, lo ritroverete finalmente nel Tempio in mezzo ai dottori meravigliati della sua prodigiosa sapienza e della facilità con cui scioglieva i dubbi più sottili, e spiegava i punti più difficili della Santa Scrittura. Ave

VI. *Rallegratevi, o Maria, che dopo essere stata tutto il venerdì e il sabato immersa in un mare di afflizioni, ne foste prodigiosamente cavata e rinvigorita con una gioia eguale al vostro sommo merito nella domenica al far del giorno vedendo risuscitato da morte a vita il vostro divin Figlio, l'anima dei vostri pensieri, il centro dei vostri affetti, e scorgendolo accompagnato dai santi Patriarchi, trionfator della morte e dell'inferno, così ricolmo di gloria, come era stato due giorni prima satollo di dolori e di ignominie. Ave*

VII. *Rallegratevi, o Maria, che terminaste la vostra Santissima vita con una morte tutta dolce e gloriosa, essendo stata unicamente cagionata dall'ardore del vostro amore a Dio; e gioite pure che, appena esalato lo spirito, foste coronata dalla SS. Trinità per Regina del Cielo e della Terra, col vostro corpo medesimo Assunta alla destra del Divin Figlio, e rivestita di un potere che non conosce confini. Ave, Gloria.*

LE SETTE ALLEGREZZE DI MARIA SS. IN CIELO

I. Rallegratevi, o Sposa dello Spirito Santo, per quel contento che ora godete in Paradiso, perché, per la vostra umiltà e verginità, siete esaltata sopra i cori angelici. Ave

II. Rallegratevi, o vera Madre di Dio, per quel piacere che sentite in Paradiso, perché siccome il sole quaggiù in terra illumina tutto il mondo, così Voi col vostro splendore adornate e fate risplendere tutto il Paradiso. Ave

III. Rallegratevi, o Figliuola di Dio, per quel gaudio che ora godete in Paradiso, perché tutte le gerarchie degli Angeli ed Arcangeli, Troni e Dominazioni e tutti gli spiriti beati Vi onorano e Vi riconoscono per Madre del loro Creatore, e ad ogni minimo cenno vi sono obbedientissimi. Ave

IV. Rallegratevi, o Ancella della SS. Trinità, per la tanta allegrezza che sentite e godete in Paradiso, perché tutte le grazie che domandate al Vostro Divin figliuolo vi sono subito concesse, anzi, come dice San Bernardo, non si concede grazia quaggiù in terra che non passi prima per le vostre santissime mani. Ave

V. Rallegratevi, o Serenissima Principessa, perché voi sola meritaste di sedere alla destra del Vostro santissimo Figliuolo, il quale siede alla destra dell'Eterno Padre. Ave

VI. Rallegratevi, o Speranza dei peccatori, rifugio dei tribulati, per la tanta allegrezza che godete in Paradiso, perché tutti quelli che vi lodano e vi riveriscono, il Padre Eterno li premierà in questo mondo colla sua santissima grazia, e nell'altro colla sua santissima gloria. Ave

---

VII. *Rallegratevi, o Madre, Figlia e Sposa di Dio, perché tutte le grazie, tutti i gaudi, le allegrezze e favori che godete in Paradiso non si sminuiranno giammai, anzi si aumenteranno fino al giorno del Giudizio, e dureranno per tutti i secoli dei secoli. Così sia. Ave, Gloria*

Thus, in this version, the Joys on Earth are Annunciation/Conception, Visitation, Nativity (with no pain), Epiphany, Finding in the Temple, Death and Resurrection of Jesus, Assumption and Coronation in Heaven. The Joys in Heaven are; Being exalted over all the choirs of angels, filling Heaven with her splendour, being honoured by and obeyed all the angels and holy souls as mother of their creator, Joy because all graces given to mankind pass to Her Hands, Joy because she sits at the right hand of her Son, who lives at the right hand of the Father, Joy because all who praise her and reverence her will be receive graces in this world and glory in the next, Joy because all the honour and graces she receives in heaven will last forever.

Another website, from the Carmelite Church and Confraternity of Cerami,[3] *http://www.madonnadelcarminecerami.com/devozioni-carmelitane/le-sette-allegrezze/ is explicit that the Joys (Allegrezze) are to be recited on Wednesdays, and end each verse or Joy with 'bella Maria, del Carmine Signora'-Beautiful Mary Lady of Carmel, Then an Ave Maria is said, and a refrain 'Del Carmelo, Maria, Madre e Signora, difendi i figli tuoi nell'ultima ora.'- 'Mary, Mother and Lady of Carmel, defend your children in their last hour' –a clear reference to the Scapular Promise.*

LE SETTE ALLEGREZZE
che si recitano nei Mercoledì

Rallegrati, Maria, predestinata
Figlia eletta del Padre Onnipotente:
Tu fosti concepita Immacolata,
rivestita di sole risplendente;
nei Cieli sei dagli Angeli esaltata,
sulla terra Regina ognor clemente.
Oggi, devoto, il nostro cuor ti onora,
bella Maria, del Carmine Signora.
Ave Maria

Del Carmelo, Maria, Madre e Signora,
difendi i figli tuoi nell'ultima ora.

Rallegrati, Maria, Vergine bella,
gran Madre di Gesù, Verbo Incarnato:
Or che splendi lassù, propizia Stella,
mostraci in questo esilio desolato,
nel buio, nel dolor, nella procella,
il Frutto del tuo Seno Immacolato.
A te noi, figli tuoi, corriamo ognora,
bella Maria, del Carmine Signora.
Ave Maria

Del Carmelo, Maria, Madre e Signora,
difendi i figli tuoi nell'ultima ora.

Rallegrati, Maria, fiamma d'Amore,
dello Spirito Santo augusta Sposa:

Trono di Sapienza e di Timore,
Maestra di Pietà, mistica Rosa;
Tu sei Fortezza e Speme nel dolore,
e ogni alma in Te confida, in Te riposa.
E con eterni canti ognun ti onora,
bella Maria, del Carmine Signora.
Ave Maria

Del Carmelo, Maria, Madre e Signora,
difendi i figli tuoi nell'ultima ora.

Rallegrati, di gioia e di sorriso
Arca divina, d'ogni Grazia piena:
l'infelice che guarda il tuo bel Viso,
nella valle del duol, si rasserena:
negli occhi tuoi c'è un dolce Paradiso,
che consola ogni lacrima e ogni pena;
la tua bellezza ogni anima innamora,
bella Maria, del Carmine Signora.
Ave Maria

Del Carmelo, Maria, Madre e Signora,
difendi i figli tuoi nell'ultima ora.

Rallegrati, Maria, Fonte di Vita,
dei Tesori del Ciel Dispensatrice:
ogni Grazia da Te viene elargita
con amorosa Mano ausiliatrice,
mentre il materno Cuor tutti ci invita
ad invocarti pia Consolatrice.

Pei figli tuoi, benigna, il Cielo implora
bella Maria, del Carmine Signora.
Ave Maria

Del Carmelo, Maria, Madre e Signora
difendi i figli tuoi nell'ultima ora.
Rallegrati, Maria, Fior del Carmelo,
Vergine e Madre, singolare Arcano:
Vite fiorita sei, splendor del Cielo,
Stella del mare nel travaglio umano.
Ai figli tuoi, difesi dal tuo Velo,
mite e materna stendi la tua Mano:
ai Carmelitani privilegi ancora
dona, Maria, del Carmine Signora.
Ave Maria

Del Carmelo, Maria, Madre e Signora,
difendi i figli tuoi nell'ultima ora.

Rallegrati, del Carmine Maria,
rifugio ed Avvocata ai peccatori:
scendi, celeste Nuvola d'Elia,
ad irrorar di Grazia i nostri Cuori,
che, un giorno, nell'eterna melodia,
canteranno coi tuoi celesti Cori:
Viva del nostro Ciel la bella Aurora,
Viva Maria, del Carmine Signora!
Ave Maria

Del Carmelo, Maria, Madre e Signora,
difendi i figli tuoi nell'ultima ora.

ORAZIONE

Assisti i tuoi fedeli, Signore, nel cammino della vita, e per intercessione della Beata Vergine Maria, fa che giungiamo felicemente alla santa montagna, Cristo Gesù, nostro Signore, che è Dio,e vive e regna con te, nell'unità dello Spirito Santo, per tutti i secoli dei secoli.

The Joys here are: The Immaculate Conception, The Virgin Mother of God, Spouse of the Holy Spirit, Consoler of the Afflicted, Dispenser of Graces, Splendour of Heaven-and giver of privileges to Carmelites-, Refuge of Sinners. Thus these are attributes of Our Lady now, and could be described as her Joys in Heaven. Again, Our Lady is exhorted to Rejoice because of particular concepts/facts.

The website of the Carmine Maggiore Palermo[4] repeats the same chaplet as the cerami website, carminemaggiorepa.blogspot.com The website http://www.airemsea.it/deserto/?p=1209 of the Deserto di Engaddi[5] repeats the same chaplet as the Cerami website, and also quotes the 'Battuti di Modena' version from the Mater Decor Carmeli website.

Another Parish Website, http://docplayer.it/17234409-Chiesa-madonna-del-carmine-san-giovanni-gemini-ag-novena-rosario-e-preghiere-in-onore-di-maria-ss-del-carmelo.html, of the Carmelite Church of San Giovanni Gemini[6] gives some of the same invocations, but in the last verse it quotes the vision of Elias

Le sette Allegrezze
Alla Madonna del Carmelo
Rallegrati, Maria, Fonte di Vita,
dei Tesori del Ciel Dispensatrice:

ogni Grazia da Te viene elargita
con amorosa Mano ausiliatrice,
mentre il materno Cuor tutti ci invita
ad invocarti pia Consolatrice.
Pei figli tuoi, benigna, il Cielo implora
bella Maria, del Carmine Signora.
Ave Maria...

Del Carmelo, Maria, Madre e Signora,
difendi i figli tuoi nell'ultima ora.
Rallegrati, Maria, Fior del Carmelo,
Vergine e Madre, singolare Arcano:
Vite fiorita sei, splendor del Cielo,
Stella del mare nel travaglio umano.
Ai figli tuoi, difesi dal tuo Velo,
mite e materna stendi la tua Mano:
ai Carmelitani privilegi ancora
dona, Maria, del Carmine Signora.
Ave Maria...

Del Carmelo, Maria, Madre e Signora,
difendi i figli tuoi nell'ultima ora.
Rallegrati, del Carmine Maria,
rifugio ed Avvocata ai peccatori:
scendi, celeste Nuvola d'Elia,
ad irrorar di Grazia i nostri Cuori,
che, un giorno, nell'eterna melodia,
canteranno coi tuoi celesti Cori:
Viva del nostro Ciel la bella Aurora,
Viva Maria, del Carmine Signora!
Ave Maria...

Del Carmelo, Maria, Madre e Signora,
difendi i figli tuoi nell'ultima ora.

ORAZIONE

Assisti i tuoi fedeli, Signore, nel cammino della vita, e per intercessione della Beata Vergine Maria, fa che giungiamo felicemente alla santa montagna, Cristo Gesù, nostroSignore, cheèDio,evive eregnaconte, nell'unità dello Spirito Santo, per tutti i secoli dei secoli

The website http://nellaseminara.altervista.org/la-storia-della-devozione-alla-ss-vergine-maria-del-monte-carmelo-la-sua-chiesa-e-la-sua-festa-a-mistretta is the website of the Church and confraternity of Our Lady of Mount Carmel of Mistretta. It gives a version of the allegrezze which is used and distributed as a leaflet during the feast and pilgrimage of Our Lady of Mount Carmel at Mistretta;[7]

Deus in ajutorium meum intende
Domine in adjuvandum me festina
Gloria Patri, etc.

I

Rallegrati o Maria del Sommo Nume
Figlia dell' Amor suo predestinata
Mentre, merce del virginal costume
Che serbasti ancor Madre Intemerata,
Piena di Gloria e maestoso lume,
Fosti degli angeli esaltata!
Quindi divoto il nostro cuor ti onora,
Bella Maria del Carmine signora.

Pater, Ave, Gloria
O Maria, Speranza mia,
Ti dono il cuore e l'anima mia,
Ora e nel ora della morte mia,
Viva, viva del Carmine Maria!

II
Rallegrati o Maria, che Madre vera,
Partoristi fatto Uom dei Santi il Santo,
Onde tu sola in gloriosa sfera
Meretasti seder del Figlio accanto;
E l'alta Trinita che a tutto impera
Ti ricopri del suo divino ammanto:
Quindi estatico il Ciel ti loda ognorsa,
Bella Maria del Carmine signora.

Pater, Ave, Gloria
O Maria, Speranza mia, ecc.

III
Rallegrati, o di grazie ampio Tesoro,
Dello Spirito Santo augusto Sposa,
Trono di maestade e di decoro
In cui la Trinita splende e riposa;
Quindi ai tuoi cenniogni celeste Coro
Pronto ubbedisce e contradir non osa,
E com eterni cantiumil ti onora,
Bella Maria del Carmine signora.

Pater, Ave, Gloria
O Maria, Speranza mia, ecc.

IV

Rallegrati, odi giubilo e di riso
Fonte a quell cuor che tue bellezze apprende,
Mentre, qual' altro sole, il tuo bel viso
Scintillante di Gloria in Ciel risplende.
Che ogni anima beata in Paradiso
Vienppiu felice e gloriosa rende.
Bel col Figlio insiem la Madre ancora
Bella Maria del Carmine signora.

Pater, Ave, Gloria
O Maria, Speranza mia, ecc.

V

Rallegrati, o dell'alta Sapienza
Madre sempre piu augusta e fortunata,
Mentre d'un Dio l'eccelsa onnipotenza
Si rese nel tuo seno umiliata.
Quindi grazia quaggiu non si dispensa
E sara sol da Dioa noi accordata
Qualora il tuo poter per noi l'implora,
Bella Maria del Carmine signora.

Pater, Ave, Gloria
O Maria, Speranza mia, ecc

VI

Rallegrati, o di bellezze eterne e rare,
Di grazie e di virtu vivo portento,
Porche Iddio nel crearti ebbe a formare
Della Gloria del Ciell'addornamento:
Ti formosi perfetta e singolare

Che mirarti non puosenza contento.
La tua bellezza ogni anima innamora,
Bella Maria del Carmine signora.

Pater, Ave, Gloria
O Maria, Speranza mia, ecc

VII
Rallegrati, o di pregi e di chiarori
Fonte perenne ed immortal sorgiva,
Mentre, cinta di Gloria e di splendori,
Per sempre goderai lieta e giuliva:
Ed a tuo onor tutti i celesti cori
Canteranno festanti eterno il viva:
Viva del nostro ciel la bella Aurora!
Viva Maria del Carmine signora!

Pater, Ave, Gloria
O Maria, Speranza mia, ecc.

In this version, there is a Pater, Ave and Gloria after each verse, and between each verse, are the words 'O Maria speranza mia, ti dono il quore e l'anima mia, Ora e nell ora della morte mia. Viva viva Del Carmine Maria'-'O Mary my hope, I give you my heart and my soul, now and in the hour of my death. Long live Mary of Carmel'. This is clearly a more folklore-oriented version.

The 'Joys' here are; Immaculate Conception-hence exaltation above the angels, Nativity so sits at the right side of her son, Spouse of the Holy Spirit, Glory of Heaven, Dispenser of Graces, Adornment of Heaven, All the choirs of Heaven sing her praises. Hence these are Our Lady's Joys in Heaven.

Another website, from Castellammare del Golfo, is based on a collector of Holy Pictures. It is this one; https://sites.google.com/site/melchiorreancona/sette-gioie-della-madonna It gives a number of versions of the Joys of Our Lady.[8] *One list is; Annunciation, Nativity, Epiphany, Jesus appears to Mary (Resurrection), Ascension, Pentecost, Assumption of Our Lady into Heaven. The website also gives a Gospel reading for each Joy.*

A further list of the seven Joys of The Blessed Virgin quoted on this website depends on a book belonging to Philip the Chancellor (thirteenth Century),[8] *These in fact are seven invocations to Mary, who is our mother, our joy, and our hope. The following are the Joys in Italian:*

1. *Ave, Maria, piena di grazia, tempio della Trinità, ornamento della suprema bontà e misericordia. Per questa tua gioia noi ti preghiamo di meritare che Dio Trinità abiti sempre nel nostro cuore e ci accolga nella terra dei viventi.*

2. *Ave, Maria, Stella del mare. Come il fiore non perde la bellezza a causa del profumo che emana, così tu non perdi il candore della verginità per la nascita del Creatore. O Madre pia, per questa tua seconda gioia, sii nostra maestra nell'accogliere Gesù nella nostra vita.*

3. *Ave, Maria, la stella che vedi fermarsi sul bambino Gesù ti invita a rallegrarti perché tutte le genti adorano il tuo Figlio. O stella del mondo, fa' che anche noi possiamo offrire a Gesù l'oro della purezza della nostra mente, la mirra della castità della nostra carne, l'incenso della preghiera e dell'adorazione continua.*

4. *Ave, Maria, una quarta gioia ti é concessa: la risurrezione di Gesù il terzo giorno. Questo evento rafforza la fede, fa rinascere la speranza, concede la grazia. O Vergine, madre del Risorto, effondi preghiere a tutte le ore affinché, grazie a questa gioia, al termine della nostra vita, siamo riuniti ai cori beati dei cittadini del cielo.*

5. *Ave, Maria, hai ricevuto una quinta gioia, quando hai visto il Figlio salire alla gloria. Attraverso questa gioia imploriamo di non sottometterci alle potenze del demonio, ma di salire al cielo, dove finalmente possiamo godere con te e con il Figlio tuo.*

6. *Ave, Maria, piena di grazia. La sesta gioia te la dona lo Spirito Santo Paraclito, quando discende dall'alto a Pentecoste sotto forma di lingue di fuoco. Per questa tua gioia noi speriamo che il Santo Spirito bruci col suo fuoco di grazia i peccati causati dalla nostra cattiva lingua.*

7. *Ave, Maria, piena di grazia, il Signore é con te. Alla settima gioia Cristo ti ha invitato quando ti ha chiamato da questo mondo al cielo, innalzandosi al di sopra di tutti i cori celesti. O Madre e Maestra, intercedi per noi affinché anche noi siamo innalzati al sommo delle virtù della fede, della speranza, della carità per poter un giorno essere uniti ai cori dei beati nella gioia eterna.*

Hence the Joys here are; Being temple of the Trinity, The Nativity and Her Virginity, Epiphany, The Resurrection, The Ascension, Pentecost, The Assumption. In all the joys, Mary's joys are linked with asking her for help in our journey to Heaven.

The same website gives another version of the joys;[8]
In it, the joys are; Immaculate Conception, Visitation, Nativity, Epiphany, Finding of Jesus in the temple, Resurrection, Assumption of Mary to Heaven.

1. *Ci rallegriamo con Te, o Maria, Vergine Immacolata, per l'allegrezza che t'inondò il cuore quando, dopo l'annuncio dell'angelo Gabriele, il Verbo di Dio per opera dello Spirito Santo s'incarnò nel tuo purissimo seno, e si realizzò il disegno eterno a cui eri stata predestinata insieme con il Figlio prima della creazione del mondo.*

---

2. *Ci rallegriamo con Te, o Maria, piena di grazia, per la consolazione che hai provato nella visita alla cugina Elisabetta, quando essa, dopo aver udito il tuo saluto, divenne profetessa e ti riconobbe vera 'Madre di Dio', e Giovanni, ancora nel grembo, veniva riempito del dono dello Spirito Santo.*

3. *Ci rallegriamo con Te, o Maria, Tuttasanta, per quel gaudio inesprimibile che hai provato a Betlemme, quando serbando illibato il giglio della tua verginità, partoristi senza dolore il tuo divin figlio Gesù, che era venuto a portare la pace e la redenzione al mondo, e lo vedesti adorato dai pastori.*

4. *Ci rallegriamo con Te, o Maria, regina della pace, per la somma letizia che sperimentò il tuo cuore, quando vedesti i Re Magi venire riverenti da terre lontane a prostarsi davanti al tuo divin figlio Gesù, e adorarlo come vero uomo-Dio, Redentore del mondo, e vedendo tu in loro l'omaggio di tutti i popoli.*

5. *Ci rallegriamo con Te, o Maria, via di salvezza, per il giubilo che provò il tuo cuore amoroso, quando cercato per tre giorni lo smarrito Gesù, lo trovasti nel tempio fra i dottori, che già spandeva i raggi della sua infinita sapienza a quanti lo cercano con cuore sincero.*

6. *Ci rallegriamo con Te, o Maria, madre della vita, per quella gioia che ti riempì il cuore quando vedesti il tuo figlio risorto da morte il giorno di pasqua.*

7. *Ci rallegriamo con Te, o Maria, porta del cielo, per l'esultanza del tuo cuore quando, dopo la morte, il Dio ti fece risorgere e fosti condotta in cielo, in anima e corpo, per regnare accanto al Figlio quale mediatrice di grazia e nostra avvocata.*

A website from Maiori gives the following version of the seven Joys;[9]

LE SETTE ALLEGREZZE DELLA VERGINE

Padre Nostro- Ave Maria. – Gloria al Padre

---

1. *Ave, Maria, Vergine gloriosa, sopra ogni altra donna voi siete beata. Sopra gli angeli siete dignitosa; da Dio Padre diletta chiamata. Siete Madonna tanto miracolosa, da dodici stelle foste incoronata. Siete adorata dalla luna santa, essa vi veste e l'angelo a voi vi canta: 'Ave, Maria'. Stella mattutina, l'angelo Gabriele vi fu mandato. Io vi saluto, o rosa senza spine, sto ginocchioni e sappia ben parlar, dicendo: Maria, di grazia voi siete piena, dallo Spirito Santo diletta chiamata. Bella Madonna mia, allegrezza prima è il vostro nome, dolcissima Regina.*
Padre Nostro. – Ave Maria. – Gloria al Padre.

2. *Ave, Maria, allegrezza eterna fu la seconda pe' me' dà cunsiglie. Bella Madonna mia, allegrezza tale, nove mesi portasti quel giglio. Senza dolore la notte di Natale partoristi Gesù, nobile figlio, senza dolore e nome d'angioletto da sì che nato, Gesù Benedetto.*
Padre Nostro. – Ave Maria. – Gloria al Padre.

3. *Ave, Maria, Vergine intercedente, che allegrezza avisteve in quel Figlio, quando li magi apparvero dall'Oriente; a vostro Figlio scesero a offerire oro, incenso e mirra, soggettamente ora conforto, o Vergine Maria, lo riceveste con tanto bello onore: terza allegrezza, o Mamma, mia Signora.*
Padre Nostro. – Ave Maria. – Gloria al Padre.

4. *Ave, Maria, Vergine fiorita, lo re di Pasqua, giorno benedetto, Gesù risuscitaie la morte mia lu terzo giorno pe' me' dà diletto. Bella Madonna mia, ricuordangillo quanne Gesù vo fa 'na crudezza, il vostro cuore è pieno d'ogni dolcezza, e ricevisteve la quarta allegrezza.*
Padre Nostro. – Ave Maria. – Gloria al Padre.

5. *Ave, Maria, è nato lu re di gloria, Gesù sagliette in cielo coi serafini; vide l'Ascensione cu gran vittoria in compagnia con gli angeli cherubini. Nessun di loro aveva ferma memoria, Gesù lo disse a grandi e piccolini. Gesù sagliette in cielo, cantann osanna. Quinta allegrezza, o figlia di Sant'Anna.*
Padre Nostro. – Ave Maria. – Gloria al Padre.

---

6. *Ave, Maria, giorno dignitoso, Pasqua rusata con diletto giorno, ai dodici apostoli santi e graziosi che adoravan Dio nel segreto loco, e a li cani giurei invidiosi, parlò lo Spirito Santo con una lampa di fuoco, sopra la testa tua un gran splendore: sesta allegrezza, o mamma, mia Signora.*
Padre Nostro. – Ave Maria. – Gloria al Padre.

7. Ave Maria, che fuste risuscitata di mezzo agosto; la scrittura dice: anima e corpo in cielo fuste purtata in compagnia con gli angeli felici. Il vostro figlio viene ad abbracciarvi, e fusteve incurunata 'n Paraviso, viva, eterna scala di fuoco, ferma speranza di ogni anima devota.
Padre Nostro. – Ave Maria. – Gloria al Padre.

The Joys (in Dialect) are here; Annunciation, Nativity, Epiphany, Resurrection, Ascension, Pentecost, Crowning of Our Lady in Heaven.

Another website, http://www.qumran2.net/materiale/anteprima.php?id=8933&anchor=documento_379&ritorna=%2Findice.php%3Fid%3D20&width=1280&height=645, is clear that the Joys of Our Lady are a Carmelite prayer for Eastertide.[10] *The entry, similar to a short play, is too long to quote here, but the Joys quoted are;Annunciation and Home of the Holy Spirit, Visitation, Nativity, Life in Holy Family, Hearing Jesus expound the word of God, Proclamation of Her Motherhood of Mankind and Being in the Cenacle, Finds in Jesus the way to the Father.*

Each Joy is attached to a bible reading, a spiritual reading and a verse. The verses are as follows:

Rallegrati, o Maria,
Dimora dello Spirito Santo.
Il tuo cuore puro e semplice,

simile ai poveri e ai miti della terra,
ha trovato grazia presso Dio.
Egli ha scelto te come Sua dimora,
egli, Parola eterna fatta carne,
è venuto ad abitare in te.
E tu l'hai accolto come una terra
buona, vergine e feconda;
l'hai generato per noi e per il mondo,
o Maria, Dimora dello Spirito Santo.

Rallegrati, o Maria, Messaggera di Pace.
La voce del tuo saluto,
eco profonda del Signore Risorto,
ci riempie di gioia,
come un tempo l'anziana Elisabetta.
Sì, nel tuo canto profetico contempliamo
le meraviglie della nostra Pasqua:
la dispersione di ogni seme
di violenza e di morte,
la liberazione da ogni forma di idolatria,
la rinascita dell'uomo nuovo.
Per questo oggi esultiamo con te
in Dio salvatore,
o Maria, Messaggera di Pace.

Rallegrati, o Maria, Madre del Signore.
Nell'umile segno della nascita del Figlio
è rivelata a noi

la presenza luminosa della Gloria:
nelle fasce la debolezza della croce,
nella mangiatoia una vita donata.
Per questo la liturgia celeste canta
l'abbraccio di pace
tra Dio e gli uomini da Lui amati.
È il canto gioioso della Pasqua,
l'annuncio di un mondo più umano e fraterno,
che noi vogliamo accogliere con te,
o Maria, Madre del Signore.

Rallegrati, o Maria, Discepola della Sapienza.
Anche tu hai vissuto il dramma dell'esilio,
la fatica del cammino
nella notte oscura della fede.
Per questo hai cercato e meditato
nel silenzio la vera Sapienza,
la sola che rivela i progetti di Dio
tra le pieghe variegate della vita quotidiana.
E l'hai trovata proprio nel tuo Figlio Gesù,
che con te a Nazaret cresceva
in sapienza, età e grazia
davanti a Dio e agli uomini.
Egli t'ha guidata verso il Regno, assieme
a coloro che sono diventati suoi familiari,
o Maria, Discepola della Sapienza.
Rallegrati, o Maria, Donna contemplativa.
La fede nel Dio dell'Alleanza,
vincolo nuziale con l'umanità,

ti ha immersa nelle situazioni della vita.
Il tuo sguardo,
affinato dall'ascolto della Parola,
ha colto ciò che viene a mancare all'uomo
quando perde il senso della vita: è l'Amore!
L'Amore che si fa dono e solidarietà,
l'Amore del Figlio tuo Gesù nell'ora della croce
invocato da te per noi,
o Maria, Donna Contemplativa.

Rallegrati, o Maria, nostra Madre e Sorella.
Nell'ora della croce,
compimento del mistero pasquale,
il tuo Figlio Gesù ha chiamato
te e il discepolo che lui amava
a vivere il dono dell'unità in un progetto
di comunione intima e profonda.
E nell'ora dell'attesa dello Spirito,
tu assieme ai suoi discepoli
eravate assidui e concordi nella preghiera.
La tua presenza accanto a loro
ravvivava la fede nel Risorto
e la memoria del suo vangelo,
come noi oggi insieme a te,
o Maria, nostra Madre e Sorella.

Rallegrati, o Maria, Immagine della Chiesa.
Tu sei il nostro modello,
il segno di sicura speranza

del nostro pellegrinare.
Per questo, nel cammino della vita,
reso arido e tortuoso dalle forze divoratrici
della violenza e del potere,
guardando te,
noi impariamo a far crescere Cristo
nel cuore degli uomini, impariamo,
nonostante tutto,
a seminare il Bene, il Vero, il Bello;
perché confidiamo nella forza del Vangelo,
la sola che ci fa assomigliare a te,
o Maria, Immagine della Chiesa.

References:

1 *http://www.materdecorcarmeli.it/preghiere-carmelitane.html*
2 *http://www.preghiereperlafamiglia.it/devozione-alle-sette-allegrezze-di-maria.htm*
3 *http://www.madonnadelcarminecerami.com/devozioni -Carmelitane / le-sette-allegrezze /*
4 *carminemaggiorepa.blogspot.com*
5 *http://www.airemsea.it/deserto/?p=1209*
6 *http://docplayer.it/17234409-Chiesa-madonna-del-carmine-san-giovanni-gemini-ag-novena-rosario-e-preghiere-in-onore-di-maria-ss -del-carmelo. html*

7 *http://nellaseminara.altervista.org/la-storia-della-devozione-alla-ss-vergine-maria-del-monte-carmelo-la-sua-chiesa-e- la-sua-festa-a-mistretta*
8 *https://sites.google.com/site/melchiorreancona/sette-gioie-della-madonna*

---

9 *https://www.santamariaamaremaiori.it/rosario-popolare/http://www.qumran2.net/materiale/anteprima.php?id=8933&anchor=documento_379&ritorna=%2Findice.php%3Fid % 3D20 & wisa '= 1280 & gholi = 645*
10 *http://www.qumran2.net/materiale/anteprima.php?id=8933&anchor=documento_379&ritorna=%2Findice.php%3Fid%3D20&width=1280&height=645*

FORTY FOUR

THE SEVEN JOYS OF OUR LADY AND THE FRANCISCANS - THE FRANCISCAN CROWN OR ROSARY

www.newliturgicalmovement.org/2015/08/the-seven-joys-of-virgin-mary.html

APART FROM THE CARMELITES, THE FRANCISCANS HAVE VERY successfully promulgated the devotion to the Seven Joys of Our Lady. This has developed into a version of the Rosary, known as the Franciscan Crown or Rosary, which is said by that order. The explanation of the origin of this devotion is described in the story below, taken from the above website, but to be found on numerous websites in English or Italian.

The devotion to the Seven Joys in and of itself, however, is much older; the story of its origin is told thus in the Manual for Franciscan Tertiaries (www.newliturgicalmovement.org/2015/08/the-seven-joys-of-virgin-mary.html). About the year 1420, a young man, known as James of the Rosary, deeply devoted to Our Lady, took the habit of St Francis with the Friars Minor, Before joining the Order, he had, among other practices, been accustomed daily to make a chaplet of flowers, and with it to crown a statue of the Blessed Virgin in his village church. Having in his novitiate no longer an opportunity of making this crown for his Most Beloved Queen, he, in his simplicity, thought that she would withdraw her affection from him; this temptation of the devil disturbed his vocation, and he resolved to abandon the cloister. But just as he was saying a final prayer in the priory chapel, the Virgin herself appeared to him, she encouraged the young novice to persevere by reminding him of the joyfulness of the Franciscan spirit (http://archives.sspx.org/third_orders/tosf/tosf_franciscan_crown_rosary.pdf), and gently rebuking him, strengthened him in his vocation by telling him to offer her instead of the chaplet of flowers, a crown much more pleasing to her, composed of seventy-two Ave Marias and a Pater after each decade of Ave Marias, and to meditate at each decade upon the seven joys she had experienced during the seventy-two years of her exile upon the earth. 'Do not be sad or downcast because you are no longer permitted to weave a chaplet of flowers for my head,' she told the novice. 'Remain here, and do not be sad and cast down, my son,because you can no longer weave a wreath of flowers for me. I will teach you how you can daily weave a crown of roses that will not wither and will be more pleasing to me and more meritorious for your soul. In place of the flowers that soon wither and cannot always be found, you can weave for me a crown from the flowers of your prayers that will always remain fresh for I will teach you to weave a chaplet from your prayers.' (mercyhour.org/2016/08/august-26th-the-seven-joys-of-mary/)(http://franciscanretreats.net/walkingcrrosary.aspx)

The novice immediately commenced reciting the new crown or rosary, and derived therefrom many spiritual and temporal graces. A coda tells us that the novice master wandered past the chapel just then and happened to notice the boy deep in prayer. Before the youth stood an angel, weaving a chaplet of roses from the prayers as they emerged from his mouth. When the chaplet was finished, the angel placed it upon the boy's head and departed into the heavens. The novice master asked the meaning of the scene he had witnessed, and the boy told him about the vision of Mary.

This pious practice spread quickly through the whole Order, and even throughout the world… St Bernardin of Siena used to say that it was by

---

the Crown of the Seven Joys that he had obtained all the graces which Heaven had heaped upon him.

The Seven Joys listed in the Manual are the Annunciation, the Visitation, the Birth of Christ, the Adoration of the Magi, the Finding of the Christ Child in the Temple, the Resurrection and the Assumption, but other versions of the list may be found. Two more Aves are added to make the number seventy-two mentioned above, and another Pater and Ave for the intentions of the Pope. The recitation concludes with a versicle and response, and with the Collect of the Immaculate Conception.

V. In thy Conception, o Virgin, thou most immaculate.
R. Pray for us to the Father, whose Son thou didst bear.

Let us pray. O God, Who by the Immaculate Conception of the Virgin, prepared a worthy dwelling place for thy Son; we beseech thee, that, as by the foreseen death of Thy same Son, Thou preserved Her from every stain, so Thou may grant us also, through Her intercession, to come to thee with pure hearts. Through the same Christ our Lord. R. Amen.

V. In Conceptione tua, Virgo, immaculata fuisti.
R. Ora pro nobis Patrem, cujus Filium peperisti.

Oremus. Deus, qui per immaculátam Vírginis Conceptiónem dignum Filio tuo habitáculum praeparasti: quaesumus; ut qui ex morte ejusdem Filii tui praevisa, eam ab omni labe praeservasti, nos quoque mundos ejus intercessióne ad te perveníre concedas. Per eundem Christum, Dominum nostrum. R. Amen.

References:

1 *www.newliturgicalmovement.org/2015/08/the-seven-joys-of-virgin-mary.html* [1]
2 *http://archives.sspx.org/third_orders /tosf/tosf_franciscan_crown_rosary .pdf* [2]
3 *mercyhour.org/2016/08/august-26th-the-seven-joys-of-mary/* [3]
4 *http://franciscanretreats.net/walkingcrrosary.aspx* [4]

FORTY FIVE

Why Does Wednesday Have a Special Significance in the Mediterranean?

The next issue that needs to be considered is why should Wednesday be chosen as a special day of devotion to Our Lady of Mount Carmel?

There is a long-standing custom to fast and abstain from meat on Wednesday and Friday. This is common in Countries which follow the Orthodox version of Christianity, such as Greece.

Orthodox Christians fast on Wednesday in remembrance of the betrayal of Christ and on Fridays in remembrance of His crucifixion and death. In other words, they believe by tradition that the meeting between Judas and the Jewish elders (Sanhedrin) occurred on a Wednesday. (https://oca.org › The Orthodox Faith › Questions & Answers › Daily Life) This website says, 'Unless a fast-free period has been declared, Orthodox Christians are to keep a strict fast every Wednesday and Friday. The following foods are avoided:

> *Meat, including poultry, and any meat products such as lard and meat broth.*
> *Fish (meaning fish with backbones; shellfish are permitted).*
> *Eggs and dairy products (milk, butter, cheese, etc.)*
> *Olive oil. A literal interpretation of the rule forbids only olive oil. Especially where olive oil is not a major part of the diet, the rule is sometimes taken to include all vegetable oils, as well as oil products such as margarine.*

> *Wine and other alcoholic drinks. In the Slavic tradition, beer is often permitted on fast days.(http://www.abbamoses .com/fasting.html)*
> *When fasting, we should eat simply and modestly. Monastics eat only one full meal a day on strict fast days, two meals on 'Wine and oil' days (see below). Laymen are not usually encouraged to limit meals in this way.*
> *Orthodox fasting must include abstaining from animal products. This form of fasting was passed on in the early Church from Jewish practice. In Matthew, Christ says, 'When you fast do not be like the hypocrites,' which indicates that the Jews fasted—it also indicates that Christ assumes that one fasts, for He says 'when you fast' not 'if you fast'. Fasting is not something that only developed alongside Christianity; rather, it is a practice that had been followed by the Jews, and even Scripture mentions that Christ fasted. (https://oca.org › The Orthodox Faith › Questions & Answers › Daily Life)*

It is worth remembering that throughout the time that southern Italy and Sicily were under the control of the Arabs and then throughout the time of the Normans and the crusades many people in southern Italy and Sicily followed the Byzantine rite, even if by now in union with Rome. These were the early centuries of the Carmelite order.

Later, after the promulgation of the Sabbatine bull, it became commonplace for Carmelite Friars to commute the obligations of the Sabbatine Bull to, (as well as wearing the scapular and observing chastity) to observe the fasts of the Church while additionally abstaining from meat on Wednesdays and Saturdays. Thus many Carmelite Tertiaries and Devotees came to fast on Wednesdays.

The obligations of the Sabbatine Privilege were

1. *To wear the Scapular faithfully after valid enrollment.*

2. *To observe chastity according to one's state.*

3. *To recite daily the Little Office of the Blessed Virgin, and other ways of commuting the third obligation was as is the common practice in our day, to have this third condition commutated to the daily recitation of five decades of the Most Holy Rosary). Because, even up to the second Vatican Council, and so in the present writer's memory, most devotees of Our Lady of Mount Carmel in Malta or Italy wished to benefit from the promises of the Sabbatine Privilege, fasting, or at least abstinence from meat on Wednesdays was commonplace in Malta and Italy up to recent times among devotees of Our Lady of Mount Carmel.*

References:

1 *https://oca.org › The Orthodox Faith › Questions & Answers › Daily Life*[1]
2 *Http://www.abbamoses.com/fasting.html*[2]

FORTY SIX

THE MADONNA BRUNA OF NAPLES AND THE DEVOTION TO OUR LADY OF MOUNT CARMEL ON WEDNESDAYS

THE ORIGIN OF WEDNESDAY AS A SPECIAL DAY OF DEVOTION TO OUR Lady of Mount Carmel is not related to Our Lady of Mount Carmel as such, but to an earlier Carmelite Devotion to the Mother of God as the Mother and Patroness of the Carmelites.

It is worth bearing in mind that the original Hermits on Mount Carmel had settled among Greek Monks, close to their 'Abbey of Saint Margaret', so one would expect that their traditions would have influenced each other. The Carmelites had dedicated their original chapel on Mount Carmel to Our Lady. Doubtless they had an Icon of Our Lady There. In the Greek Theology of Icons[1], an Icon represents the person painted itself, (and furthermore, if a copy of the icon is touched to the original, it too represents the person painted) - so the Chapel belonged to Our Lady. She was the 'Lady of the Place', the Lady of Carmel in a special way. Thus the Carmelites viewed Her as their Patron. Later John Baconthorpe and other Carmelite Writers were to continue referring to Our Lady as the 'Domina Loci', the Lady of the Place. (see Emanuele Boaga 'The Lady of The Place' 2001 Roma Edizioni Carmelitane)[2]. The Carmelites therefore came to see Our Lady as their Special Patron, their Queen, Mother and Sister, and saw themselves as the 'Brothers of Our Lady of Mount Carmel' par excellence. The Carmelites went to great extent to promote the idea that they were the 'Brothers of Our Lady of Mount Carmel'. It gave them their special identity as 'Our Lady's Order', as distinct from other mendicant Orders. In 1374 the Carmelite John Hornby defended this Marian Title of the order against the Dominicans at the University of Cambridge. This was one of the major occasions which led to the final papal approval of the order. A story, not linked with the scapular vision itself, but emphasizing the order's earlier special devotion to Mary, would be extremely important to the Order. One such story is that of the Madonna Bruna of the Carmine Maggiore in Naples.[3,4,5]

The story starts in the Carmine Maggiore in Naples which houses an ancient Icon of Our Lady which was said to have been painted by Saint Luke and to have been brought to this church and monastery by the Carmelites directly from Mount Carmel and is known as the Madonna Bruna (could it be the original Icon from Mount Carmel or a copy touched to it?).

In the Holy Year of 1500, the confraternity of tanners, which was based in a church near the Carmine Maggiore, made a pilgrimage to Rome to gain the indulgences of the jubilee proclaimed by Pope Alexander VI. They were joined by many other faithful.

The pilgrimage left Naples on April 7. The Pilgrims brought with them the icon of the Virgine Bruna. They walked the whole route on foot, passing through Traietto and Sermoneta. During the journey, through the intercession of Our Lady there took place 'many miracles to several men in various lands.' In particular, a crippled beggar called Tommaso Saccone was cured when he watched the procession and wished to go with them to Rome.

When they arrived in Rome on April 13, the image of the Madonna Bruna was exposed for veneration in the Vatican Basilica, where it received the homage of Alexander VI, the Pope himself.

The turnout of the Roman people and the pious pilgrims present in the Eternal City was so extraordinary that the Pope a few days later, gave the order to the pilgrims from the city of Naples to leave Rome with their Icon 'to prevent this icon from becoming more important a site of pardon than Saint Peter's or other places of Rome.'

So the pilgrims on April 18 began their return journey, reaching Naples on the twenty-fifth of the same month, On the return journey they were joined by other pilgrims along the way, and there were repeated miracles along the route through the intercession of the Madonna, so that many gave thanks to Her.

The welcome of the city of Naples to the on the return of the venerated image was triumphant. Later the skilful brush of Luca Giordano would immortalize the event in a painting, which is in the church of Donnaregina in Naples. Through the intercession of the Madonna Bruna there continues to be 'many miraculous healings of the Deaf, the Blind and the crippled' and many spiritual and temporal graces, Soon 'almost all the kingdom was coming to Naples with processions to visit the said figure of Santa Maria della Bruna, all were barefoot, some with torchlights and some with silver chalices.[3,4,5]*'*

For this reason, the Marian icon was not placed in its original site, but was placed on the high altar on a wooden stand, instead of the picture depicting the Assumption, which was then placed in the chapter room of the convent.

By order of Frederick II of Aragon on June 24 of that year 1500 many sufferers were gathered in the Carmelite church to implore from heaven, through the maternal intercession of Mary, the desired cure. He later had recorded the healings that took place. Now 24 June was a Wednesday.[3,4,5]

This determined the choice to worship the Madonna Bruna especially on Wednesday. Thus were born the 'Wednesday of Carmel,' a pious devotion which soon spread from Naples not only throughout the ancient Kingdom of Naples, but also out of it especially in all the churches of the Carmelite order. The pious practice of 'Wednesday' still continues, and the pious pilgrimage remains as a living reality in the piety of the Neapolitans to the 'Vergine Bruna'.[3,4,5]

The Wednesdays of Our Lady were introduced into the Roman Church of Traspontina in 1724 and was granted indulgences by Pope Benedict XIII in the bull Alias pro parte. In Traspontina, the Wednesdays between Easter and Pentecost had a special character. There would be a sermon on the seven joys of Our Lady.[3,4,5]

In other churches and in those of the confraternities, the nine Wednesdays preceding the feast of St. Joseph were celebrated solemnly.This practice was given indulgences by Pope Clement XIII in 1765.[3,4,5]

References:

1 *Leonid Ouspensky, Vladimir Lossky The Meaning of Icons SVS Press 1989*

2 *Emanuele Boaga 'Our Lady of the Place' 2001 Roma Edizioni Carmelitane*

3 *Breve Racconto Della Miracolosa Immagine Della santissima Vergine Detta La Bruna che si venera nella regal chiesa del Carmine Maggiore di Napoli MDCCXCVI Stamperia Del Paci.*

The Madonna Bruna Carmine Maggiore Naples
(credit http://karmelitaikon.blogspot.com/2010/)

---

4 *La 'Bruna'e il Carmine di Napoli Napoli Fede-Storia-Arte Napoli 2001*
5 *S.Maria Del Carmine detta 'La Bruna' Storia, Culto. Folclor Dott. Gabriele Monaco Laurenziana. Napoli 1975.*

FORTY SEVEN

THE SEVEN WEDNESDAYS AFTER EASTER - WEDNESDAYS 'OF AUDIENCE' (*TAL-UDIENZA*)

WITHIN A SHORT TIME OF FIFTY DAYS, THREE MYSTERIES OCCUR which cause great Joy to Mary and which are very dear to the heart of every Christian. These are the Resurrection of Jesus from the dead, his Ascension into Heaven, and the Descent of the Holy Ghost upon the apostles. The Carmelites had the holy custom of every Wednesday giving honour to Our Lady with devotion to Her seven greatest Joys. So, in order to show their joy at such extraordinary events and at the same time to share the Joy of their beloved Mother, the Blessed Virgin Mary, the Carmelites began to solemnise more than usual the seven Wednesdays which occurred in this period of fifty days after Easter. As well as the three mysteries which we have mentioned, they would celebrate four other circumstances during which Mary's heart would certainly have overflowed with joy. In their prayer, as well as the chaplet of the Joys, with the recital of an 'Our Father, Hail Mary and Glory Be' after each Joy, they would also make a short meditation on each one[172]. In some churches, such as S. Martin Major in Bologna, The Traspontina in Rome, Our Lady of Mount Carmel in Valletta and in Mdina, Malta, they would also organise a sermon about the Joy which was being celebrated on that Wednesday[173].

NOTES

172 *See LEOINDELICATO, Giardino Carmelitano, p. 218: MARUGGI, Tesoro spiritual, p.150; Modo di recitare le sette Allegrezze....di Monte Santo, p.19; HOPPENBROUWERS, Devotio Mariana, p.281.*

173 *In San Martino Maggiore, Bolognia and in the Church of Traspontina in Rome, the sermon would be held during the first mass, called 'of the Scapular': 'La messa dell'Abito'; In Malta, as far as we know, the sermon would always be held in the evening. See DAL BUONO, Divozione, pp.13-14; BAGNARI, Divozioni, pp.12-13; VELLA, id-devot, pp.5, 289-290.*

FORTY EIGHT

The Relationship Between the Carmelite Order and Our Lady

OVER TIME, HOWEVER, BECAUSE OF CIRCUMSTANCES, THE SUBJECT of these sermons began to change. Importance began to be given to some aspects of the relationship of the Carmelite Order to Our Lady, Mainly because of the Giving of the Scapular (by Our Lady to Saint Simon Stock) and the promises linked with it, among them the promise of salvation to the true devotees of the Scapular and their early release from Purgatory (on the first Saturday after their death, according to the traditional understanding of the Sabbatine Privilege).

We have not been able to identify exactly when this change happened, but we think that the conclusion which we have come to is not far from the truth.

(i) The General Chapter of 1575

The advent of Protestantism in the history of the Church at the beginning of the sixteenth century served as an occasion for the devotion of the scapular to develop further.[174] In 1535, Luther himself attempted to ridicule the Scapular.[175] The reaction was that this devotion so spread across the world that we can say that, together with the rosary, we can consider it the main Marian Devotion with which the Catholics challenged the anti-marian spirit of Protestantism.[177] It is not therefore surprising that the General

Chapter of 1575 decided that, in order to further encourage the devotion of the scapular[178], there should, every Saturday, be a sermon held in all Churches of the Carmelite Order which would be entirely or at least partially about Our Lady of Mount Carmel.[179]

(ii) The decree of 1595 of Prior General Chizzola

Twenty years later, the Prior General of the Carmelite Order, P. Sephen Chizzola issued a decree in which he confirmed the obligation or statute of the General Chapter which we have just mentioned. He says, in fact, that every Saturday, Carmelite preachers should, as well as the explanation of the Gospel, and other Christian teaching, say something about Mary, Our Lady of Carmel. They should also preach about the saints of the Order and its Antiquities and how the Order had spread, as well as the indulgences granted to it by the Popes. Whoever did not do this was not to be allowed to continue to hold the office of preacher.[180]

(iii) The Carmelite Constitution of 1626

The decree of Chizzola was included word for word in this constitution, which was issued during the tenure of Prior General P. Gregorio Canali. However this limited the obligation which bound Carmelite Preachers to the time of Lent. On other Saturdays of the year, preachers were not obliged to preach about Our Lady of Mount Carmel.[181] There were also some additions and warnings. Not only were preachers obliged to preach about the saints of the Order and its Antiquities and how the Order had spread around the world, but they were also expected to speak about the Scapular Confraternity and the indulgences which both it and the Order were adorned with. On the other hand, preachers were warned to be careful not to exaggerate these things.[182]

Here one should ask why the Constitution required that sermons should be made to speak about the Scapular Confraternity and the indulgences which it was adorned with. The only possible reason must be the decree of the Holy Inquisition (Holy Office) of the twentieth of January 1613.[183]

The Carmelites had appealed to Rome in the dispute that the Portuguese Carmelites had had with Inquisitor General Don Pedro de Castillo because of a booklet which he had prohibited on pain of excommunication 'ipso facto' should anyone read it or did not surrender any copy of it, whether whole or in part. This booklet summarised all the indulgences received by the Carmelite Order including the Sabbatine Privilege. After hearing their defence, made by Father John of Saint Thomas, the Roman Inquisition issued a decree in favour of the Carmelites on the twentieth of January 1613. It said that Carmelite Religious could preach the Sabbatine Privilege, so long as they explained it correctly. Mary did not free her scapular devotees by descending into purgatory, but by helping them with her continual intercession and merits.[184]

The instructions of Canali's Constitution were followed exactly by Filocalo Caputo. Every Saturday of Lent he would give an excellent sermon on the Carmelite Scapular.[185] However, later, in Naples, these sermons were transferred to Wednesdays. An example are the sermons by Andrea Mastelloni published under the name of 'The Wednesdays of Santa Maria della Vita'. They discuss the miracles and graces which Our Lady had given to her Carmelite Scapular devotees applied to the gospel readings throughout the year.[186]

Some also transferred the sermons to Sundays. Among the famous preachers were George of the Queen of Angels Gaillard, Isidor of Saint Egidius and Thomas of the Virgin. The first wrote about the Confraternity of the Virgin Mary of Mount Carmel, while the last used to split every sermon into two, the first part would be about Christ, while the second part would be about Our Lady.[187]

According to this author, in the relics of the scapular we have a mirror of the presence of God and of his Mother Mary, so that after this life we will enjoy in a more intensive way our union with God and Mary.[188]

Therefore we believe that because of a reaction against Protestantism, given that even Luther himself had criticized the devotion of the Scapular, and also because of opposition of Catholics against the promises attached to the scapular, that is of salvation and of early release from purgatory, the sermons which were originally about the Joys of Our Lady changed into sermons about the relationship between the Carmelite Order and Our Lady and in particular about the Scapular Devotion. Finally, we believe that it was the three documents which we have examined; that is, The Chapter General (1575), the Decree of Chizzola (1595) and the Carmelite Constitution (1626) which were the main means which brought about this change.

Notes

174 *ESTEVE, De valore spirituali devotionis S. Scapularis, p.59; 'Apparitio protestantismi in historia Ecclesiae ineunte saeculo XVI, signat novam periodum in evolutione devotionis (S. Scapularis), Etenim haec* *altera periodus correspondet plenae reactioni spiritus catholici adversus positionem negativam protestantismi'.*

175 *'Les moines armes de leurs rosaries, scapulaires... condusant les foules 'ad muta simulachra', See G. PHILIPS, l'opposition protestante a la Mariologie, in Marianum, 11(1949) 474.*

176 *XIBERTA, De vision s. Simonis Stock, p.42: 'S.Scapulare altera mendietate saeculi XVI [ESTEVE, ib.,p.50] 'quasi flumen exundans....,per totum orbem se diffudisse'.'*

177 *ESTEVE, ib., p.50: 'Devotio enim, iam antea evulgata, decursu catholicis..., tamquam magna devotio mariana catholicismi una cum ss.Rosario adversus protestantesimi spiritum, antidicomarianum....'*

178 *ESTEVE, ib., p.100: 'Ut autem vera devotion mariana S. Scapularis foveretur, praescriptum fuit ab ordine ut de ea frequens sermohaberetur.Ita in Capitulo generali a.1575'.*

179 *Acta Capitulorum Generalium Ordinis Fratrum B.V. Mariae de Monte Carmelo, ed.Gabriel Wessels O. Carm.,v.1, Romae, 1912. P.518; 'Quolibet sabbato totam praedicationem, aut praedicationis partem habebunt de B.ma Virgine, Dei Genitrice, Montis Carmeli Domina.'*

180 *STEPANUS CHIZZOLA, O. Carm., Decreta pro conservanda et amplificanda vitae regularis observandia, Hispali, 1595, p.32: 'Predicatores omni tempore diebus sabbati in praedicationibus suis ultra explenationem evangelii et aliarum doctrinarum semper aliquid praedicent de beatissima et felicissima Virgine Maria Dei Genitrice, Domina huius nostrae religionis montis Carmeli; idque faciant ob devotionem populi in laudem eiusdem piissimae Matris. Amplius recordabuntur praedicare de sanctis nostri ordinis et saepissime aliqua exponent de antiquitate et amplitudine ordinis nostri ac indulgentiarum illus, et secus facientes non admittentur ad illud sacrum munus obeundum'.*

181 *Costitutiones Ordinis Carmelitarum, Romae, 1626, p.30, n.9:*

'Praecipimus ut praedicatores nostril omni tempore Quadragesimae diebus sabbatisin concionibus suis intra explicationem evangelii et aliarum doctrinarum semper aliquid praedicent de beatissima et felicissima V. Maria Dei Genitrice Domina huius nostrae religionis montis Carmeli; idque faciant ob devotionem populi in laudem eiusdem pissimae Matris'.

182 *Costitutiones O. Carm., ib., p.30; 'Amplius recordabuntur praedicare de sanctis ordinis et saepissime aliqua exponere de antiquitate et amplitudine religionis et confraternitatis Scapularis ac de earum indulgentiis, et secus facientes non admittentur ad illud sacrum munus obeundm; simper tamen caveant a nimia exageratione'.*

183 *As we find in Bullarium Carmelitanum, this decree was given on 20th January 1613 (see I, pp.62-63), but was promulgated on 15th February 1613 (see II, p.601). Therefore we think that P.Melchiorre di S. Maria was mistaken when he said that this decree was promulgated on 11th February 1613 (see Il Privilegio Sabatino, in Lo Scapolare, a cura del comitato italiano VII centenario dello Scapolare, 2 [1951] 73).*

184 *About this dispute, see especially ELISEO MONSIGNANI O. Carm., Relazione di tutti i successi, provisioni, e decreti emanati circa il Privilegio, o sia Bolla chiamata Sabatina, dall'anno 1603 sino al presente 1718, in Arch.Gen. O.Carm., Confr. II, 1; MELCHIORRE DI S. MARIA, O.C.D., Il Privilegio Sabatino, in Lo Scapolare, p.73.*

185 *See PHILOCALUS CAPUTO, O.Carm.,I discorsi quares-imali, Napoli, 1628;ESTEVE, De valore spirituali devotionis S. Scapularis, p.101.*

186 *MASTELLONI, I mercoledì di Santa Maria della Vita: miracoli e favori della Beate Vergine a suoi divoti applicati agli evangelji dell'anno, 2.v., Napoli, 1704. See VALENTINO BORG GUSMAN, O. Carm., Un predicatore mariano, in Carmelus, 12 (1965) 30, 34; Dottrina mariologica di Andrea Mastelloni, Romae, 1966, pp.30, 34(n.19); ESTEVE, ib., p.101.*

187 *See GEORGIUS (a Regina Angelorum) GAILLARD, O.Carm., Trifoedus marianum, sive conciones historico-theologico-ascetico-morales de alma confraternitate gloriosissimae Virginis Mariae de Monte Carmelo sive sacri Scapularis in omnes totius anni Domenicas, 1683;ISIDORUS A. S. AEGIDIO, O.Carm., Corona Stellarum duodecim, Antverpiae, 1685; THOMAS A VIRGINE MARIA, Concordia evangelica Christi cum Maria super quodlibet evangelium dominicale, 'concionem complectens bipartitam: cuius pars prima est de Christo evangelizante; pars secunda de Deipara cum Christo concordante', Antverpiae, 1673.*

188 *THOMAS A VIRGINE MARIA, Concordia evangelica... p.344: 'Sic igitur Deum et Mariam in Deo praesentem sub reliquiis Scapularis habeamus, illos....quasi per speculum in aenigmate incessanter intuentes, ut post mortalem vitae decursum, intensius Dei et Mariae in Deo unione perfruamur'.*

FORTY NINE

A Special Name for the Seven Wednesdays after Easter

The Carmelites have the custom of celebrating the Wednesdays between Easter and Pentecost with greater solemnity than usual. In Malta they have a special name, we call them 'Tal-Udienza', a name which has a little-known history behind it. We tell whoever asks us what these words mean that we do not know, however there must be some explanation.

Professor P. Anastasju Cuschieri O.Carm. says that 'we cannot say what this term means', however he himself tells us that 'some say that these Wednesdays are called 'Tal-Udienza' because during them, prayers are more likely to be heard'.[189]

Is it true that we cannot find the true meaning of these words? And who are the persons that Cuschieri is referring to? We have often asked ourselves these questions. To answer them we have had to use our brains, and also to search many books and documents which we have thought might give us some information. What follows is the result of the research which we have carried out.

It appears that the name given to these Wednesdays is linked to a miraculous statue of Our Lady, which is venerated in the church of Our Lady of Mount Carmel in Sambuca, Sicily. In the past this church belonged to the Carmelites, but now it is in the hands of the secular clergy. At present it serves as the Archepretal Church of

Sambuca. This year [1979] we visited it in July, and we said mass in it several times and also preached.

According to tradition, this statue was brought to Sambuca from Cellaro during the plague epidemic of 1575-6.(190) However, before this it had been brought to Cellaro from Mazara del Vallo.(191) It was the property of the Xarrino family, which held a fiefdom in Cellaro, which had been given to them on a perpetual lease by the Commander of the Order of the Knights of Malta[192] This family itself held the title of Knights of Malta.[193]

This marble statue is called the Madonna dell'Udienza, and there are two opinions about the origin of this name. Some say that the Carmelites of Sambuca gave it this name because it is usual for Carmelites to honour images of Our Lady with this title in their churches, in the same way as Augustinians often prefer the title 'Of Help' - Soccorso.[194] This opinion is appropriately criticised and discarded by De Ruberto, because there are only a few places where Our Lady is honoured under this title[195], and indeed this title is practically unknown in other Carmelite churches.[196]

The other opinion is that this name was given to the statue by the people of Sambuca. The people gave the statue this name as a sign of gratitude and in thanksgiving because when the image entered the town for the first time, Our Lady listened to the cries and sobs of those who were ill with plague and healed them and ended the epidemic[197]. Di Ruberto accepts this view because it is more probable than the other, it is more natural and spontaneous, and it is in keeping with the local tradition.[198]

Regarding devotion, Rocco Pirro had written that 'In the Church of the Carmelites (of Sambuca) there was an image of Santa Maria dell'Udienza, which, in all times of necessity, would be carried in procession by the people with great devotion'[199]. Over time, this devotion grew, as can be witnessed today by the feast and procession which is celebrated every year on the third Sunday of May.[200]

To give an idea of how great the devotion to the Madonna dell' Udienza is, we can mention three facts or happenings. Firstly, we mention the Confraternity of the same name. In the Carmelite church of Sambuca is founded the Confraternity of the Madonna dell'Udienza. The members wear light blue, with a scapular with an Image of the Madonna dell'Udienza embroidered on it. Because the members of the Confraternity go bare foot, this confraternity used to be referred to as that of the 'nudi'.[201]

In the second place, we should mention the decree by which the Sacred Congregation of Rites, on the 17th September 1847 declared the Madonna dell Udienza patroness of Sambuca in Sicily.[202]

To finally crown this devotion, the Vatican Chapter solemnly crowned the statue of the Madonna dell'Udienza on the 17th of May 1903.[203]

Sambuca is a town in the province and diocese of Agrogento, Sicily. The Sicilian Carmelites of the province of Saint Angelus, that is those of the province of Mazara del Vallo [204], had opened a convent in this town and named it for Saint Elias. The part of the town around that convent started to be called 'the quarter of Saint Elias'.[205]

At first, the Carmelites did not build a church in this town. They used to officiate in the church of Saint Leonard, which was close to their convent. Later the church began to be called that of Saint Lucy.[206]

Although we do not know when the first Carmelite religious opened the convent of Saint Elias, it was definitely before 1530. Indeed, in 1530, Salvatore Bardi Mastrantonio, baron of Sambuca and prince of Iaci, built them a convent beside the church of Saint Anthony the Abbot. They began to officiate in this church and changed its name to that of the convent: Santa Marija Annunzjata.[207]

During the plague of 1575/76 this church was dedicated to Our Lady and officiated by the Religious of the Carmelite Order, which is also known as the Order of Our Lady. Since the Xarrino family, who were the owners of the statue of the Madonna dell'Udienza, were very great devotees of Our Lady of Mount Carmel, it was placed in the church of the Carmelites, where it is till this day.[208]

Madonna del Udienza Sambuca Sicily
(Credit Guzzman85)

NOTES

189 *ANASTASJU CUSCHIERI O.Carm., l'Erbgħat tal Udienza, in Ir Regina tal Carmelu, 9 (1917) 264.*

190 *SALVATORE DI RUBERTO, Sambuca-Zabut e la Madonna dell' Udienza, Napoli (s.a.), p.82; 'La Statua venne nel tempo della peste...; degnissima di fede la tradizione, la quale asserisce che la traslazione di Maria SS. Dell'Udienza, da Cellaro a Sambuca, sia avvenuta in tempo di peste, e propriamente in quella del 1575-6'. See also p.66.*

191 *DI RUBERTO, Sambuca-Zabut...., p.45: 'La tradizione ci dice pure che l'Immagine fu trasportata da Mazzara a Cellaro';p.50; 'La statua della Madonna dell'Udienza venne fatta trasportare, per la prima volta, da Mazara del Vallo, da un signore della famiglia Sciarrino'.*

192 *Ib, p.51; 'Noi infatti sappiamo dagli atti piu antichi che l' Immagine fu in origine proprieta della famiglia Sciarrino, la quale era oriunda appunto da Mazzara'. He then quotes a notarial act of 9th March 1670, where are the words 'Cappellam vocatam olim di Xarrino con una Madonna di marmot dentro chiamata la Madonna dell' Audientia'. Later he publishes the whole document (pp.168-171). In it is mentioned another notarial act of 1628, where it is said again that the chapel with the statue of the Madonna dell'Udienza was property of the family Xarrino. He then continues talking about the fiefdom which we have mentioned: 'Infatti e cosa certissima, che, nel 10 Aprile 1503, per mezzo del notaro Pietro Buxerra, il commendatore dell'Ordine Gerosolimitano di S. Giovanni di Rodi (Cavalieri di Malta) dette a censo, per tari 25 all'onorevole Giacomo Sciarrino, della citta di Mazara, per sé e suoi eredi e successor in pepetuum, un tenimento di terre nei feudo di Cellaro, presso Sambuca e presso il fiume ed il mulino' (pp.53-54).*

193 *GIUSEPPE GIACONE FU DOMENICO, Zabut: notizie storiche del Castello di Zabut e suo contiguo casale oggi Comune di Sambuca di*

Sicilia, (s.n.t.), p.109: 'La cappella della Madonna dell'udienza, diligentemente tenuta dai Monaci, era chiusa da una magnifica e lavorata grata in ferro, alla cui sommità era posta la croce di Malta, la quale ricordava che i padroni ebbero il titoli di Cavalieri di Malta'.

194 *DI RUBERTO, Sambuca-Zabut, pp.46-47: 'Vi e chi dice, che questo titolo Le sia stato imposto dai Carmelitani, nella cui Chiesa e collocate, appunto perché questo titolo è solito trovarsi nelle immagini venerate nelle chiese di quei frati, allo stesso modo che, presso gli Agostiniani, troviamo spesso il titolo del Soccorso'.*

195 *PLACIDO SEMINERI, in his book Iconologia della Vergine Madre di Dio Protettrice di Messina (Messina 1644, pp.386, 436-4) mentions two monasteries in Messina where Our Lady is honoured under the title of 'dell Udienza'. These are the monastery 'dell'Alto' and that of 'S.Caterina di Valverde'. SALVATORE DI PIETRO also mentions Mezzoiuso. In this village there was a church dedicated to Madonna dell'Udienza, to which many pilgrims went every day.(see L'Assunzione di Maria in cielo secondo la storia e la tradizione, S.Benigno Canavese, 1902, p.109). Finally DI RUBERTO tells us about three other places where there is devotion to la Madonna dell'Udienza: Salemi, S. Margherita Belice and Sciacca (see Sambuca-Zabut, p.48).*

196 *DI RUBERTO, ib p.47: 'Ma a dire il vero, questa opinion non ci piace; perché sono pochissime quelle parti, dove la Madonna si venera sotto questo titolo, anzi, nella maggior parte delle stesse chiese Carmelitane, e affatto sconosciuto'.*

197 *Ib.: 'Si dice da altri, che questo titolo fu dato alla Madonna di Sambuca quando, entrando nel paese la prima volta, lo liberò dalla peste, prestando Udienza ai gemiti degli appestati, Ella dunque presto il suo benevolo orecchio in quell immane sciagura, e percio per gratitudine, Le fu dato questo titolo dal populo bene-ficato'.*

198 *Ib.: 'Quest'opinione, poggiata sulla tradizione, ci sembra piu spon-*

tanea, e l'accettiamo, tanto piu che, alla sua volta, conferma la tradizione medesima'.

199 *ROCCO PIRRO, Sicilia Sacra: Notizia Agrigentina, Palermo, 1733. V.1, p.750: 'Carmelitarum...aedes...nobilitata est... simulacro Sanctae Mariae de Audientia quod magna populi pietate in cunctis necessitatibus circumducitur'. According to Di Ruberto, Pirro wrote his notes on Sambuca between 1606 and 1633 (See Sambuca-Zabut, pp.97, 123).*

200 *DI RUBERTO, o.c., p.124: 'La devozione, rinforzata dal benefico della liberazione della peste andò sempre crescendo, e ne è prova non dubbia la processione della terza Domenica di Maggio.....Questa processione, ...continua ad essere l'attestato solenne della devozione dei Sambucesi verso la Madonna dell'Udienza. I continui beneficii della Madonna sono sempre concorsi a mantener viva la devozione.'*

201 *Ib.,p.153: 'Confraternita di Maria SS. Dell'Udienza. I Confratelli indossano il ricco scapolare adornato dall'Immagine in ricamo della Madonna dell'Udienza'; p.83 '....la confraternita dei cosidetti nudi, ...Questi nudi vestono un abito tutto quanto azzurro e vanno scalzi'.*

202 *Ib., p.130: 'La sacra Congregazione dei Riti, prefetto il Cardinale Lambruschini, riunita nel palazzo del Quirinale il giorno 11 Settembre 1847, approve la domanda. E, nel 17 Settembre dello stesso anno, coll' approvazione del Pontefice Pio IX, emano il decreto, concedendo che la Madonna dell'Udienza fosse dichiarata Patrona di Sambuca'. In pp.175-178, Di Ruberto gives a complete copy of the decree he mentions, as well as a full translation from latin into Italian.*

203 *See ib.,pp.130-154 where he recounts the story of this coronation; pp.185-192, where he presents a full copy of the decree of coronation and a translation into Italian.*

204 *In the General Chapter of 1472, the Prior General of the Order of the time divided the province of Sicily into two provinces: 'divisi....Provinciam*

Siciliae in duabus Provinciis; videlicet in Provinciam Vallium Noti et Demonum...et Provinciam Vallis Mazariae Sancti Angeli Ordinis nostri' (Acta Capitulorum Generalium, v.1.p.260). That of Vallium Noti et Demonum continued to be called the province of Sicily and the other of Vallis Mazariae began to be called 'of Saint Angelus': 'divisit, ...Provinciam Siciliae in Prov- inciam communiter dictam Siciliae, ...et Provinciam Vallis Mazzariae, quae Sancti Angeli dicitur' (LEZANA, Annales, v.4, p.931).

205 *GIACONE, Zabut: notizie storiche..., p.107: 'L' antico convento del Carmine, sotto il titolo di S. Elia...Quella contrada del paese perciò prese il nome di Quartiere di S. Elia'.*

206 *DI RUBERTO, Sambuca-Zabut, p.15: 'I Carmelitani, i quali dapprima si erano stabiliti presso l'antica chiesa di S. Leonardo, che oggi chiamasi Santa Lucia'; GIACONE, o.c.,p.107: 'L, antico convento del Carmine, ...era nel fabbricato contiguo all'odierna Chiesa di S. Lucia.... In antico la cennata Chiesa era detta di S. Leonardo, la quale, per il suo vicinato al convento era officiata dai Carmelitani'.*

207 *DI RUBERTO, o.c., p.30: 'Al 1530 Salvatore Bardi Mastrantonio, barone di Iaci,....fece costruire il convento dei Carmelitani, e la Chiesa (di S.Antonio) ebbe il titolo della SS.Annunziata' (see also pp.15, 116); PIRRO, Sicilia Sacra, v.1, p.750: 'Carmelitarum ab anno 1530 aedes divi Antonii a Salvatore de Mastrantonio, huius oppidi Iacisque domino, fundata, nunc sub titulo 'SS. Annuntiatae', opibus Ignatii Marchionis et studio F. Leonardi Contini Prioris, viri virtutibus noti, aucta atque nobilitata est'; D'AMICO, Lexico Topografico Siculo, t.2, p.155: 'Carmelitarum conventus ad S. Antonii aedem a Salvatore Bardi Magistrantonio 1530 aedificatus, sub titulo nunc Deiparae Annuntiatae, quem Ignatius Marchio opibus et Leonardus Contini prior vir virtutibus clarus aedificiis auxit'; See also GIACONE, o.c., p.108.*

208 *DI RUBERTO, ib.,pp.116-117: 'La Chiesa del Carmine, all'epoca della peste, era una Chiesa già dedicate alla Madonna, ed era servita dai frati Carmelitani, appartenenti a quell'Ordine che chiamasi per antonomasia l'Ordine della Madonna, i quali fin dal 1530 come dicemmo, s'erano stability cola'. Questi religiosi avrebbero mantenuto piu vivo il culto alla Madonna...(Inoltre) La famiglia Sciarrino, proprietaria dell'Immagine, era devotissima della Madonna del Carmine'.*

FIFTY

OTHER PLACES IN ITALY IN WHICH THE TITLE MADONNA DELL'UDIENZA IS USED

APART FROM SAMBUCA, THERE ARE A NUMBER OF PLACES IN ITALY where Our Lady is reverenced as patron under the title 'Dell'Udienza'. Each has its own story which accounts for the derivation of the title, so that this title - which means in general 'Our Lady who gives Audience - as a Queen to her Devotees - ' has not one origin but several, with a different origin from each place.

There are a number of different places, mainly in Sicily, where Our Lady is venerated under the title of Madonna Dell'Udienza[1,2]. Apart from Sambuca, a Google Search revealed the following locations.

In Giuliana, the title of the sanctuary is 'dell'Udienza", because of an ancient Carmelite tradition according to which Mary every year after Easter goes to Mount Carmel to listen to the supplications of her faithful. Thus, for seven consecutive Wednesdays the seven joys of Our Lady are recited and the rosary is sung in Calabrian dialect.The image of Our Lady in Giuliana seems a copy of Our Lady of Trapani. The origin of the cult in Giuliana could be at the end of the fifteenth or beginning of the sixteenth century, but the cult became much greater from 1837, the year when there was an epidemic of cholera in Giuliana. It is said that that year the statue sweated six times, and the end of the epidemic was attributed to the intercession of Our Lady.

In Bovalino Superiore[3], there is a specific text for the Seven Joys, which is kept in a manuscript written in dialect in the Church of Saint Catherine. In Augusta (Sicily), the seven Wednesdays between Easter and Pentecost are known as the Wednesdays 'Dell'Udienza' -'of Audience'. In these days it is considered particularly propitious to implore graces of Our Lady. It was considered in popular devotion that the faithful, having shared Our Lady's suffering during Lent, should now go and congratulate Mary on the resurrection of Her Son, confident that after such suffering She would be more inclined to hear and respond to her clients' supplications. Thus She, as queen of Heaven, gave seven appointments in which to listen to and respond to her faithful 'subjects'.

Public devotion demanded that on these days, solemn masses be said, the Seven Joys of Our Lady and litanies be recited, and the Image of Our Lady of Mount Carmel should be exposed, covered with ex-votos, whereas for most of the year it is covered.

In Augusta, the name 'Dell'Udienza'[4] is identically interchangeable with Our Lady of Mount Carmel. This same identification of the two titles occurred in Sambuca and Giuliana. In the past, in Augusta, the feast of Our Lady of Mount Carmel used to be held on the last Wednesday 'Dell'Udienza'. In Augusta, the Carmelite Third Order now organises these Wednesdays, with mass preceded with an hour 's exposition of the Blessed Sacrament, rosary and recitation of the seven Joys before Mass, while after mass, the chaplet of Our Lady of Mount Carmel is recited.[5]

In Roccella Valdemone (Messina)[6], the feast of its patron, Maria

Santissima dell'Udienza is considered very important. It is held on the feast of the Assumption. The procession starts from the Mother Church of the town. When the statue comes out of church, the men who are carrying the statue on its pedestal ('baiardu') must lower it and then raise it to shoulder height again, to cries of'e chiamamela, chi n'aiuta! Evviva la Vergine Maria.' The crowd used to kneel as the statue left the church. During the procession, when the Church of Our Lady of Mount Carmel is reached, one of the poles attached to the pedestal is touched to the door of the church, to honour the dead, and so that the 'two sisters' (statues of Our Lady) could meet each other. Later, at the square before the Cathedral, the statue stops to 'give audience to its children', and at this point, parents present their children and babies to Our Lady. Thus, at Roccella Valdemone Udienza refers to a Queen giving audience to Her Children or subjects.[6]

Another church near Palermo dedicated to the Madonna dell'Udienza is in Mezzojuso near Palermo.[7] It dates to the seventeenth century. There is also the Church of the Madonna dell' Udienza in Castronuovo Di Sicilia (PA), once the Mother Church of the town. It has recently been reopened. A mountainside shrine called Madonna dell'Udienza exists in Castroreale.[8]

The Madonna dell'Udienza, of Melissa has recently (2013) been crowned again after its crowns were stolen.[9]

It has also been reported that the ancient icon of the Madonna Delle Perle was originally known as the Madonna[10]. It became known as 'delle perle' because of pearls appended to it as ex-votos. It was donated to the Church and Abbey of Santa Maria de Latinis in Palermo, and was venerated there for eight centuries, until the destruction of the church in the second world War and is now in the Palermo Diocesan Museum. The donor was Matteo Ajello, Grand Chancellor of William II and Tancred.

Also in Palermo, the Carmine Maggiore of Palermo reports on its website that it contains an altar dedicated to the Madonna dell-Udienza. The statue on this altar used to be known as Our Lady of Mount Carmel and was used in the procession of the last Sunday of July until it was substituted by another statue. The statue is of Marble and is by Domenico Gagini (1456 -1571).[11]

The Carmelites note that the cult of the Madonna dell'Udienza was introduced into Sicily by the Carmelites, The title derives from an ancient Carmelite tradition that every year after easter Mary would go to Mount Carmel to listen to the supplications of the faithful who lived their moments of passion or suffering. The Virgin Mary would give 'audience' to them because, having just experienced the passion and death of her Son she can understand the needs of those who call on her. It is noted that every location has a different version of this legend.[11]

This popular devotion to Mary under this title has continued from the fifteenth till the twentieth century.

Each place has its own local stories about its origin and how the devotion is expressed, but the tradition is always linked with the recitation of the seven Joys of Our Lady. In many places (presumably also in the Carmine Maggiore of Palermo) these seven Wednesdays of Udienza-Audience continue as a way of preparing for Pentecost with the Mother of God.

Thus, the title of Our Lady Dell'Udienza occurs in Sicily, not only in Sambuca but in several other places. Many have legends or historical facts attached to the devotion, which is linked, but not always, with the Carmelites and with the Joys of Our Lady, sometimes it is linked with protection from various epidemics, but the most common underlying factor is the concept of Our Lady, as Queen and Mother giving audience to and helping the faithful who have recourse to Her.

References:

1 *tradizioniditalia.wordpress.com › sicilia › madonna...Madonna dell' Udienza a Giuliana | tradizioni e feste d'Italia*

2 *www.parrocchiasantarosalia.it ›, ..il santuario della madonna dell' udienza di giuliana etnaportal.it ›, .. › Giuliana › Cosa vedere qui Madonna dell?Udienza, Giuliana – Etnaportal*

3 *www.facebook.com ›, .. › Religious Organization Arciconfraternita Maria SS. Immacolata Bovalino Sup. - Home*

4 *tradizioniditalia.wordpress.com›sicilia › festa-dell...festa della Madonna del Carmine ad Augusta/ tradizioni e feste d'Italia.*

5 *www.facebook.com ›, .. › Madonna Dell'Udienza - Roccella Valdemone*

6 *Madonna Dell'Udienza - Roccella Valdemone - Home*

7 *Mezzojuso - Festa della madonna dell'Udienza - 15 agosto 2002, Nicolo Perniciaro youtube.com*

---

8 www.facebook.com › posts › preghiera-alla-madon...Preghiera alla Madonna dell'Udienza... - Melissa on line

9 *www.e-borghi.com ›, .. › Calabria › Crotone › Melissa The Church of Santa Maria dell'Udienza - What to see in Melissa*

10 *http://www.reginamundi.info/icone/perle.asp*

11 *http://carminemaggiorepa.blogspot.com/2012/04/i-mercoledi-delludienza.html*

FIFTY ONE

OUR THEORY ABOUT THE ORIGIN OF THE NAME WEDNESDAYS 'TAL-UDIENZA'

As we have already said, in our opinion, the special name that is given in Malta to the first seven Wednesdays after Easter - the Wednesdays 'Tal-Udienza' is linked with the name of the statue of Our Lady venerated in the church of Our Lady of Mount Carmel – or better of the Annunciation - in Sambuca. We shall now discuss the reasons and circumstances which led us to this conclusion.

(i) That from most distant times Malta's destiny has been linked with that of Sicily is historically certain. Furthermore, there have always been strong links between the area of Agrigento (Girgenti in Maltese) and Malta. Indeed, from the time that the Normans joined Malta to the Kingdom of Sicily till the reign of William II we do not meet with the name of one Maltese Bishop. From 1156 onwards our diocese was suffragian to that of Palermo together with those of Agrigento and Mazzara[209]. When, in 1222, the Arabs revolted against Frederick II, they made the Province of Agrigento in Sicily their fortress and used Malta (much as it was used as an 'unsinkable aircraft carrier' in World War II) as a staging post to bring in further forces from North Africa.[210]

We also know from history that, after the death of Frederick IV (1377) till 1396, Sicily and Malta suffered a period of anarchy with confusion, betrayals, revolts, sieges, and religious and civil schisms.

Sicily was divided into four Vicarates who took power into their own hands. Malta owed allegiance to the Vicar Chiaramonte who also ruled Palermo, Trapani, Val di Noto, Modica and Agrigento. Fortunately, during the Schism of the Church, when there was a Pope in Rome and an Antipope in Avignon or elsewhere, Chiaramonte had sided with the true Pope. Thus, when the Archbishops of Palermo and Monreale called a provincial Synod, in which the suffragan dioceses of Agrigento, Mazzara and Malta participated, the Bishop of Malta, Antonio de Volpunno was with them.[211] It may be that because of this link between the Maltese Islands and Agrigento, there is a place name in Malta called Girgenti.

(ii) However, we are interested here in the misfortune which befell the Maltese and the Sicilians, particularly those of Agrigento in the second half of the sixteenth century. Both countries suffered an epidemic of plague which caused the death of thousands of people. In Agrigento, particularly in the province of Sambuca, this occurred in 1575-76: in Malta, about twenty years later. According to the historian Arthur Bonnici, the epidemic of plague began in Malta in June of 1592 and continued for about a year and three months. When it ended, in September 1592, it had caused the death of 3,800 victims.[212]

It is said that it was the Madonna dell'Udienza who saved Sambuca from this destructive plague. As soon as the statue was brought from Cellaro to Sambuca, the plague ended at once.[213] For this reason, this miraculous statue, which was placed in the church of the Carmelites, for the reasons which we mentioned, began to be called Dell'Udienza', because it had heard the sobs and cries of the plague victims and all the people and had listened to their plea.[214]

(iii) The Carmelites of Malta inevitably knew about this miraculous happening. They had very important links with the Sicilian Carmelites, particularly with those of the province of Saint Angelo of Mazzara del Vallo.Both the Maltese Carmelites and those of Sambuca belonged to the same province, and the Maltese remained part of this province till 1819.[215] Furthermore, many Sicilian Carmelites had lived in Maltese convents. In the opinion of Cuschieri, the first Carmelites in Malta came from Sicilian Convents and probably 'they would stay for a short time and be replaced by others.'[216] On the other hand, various Maltese Carmelites had lived, and even been superiors or professors in Sicilian convents of the province of Saint Angelo.[217] Two of them even became provincials of this province: P. Tonin Agius and P. Baldassere Azzopardi.[218]

Regarding the convents where the Maltese spent time in Sicily, these were usually Palermo, Licata, Trapani, Caltanissetta, Agrigento, Caltabellotta.[219] Most of these convents were close to the convent of Sambuca.

Finally, it is worth mentioning that the first provincial visitation to the Convent of Valletta, Malta, in 1587, was carried out by a friar from the convent of Agrigento, P. Jacobo.[220]

All these circumstances demonstrate the link between the Maltese Islands and Sicily, particularly with Agrigento, to which the Town of Sambuca is associated, and in particular show the link between the Maltese Carmelites and the Sicilian Carmelites of the province of Mazara del Vallo, otherwise known as the province of Saint Angelo, which owned the convent in Sambuca in which was the miraculous statue of the Madonna dell'Udienza.

It was inevitable that, as there was one Province with one provincial, and friars would move between Sicily and Malta so that there would be Sicilian Friars living in Maltese convents and vice versa.

As a consequence of this strong link, we must suppose that the Maltese Carmelites knew about the Madonna of Sambuca, about the devotion to it, and about the reason for this devotion, that is, being freed from the terrible illness of plague. Hence, when, a few years later, plague appeared in Malta and began to cause the death of hundreds and thousands of persons, we believe that the Carmelites remembered this Miraculous Statue and turned to Our Lady to beg Her to drive the plague from Malta. Who knows how many promises they made Her, assuring Her that they would never forget her Feast on the third Sunday of May!

So, because as we have seen, several Carmelite Provinces of Italy, including that of Sicily of Saint Angelo, from which our own Maltese Province emerged, had the custom of celebrating, with more solemnity than usual, the first seven Wednesdays after Easter Sunday, and because these Wednesdays usually come to an end around the time of the third Sunday of May, feast of the Madonna dell'Udienza, the Miraculous Madonna of Sambuca, we Maltese continue to call these Wednesdays 'Tal-Udjenza'.

NOTES

209 *See ANDREW P. VELLA, O.P., Storja ta' Malta, v.1, Marsa, 1974 pp.88-89. According to R. Valentini, it was Pope Adrian IV who united the Diocese of Malta with that of Palermo, because in the time of Gregory I (598) it was part of the Diocese of Syracuse (See ib., p.104, n.67).*

210 *See VELLA, o.c., p.92.*

211 *See VELLA, o.c., pp.123-124.*

212 *For the plague of Sambuca of 1575-76, see DI RUBERTO.Sambuca Zabut, part3, kap.4 (pp.66-82) which describes this issue; for the plague of Malta of 1592-93, see ARTHUR BONNICI. History of the Church in Malta v.2, Malta (Catholic Institute), 1968. He says: 'When the same epidemic raged in Malta from June 1592 to September 1593 with a death-toll of 3,800 persons...' (p.72).*

213 *See DI RUBERTO, o.c., pp.47, 83.*

214 *See note 197 of this study.*

215 *See CUSCHIERI, Il-firda tal-kunventi ta' Malta mill-Provinċja ta' Sqallija, in Ir-Regina tal Carmelu, 3 (1916) 91-93.*

216 *CUSCHIERI, Il-Patrijiet tal-Kunvent tax-Xaghra jew tal Lunzjata il-qadima in Ir-Regina tal Carmelu, 8 (1917) 240.*

217 *The following had been Priors; P.Injazju Caruana, P. Indri Bonnici, P. Bennard Gutiglion, P. Baldassere Azzopardi and P. Elizew Balzan; this latter and P. Salv Caruana were for a time masters of novices. Also, while P. Baldassere Azzopardi taught in the convents of Palermo and Licata, P. Tumas Grech used to teach in Caltanissetta. (See CUSCHIERI, in Ir-Regina tal Carmelu, 11 (1916) 337. 341: 12 (1916) 369.370;8 (1917) 242).*

218 *P. Tonin Agius was also Vicar Provincial and Commissioner General, consultor of the Inquisition, and once presided over the provincial chapter of the Province of Saint Angelus, P. Baldassere Azzopardi for nine years*

---

was prior of two convents in Sicily, probably those of Palermo and Licata where he used to teach. After he ended his time as Provincial, he came to Malta and became Prior of the Mdina convent. (See CUSCHIERI, ib.,11 (1916) 341;8 (1917) 242.

219 *See CUSCHIERI, Il-Patrijiet tal-Kunvent tal-Belt, in Ir-Regina tal Carmelu, 11 (1916) 336.337.339.341; 12 (1916) 369.370.372; Il-Patrijiet tal-Kunvent tax-Xagħra, in Ir-Regina tal Carmelu, 8 (1917) 241.243.*

220 *See art.cit., 8 (1917) 243.*

FIFTY TWO

WHERE THE WEDNESAYS 'TAL-UDJENZA' ARE HELD AND WHAT THEIR CONTENT IS

We close this study by seeing where the Wednesdays 'Tal-Udjenza' are held in Malta and what is discussed in them. In other words, in them do we discuss the seven Joys of Our Lady or do we discuss the relationship which the Carmelite Order has with the Blessed Virgin Mary?

Firstly we must mention the churches of the Carmelite Friars of the Ancient Observance. These Wednesdays are held in the Basilica Sanctuary of Our Lady of Mount Carmel in Valletta and in the Carmelite Church of Mdina (dedicated to the Annunciation), as well as in the four parishes which are serviced by these religious- three dedicated to Our Lady of Mount Carmel, that is Fgura, Saint Julians (Balluta) and Fleur-de-Lys, as well as another dedicated to Santa Venera in the village which has the name of this saint from Acireale. They are also held in the new church of Santa Venera, which is dedicated to Our Lady of Mount Carmel.

Next we should mention two churches of the Discalced Carmelites, or, as they are often called in Malta, of the 'Teresians'. These are the one in Cospicua, whose dedication is Saint Teresa of Avila, and the shrine in Birkirkara dedicated to Saint Therese.

Because the Franciscan Friars Minor also have devotion to the seven Joys of Our Lady, they also celebrate the Wednesdays

'Tal-Udienza'(221). This they do in their Sliema parish of 'Sacro Cuor', and in the chapel of the Madonna ta' Liesse in Valletta. There is a very good reason for holding them in ta' Liesse, because, in French, the word Liesse means happiness. Hence the dedication of this chapel is 'Our Lady of Happiness', in honour of a miraculous event which led to much devotion, and the founding of Churches with this name in both France and Malta (222).

Finally, we are sure that there are eight other parishes where the Wednesdays 'Tal-Udjenza'are celebrated. Seven of these parish churches are in the hands of the Secular Clergy: they are Żurrieq, Mosta, Rabat (Malta), Ħamrun (Saint Cajetan), Senglea, Sliema (Stella Maris) and Msida.In this latter parish they were re-started in 1978. Another parish in which they are held is San Ġwann, run by the Franciscan Capuchin Fathers.

Unfortunately these Wednesdays are no longer held in Gzira. They were stopped a few years before 1979. This is indeed a paradox, since these Wednesdays are celebrated in some Churches which are not even dedicated to Our Lady, but they have stopped being held in Gzira parish, which is dedicated to Our Lady of Mount Carmel, although commonly known as Our Lady tal-Gebla (Of the Stone).

If we then turn to the content of the sermons preached on those Wednesdays, we find that in the churches which belong to both branches of the Carmelite Order, when the preacher is a Carmelite or Teresian friar, importance tends to be given to the devotion of the Scapular of Our Lady of Mount Carmel, and within this, the history of the Order is discussed as well. The same can be said of the Parish

---

of Żurrieq, where there is great devotion to Our Lady of Mount Carmel, as she is the secondary patroness of the town. However, when the preacher is from the secular clergy, and so he may not know very much about the history of the Carmelite Order or indeed about the devotion of the Carmelite Scapular, the sermons are usually about various main Joys of Our Lady or some other Marian privileges.

In some of the other churches and parishes we have mentioned, even if the preacher is a Carmelite or Teresian, sometimes a parish priest or the rector of a church specifies or limits the subject of the sermons to the seven Joys of Our Lady or some other Marian aspects.

Notes

220 *See n.17 of this study.*

221 *See S.C.Z., Il-Madonna ta' Liesse, in Ir-Regina tal Carmelu, 10 (1917) 310-311.*

FIFTY THREE

CONCLUSION BY FATHER BORG GUSMAN

BEFORE CLOSING THIS STUDY, LET US DRAW ALL THE POINTS WE HAVE made into one picture.

We saw that the devotion of the seven Joys of Mary is a devotion which is particular to the Carmelite Order, Its origin in Carmel is linked with the custom of Saint Bertold and, finally, with the cloud which was seen by Saint Elias when for seven times he sent his servant to look to see if something appeared. Since, according to tradition, the prophet saw the Virgin Mary figured in the cloud rising from the sea, Saint Bertolt used to salute the Mediterranean Sea seven times a day by saying the Hail Mary.

Because they were trained in this custom, the Carmelite Hermits found it easy, when they came to England, to adopt the devotion which had been promoted by Saint Thomas Becket. This devotion of the seven Joys of Mary gradually spread throughout the whole Order., Not everyone commemorated the same Joys. Some preferred the Seven Joys which Mary enjoyed in this world, while others preferred the same number of Joys which she now enjoys in Heaven. Others composed a composite series of Joys which included some of each kind.

The first seven Wednesdays after Easter used to be celebrated by the Carmelites with a greater solemnity than the others of the year. On each of these seven Saturdays they would have a meditation, or even a major sermon about a Joy of Our Lady. However overtime, and because of certain circumstances the content of these sermons changed. The sermons began to be focussed on certain special relationships which the Carmelite Order has with Mary.

These seven Wednesdays are known in Malta as 'Tal-Udienza', We believe that the origin of this name is in the last years of the six-teenth century, when Malta was freed from the plague as a result of devout prayer to a miraculous statue of the 'Madonna Dell'Udienza' which is in the Carmelite Church of Sambuca (Sicily).

In Malta the devotion to these Wednesdays is very widespread. They take place in at least nineteen Churches, of which thirteen are parishes. There still is the custom that a sermon should be given on each Wednesday. The sermons are held in the evening, as opposed to the custom in some Italian churches, such as that of the Traspontina in Rome or the Basilica of Our Lady of Mount Carmel in Florence, where they are held in the morning, during or after the first mass.

The subjects of the sermons vary, as this depends on the preacher, and on the parish priests. If the preacher is not schooled in Carmelite culture, the content of the sermons is on the seven Joys of Our Lady, particularly Joys Our Lady experienced on earth, or Our Lady in a general way, especially some of her great and well known privileges. Sometimes the parish priest orders the preacher to preach about the seven Joys of Our Lady. We Carmelites cannot accept this, because the devotion of the Joys of Our Lady is a particular devotion of the Carmelite Order. Furthermore, both the

Chapter General and a decree of the Prior General and the Carmelite Constitution of 1626 have made it clear that in sermons such as these importance has to be given to diverse aspects of the special relationship that Our Order has with the Blessed Virgin Mary, Mother and Queen of Carmel.

Therefore it is right that in Carmelite and Teresian Churches, the sermons of the Wednesdays Tal-Udjenza should be given by a Carmelite or Teresian friar. Should someone else be employed, who does not belong to one of the two branches of the Carmelite Order, we should clarify to the preacher that the content of the sermons should be essentially both Marian and Carmelite. That is, it should be about devotion to Our Lady of Mount Carmel and about the Order which bears Her name. If the preacher has no literature on the subject, then we should provide it to him, by lending him books, magazines, and up to date articles, of which there are many. We also insist that the material for the sermons, as well as those in all Novenas, Triduums, and Panegyrics about Our Lady of Mount Carmel should be free 'of every false exaggeration', and of 'anything which could lead into error regarding the doctrine of the Church' (LG, n67), Therefore, in the second part of this book we are pres-enting some sermons which could be preached on these occasions.

Assuming there is no objection from the parish priest, we should, even when preaching in churches which are not Carmelite, we should, when preaching on these Wednesdays, give the sermons a Carmelite flavour, indeed a Carmelite structure. It was the Carmelites who made these sermons popular in Malta. In parish churches, these Wednesday sermons are usually a foundation.

Whoever left the foundation has probably done so on the advice of a Carmelite friar, so that the people of the parish can hear what is usually preached in Carmelite Churches about the devotion of the scapular and other things related to Our Lady of Mount Carmel.

May the devotion of the 'Tal-Udienza' Wednesdays continue, so as to spread honour and glory to Our Mother Mary, Queen of Carmel.

P. Valentin Borg Guzman, O.Carm.
Convent of Our Lady of Mount Carmel
Valletta, Malta.

FIFTY FOUR

The Link Between the Joys of Our Lady, the Scapular and the Rosary

It will be noted that the obligations of the Sabbatine Privilege, which we will discuss in the second part of this book, were/are:

1.To wear the Scapular faithfully after valid enrollment;
2. To observe chastity according to one's state;
3. To recite daily the Little Office of the Blessed Virgin.

One commutation of the third condition was to daily recite five decades of the Most Holy Rosary. This therefore associated the Rosary with the scapular.

There is the statement by Lucia, the Visionary of Fatima who became a Carmelite Nun that 'The rosary and the scapular are one', but this is only a statement, not evidence. There is also the legend that Saint Francis, Saint Dominic and Saint Angelus once met in Rome and there St. Dominic prophesied that 'One day, through the Rosary and the Scapular, Our Lady will save the World'- significant because here we have the originators of the Franciscan and Dominican orders (and so rosaries) both present, but again this is really a legend.

However, the fact that the recitation of the Little Office of Our Lady, in a time when most lay persons could not read could be commuted to the Rosary provides an important real link between the Joys of Our Lady, the Scapular and the Rosary.

Let us briefly discuss the development of the Rosary outside of the Carmelite Order..

It was a Dominican, Alain de La Roche (c.1428-75) who did so much to promote the rosary in the late 15th century. He did this by founding Confraternities, the first one being 'The Confraternity of the Psalter of the Glorious Virgin Mary' at Douai between 1468-70. **(Beads and Prayers: The Rosary in History and Devotion John Desmond Miller June 2002)**[1] These Rosary Confraternities had their counterpart in the Scapular Confraternities through which the Carmelites spread the Scapular Devotion. In further developing the Rosary, Michael Francisci, a professor at Cologne University, presented a series of lectures in December 1475 in which he suggested that during the rosary one should meditate on 1) Mary's earthly joys, 2) her Passion sorrows, and 3) her heavenly joys. **(Beads and Prayers: The Rosary in History and Devotion John Desmond Miller June 2002)** This is what the present Joyful, Sorrowful and Glorious mysteries do; thus he linked the Rosary with the devotion of the Joys of Our Lady. In the meantime, the Franciscans had developed their own version of the 'Rosary', also based on the Joys of Our Lady. We have recounted the origins of this devotion earlier in this book.

The devotion of the Joys of Our Lady is also linked with the Carmelites, as we have already seen, and through the Carmelites it is linked with the scapular. One should note that Aylesford, the Mother House of the Carmelites, is 'one day's march' from Canterbury, and the Carmelites would encourage pilgrims to stay the night at their pilgrim hall before moving on to Canterbury the next day. This is evidenced in the BBC TV Programme 'Pilgrimage' (Pilgrimage DVD Simon Reeve BBC 2013).[3] It seems plausible that they would entertain the pilgrims, who might well sing songs about the Joys of Mary, both Earthly and Heavenly, and recount how these latter had been revealed to Saint Thomas Becket, the goal of the pilgrimage. It seems logical that from this milieu of the joys of Our Lady and the need to encourage meditation on them, the rosary gradually, over time emerged.

Across Italy, Carmelite Confraternities had developed numerous chaplets of the Joys of Our Lady, many of which are still in use locally, as we have seen. In Verona, the Carmelites had unusually named their church, in which the Joys of Our Lady were celebrated weekly at the Altar of Our Lady of Mount Carmel after Saint Thomas Becket, clearly to celebrate his link with their Devotion to The Joys of Our Lady and the chaplet commemorating them.

Hence, across Medieval Europe, the mendicant Orders of Dominicans, Franciscans and Carmelites – and also the Augustinians, especially with regard to the Servites who celebrated the Seven Sorrows of Our Lady - solved the problem of enabling Lay Persons to Meditate on the Life and Teachings of Christ by a complex of Chaplets, and Rosaries about the Joys (and Sorrows) of Our Lady from which evolved the Rosary which we know now.

In the meantime, the Scapular Confraternities provided the possibility for laypersons to show in a palpable form commitment to Christ and His Mother by enrolling in and wearing the habit of the Carmelite order.

By the nineteenth Century Apparitions of Lourdes (linked with the Carmelites because the last Apparition was on 16th July, feast of Our Lady of Mount Carmel) and the Apparitions of Fatima in the early Twentieth century (1919), (linked with the Carmelites because Our Lady appeared in the last Apparition dressed as a Carmelite),[3,4] the rosary was established as one of the most popular prayers of the church in the form we know today.

On the other hand it is worth noting that on the return of the Friars to Aylesford in the 1950s, they set up a Rosary Way which pictorially showed pilgrims '1) Mary's earthly joys, 2) her Passion sorrows, and 3) her heavenly joys'. Every celebration of Our Lady of Mount Carmel in Modern Aylesford entails carrying the Statue of Our Lady presenting the Scapular to Simon Stock round the Rosary Way while reciting the rosary. In Restored Aylesford the Carmelites did not, other than this, promote a specific separate devotion to the Joys of the Virgin, despite Canterbury being close by. Instead they celebrated the Joys of Our Lady by setting up the artistic Rosary way which is both very artistic and also provides the venue for all the processions there in honour of Our Lady of Mount Carmel. They later replicated this Rosary Way in Hazelwood Castle in Yorkshire. Thus they 'closed the cycle over centuries'...the rosary was now in the 20th Century the main method within the Catholic Church of Meditating on the Joys of Our Lady, and, indeed, wherever Our Lady of Mount Carmel is celebrated, including where the Joys of Our Lady are celebrated by recitation of a chaplet (as in many feasts of Our Lady of Mount Carmel in Italy) or in a sermon (As in the Wednesdays Tal-Udienza in Malta) the rosary is recited, and also the Scapular is worn. Thus it is, today that 'The Rosary and the

Scapular are truly One', linked together as the main form of lay meditation on the Joys of Our Lady.

References:

1 *Beads and Prayers: The Rosary in History and Devotion John Desmond Miller June 2002*

2 *Pilgrimage DVD Simon Reeve BBC 2013*

3 *Fatima in Lucia's own words Fr. Louis Kondor SVD 1963*

4 *Our Lady of Fatima and the Brown Scapular Fr. Kilian Lynch O.Carm 1980 The Carmelite Press*

FIFTY FIVE

The Crowned Icon of Our Lady of Mount Carmel in the Valletta Basilica

The Crowned Icon of Our Lady of Mount Carmel In the Basilica in Valletta provides the focus of the Wednesdays known as the Erbgħat Tal-Udienza, and indeed for all Ceremonies in Honour of Our Lady of Mount Carmel, It clearly depicts Our Lady as Queen, giving Audience to her devotees. She clearly offers the habit of her Order - The Scapular - to the Devotees as a sign of their commitment to Her, and as a sign of salvation, and by the symbolism in which the scapular appears to touch a church which is similar to the Naples Carmine Maggiore, the 'home' of the Madonna Bruna, it suggests to the friars a link with the Wednesdays of Our Lady, which originated around the Madonna Bruna, and thence with the ancient devotion to the Joys of Our Lady; therefore a link between the Joys and the scapular.

In the following pages we publish in its entirety the excellent pamphlet by Fr. Charlo Camilleri, which describes in detail these links as depicted by this holy Icon, which remains beloved by the People of Valletta.

The Miraculous Painting of Our Lady of Mount Carmel in The Basilica of Valletta (Credit Mark Micallef Perconte)

FIFTY SIX

THE SANCTUARY OF OUR LADY OF MOUNT CARMEL IN VALLETTA MARIOLOGY IN COLOUR

FATHER CHARLO CAMILLERI O. CARM

'Paradisi clavis et ianua, fac nos duci quo, Mater, Gloria coronaries. Amen, Alleluia.' from the 'Flos Carmeli'

PREFACE

It gives me great pleasure, as Prior of the Carmelite Community of Valletta and Rector of the Basilica Sanctuary of Our Lady of Mount Carmel, Valletta, to write the introduction to this booklet: '*The Sanctuary of Our Lady of Mount Carmel in Valletta; Mariology in Colour*', by Father Charlo Camilleri, O.Carm.

We, both as Carmelites and as Maltese, have had love and devotion to Our Lady of Mount Carmel for centuries. We can say with certainty that this devotion began with the arrival among us of the Carmelite Order, and that it was encouraged and spread because of the veneration in which the crowned painting in the Sanctuary of our Capital City is held. Our fathers always had a special love for this painting and held it in great honour. Father Charlo, who is a person who is trained in both spiritual Theology and Art, offers us an excellent mistagological description of its symbolic and deep meaning.

On the one hundredth and thirty fifth anniversary since Malta saw a Holy Image being Crowned in Our Islands, we wished to publish this explanatory booklet so that we can understand the deep meaning represented by this Miraculous Painting which was crowned by the Vatican Chapter on the 15th of July 1881.

In the name of the Carmelite Community, and all the devotees of the Sanctuary, I hope that this booklet will help to spread among us love and devotion to Our Lady of Mount Carmel.

May the Virgin Mary, Mother and Beauty of Carmel, give the grace to all who read this booklet that they should become closer to her Son, Our Lord Jesus Christ.

Father Alex M. Scerri O.Carm
Prior and Rector of the Sanctuary
11th May 2016
The Last Wednesday of Our Lady.

The Sanctuary of our Lady of Mount Carmel in Valletta
Mariology in Colour

Introduction

Saint John of the Cross observes that God often uses a work of art to draw mankind to Him, and he usually does not use works which have a major artistic value, rather He uses works which are not worth a great deal by human aesthetic and artistic standards.[1] He teaches those who wish to grow in their spiritual life that things which please our senses, although good in themselves, can impede our journey towards God because our hearts may become bound to spiritual things and to things which we like but are not God, so that even holy things can draw us into idolatry, Therefore, Saint John of the Cross argues, God chooses art works which by human criteria appear ugly, so that He can touch the hearts of men and lift them from earthly things to spiritual things.

This can be said of the 'prodigious painting of the image of the Madonna of Mount Carmel'[2], as Father Lawrenz Sammut calls it, because 'although the painting is possibly not of great artistic merit, it none the less induces devotion and love in those who look at it.'[3]

The origin of this painting, like that of many other miraculous paintings or icons, is lost in time. We do not know exactly where it came from and neither do we know the artist who was inspired to design it and painted it. What we do know is that Father Ġwann Vella brought a painting for the Church from Sicily around 1570, but we do not know whether it is the one which we have now because at some point the painting was changed. Father Lawrenz Sammut quotes the opinion of Giuseppe Bonnici Cali that the painting which we have is the titular of the Basilica Sanctuary. Sammut tells us that Cali attributes it to the artist Filippo di Benedetto Paladini (1544-1614), one of the last masters of Tuscan Mannerism who escaped to Malta in 1590.[4] When in 1924 the painting was taken down for restoration another painting was found beneath it which resembled it, except that the Madonna is holding the Child Jesus on her right rather than her left hand. This is probably the painting which suffered serious damage as a result of the fire caused by the lightning bolt in 1797 so that, according to Father Lawrenz, only the faces of The Virgin Mary and the Child Jesus were left.[5]

There is a resemblance, mostly in the face of Our Lady and in the folding of the clothes, between the present painting and another interesting very old painting, which is to be found in the Sanctuary of the Madonna of the Vision in Pallestrina, Venice. The resemblance with this painting struck me immediately when I saw it in Venice. According to tradition, the Pallestrina painting was painted by a pilgrim on a board made from a barrel of wine in order to thank a family which had been very hospitable to him. This image included, in the manner of a Sacra Conversazione, Saint Vito and Saint Modesto, which have now been removed from the Image of the Virgin Mary. Some claim that this painting is of the Spanish School.

Mannerism, especially in Italy, is a transitional style between the Renaissance and the Baroque. This style is characterised by deep thought, and by artificiality in the sense that it avoids reproducing exactly how things are in nature, and also avoids perfect symmetry in composition without losing equilibrium. These are elements which we can see in the painting of Our Lady of Mount Carmel which is to be found in the Basilica Sanctuary.

The painting was originally larger in size. For one reason or another, presumably so that the painting could fit within the picture frame over the Main Altar, Saint Lucy (?), who was beside Saint Agatha was removed, Saint Agatha is a virgin martyr, who is patron of Sicily and Malta. Also removed was another figure who was beside Saint Simon Stock, the Prior General of the Order who is linked with the transition of the Carmelites from hermits to mendicant friars and with the Scapular Vision[6]. The positions of the saints are hieratic, and they lack a certain naturalness, as if they had been brought from another scene and placed within the composition of the picture. Naturally this style is not due to lack of artistic skill, but is intended to create an effect of stability, almost as if there is an attempt at immortalisation so that the timing of the scene is eternal. Thus we need to begin to interpret the painting; from the religious, theological and spiritual points of view.

The sense of equilibrium, the use of few figures in a scene limited to those which are essential, together with the absence of secondary elements, remind us of the artistic work of Fabrizio Santafede (1560-1635), a Neapolitan Mannerist artist who worked in the South of Italy as well as the North, and who also has works in Spain. We can say that the painting of Our Lady of Mount Carmel, like the work of Santafede attempts to interpret sacred art with that seriousness and gravity required by the Catholic Counter-reformation of the Council of Trent, and is also adjusted to cause devotion in those who contemplate it because the image does not simply draw the viewer to itself, but also draws him into the mystery.[7]

A great sign appeared in Heaven... (Apocalypse 12:1)

Naturally the most prominent figure is that of the Virgin Mary, who appears to be emanating from the golden glow of heaven which has opened up to allow her to come down or pass through. The white cloud opens like a theatre curtain or a door in order that the Blessed Virgin Mary may go through. Here it is clear that the artist was inspired by the biblical text of the Apocalypse which the Tradition of the Church applies to the Blessed Virgin:

'The temple of God opened and the Arc of His Covenant appeared... A great sign appeared in heaven, a Woman clothed in the sun with the moon beneath her feet and a crown of twelve stars on her head. She was in pain from childbirth...' (Revelations 11:19; 12:1-10), Mary coming down from the open temple of God in heaven is the Woman clothed in the sun with all that glow behind her, with the moon beneath her feet to indicate her spotless beauty. She is the woman who is victorious over the Dragon of old, the Devil, and who has been conquered by the strength of Christ with whom she is always united as beloved, disciple and mother. The Bridegroom in the Song of Songs sings to his beloved that she is 'as beautiful as the moon, shining as the sun, and terrible as an army ready for battle'(Song 6:10). The figure of Mary is imposing and overawes in all senses. Her breast is uncovered with a girdle under her breast and above her womb to depict her as the Mother of the Son of God who became man, while in the picture, her Son appears naked, as a human person in Mary's hands, facing towards us because He became a man like us and for our salvation.. The nakedness of Jesus reminds us of the kenosis, His making Himself nothing in the Incarnation and on the Cross. His nakedness is also a statement of the belief that Jesus is truly man, 'like us in everything except sin' (Hebrews 4:15). In the history of sacred and religious art, the nakedness of Jesus with the showing of His genitals (ostentatio genitalium) both as a child and as a fully formed young man, was common in the Renaissance, from the fourteenth till the seventeenth centuries, and was as important as the showing of His wounds (ostentatio vulnerum). The emphasis is on the true humanity of Christ in the Incarnation and the goodness and beauty of human nature which, although sinful, remains fundamentally good because man remains created in the image of God (Genesis 1:27). This was in contrast with the Protestant reformation Iconoclasm at whose root was the belief that human nature was fundamentally corrupt and bad. The nakedness of the body of Jesus, the new Adam, uncovered before us without any shame is also a sign of the theological truth that the Incarnation of the Son of God, who has a body just like ours returned to man (Adam) the beauty and dignity that God had given the first man in Eden, where he was naked. Shame at man's nakedness came about only after the fall of man, who then became ruled by his passions and lost the dignity that God had adorned him with, so that he became very vulnerable. During the Mannerist and Baroque periods, although the nakedness of Jesus remained quite common, his genitals used to be hidden with an undergarment or by one leg being raised. This detail gives us a rough idea of in which period the painting was made. This situation of Christ making himself nothing (kenosis) gives us the dignity of children of God. The first fruit of this is Mary herself, since 'first Christ, then those who belong to Christ, everyone in his order' (1 Corinthians 15:22). A sign of this dignity is the purple imperial or royal garment which Mary is wearing, Over the red garment representing Her Humanity she is clothed with a blue mantle which signifies the life of heaven, or the divinity. This is what is called the mirabile commercium, or amazing change: God becomes man in the form of a slave, so that man, from being a slave takes the form of God, partaking in the divine nature. Through the divine Maternity of Mary, God again united earth and heaven in the person of His Son made man. Through this mystical marriage between God and man in Mary's womb, God brought us back to the Garden of Eden where our first parents had destroyed by their pride the harmony between humanity and the divine. The humility of Mary in her disponibility to accept what pleases God made possible the redemption. Her inclined face, radiating the sweetness of heaven reminds us of the beatitudes: 'Blessed are the meek for they shall inherit the earth' (Matt. 5:5), or the Kingdom of Heaven. Her gaze, full of sweetness and mercy also shows her attention focussed on us. From her divine maternity arises her spiritual maternity of the Church, of her children who are still living 'in this vale of tears' until we reach our home in heaven. This is shown by the milk which Christ is squeezing from the nipple on Mary's breast, and which is dripping to refresh the souls in purgatory. These souls are 'in a dry, parched land without water' (psalm 62), behind which appears a Church with four floors, which reminds us very much of the basilica of Our Lady of Mount Carmel in Naples, which had been restructured in 1622 by the architect Giovann Giacomo di Conforto.[8] Our Lady is placing Her Scapular directly on this church as a sign of her protection of the people of God who in this world struggle to achieve perfect love in the practice of the will of God. Thus here we have painted in a marvellous way the link between the pilgrim church on earth, the church which is becoming purified after death, and the church which participates in the glory of Heaven. A circle can be drawn linking the gate of Heaven, where the Throne of God is located (this is not shown) to the face of Mary, to her hand holding the scapular, to the church-tower, to the Holy Souls, whose gaze points towards the gaze of Christ. Thus this circle links the militant Church (represented by the building of the church), the purgative Church (the Holy Souls in Purgatory), and the Church Triumphant represented by Mary, the woman of the Apocalypse who is also the Church of Christ. When Mary clothes us with the scapular she clothes us with her life and protects us with her example and her intercession during our journey following Jesus until we achieve perfect love of God and like her we see him face to face in the glory of Heaven. Mary is resting on a black cloud, which seems full of and about to rain, which reminds us of the cloud which Elias saw rising from the sea and raining on the land which had been dry and parched after three years of drought. The Carmelites follow the allegorical interpretation which the Fathers of the Church give of the cloud of Elias, in which they see the Blessed Immaculate Virgin Mary pregnant with the fullness of grace which is Christ who 'falls like rain on dry land, like rain which waters parched land' (Psalm 72:6-7). The cloud beneath Mary gives us a historical clue regarding the dating of the painting because it points to the development of devotion to Our Lady of Mount Carmel which is linked to the promise of the Bolla Sabatina which is said to date to 1322 and which led to a belief that Our Lady herself went down to purgatory on Saturday to take the souls who wore the scapular to heaven, While the popes have always confirmed the content of this Bull as an expression of faith in the protection by Mary of her children when in this world and when they are being purified while on their road towards heaven, they have always intervened to prevent mistakes which may arise because of exaggeration of devotion. One of these interventions regarded the iconography of Our Lady of Mount Carmel. By a decree of the 20th of January 1613, published on the eleventh of February of that year, the Congregation of the Inquisition gave a directive that in images of Our Lady, she should not be shown descending into purgatory to take up the Holy Souls, but she should be separated, by a cloud which holds her in heaven, from the souls who under her protection are being purified by the fire of the Love of God, as we see in the iconography of Our Lady and the Holy Souls (which we see in this painting). This historic detail helps us to date this painting of Our Lady of Mount Carmel to 1613 or later.[9]

Finally, we see two angels flying over the Virgin Mary holding a royal crown. Mary is presented here as the Queen of Heaven and Earth. One angel represents God, Lord of everything and everyone, while the other angel represents the spiritual and civil leaders of the world.

Mary was assumed into Heaven and was crowned in Heaven as Queen, meaning that she is fully taking part in the Glory of God because she followed Jesus and shared his victory over sin and death. In the Apocalypse Jesus promises ' I will give the victor the crown of life' (Apocalypse 2:11) and ' I will grant to the victor that he will stay beside me on my throne; in the same way as when I, when I was victorious, sat beside my Father on His Throne.' (Apocalypse 3:21), Mary alone has received in its entirety this crown of life or glory because she is in Heaven Body and Soul. All the rest of mankind, including the saints, are expecting the fullness of glorification on the last day when Christ will raise our bodies and make them put on immortality.[10] The angel who represents God is to the left of the person who is looking at the painting. He is wearing a golden garment and a red purple mantle to show the divinity and royalty of God.

The angel on the right who represents the leaders of this world, wears green and a red /purple mantle to show temporal royalty and shows that the Pope, the Church and all the kingdoms of this world recognise this Woman of Heaven as their Lady. This iconographic symbolic motif is a Neapolitan Characteristic which still exists in the symbolism of Nativity scenes.

In 1881 the painting was crowned by a decree of the Vatican Chapter, and so the church which holds it became the first Sanctuary containing a crowned painting in Malta because of the great devotion of the people, This is in eternal remembrance of all the graces which God scattered upon the Maltese people through this image. After the coronation of this picture of Our Lady of Mount Carmel it appears that there developed an appetite among the Maltese to crown more devotional images of Mary.

Indeed it appears that this painting is even privileged by Heaven! The profundity and theological beauty with which it is adorned make it a true Icon, an image of a spiritual reality of God which it makes real to us and towards which we are travelling in faith.

You for us are a door and key to Heaven!

Oh Mother draw us to heaven where you reign Crowned!

Notes

1 *Juan de la Cruz, Subida del Monte Carmelo, 3/372.*

2 *Lawrenz Sammut, Is-Santwarju tal-Karmnu Valletta 1952, 36.*

3 *Ibid.*

4 *Actually the figures of Paladini are more elegant than those which we see in the picture of Our Lady of Mount Carmel, and this, as well as the fact of his travels - he went to Mazzarino in 1595 and died there in 1614, Furthermore theological iconographic factors such as the cloud beneath the Madonna and the positioning of the leg to hide the genitals of Baby Jesus make us feel that the painting was made from 1613 onwards. All these factors make the attribution to Paladini unlikely. See note 5.*

5 *It could be that this is the now lost painting brought over from Sicily in 1570, which is now lost. Sammut tries to argue that the painting which is there today was acquired in 1570 and was then used to replace another which had been destroyed by a lightning strike, and finally this painting was again put in place. It makes more sense to say that the original painting was destroyed and that thus it was replaced by the one which we have today, and that, out of devotion, behind it were placed the faces of Our Lady and Jesus which had survived, which have now also been lost. CF.: Sammut, 36-37.*

6 *t is not for this mystagogical article to go into the finer historical details of the dating of this painting, however we should simply mention that if what Father Lawrenz Sammut reports is true, (see note 5) it is possible that the painting originally filled the whole facade of the choir, as, for example in the Collegiate Church of Saint Lawrence in Birgu or in the Oratory of the beheading of Saint John in the Co-Cathedral. Father Lawrenz mentions that the first among many changes in the facade of the choir happened in 1705 when, during the changes, two statues of Saint*

Elias and Saint Elishua were added on either side of the painting, Is it possible that during this time of change in the structure of the facade of the choir the painting was indeed changed for another one which is now destroyed or lost? The size of the two statues which fell when the facade collapsed in 1797 and which today stand by the stairs of the convent appear small beside a large painting. Can we therefore say that it is true that the original painting was changed for another one which was then destroyed by lightning in October 1797? If this is the case, then the painting which we have today is the original one which arrived in 1570 which had been put back to act as Titular, as father Lawrenz says, after it had been changed for another one, but which now had to be cut in order to fit within the choir which had collapsed and had then been rebuilt including the statues of Saint Elias and Saint Elishua in 1805. These and other questions require study and deep research so that we can achieve a final definitive chronology, attribution and dating. While Father Lawrenz Sammut has the merit that he collected into a book the historic memory, from the documents which he found and sayings and oral tradition, he sometimes appears uncertain and confused, while attempting to put together loose ends to account for lack of information and information which is often contradictory. What most does not fit in with his suggested chronology is the issue related to the Bolla Sabatina, as we will see later: Regarding this note see Sammut Is-Santwarju, 34-37.

7 *I am proposing the similarity of Santafede in this writing because I see a great similarity, for example, in the face of Our Lady and the positioning of Baby Jesus in the painting of Our Lady of Mount Carmel and that in the painting of Our Lady of the Rosary which is in the Gesu Nuovo of Naples. There is also a great similarity between Saint Simon Stock and Saint Dominic. Furthermore in the Fine Arts Museum of San Francisco, California, there is a pencil and ink drawing of Santafede which shows the*

Coronation of Our Lady by the Holy Trinity. The crown on the head of Our Lady is identical with that painted in the painting of Our Lady of Mount Carmeland like it, it appears to be of Spanish style. Naturally I am here speaking of a similarity which may serve as a spur so that a deep study at artistic level should be made of the painting. The use of angels holding a crown is a characteristic of Fabrizio Santafede and is commonplace in Italian Marian art in the south of Italy, especially in images of Our Lady of Mount Carmel, Ippolito Borgese (+1627) also uses this important iconographic motif, and in a picture which shows the Madonna with the Holy Souls beneath Her, which is to be found in the Capuchin Church in Vico del Gargano, there is a great similarity with another picture dated 1613 of Our Lady of Mount Carmel which presently is found in the Church of the Annunciation in the limits of Rabat, Malta. In the Castel Nuovo in Naples there is a conserved painting of his which shows the Crucifix with Saint Catherine and Saint Egidius, the face of Saint Catherine resembles that of the Madonna in the painting which we are writing about.

8 *Dr. Simon Mercieca also suggests a similarity with the Siculo-Norman Bell-tower of the Old Cathedral in Mdina which fell in the earthquake of 1693.*

9 *See note number 3. So as to get an idea of how it was prohibited to paint Our Lady of Mount Carmel, we can mention the masterpiece of Rubens which goes back to the years 1630-35 and which shows a scene from the Book of the life of Saint Teresa of Jesus in which she recounts how, during her life, she had prayed for the soul of Bernardino de Mendoza, who had died young after a carelessly lived life, but who had never refrained from doing works of mercy and charity with the monastery, and so was not lost. In the painting, Jesus appears as if descending into Purgatory so as to take Bernardino up at the prayer of the saint, who is also painted by Rubens in Purgatory, The painting was originally in the Carmelite Church of*

Antwerp, but now is in the Royal Museum of Fine Arts of the same city. Naturally the scene is shown within purgatory because it illustrates an incident from the autobiography of Saint Teresa. See note 4.

10 *For this reason, the Church, with occasional exceptions only crowns images of Jesus or Mary and not of other saints, since these two are the only ones who live Body and Soul in their life of Glory. To crown images of other saints, no matter how great, may be a devotional act but it is a poor theological gesture, or even a wrong one. Such an act can be criticised because the Church always acts on the principle of lex orandi, lex credendi, lex vivendi.*

FIFTY SEVEN

CONCLUSION OF THE TRANSLATOR

THE CEREMONIES OF THE ERBGĦAT TAL-UDIENZA IN MALTA usually take place in the evening. Recitation of the Rosary and the chaplet of Our Lady of Mount Carmel is followed by Mass and Benediction. Pride of place is given to a sermon on Our Lady, given, often by an invited preacher, after the Gospel Reading of the Mass.

In the sanctuary in Valletta, The Miraculous Icon of Our Lady is exposed from behind its curtain; the Icon leaves no doubt that Our Lady is enthroned in Glory, as Queen ready to give audience to Her Devotees.

However, the Icon depicts the scapular vision of Saint Simon Stock, as well as how the devotees of Our Lady of Mount Carmel are helped in Purgatory. Thus, both the idea that wearers of the Scapular are Consecrated to Our Lady and that they will be saved from purgatory are both represented.

The fact that the scapular which Our Lady presents to Simon Stock touches the church, which is reminiscent of the Naples Carmine Maggiore, the 'Home' of the Madonna Bruna, the original icon linked with the Wednesday devotion brings the concepts full circle, linking the Scapular devotion with the Wednesdays of Our Lady.

It is clear that one major issue faced by the Church has always been to encourage its members to think about the significance of the life and teachings of Christ. It is only by considering or meditating on Christ's Life and teaching that the members of the church would live their life as Christ had wished them to live, and the significance of the redemption.

In the 12th century, the idea of the Joys of Our Lady, linked with the belief that Our Lady had appeared to Thomas Becket was a very good way in which meditation on the Joys, which were also the main episodes of the life of Christ, could be promoted, and the Carmelites of Aylesford, only one day's march away from Thomas' shrine, came to make these Joys a major part of their teaching.

As time went on, the Joys became included in other devotions, particularly those of the Dominican and Franciscan Rosaries.The Carmelites developed the same Joys into chaplets. All these devotions developed but the aim was always the same, meditation on the life of Christ and His Mother.

The Franciscan and Dominican Rosaries were both accompanied by stories of visions relating to their origin. They became very similar so that eventually, they became the most popular of many other devotions promoted by mendicant friars.

Meanwhile, the story of the Scapular Vision gradually became more popular and contributed to another fundamental requirement of the Church - which was consequent on the first; having meditated or contemplated on the life of Christ and his Mother and the salvation which Christ had brought mankind, the individual Christian could become committed to Christ and His Mother, and the Scapular, which showed the Christian's total belonging to Our Lady, in the fundamental meaning of belonging or consecration to a Mistress, Mary. Hence the meditation on the life of

Christ, represented by the Rosary and the Consecration to Mary, and hence to Christ, represented by the brown Scapular, became together important aspects of the spiritual life of the Catholic Christian.

As this development continued over the centuries, particular devotions in particular locations remained, taking a form of their own depending on their location and the circumstances which brought them about. This is particularly true of the Carmelite Devotion of the Chaplet of the Joys of Our Lady, which took many local forms across Italy, and which was recited in some places on Wednesdays, linked with the Madonna Bruna of Naples, and in some places recited as part of the Feast of Our Lady of Mount Carmel. It was always linked with the scapular, since in many areas it was Scapular Confraternities which maintained the devotion, especially when the Carmelites had been forced by circumstance, such as suppression of monasteries, to leave particular locations. In the same way deliverance of a locality from Plague or Cholera, as in the case of Sambuca, led to the idea in those places that Our Lady particularly listened to her Devotees, so that, in some of these places, the appellation 'Dell'Udienza' – Our Lady who gives Audience – became applied to these devotions in particular locations. But since it is a Queen who usually gives Audience - indeed, since Byzantine times, Audience with a Ruler could be a very solemn, awe inspiring occasion- much ceremony came to be held in Her honour, and so the association, as in the case of the Basilica of Valletta, with an Icon of Our Lady, as Queen, giving Audience - thus in Valletta a curtain is raised to reveal the Icon and a fanfare is sounded at the beginning of the service- became an obvious link with the title 'tal-Udienza'. Finally, in particular locations, one particular component of the ceremonies might become particularly important, thus, in Malta, the Sermon by an invited preacher, became a particular hallmark of the Wednesdays between Easter and Pentecost, called Tal-Udienza'.

Seen in this way, the development of the devotion of the Joys of our Lady, from the 12th century, into the devotions of the Rosary and the Scapular, and other less widespread Devotions like the Wednesdays 'Tal-Udienza' are linked 'psychologically' as part of the effort of the Church in teaching its faithful to meditate on the life of Christ and commitment as consecration to Him.

One simple illustration of this is that, whereas it is very likely that the Carmelites at Aylesford used to teach pilgrims to Saint Thomas Becket's Tomb about the Joys of Our Lady in the Middle Ages, they did not do so after their return to Aylesford in the 1950s. Instead they set up a Rosary Way, which is regularly used; the mysteries of the Rosary had totally supplanted the Joys of Our Lady by the twentieth century, but this did not matter, since the Rosary incorporated the same events of the Life of Christ, and had become the main method of meditation on the life of Christ for today's faithful.

The Development of devotion which we suggest, based on the evidence which we have seen in this book can be said to be paralleled by the development within the Carmelite Order of Devotion to Mary, its Patron. Thus, Emanuele Boaga has traced this development of this devotion in his book 'The Lady of the Place' (Roma Edizioni Carmelitane 2001)[1]*. His description is summarised in the following paragraph:*

> *In the Beginning, on Mount Carmel, the Carmelite Hermits expressed Allegiance to Mary, to the 'the Lord and to the Lady of The Place'. By the thirteenth century (1252 and later) their emphasis was on the Patronage of Mary; she was seen as the patroness of the Order, the 'Domina Loci'. By the XIV centuryshe was seen as Immaculate, theVirgo Purissima, but also as Sister and Mother of*

the Order and its members. This lead toImitation of her in Listening to the word, Faith, Prayer to Her in time of need and Contemplation of the life and virtues of Mary. By the fifteenth century, the emphasis was on Imitatio Christi, Imitation of Christ, and Intimacy with Her by total giving of self to Mary, and through her to Jesus, thus Imitation and Union with both Mary and Christ. By the Sixteenth Century, Teresa of Jesus and John of the Cross in Spain had developed further the notion of Union with Christ, and were seeing Mary as a model of Perfection on the Journeyinto God, while in Italy, Mary Magdalene de' Pazzi wrote of Mystical union with Mary. By the seventeenth century, Michael of St. Augustine was writing about a Mystical union with Mary in perfect harmony with the central position of Christ, The Brown Scapular becomes prominent as a popular devotion in the seventeenth till the twentieth centuries, With this comes the devotion to Our Lady of the Scapular, with development of Scapular Confraternities, the development of emphasis on the Holy Scapular as a pastoral instrument, Privileges and Popular devotion. Finally, in the nineteenth and twentieth centuries, many Carmelites, including Therese of the Child Jesus, Elizabeth of the Trinity, Edith Stein and Titus Brandsma saw Mary as an example to follow- emphasizing the Exemplarity of Mary, seeing Imitation as the best form of devotion, taking a Biblical Approach, and seeing Mary, as a way to holiness, aiming to be a 'Theotokos' (God Bearer) like Mary. The above describes in brief the history of the development of prayer, as a form of union with God, within the Carmelite Order itself.

In parallel to this development, as we have argued, is a development of teaching of the persons who were evangelised by the Carmelites. Thus Thomas Becket died in1170 the twelfth Century, so the teaching about the Joys of Our Lady and His Vision can only have started after this and, since the Carmelites arrived in Aylesford in 1242, they can only have begun to be associated with it after that date. The Scapular Vision is said to have occurred in 1251(thirteenth Century), it became popularised according to Boaga in the seventeenth century, however, Scapular Confraternities must have existed in the fourteenth century, since John of Gaunt, who died in 1399 is said to have been a member. Indeed they are known to have existed from the 13th century onwards as groups of persons affiliated with the order, The earliest confraternity of Battuti of Modena, who met in a Carmelite Church, used a Chaplet of Joys dated 1300. In the meantime, rudimentary Rosaries were first being described by William Schaffener of Rappeltsweiler in 1498 (fifteenth Century) while the story of the Franciscan Crown is dated 1422.Thus, the assimilation of the concepts of the Joys into meditating the Mysteries of the rosary begins in the fifteenth century. The Wednesdays of Our Lady of Mount Carmel in Naples begin from 1500, that is the sixteenth century. The liberation from the Plague of Sambuca by the Madonna Dell'Udienza is dated 1575, while that in Malta is dated 1592.

Hence, there is a development from the twelfth till the sixteenth centuries, in which the Devotion of Joys of Our Lady developed into the meditation of the Mysteries of the Rosary and a development in which the story of the Scapular Vision developed from the thirteenth century up to the sixteenth and seventeenth century into a popular form of consecration to Mary and Christ. At the same time, within the friars of the Order, there was a movement from declaring Mary their Patron in the thirteenth century to deep union with God as an aim of prayer by the sixteenth century, This spiritual movement within the clergy of the order can be seen as being in parallel with or mirroring their teaching of their devotees. What the

Scapular, Rosary and Chaplet of Joys offered was equal meditation and full consecration to Mary and Christ for the multitude on a par with the union with Mary and Christ of the clergy of the order.

It is indeed true to say, then, 'The Rosary and the Scapular are One'. The Wednesdays of Our Lady, known as l-Erbgħat Tal-Udienza' are a reflection and a product of the development of these two great devotions in the Catholic Church.

References:

1 *Emanuele Boaga 'The Lady of the Place' (Roma Edizioni Carmelitane 2001).*

Part 5

The Carmelite, The Scapular Wearer, and their Relationship with God

FIFTY EIGHT

THE CARMELITE AND HIS RELATIONSHIP WITH GOD - THE CARMELITE RITE AND THE SCAPULAR

LET US CONSIDER HOW THE CARMELITES FRIARS, NUNS AND MEMBERS of the third Order, as well as all the Carmelite Devotees who wear the scapular and are enrolled in the Confraternities of the scapular, or of Our Lady of Mount Carmel, come to use this relationship to Mary as a way of relating to God, who created us all and loves us.

It is now a commonplace assertion that Carmel is Mary's Order, and the Scapular of Carmel is an external sign of this. However, how does this relationship with Mary affect the way in which the Carmelite prays to the God who made him? How does it come about that the Carmelite Order has produced great figures such as Saint Teresa of Avila and Saint John of the Cross, and so many others, whose deep relationship in prayer with God has become an example to all of how to pray, in friendship with God.

True, these great doctors of prayer were Carmelites, who wore their scapular and had a deep devotion to Mary - Remember Saint Teresa's commitment to Our Lady that she (Our Lady) would be her Mother- but was there something which was there from the beginning of the Carmelite Order which made this order more prolific than others in producing Doctors of the Church who had deep prayer lives and taught the whole Church how to pray?

One answer must lie in their imitation of their patron the Prophet Elias, who was zealous for the Lord God of Hosts. Another answer must lie in their way of praying, or Rite, which they adopted once they were recognised as a group (or 'order') within the local diocese of Jerusalem by Saint Albert, who gave them a rule.

In this rule, which was one oriented to the way of life of hermits, they were each to live in a cell, and to meet for prayer in a chapel in the centre of the hermitage site. We know that the chapel contained an Icon of Our Lady and was dedicated to Her- hence the beginning of the Marian Tradition of the Order, as Our Lady was seen as 'The Lady of the Place'[2]- but in that chapel, was also the altar where the Mass would be said, as well as round which the hermits would recite the Holy Office.

So, within that chapel the early Carmelites would practice the Rite of Mass and the Office in accordance with the custom, or rite, of the diocese with which they were affiliated, that diocese being Jerusalem. This Rite gave them an orientation to their prayer life which became part of the Carmelite Tradition, as much as did their Marian Devotion.

The rite of this diocese was the rite of the Holy Sepulchre, in other words, the liturgy as practiced in the Church of the Holy Sepulchre. It was not an Eastern Rite, but a Gallican (From France) Rite[3], brought from France by the Franks who participated in the Crusades, but it was inevitably focussed on the place in which it was carried out- the Church of the Holy Sepulchre, built around the Holy Sepulchre of Christ. Hence the whole emphasis of this Rite was on the Resurrection of Christ, and the Celebrant's relationship with and celebration of that mystery.

One important part of the Rite of the Church of the Holy Sepulchre is that of frequent processions, which started as processions to the Holy Sepulchre itself. These processions became an important characteristic of the liturgy of the order. In Jerusalem, the Canons of the Holy Sepulchre 'instituted various processions and other ceremonies on the principal feasts of Our Lord, such as Easter, the Ascension, etc. Two of the processions proper to the Carmelite Rite, and still prescribed in our Missal, namely, the processions before the Conventual Mass on the feasts of the Ascension and the Assumption, are precious relics of the solemnities performed by the Canons of the Holy Sepulchre in the very places where these Mysteries actually occurred'[1] *(Bartholomew Quinn, O.Carm Carmelite Rite, the history of the Carmelite Liturgy).*

In a recent lecture, it was said that, to celebrate the Resurrection, in the Carmelite Rite, the celebrant stands and bows, rather than genuflects.[4] I well remember that before the Second Vatican Council, after the Consecration, the celebrant was standing straight upright, with his arms outstretched in the form of a cross. That shape of a cross formed by the celebrant reminded both the Carmelite Friars and the Congregation of the link between Christ's death and Resurrection and the Eucharistic mystery and union with Christ that they were celebrating.

The Carmelite Rite, based on the Rite of the Holy Sepulchre, also dictated how the Holy Office was recited.[3] This is confirmed by some of the most ancient Carmelite liturgical documents we possess. Thus, in the Ordinal written by Sibert de Beka[5,6] at the beginning of the fourteenth century, we read: 'Here begins the Ordinal of the Brothers of the Blessed Virgin Mary of Mount Carmel, extracted and drawn from the approved usage of the Church of the Holy Sepulchre at Jerusalem, within the boundaries of which the Order of the aforesaid Brothers had its beginning.'[1] Again, the Constit-utions of the Chapter of Barcelona prescribe: 'Let them celebrate the Divine Office uniformly, according to the Rite of the Holy Sepulchre.'[1]

So, this rite, being part of the life of the order from the beginning, prepared the members of the order for a prayer life grounded on the celebration of the mysteries of the Redemption, and especially of the Resurrection; a prayer life which must involve a joyful relationship with the Risen Christ.

At the same time, the Carmelites' relationship with Our Lady, which began in the revering of Her as 'The Lady of the Place' on Mount Carmel had developed into the concept of Mary as a model of Perfection on the Journeyinto God (Boaga Our Lady of the Place)[2], so that Carmelites, Including John of The Cross, Teresa of Avila and Mary Magdalene of Pazzi used Our Lady of a Model for their prayer life.

So the two trends - to relate to the risen Christ and to see Mary as a Model in their deep prayer life,- are inextricably intertwined, and both are intertwined with the idea of the Scapular as a sign of commitment and Consecration to God and Our Lady.

References:

1 *Bartolomew Quinn, O.Carm Carmelite Rita, Carmelite Rite, The history of the Carmelite Liturgy (wwwocarm.org)*
2 *Emanuele Boaga O.Carm. The Lady of the Place, Mary in the History and in the life of Carmel Edizioni Carmelitane Roma 2001.*
3 *Shawn Tribe; The Carmelite Rite: A quick summary New Liturgical Movement Saturday Nov 25, 2006.*
4 *This lecture was given by Fr. Kevin Alban O.Carm to whom this chapter is dedicated.*
5 *Paul Anthony Chandler, Reflections on the Ordinale of Sibert de Keka (1312) July 1 2010. hhtps://zenodo.org/record/1872069.*
6 *The Carmelite Order and its liturgy. https://cambridge.org/core/services/aop-cambridge-core/content/view/8FO426A70D363D9BDO86E737569FB89D/SO143491800001252a.pdf/div-class-title-introduction-div.pdf*

FIFTY NINE

THE CONTRIBUTION OF THE CARMELITES TO THE CONCEPT OF THE IMMACULATE CONCEPTION

Mark Agius
After Emanuele Boaga

THE CARMELITE ORDER WAS AMONG THE FIRST TO BEGIN TO describe the concept of the Immaculate Conception, especially in the 14th and 15th Century.[3]

The basic legend of the Carmelite order is that they were founded by Elijah, who saw Mary in a cloud rising from the sea. Elijah was followed by Elisha, and the sons of the prophets, Mary was said to visit the sons of the prophets in Carmel, and then to bring Jesus to visit them, and the sons of the prophets were said to have become some of his followers.[1,4]

Furthermore, the basis of the Carmelite devotion to the Immaculate Conception included their interpretation of the 'Little Cloud' of Elijah, the legend that the Carmelite Convent in Jerusalem was constructed in the place where the conception of the Virgin was said to have taken place, and reference to the person and work of Saint Cyril of Alexandria, who was said to have been a Carmelite.[1]

The Carmelites understood their relationship to Our Lady in a living way. They saw her presence in their life as a sister accompanying them on their journey. They praised her purity and saw this as in fact her attitude of total self-abandonment to God and conformity with the divine will.[1]

The Carmelites saw the similarity and sisterhood between the order and Our Lady since they both lived in Virginity. Elijah, founder of the order, and Mary, patroness and later founder, are from the family of Aaron and so are of the same family. Elijah, Elisha, and the sons of the prophets preserved their virginity. In Mary virginity flourished. The Carmelites, descendants of Elijah, saw Mary, prefigured in the Cloud seen by Elijah, hence they saw Mary as a sister, who was linked with them.[1]

Therefore the Carmelites saw Mary as being their Sister. This is so with many early Carmelite writers. For example, Arnold Bostius sees Mary as a sister, as well as seeing Mary as mother since there is a connection between her virginity and that of the Carmelites which makes a deep loving fraternal relationship between them[1]. Paleonidorus, John Baconthorpe, John of Cheminot, John of Hildesheim, John Baptist de Lezana, Daniel of the Virgin Mary give similar arguments.[1]

The most important Carmelite Theologians who argued in favour of the Immaculate Conception were John Baconthorpe in England (Cambridge), Michael Aiguani in Italy (Bolognia) and Francis Marti (Spain).[1]

The Argument of John Baconthorpe to support the Immaculate Conception was as thus; Mary had a unique position in the realm of grace because she was predestinatined to be Mother of God. Thus in order to be the habitation of the Son of God, Mary was destined to be holy and without stain of sin. Thus he elaborated Gn.3.15.[1]

St.Augustine and St.Anselm provided the basis for the arguement of Michael Aiguani to support the Immaculate Conception was based on. At that time there were understood to be two parts to conception; first material conception, then the infusion of the soul. Hence Aiguani argued that Mary was 'purified and sanctified before the infusion of the soul, in the first moment of her conception'.[1]

It was mainly because of the writings of John Baconthorpe, that the Carmelites took the decision to change their cloak from the striped cloak to the white cloak in order to honour the Immaculate Virgin. Therefore, the white cloak was seen as a sign of the Immaculate Virgin. John Baconthorpe at the beginning of the 14th century called the white cloak 'Mary's Mantle'.[1]

For John of Hildesheim, Philip Ribot, John Grossi (14th Century) the white cloak symbolised the Purity and Virginity of Mary. For Ribot, the use of the white cloak meant conserving purity of mind and body.[1] In the Mantuan Congregation, the white cloak was a sign of the Immaculate Virgin.[1] In a sermon on the feast of the Immaculate Virgin in the Carmelite church of Avignon, Bishop Richard Fitzralph said 'This holy and ancient order of Carmelites, which celebrates this feast with special solemnity, underlines it and relates it, prudently and devoutly, to the whiteness of the cloak.'[1] In 1370, John of Hildesheim related the white cloak to the purity of the followers of Elijah and in praise of Mary, who, he alleged, also used the white cloak to be like the angels and in honour of her son in the Transfiguration.[1]

How the Carmelites Celebrated the feast of the Immaculate Conception[1] in the late thirteenth and early fourteenth century is illustrated by the following facts;

In 1296, they requested that indulgences be given to those who visited their churches in Germany on the feast of the Immaculate Conception. In 1306 the feast on the Immaculate Conception was kept as the order's patronal feast in Avignon while the popes resided there (1309-1377), and this continued till the 15th century[1]. When the patronal feast of the order was changed to July, the General Chapter of the of 1609 ordered that the feast of the Immaculate Conception be kept in a special way.[1] In the 14th century, the word 'Virgin', and in 1478 'Ever Virgin' was inserted into the Order's Name.[1]

The virginity of Mary and the Immaculate Conception are related to the nature of the Order, its habit and its Title

The Carmelite devotion to the Immaculate Conception took two forms, which were related to each other. The first of these forms was that the virginity of Mary and the Immaculate Conception were and are related to the nature of the Order, its habit and its Title. This concept was rooted in the mystery revealed to Elijah in the 'Little Cloud' and is connected with the divine maternity.[1]

Until to the 18th Century, it was considered important to defend the Marian Privilege of the Immaculate Conception. Thus the Carmelites of the Iberian Peninsula made a promise to defend this privilege in sermons and debates.[1] The Portuguese Carmelites renewed their vows on the feast of the Immaculate Conception

(1617) and made a promise to defend this privilege.[1] In 1624, the Carmelites of Aragon swore an oath to defend this privilege.[1] In Betica (Spain), in 1758, the Carmelites introduced a fourth vow to defend this privilege.[1] Lay Carmelites and confraternities in Spain were encouraged to defend this privilege.[1] Also, in the 17th Century, The Mantuan Congregation honoured the Immaculate Conception in spiritual exercises and sermons to the public.[1]

THE IMMACULATE CONCEPTION AND PURITY AND THE INTERIOR LIFE

The second form by which the Carmelites related to the concept of the Immaculate Conception was that it related the Immaculate Conception to the concepts of Purity and the Interior Life.[1]

The conformity of the Carmelites to Mary in relation to her Virginity or purity was important because they therefore saw Themselves as therefore committed to defending themselves against concupiscence in the mind and heart, guarding against every form of sin, in particular sins of the flesh.[1] Thus, Ribot, John of Hildesheim, and John of Chemont all argued that Carmelites were virgins, and *to climb Mount Carmel meant offering to God a Holy Heart, purified from all stains of sin. This they did in conformity with Elijah, the first virgin and Mary, who became the model of the perfect Carmelite who desires to adhere to God with the greatest purity.*[1] At the time, purity was understood as having to do with Union with God. Thus there was a connection between the Most Pure Virgin and the characteristic Carmelite way of understanding the interior life.[1] This is important because it shows a link between Carmelite Devotion to the Immaculate Conception and the Union with God [in imitation of Mary] in the practice of Contemplative Prayer as advocated by the

Carmelite Mystics including Teresa of Avila, John of the Cross, and Mary Magdalene de' Pazzi.[1] Carmelites thought of the Immaculate Virgin as 'Tota Pulchra' (all Beautiful - this antiphon possibly written by Baconthorpe), 'Virgo Virginum' (Virgin of Virgins), The Woman of the Apocalypse, The One who was totally available for union with God.[1]

This devotion to the Most Pure Virgin is the continuation of the remembrance of the Annunciation, in the sense that it was purity which united Mary to God in the Annunciation.[1] The Carmelites were very aware that they could not imitate Mary in that singular privilege, but they could imitate her in her Union with God by means of Prayer and their faithful listening to the Word of God.[1]

In the 17th and 18th centuries the cult of the Immaculate Conception was carefully developed in Carmelite churches, in the Third Order, and the whole Order. Members of the confraternity of the scapular were recommended to 'observe chastity according to their own state of life.'[1] These terms were considered synonymous; Mary Immaculate, Most Pure Virgin, Virgin of Virgins, Mater Purissima, and this affected the litanies of Our Lady.[1]

In the 19th and early 20th Centuries, the term 'Most Pure Virgin' tended to be less used in Carmelite Writings. However there is now more emphasis on the Carmelite Devotion to the 'Most Pure Virgin' in the writings of Albert Grammatico, Valerius Hoppenbrouwer and Ludovico Saggi.[1]

Saint Mary Magdalene de' Pazzi on Mary, Purity and the Interior Life (After Boaga)

How the Carmelite Writers of the sixteenth and seventeenth century related the Immaculate Conception to the Interior Life can be exemplified by the writing of Saint Mary Magdalene de' Pazzi.[1]

St Mary Magdalene de' Pazzi (1607) uses the word purity in connection with the symbolism of the white cloak; thus,in the purity of the Virgin her beauty shines out, which attracts God to Her. An important aspect of purity is the capacity to be available for God by means of an ascetical-mystical journey that begins with the recognition of one's own nothingness and reaches out towards participation in contemplative union with God. For Saint Mary Magdalene de' Pazzi, Mary the Most Pure Virgin is an example of this mystical purity. She presents Our Lady as recommending Purity, inviting us to live a pure life, being for all a transient witness to purity. She speaks of Mary as 'Purifying and washing the nuns with the blood of Christ', 'Feeding them with her milk', 'So that they might always be available to choose and accept the divine ',and 'Transforming them into white doves that fly to the heart of Jesus'. In this ascetical-mystical dimension, the human being learns a lesson; humans learn the need for 'Availability for God', for 'Conformity with his will', and the need for 'Spiritual fruitfulness, bearing witness and prophecy'. This ascetical-contemplative panorama goes well beyond a mere psychological fact. It is a mystical adventure that tends to develop within the mystery of the Church, fed with hope in the incarnation. The prophetic function of virginity within the Church consists in living in a situation of availability and fruitfulness like Mary, the Most Holy Virgin.[1]

Thus, the virtue of purity in relation to the Immaculate Conception is much more than what may be traditionally understood, but relates to Union with God, the deepest goal and final destiny of the human person, as understood by the Carmelite Mystical Writers. When recommending members of the confraternity of the scapular to 'observe chastity according to their own state of life, 'this relationship to union with God needs to be remembered, because what is in fact being recommended is that the scapular wearer should be aiming to lead a life of Union with God, no less than the Carmelite Mystics, and both the scapular and that observance of chastity according to their own state of life are signs of this. Thus, through the scapular all are called to perfection.

References:

1 *Emanuele Boaga O.Carm. The Lady of the Place, Mary in the History and in the life of Carmel Edizioni Carmelitane Roma 2001.*

2 *https://en.wikipedia.org/wiki/Carmelites*

3 *https://www.stjudeshrine.org.uk/news/carmelite-pirituality-series-our-lady-immaculate*

4 *https://www.carmelite.org/carmelite-spirituality/saints-of-carmel/st-elijah-prophet*

SIXTY

SOME CARMELITE SAINTS AND CONSECRATION TO THE VIRGIN MARY

Mark Agius

THE PROBLEM

THERE ARE MANY CARMELITE SAINTS WHO HAVE DEVELOPED A VERY great reputation as the greatest experts on Mystical Theology in the Church. These include Teresa of Avila and John of the Cross, but there are many others including Mary Magdalene de'Pazzi, Lawrence of the Resurrection, Therese of Lisieux, Elizabeth of the Trinity, and Edith Stein.

The difficulty is that some of these saints, particularly Teresa of Avila and John of the Cross, have been popularised in the English Literature by persons who have not discussed them from a Catholic point of view (indeed they are very popular within the Anglican Community among others), and hence these persons have not emphasized their relationship with the Virgin Mary, concentrating on their commitment to developing a relationship of deep union with God. On the Other Hand, Emanuela Boaga O.Carm says of some of these saints that in the sixteenth century, within the Carmelite Order, Mary was seen as model of Perfection on the Journeyinto God, quoting as exemplars of this Teresa of Jesus, John of the Cross and Mary Magdalene de' Pazzi. The Carmelite order in that Century was also said by Boaga to be committed to Mystical union with Mary, presumably also linked with the 'Journey into God'.

Mary Magdalene de' Pazzi has been amply analysed by Boaga as quoted in another of these Essays, and her work has been said by Boagato to link union with God with the 'situation of availability and fruitfulness like Mary'. Thus he says, *'In this ascetical-mystical dimension, the human being learns a lesson; humans learn the need for 'Availability for God', for 'Conformity with his will', and the need for 'Spiritual fruitfulness, bearing witness and prophecy'. This ascetical-contemplative panorama goes well beyond a mere psychological fact. It is a mystical adventure that tends to develop within the mystery of the Church, fed with hope in the incarnation. The prophetic function of virginity within the Church consists in living in a situation of availability and fruitfulness like Mary, the Most Holy Virgin'.* [27]

The question is whether there is a similar link between union with God and a Marian Dimension in the other Carmelite Authors; Teresa of Avila and John of the Cross.

Teresa of Avila

'Saint Teresa of Jesus and the Virgin Mary' is an excellent article on the website of the Discalced Carmelite Order. In it, the point is made that 'St Teresa's whole Marian experience is found scattered throughout her writings, from which we can put together a lovely mosaic of Mary.'(1) From this, let us try and identify points which suggest a commitment by Teresa to live in union with, or be consecrated to Mary. They are easy to find; the quoted article recounts 'The episode of her prayer to Our Lady after the loss of her mother at the age of thirteen is very moving: 'in my affliction I went to an image of our Lady and begged her with many tears to be a mother to me. It seems to me that though I did this in simplicity, it has been of much help to me; for I know that I have always found favour with this sovereign lady when I have commended myself to her and in the end, she has drawn me to herself'.[2]

With the words 'She has drawn me to herself', Teresa attributes to Our Lady the grace of a constant protection and in a special way the grace of her conversion.[1] Later it is clear that in her prayer life, she has very deep insights into the Mystery of the Incarnation[3], the presentation of Jesus in the temple.[4] She had a special intuition of the presence of Mary in the paschal mystery of her Son, on the pain of her desolation and the joy in the Lord's resurrection.[1,5,6,7,8] When it was given to her to know the mystery of the Trinity, she perceived the closeness of the Virgin to this mystery.[1,9]

Thus, It can be stated that the Holy Mother had a profound mystical experience of Mary, that she enjoyed her presence. Teresa also experienced the mysteries of Mary's life. Consequently, in Teresa's doctrine there runs a deep conviction that the mysteries of the Humanity of Christ and those of his Virgin Mother form part of the mystical experience of those tending to perfection.[1,10] This shows how deeply and personally Teresa lives in Union with both Mary and Jesus, which is what we were seeking in this enquiry.

Furthermore, it can be said that Teresa saw such a relationship with Mary as important for every Carmelite. For example, when she was appointed Prioress of the Incarnation in 1571, she placed a statue of Mary in the first place in the choir for she knew that the devotion, love and respect of all the religious converged on Mary. This gesture had a delightful epilogue in the apparition of the Virgin.[1,11] Within her monasteries, Teresa's idea of fraternity, with its reciprocal love and sharing of goods, has for its foundation love of the Virgin and the sense of belonging to the same family, as this text suggests[1]: 'And so my daughters, all belong to the Virgin and are sisters and should seek to love one another greatly'.[12]

Teresa was very conscious of the origins and traditions of the Carmelite Order, as well as their devotion to Mary. On various occasions the thought of the Virgin arouses in Teresa an understanding of the Carmelite vocation inspired by Mary. Here, for example, with an implicit reference to Mary[1] she writes, 'All of us who wear this holy habit of Carmel are called to prayer and contemplation. This call explains our origin; we are descendants of men who felt this call, of these holy fathers of Mount Carmel who in such great solitude and contempt for the world sought this treasure, this precious pearl we are talking about.'[13]

Very pertinent to this book on the Scapular, it is clear that Theresa was very aware of the relationship between the Carmelite Scapular, the Carmelite Order and Our Lady. She was fully conscious of the privileges of the Holy Scapular as appears in this sentence referring to the death of a Carmelite Friar[1]: 'I understood that having been a friar who was very faithful to his profession, he had profited by the Bulls of the Order so as not to enter purgatory.'[14] Thus Teresa is aware of the Sabbatine Privilege linked with the scapular. Hence Teresa lived in union with Mary and with God, and was also very faithful to her Order, of which she knew the customs, traditions, and privileges including those of the Scapular as they were known in her time.

Saint John of the Cross

'The Mariology of Saint John of the Cross' by Br. John-Mary of Jesus Crucified, OCD provides a useful overview of Saint John's Mariology.[15] The author raises the question which this essay raises: 'How is it that a man known for his spiritual wisdom, who devoted his entire life to achieving union with God in a religious order dedicated to living in imitation of Mary, is rarely recalled in relation to Our Lady?'[15] It is pointed out that; 'In all his extant writing (four major spiritual treatises, fifteen poems, thirty-three letters, and several other minor works) John mentions Mary explicitly only twelve times, and most of these references are only incidental'.[15] Despite these few references to Mary, it has been claimed that John offers a complete and systematic Mariology. Fr. Emmanuel Sullivan, OCD explains that 'while the explicit references to Mary are very few, all of John's writings are really centered on Mary. Actually, there is little about Mary that John has left unsaid. His whole spiritual doctrine conveys an implicit Mariology.'[15]

The life of the Saint gives substantial proof of the centrality of Mary in his mind and heart[15], On two occasions, John was saved from drowning when he was a boy.[15] Once, John was playing near a lagoon when he fell into the water and began to drown. Later he would recall that a beautiful lady, whom he later identified as Our Lady, came to his aid.[15] On a second occasion, John fell into a deep well but was pulled out without injury. He attributed this miracle to the Blessed Virgin Mary.[15]

John's early biographers also affirm that his decision to enter the Carmelites was largely influenced by the Marian character of the

Order and his great love for Our Lady,[15] and this same love of Our Lady that enabled Teresa of Avila is said to have convinced him to stay and become the co-founder of her reform.[15]

John was also known to attribute his miraculous escape from prison to the strength given to him from the Mother of God.[15]

Br. Martin of the Assumption, a regular travelling companion of St. John of the Cross, testified following John's death: 'He was so devoted to Our Lady that every day he prayed the Office of Our Lady on his knees.'[15] And Martin added that, during their many journeys together, John would sing hymns to Our Lady.[15]

At the hour of his death, upon hearing the bell for Matins, John of the Cross said, 'And I, too, through the goodness of the Lord, will have to say them with our Lady in heaven.'[15]

All the above suggests that the Blessed Virgin was central in his mind and heart from his earliest childhood until the moment of his death.(15) Br. John-Mary of Jesus Crucified OCD therefore says that John lived and breathed devotion to Our Lady.[15]

Br. John-Mary of Jesus Crucified OCD points out that 'All that John says about union with God can be applied pre-eminently and perfectly to the Blessed Virgin. Considering that union with God is the central focus of all of his writing, his works are a treasury of rich insights into the life and holiness of Mary'.[15]

One example of John's devotion to Mary which gives a Marian gloss to his writing is from one of the poems in John of the Cross' *Romances*, In it, talking of the Annunciation, the Angel Gabriel is sent not to give a message to Mary but to take back a message from Mary to God - Her Consent.[15]

In the article 'The Virgin Mary, St John of the Cross and other Carmelite authors[16], further reference is made to the Marian Doctrine in the *Romances*, In the *Romances* on the Gospel of John, numbers 8-9 Mary is seen *In communion with the mystery of Christ.* The Virgin appears in the splendour of her communion with the Trinity, in her privilege and mission as Mother of the Incarnate Word, in her acceptance and consent to the work of redemption.[16] The Virgin Mary is witness of the mystery, the 'Mother of Grace' who bears in her arms God, the Spouse - Church and Humanity in that the wedding of God with Man was consummated in Her: 'He whom she bore in her arms embraced her as his spouse.'[16] The peak of this communion is reached in the cross, when the Virgin shared in the redemptive suffering of Christ, although exempt from sin, and having no need of suffering as a purification, but because Christ associates her with his saving action.[17]

Next, John describes Mary as *Moved by the Holy Spirit.* In a significant context, speaking of souls so entirely identified with the will of God that all their acts, works, petitions, are inspired by God.[16] St John writes: 'Such were those of the glorious Virgin our Lady, who, having been raised to this high estate from the beginning, never received in her soul the impress of any creature, nor was moved by it, but was always moved by the Holy Spirit.'[18] Here he affirms a principle of the constant and total action of the

Holy Spirit in Mary, raised to this high state, right from the beginning, of communion with God in a growing dynamism of fidelity and cooperation with the inspirations of the Holy Spirit.[16] This Union between Mary and the Holy Spirit is used by John to illustrate the deep union between human souls and God, such that He himself must have experienced.

John describes Mary as a *Model of contemplation and intercession* and gives her intersession at the Marriage of Cana as an example.[19]

The Virgin's presence is implicit in this thought of the Saint, in which John talks about union between the soul and God the Father and the Son: 'The Father has spoken one Word, which is the Son, and he speaks the Word ever in eternal silence, and in silence the soul hears it.'[20] It is Mary who is the contemplative silence that has received the Word, and in Christ 'the Mother of God is mine'.[21] That statement 'the Mother of God is mine' shows that John is in union with both Mary the Mother of God and God Himself.

Before leaving our consideration of John of the Cross, it is worth noting his devotion to the brown scapular, which he wore as part of the Carmelite Habit. Fr. Peter Davis O.Carm has recorded some quotes from his life.[22] On receiving the habit John is recorded as having said 'I desire to practice with fervour all the virtues of Mary which this holy habit symbolises.'[22] John appears to have been well aware of the Sabbatine Privilege associated with the scapular. The great Carmelite mystic, St. John of the Cross, used to pray for the grace to die on a Saturday, and his prayers were answered.[22] Before he died, in the year 1591, he said: 'The Mother of God and of Carmel hastens to Purgatory with grace on Saturday and delivers those souls who have worn her Scapular. Blessed be such a Lady who wills that, on this day of Saturday, I shall depart from this life!'[22]

From all of the above it is clear that Saint John of the Cross lived in union with Mary and with God, and was faithful to the Order, and was well aware of the Scapular and the privileges thereof as they were known in his time.

Thérèse of Lisieux

Thérèse grew up in a family which was very devoted to Our Lady. Fr. John A. Hardon, S.J.provides an excellent study *'Devotion of St. Thérèse of Lisieux to the Blessed Virgin Mary'*[23]. Her mother died at the early age of forty-six, when Thérèse was 5 years old, Until Thérèse was nine years old, her sister Pauline took the place of her mother. But in 1881 when Pauline entered the Carmel at Lisieux, her younger sister felt the shock so severely that she came down with an apparently incurable nervous malady.[23]. She was cured of this illness through a statue of Our Lady, which came to life during her delirium. This clearly strengthened her devotion to Our Lady and her wish to be Consecrated to Our Lady.[23]

In the afternoon of her first Holy Communion, aged 10, she solemnly ratified Mary's gift to her by consecrating herself 'with all the affection of my heart' to the Blessed Mother of God. 'I pronounced the Act of Consecration to the Blessed Virgin in the name of my companions. Doubtless I was chosen for this because I was left without my mother on earth…In consecrating myself to the Virgin Mary, I asked her to watch over me, placing into the act all the devotion of my soul, and it seemed to me, I saw her once again looking down and smiling on her 'petite fleur.'[24]

However this general consecration to Mary did not satisfy her, She wished to dedicate herself in a very special way. 'I resolved therefore,' she says, 'to consecrate myself in a particular way to the Most Holy Virgin, begging for admission among the Daughters of Mary.'[25] And so, on May 31, 1887, she was enrolled in the Association of the Daughters of Mary, at the convent of the Benedictine Abbey of Lisieux, among whom were admitted only those students who were distinguished for their piety and good example.[25]

Once she entered the Carmel of Lisieux, Thérèse' life of union with the Mother of God became daily more intense. According to the late Prioress of Carmel at Lisieux, what contributed not a little to this was the classic treatise, 'On the True Devotion of Blessed Virgin Mary,' by St. Louis de Montfort, which Thérèse frequently read and meditated upon. Following Louis de Montfort's advice, she did everything with Mary, or rather, in the presence of Mary, under Mary's influence and according to her example.[23]

Not only did she live in Union with Our Lady, but also with Our Lord. The very name of Mary was enough 'to transport her heart with joy.'[23] Her prayer to Our Lord was that He would always remember her as thc daughter of the same Mother as Himself.[23] This thought so fascinated her that she never tired of repeating it. 'Everything is mine,' she wrote Oct. 19, 1892, to her sister Céline, 'God is mine, and the Mother of God is also my Mother, ...

something I find myself saying to her, 'You know, dear Mother, that I am happier than you? I have you for Mother, whereas you do not have the Blessed Virgin to love…[23]

Naturally the Carmelite nuns distributed scapulars, and Thérèse clearly was very aware of the significance of the Scapular. On the Feast of Our Lady of Mt. Carmel, in 1894, Thérèse wrote to her cousin, Mme. Pottier. She wrote 'I had asked Our Lady of Mt. Carmel for the grace you obtained at Lourdes.' And she adds, 'I am so happy that you are wearing the Blessed Scapular; it is a sure sign of predestination.'[23]

So, also in the case of Thérèse of Lisieux, we have a person who is consecrated to Mary, and lives in union with Mary and with God, and is well aware of the significance of the scapular.

Edith Stein

Edith Stein, the philosopher saint who discovered empathy also experienced living in union with Our Lady and with God as a Carmelite, Sister Benedicta of the Cross. Shewrote of Mary in an essay called 'Woman's Place in the Mystical Body of Christ' 'she (Mary) has borne us into our life of grace, by casting her whole being, body and soul, into the divine maternity. Therefore she is intimately united to us: she loves us, she knows us, she is anxious to make each of us what he ought to be, especially to bring each of us into as close a relationship, as possible to our Lord.' Thus she understood the concept both of living in union with Mary, and consequently in union, through Mary, with our Lord.

CONCLUSION

Finally, what can we say about Elizabeth of the Trinity, the 'Praise of His Glory' who lived such a deep life of Union with God in the Carmel of Dijon, and what can we say of Lawrence of the Resurrection, who gave us the Practice of the Presence of God? Their writings talk of a deep union with God, and they lived the Carmelite Life, wearing their scapular as part of their Habit. Their writings are not on our Lady, but only on living in deep union with God, but the truth is this. They lived as Brothers and Sisters of the Blessed Virgin of Mount Carmel. Therefore they lived in union with Mary, their Sister and Mother.

References:

1 *'Saint Teresa of Jesus and the Virgin Mary' Updated 04 giu 2003 by OCD General House Corso d'Italia, 38 - 00198 Roma – Italia*

2 *Teresa of Jesus Life 1:7.*

3 *Teresa of Jesus Way, Escorial 48:22.*

4 *Teresa of Jesus Relations 36:1.*

5 *Teresa of Jesus Way 26:8.*

6 *Teresa of Jesus Concepts 3:11.*

7 *Teresa of Jesus Relation 58*

8 *Teresa of Jesus Relation 15: 1, 6.*

9 *Teresa of Jesus Relation 25:1.*

10 *Teresa of Jesus See Mansions VI 7:13 and the title of the chapter; 8:6.*

11 *Teresa of Jesus Relation 25.*

12 *Teresa of Jesus Letter to the nuns of Seville, January 13th 1580: 6*

13 *Teresa of Jesus Mansions V: 1:2.*

14 *Teresa of Jesus Life 38:31.*

---

15 *Br. John-Mary of Jesus Crucified, OCDhttps://discalcedcarmel.org/the-mariology-of-saint-john-of-the-cross/The Mariology of Saint John of the Cross 1918*

16 *'The Virgin Mary, St John of the Cross and other Carmelite authors' Updated 04 giu 2003 by OCD General House Corso d'Italia, 38 - 00198 Roma – Italia*

17 *John of the Cross Canticle B 20:10; Canticle A 29:7.*

18 *John of the Cross Ascent III: 2:10*

19 *John of the Cross Jn 2:3; Canticle A & B 2:8.*

20 *John of the Cross Sayings of Light and Love 104; See Ascent II: 22: 3-6.*

21 *John of the Cross Prayer of the enamored soul.*

22 *Fr. Peter Davis O.Carm Our Lady's Brown Scapular Sign of Consecration to Marywww.ecatholic2000.com › cts › untitled-328.*

23 *Fr. John A. Hardon, S.J.Devotion of St. Thérèse of Lisieux to the Blessed Virgin Mary https://hardonsj.org/devotion-of-st-therese-of-lisieux-to-the-blessed-virgin-mary/*

24 *Thérèse of Lisieux Autobiography 60*

25 *Thérèse of Lisieux Autobiography 68*

26 *Mary Julian Baird 1958 Edith Stein and the Mother of God, https://ecommons,udayton,edu/cgi/viewcontent.cgi?article=1058&context=marian_reprints*

27 *Emanuele Boga O. Carm. The Lady of the Place, Mary in the History and in the life of Carmel Edizioni Carmelitane Roma 2001*

SIXTY ONE

The Carmelite Mystics, Models of the Human Person, and Relationship with God

Mark Agius

According to Wikipedia, a person is a being that has certain capacities or attributes such as reason, morality, consciousness or self-consciousness, and being a part of a culturally established form of social relations such as kinship, ownership of property, or legal responsibility. The defining features of personhood and consequently what makes a person count as a person differ widely among cultures and contexts. In addition to the question of personhood, of what makes a being count as a person to begin with, there are further questions about personal identity and self: both about what makes any particular person that particular person instead of another, and about what makes a person at one time the same person as they were or will be at another time despite any intervening changes.[1]

This is a very complex definition.

One interesting way of looking at the Carmelite writers on mystical theology is looking at whether their writing gives insights into a 'model' of what a human person is, and thence at how the human person is able to relate to that other person - the Infinite God.

Indeed, a human person might be described as a person who is able to relate, in all the aspects mentioned above, to God, the Infinite Person.

Carmelite writers have described a number of 'models' both of human persons, and of the way in which the human person relates to God in prayer. Sometimes they have used the same model, and sometimes they have thrown light on aspects of the human personhood which are often ignored.

Depth

One such aspect of human personhood is depth. This is an aspect of being human in which persons ponder on information they receive and see deeper meanings in it. Such persons are aware of an interior life. This is an aspect of 'interiority' which is not related to anatomical interior organs but to an awareness of an interior life which human persons experience.

Thus, Teresa of Avila, describes how, as a person deepens their prayer life in her book 'The Interior Castle', which is made of several concentric mansions, and as the person grows in holiness and in her / his prayer life, he / she moves from one mansion to the next, till complete union with God is achieved in the innermost mansion.[9]

Elizabeth of the Trinity is quite clear about her sense of interiority when she says, **'Make my soul…Your cherished dwelling place, Your home of rest. Let me never leave You there alone, but keep me there all absorbed in You, in living faith, adoring You.'** Or **'It seems to me that I have found my heaven on earth, because my**

heaven is you, my God, and you are in my soul. You in me, and I in you – may this be my motto.' Also, 'What a joyous mystery is your presence within me, in that intimate sanctuary of my soul where I can always find you, even when I do not feel your presence. Of what importance is feeling? Perhaps you are all the closer when I feel you less.' Or, in a letter to a friend, **'Try as I do, to build a small cell in your heart. Think of God who resides there....When you feel nervous and troubled..., enter that cell quickly and entrust everything to Jesus. If you confide in Him, prayer will not trouble you any more. Prayer is rest, relaxation, a visit by us in simplicity to the person who we love. Let us stay beside Him as a child stays in his mother's arms and lets his heart become one with hers'**. Thus Elizabeth was able to be clear that God lived within her heart.[7]

A JOURNEY BY A PERSON TOWARDS HIS/HER BELOVED, FOLLOWED BY UNION WITH THE BELOVED.

John of the Cross describes the human person as on a journey, climbing a mountain, or through a dark night, to his / her beloved, which is then, in union with the beloved, becomes a complete intimate union between two persons, lover and beloved. He does this in a series of books- the ascent of Mount Carmel, The Dark Night of the Soul, the Spiritual Canticle and the Living Flame of Love. There is a progressive purification of distractions first by the senses then by spiritual distractions, as the person, or soul, comes to be more and more centred on God, until God alone suffices. However the model is one of ever deepening love between two persons, culminating in the living flame.[2,3,4]

'Spiritual childhood'

Therese of Lisieux developed a very direct way of relating to God. It became known as 'Spiritual Childhood' after her death when her sister Pauline adopted the phrase 'the little way of spiritual childhood' to interpret Thérèse's path. Therese wrote 'I will seek out a means of getting to Heaven by a little way—very short and very straight little way that is wholly new. We live in an age of inventions; nowadays the rich need not trouble to climb the stairs, they have lifts instead. Well, I mean to try and find a lift by which I may be raised unto God, for I am too tiny to climb the steep stairway of perfection. [...] Thine Arms, then, O Jesus, are the lift which must raise me up even unto Heaven. To get there I need not grow. On the contrary, I must remain little, I must become still less.' Essentially this is about one person, Therese, relating to another, Jesus, as a child does, with total confidence and total love, as a child would do. She referred to this saying 'My way is all confidence and love.'[6]

Conversation and friendship with God

Therese of Lisieux saw prayer as a direct conversation with God. 'I have not the courage to force myself to seek beautiful prayers in books; not knowing which to choose I act as children do who cannot read; I say quite simply to the good God what I want to tell Him, and He always understands me.'[8] However, Teresa of Avila also saw prayer as a direct conversationwith God; 'For prayer is nothing else than being on terms of friendship with God.'[10]

Love

However, the core of the relationship we are describing is love. This is what makes the 'Little Way' possible. It is about the love of the human person for God and much more importantly the Infinite love of God for the human person. Teresa of Avila says of us 'The important thing is not to think much, but to love much.'[11] It is love for the Beloved that impels John of the Cross to go out on a journey

> 'One dark night,
> fired with love's urgent longings
> — ah, the sheer grace! —
> I went out unseen,
> my house being now all stilled.'[2]

Of God's love Teresa says

> 'This Beloved of ours is merciful and good. Besides, he so deeply longs for our love that he keeps calling us to come closer.'[12]

Of the meeting between human person/ himself and God, John of the Cross says

> 'O guiding night!
> O night more lovely than the dawn!
> O night that has united
> the Lover with his beloved,
> transforming the beloved in her Lover.[2]

Elisabeth of the Trinity says,

> **'May my life be a continual prayer, a long act of love.'**[13]

LOVE OF OTHERS

In all the Carmelite writers, love of other persons is how the love of God is expressed.

Thus, for Teresa of Avila, 'The important thing is not to think much but to love much[11]; and so do that which best stirs you to love.' 'It is love alone that gives worth to all things.'[14]

For Therese of Lisieux,'Our Lord does not so much look at the greatness of our actions, or even at their difficulty, as at the love with which we do them.'[15] And 'Miss no single opportunity of making some small sacrifice, here by a smiling look, there by a kindly word; always doing the smallest right and doing it all for love.'[16] These are the small simple acts of lovewith which she expressed to God her love of him, because 'I understood that love comprises all vocations – that love is everything, and because it is eternal, embraces all times and places.'[6,17]

Empathy

To love others, it is necessary to empathise with them (Feeling for Others), Edith Stein, the trained philosopher among the Carmelite Saints, had written on Empathy for her PhD thesis. Perhaps it is because of Empathy with others, in particular with those of her Jewish Origins that she became impelled to petition her prioress to 'allow [Stein] to offer [her]self to the heart of Jesus as a sacrifice of atonement for true peace' and, on her arrest she said 'Come, we are going for our people.'[8]

The Practice of the Presence of God

It can be said that all the models of the life of prayer described by Carmelite Writers are with different imagery but are essentially the same. The most straightforward 'model' for the life of Prayer, and therefore of the relationship between the human being and God is The Practice of the Presence of God, which was written by the Discalced Carmelite Lay Brother Friar Lawrence of the Resurrection. He describes an experience where lives constantly in God's Presence. The great attraction for the modern reader is because this friar spent his life doing ordinary things, such as working in the kitchen of his monastery, Hence it is true that this is a form of deep relationship with God which is clearly possible for the modern Man. 'Brother Lawrence told me he had always been governed by love without selfish views. Since he resolved to make the love of God the end of all his actions, he had found reasons to be well satisfied with his method. He was pleased when he could take up a straw from the ground for the love of God, seeking Him only, and nothing else, not even His gifts.[5]

He said he had been long troubled in mind from a certain belief that he should be damned. All the men in the world could not have persuaded him to the contrary. This trouble of mind had lasted four years during which time he had suffered much.

Finally he reasoned: I did not engage in a religious life but for the love of God. I have endeavoured to act only for Him. Whatever becomes of me, whether I be lost or saved, I will always continue to act purely for the love of God.[5]

I shall have this good at least that till death I shall have done all that is in me to love Him. From that time on Brother Lawrence lived his life in perfect liberty and continual joy.[5]

He placed his sins between himself and God to tell Him that he did not deserve His favours, yet God still continued to bestow them in abundance.[5]

Brother Lawrence said that in order to form a habit of conversing with God continually and referring all we do to Him, we must at first apply to Him with some diligence. Then, after a little care, we would find His love inwardly exciting us to it without any difficulty. He expected after the pleasant days God had given him, he would have his turn of pain and suffering. Yet he was not uneasy about it. Knowing that, since he could do nothing of himself, God would not fail to give him the strength to bear them. When an occasion of practicing some virtue was offered, he addressed himself to God saying, 'Lord, I cannot do this unless Thou enablest me'. And then he received strength more than sufficient.'[5]

It can be seen from the above extract that all the criteria which have been identified from the other Carmelite Writers are summarised in the 'Practice of the Presence of God'.

All these writers we have quoted wore the Carmelite Scapular, and so were consecrated to Our Lady, and hence to Christ. Hence we can confidently argue that wearers of the Carmelite Scapular should all aim, being likewise consecrated, to practice either the Practice of the Presence of God or Therese's Spiritual Childhood as a way of life. In other words, all wearers of the Carmelite Scapular should live in the Presence and Love of God as a way of life.

References:

1 *Wikipedia, definition of Person*

2 *John of the Cross, Dark Night of the Soul*

3 *John of the Cross, Spiritual Canticle*

4 *John of the Cross, Living Flame of Love*

5 *Brother Lawrence of the Resurrection Practice of the Presence of God*

6 *Fr. John A. Hardon, S.J.Devotion of St. Thérèse of Lisieux to the Blessed Virgin Mary https://hardonsj.org/devotion-of-st-therese-of-lisieux-to-the-blessed-virgin-mary/*

7 *ttps://www.goodreads.com/author/quotes/202324.Elizabeth_of_the_Trinity*

8 *Mary Julian Baird 1958 Edith Stein and the Mother of God https://ecommons.udayton.edu/cgi/viewcontent.cgi?article=1058&context=marian_reprints*

9 *Teresa of Avila The Interior Castle*

10 *Teresa of Avila https://www.goodreads.com/quotes/93574-for-prayer-is-nothing-else-than-being-on-terms-of*

11 *Teresa of Avila https://www.goodreads.com/quotes/281378-the important-thing-is-not-to-think-much-but-to*

12 *Teresa of Avila https://www.goodreads.com/quotes/350845-this-beloved-of-ours-is-merciful-and-good-besides-he*

13 *https://www.ncregister.com/features/eliabeth-of-the-trinity-may-my-life-be-a-continual-prayer*

14 *Teresa of Avila https://www.goodreads.com/quotes/49762-it-is-love-alone-that-gives-worth-to-all-things*

15 *Theresa of Lisieux https://www.goodreads.com/quotes/783758-you-know-well-enough-that-our-lord-does-not-look*

16 *Theresa of Lisieux https://www.goodreads.com/quotes/243930-miss-no-single-opportunity-of-making-some-small-sacrifice-here*

17 *Therese of Lisieux Story of a Soul TAN 2010*

SIXTY TWO

Some Carmelite Saints, Consecration to the Virgin Mary, Living in Union with God and the Scapular of Carmel

Mark Agius

The Problem

There are many Carmelite Saints who have developed a very great reputation as the greatest experts on Mystical Theology in the Church. These include Teresa of Avila and John of the Cross, but there are many others including Mary Magdalene de' Pazzi, Lawrence of the Resurrection, Therese of Lisieux, Elizabeth of the Trinity, and Edith Stein.

The difficulty is that some of these saints, particularly Teresa of Avila and John of the Cross, have been popularised in the English Literature by persons who have not discussed them from a Catholic point of view (indeed they are very popular within the Anglican Community among others), and hence these persons have not emphasized their relationship with the Virgin Mary, concentrating on their commitment to developing a relationship of deep union with God. On the Other Hand, Emanuela Boaga O.Carm says of some of these saints that in the sixteenth century, within the Carmelite Order, Mary was seen as model of Perfection on the Journey into God, quoting as exemplars of this Teresa of Jesus, John of the Cross and Mary Magdalene de' Pazzi. The Carmelite order in that Century was also said by Boaga to be committed to Mystical union with Mary, presumably also linked with the 'Journey into God'.

Mary Magdalene de' Pazzi has been amply analysed by Boaga as quoted in another of these Essays, and her work has been said by Boaga to link union with God with the 'situation of availability and fruitfulness like Mary'. Thus he says, '*In this ascetical-mystical dimension, the human being learns a lesson; humans learn the need for 'Availability for God', for 'Conformity with his will', and the need for 'Spiritual fruitfulness, bearing witness and prophecy'*. This ascetical-contemplative panorama goes well beyond a mere psychological fact. It is a mystical adventure that tends to develop within the mystery of the Church, fed with hope in the incarnation. The prophetic function of virginity within the Church consists in living in a situation of availability and fruitfulness like Mary, the Most Holy Virgin'.[27]

The question is whether there is a similar link between union with God and a Marian Dimension in the other Carmelite Authors, Teresa of Avila and John of the Cross.

Teresa of Avila

'Saint Teresa of Jesus and the Virgin Mary' is an excellent article on the website of the Discalced Carmelite Order. In it, the point is made that 'St Teresa's whole Marian experience is found scattered throughout her writings, from which we can put together a lovely mosaic of Mary.'[1] From this, let us try and identify points which suggest a commitment by Teresa to live in union with, or be consecrated to Mary. They are easy to find; the quoted article recounts 'The episode of her prayer to Our Lady after the loss of her mother at the age of thirteen is very moving: 'in my affliction I went to an image of our Lady and begged her with many tears to be a mother to me. It seems to me that though I did this in simplicity, it has been of much help to me; for I know that I have always found favour with this sovereign lady when I have commended myself to her and in the end, she has drawn me to herself.'[2]

With the words 'She has drawn me to herself', Teresa attributes to Our Lady the grace of a constant protection and in a special way the grace of her conversion.[1] Later it is clear that in her prayer life, she has very deep insights into the Mystery of the Incarnation,[3] the presentation of Jesus in the temple.[4] She had a special intuition of the presence of Mary in the paschal mystery of her Son, on the pain of her desolation and the joy in the Lord's resurrection.[1, 5, 6, 7, 8] When it was given to her to know the mystery of the Trinity she perceived the closeness of the Virgin to this mystery. [1, 9]

Thus, It can be stated that St. Teresa had a profound mystical experience of Mary, that she enjoyed her presence. Teresa also experienced the mysteries of Mary's life. Consequently in Teresa's doctrine there runs a deep conviction that the mysteries of the Humanity of Christ and those of his Virgin Mother form part of the mystical experience of those tending to perfection. [1,10] This shows how deeply and personally Teresa lives in Union with both Mary and Jesus, which is what we were seeking in this enquiry.

Furthermore, it can be said that Teresa saw such a relationship with Mary as important for every Carmelite. For example, when she was appointed Prioress of the Incarnation in 1571, she placed a statue of Mary in the first place in the choir for she knew that the devotion, love and respect of all the religious converged on Mary. This gesture had a delightful epilogue in the apparition of the Virgin.[1,11]

Within her monasteries, Teresa's idea of fraternity, with its reciprocal love and sharing of goods, has for its foundation love of the Virgin and the sense of belonging to the same family, as this text suggests (1): 'And so my daughters, all belong to the Virgin and are sisters and should seek to love one another greatly.'[12]

Teresa was very conscious of the origins and traditions of the Carmelite Order, as well as their devotion to Mary. On various occasions the thought of the Virgin arouses in Teresa an understanding of the Carmelite vocation inspired by Mary. Here, for example, with an implicit reference to Mary[1] she writes, 'All of us who wear this holy habit of Carmel are called to prayer and contemplation. This call explains our origin; we are descendants of men who felt this call, of these holy fathers of Mount Carmel who in such great solitude and contempt for the world sought this treasure, this precious pearl we are talking about.'[13]

Very pertinent to this book on the Scapular, it is clear that Theresa was very aware of the relationship between the Carmelite Scapular, the Carmelite Order and Our Lady. She was fully conscious of the privileges of the Holy Scapular as appears in this sentence referring to the death of a Carmelite Friar[1]: 'I understood that having been a friar who was very faithful to his profession, he had profited by the Bulls of the Order so as not to enter purgatory.'[14] Thus Teresa is aware of the Sabbatine Privilege linked with the scapular. Hence Teresa lived in union with Mary and with God, and was also very faithful to her Order, of which she knew the customs, traditions, and privileges including those of the Scapular as they were known in her time.

Saint John of the Cross

'The Mariology of Saint John of the Cross' by Br. John-Mary of Jesus Crucified, OCD provides a useful overview of Saint John's Mariology[15]. The author raises the question which this essay raises: 'How is it that a man known for his spiritual wisdom, who devoted his entire life to achieving union with God in a religious order dedicated to living in imitation of Mary, is rarely recalled in relation to Our Lady?'[15] It is pointed out that; 'In all his extant writing (four major spiritual treatises, fifteen poems, thirty-three letters, and several other minor works) John mentions Mary explicitly only twelve times, and most of these references are only incidental.'[15] Despite these few references to Mary, it has been claimed that John offers a complete and systematic Mariology. Fr. Emmanuel Sullivan, OCD explains that 'while the explicit references to Mary are very few, all of John's writings are really centered on Mary. Actually, there is little about Mary that John has left unsaid. His whole spiritual doctrine conveys an implicit Mariology.'[15]

The life of the Saint gives substantial proof of the centrality of Mary in his mind and heart[15], On two occasions, John was saved from drowning when he was a boy.[15] Once, John was playing near a lagoon when he fell into the water and began to drown. Later he would recall that a beautiful lady, whom he later identified as Our

Lady, came to his aid.[15] On a second occasion, John fell into a deep well but was pulled out without injury. He attributed this miracle to the Blessed Virgin Mary.[15]

John's early biographers also affirm that his decision to enter the Carmelites was largely influenced by the Marian character of the Order and his great love for Our Lady[15], and this same love of Our Lady that enabled Teresa of Avila is said to have convinced him to stay and become the co-founder of her reform.[15]

John was also known to attribute his miraculous escape from prison to the strength given to him from the Mother of God.[15]

Br. Martin of the Assumption, a regular travelling companion of St. John of the Cross, testified following John's death: 'He was so devoted to Our Lady that every day he prayed the Office of Our Lady on his knees.'[15] And Martin added that, during their many journeys together, John would sing hymns to Our Lady.[15]

At the hour of his death, upon hearing the bell for Matins, John of the Cross said, 'And I, too, through the goodness of the Lord, will have to say them with our Lady in heaven.'[15]

All the above suggests that the Blessed Virgin was central in his mind and heart from his earliest childhood until the moment of his death.[15] Br. John-Mary of Jesus Crucified OCD therefore says that John lived and breathed devotion to Our Lady.[15]

Br. John-Mary of Jesus Crucified OCD points out that 'All that John says about union with God can be applied pre-eminently and perfectly to the Blessed Virgin. Considering that union with God is the central focus of all of his writing, his works are a treasury of rich insights into the life and holiness of Mary.'[15]

One example of John's devotion to Mary which gives a Marian gloss to his writing is from one of the poems in John of the Cross' *Romances,* In it, talking of the Annunciation, the Angel Gabriel is sent not to give a message to Mary but to take back a message from Mary to God - Her Consent.[15]

In the article 'The Virgin Mary, St John of the Cross and other Carmelite authors[16], further reference is made to the Marian Doctrine in the *Romances,* In the *Romances* on the Gospel of John, numbers 8-9 Mary is seen *In communion with the mystery of Christ.* The Virgin appears in the splendour of her communion with the Trinity, in her privilege and mission as Mother of the Incarnate Word, in her acceptance and consent to the work of redemption.[16] The Virgin Mary is witness of the mystery, the 'Mother of Grace' who bears in her arms God, the Spouse-Church and Humanity in that the wedding of God with Man was consummated in Her: 'He whom she bore in her arms embraced her as his spouse.'[16] The peak of this communion is reached in the cross, when the Virgin shares in the redemptive suffering of Christ, although exempt from sin, and having no need of suffering as a purification, but because Christ associates her with his saving action.[17]

Next, John describes Mary as *Moved by the Holy Spirit.* In a significant context, speaking of souls so entirely identified with the will of God that all their acts, works, petitions, are inspired by God.[16] St John writes: 'Such were those of the glorious Virgin our Lady, who, having been raised to this high estate from the beginning, never received in her soul the impress of any creature, nor was moved by it, but was always moved by the Holy Spirit.'[18] Here he affirms a principle of the constant and total action of the Holy Spirit in Mary, raised to this high state, right from the beginning, of communion with God in a growing dynamism of fidelity and co-operation with the inspirations of the Holy Spirit[16]. This Union between Mary and the Holy Spirit is used by John to illustrate the deep union between human souls and God, such that He himself must have experienced.

John describes Mary as a *Model of contemplation and intercession* and gives her intersession at the Marriage of Cana as an example.[19]

The Virgin's presence is implicit in this thought of the Saint, in which John talks about union between the soul and God the Father and the Son: 'The Father has spoken one Word, which is the Son, and he speaks the Word ever in eternal silence, and in silence the soul hears it.'[20] It is Mary who is the contemplative silence that has received the Word, and in Christ 'the Mother of God is mine.'[21] That statement 'the Mother of God is mine' shows that John is in union with both Mary the Mother of God and God Himself.

Before leaving our consideration of John of the Cross, it is worth noting his devotion to the brown scapular, which he wore as part of the Carmelite Habit. Fr. Peter Davis O.Carm has recorded some quotes from his life.[22] On receiving the habit John is recorded as having said 'I desire to practice with fervour all the virtues of Mary which this holy habit symbolises.'[22] John appears to have been well aware of the Sabbatine Privilege associated with the scapular. The great Carmelite mystic, St. John of the Cross, used to pray for the grace to die on a Saturday, and his prayers were answered.[22] Before he died, in the year 1591, he said: 'The Mother of God and of Carmel hastens to Purgatory with grace on Saturday and delivers those souls who have worn her Scapular. Blessed be such a Lady who wills that, on this day of Saturday, I shall depart from this life!'[22]

From all of the above it is clear that Saint John of the Cross lived in union with Mary and with God, and was faithful to the Order, and was well aware of the Scapular and the privileges thereof as they were known in his time.

Thérèse of Lisieux

Thérèse grew up in a family which was very devoted to Our Lady. *Fr. John A. Hardon, S.J. provides an excellent study* 'Devotion of St. Thérèse of Lisieux to the Blessed Virgin Mary'.[23] Her mother died at the early age of forty-six, when Thérèse was 5 years old, Until Thérèse was nine years old, her sister Pauline took the place of her mother. But in 1881 when Pauline entered the Carmel at Lisieux, her younger sister felt the shock so severely that she came down with an apparently incurable nervous malady.[23] She was cured of this illness through a statue of Our Lady, which came to life during her delirium. This clearly strengthened her devotion to Our Lady and her wish to be Consecrated to Our Lady.[23]

In the afternoon of her first Holy Communion, aged 10, she

solemnly ratified Mary's gift to her by consecrating herself 'with all the affection of my heart' to the Blessed Mother of God. 'I pronounced the Act of Consecration to the Blessed Virgin in the name of my companions. Doubtless I was chosen for this because I was left without my mother on earth…In consecrating myself to the Virgin Mary, I asked her to watch over me, placing into the act all the devotion of my soul, and it seemed to me, I saw her once again looking down and smiling on her 'petite fleur.'[24]

However this general consecration to Mary did not satisfy her, She wished to dedicate herself in a very special way. 'I resolved therefore,' she says, 'to consecrate myself in a particular way to the Most Holy Virgin, begging for admission among the Daughters of Mary.'[25] And so, on May 31, 1887, she was enrolled in the Association of the Daughters of Mary, at the convent of the Benedictine Abbey of Lisieux, among whom were admitted only those students who were distinguished for their piety and good example.[25]

Once she entered the Carmel of Lisieux, Thérèse' life of union with the Mother of God became daily more intense. According to the late Prioress of Carmel at Lisieux, what contributed not a little to this was the classic treatise, 'On the True Devotion of Blessed Virgin Mary,' by St. Louis de Montfort, which Thérèse frequently read and meditated upon. Following Louis de Montfort's advice, she did everything with Mary, or rather, in the presence of Mary, under Mary's influence and according to her example.[23]

Not only did she live in Union with Our Lady, but also with Our

Lord. The very name of Mary was enough 'to transport her heart with joy.'[23] Her prayer to Our Lord was that He would always remember her as the daughter of the same Mother as Himself.[23] This thought so fascinated her that she never tired of repeating it. 'Everything is mine,' she wrote Oct. 19, 1892, to her sister Céline, 'God is mine, and the Mother of God is also my Mother, ... something I find myself saying to her, 'You know, dear Mother, that I am happier than you? I have you for Mother, whereas you do not have the Blessed Virgin to love...[23]

Naturally the Carmelite nuns distributed scapulars, and Thérèse clearly was very aware of the significance of the Scapular. On the Feast of Our Lady of Mt. Carmel, in 1894, Thérèse wrote to her cousin, Mme. Pottier. She wrote 'I had asked Our Lady of Mt. Carmel for the grace you obtained at Lourdes.' And she adds, 'I am so happy that you are wearing the Blessed Scapular; it is a sure sign of predestination.'[23]

So, also in the case of Thérèse of Lisieux, we have a person who is consecrated to Mary, and lives in union with Mary and with God, and is well aware of the significance of the scapular.

Edith Stein

Edith Stein, the philosopher saint who discovered empathy also experienced living in union with Our Lady and with God as a Carmelite, Sister Benedicta of the Cross. She wrote of Mary in an essay called 'Woman's Place in the Mystical Body of Christ' 'she (Mary) has borne us into our life of grace, by casting her whole being, body and soul, into the divine maternity. Therefore she is intimately united to us: she loves us, she knows us, she is anxious to make each of us what he ought to be, especially to bring each of us into as close a relationship as possible to our Lord.' Thus she understood the concept both of living in union with Mary, and consequently in union, through Mary, with our Lord.

Elizabeth of the Trinity

What can we say about Elizabeth of the Trinity, the 'Praise of His Glory' who lived such a deep life of Union with God in the Carmel of Dijon?

Elizabeth loved Our Lady very deeply. The proof of this is scattered in her writings. Here are a few examples; *'Oh ! I never loved her so much! I cry with joy at the thought that this very serene, all luminous Creature is my Mother and I rejoice in her beauty like a child who loves her mother; I have a very strong movement towards her, I have restored her Queen and Guardian of my sky.'*[28]

Like Mary who keeps everything in her heart, she prefers silence to welcome the deepest gift of love from God. Thus Mary was for her a model of contemplation and union with God.'*If you knew the gift of God, ..' 'There is a creature which knew this gift of God, a creature which did not lose a piece of it, a creature which was so pure, so bright, that it seems to be the Light itself. A creature whose life was so simple, so lost in God that almost nothing can be said about it. She is the faithful Virgin, 'the one who kept all things in her heart' It seems to me that the attitude of the Virgin during the months which passed between the Annunciation and the Nativity is the model of inner souls, beings that God has chosen to live inside, at the bottom of the bottomless abyss. In what peace, in what meditation Mary surrendered and lent herself to all things! How the most banal were deified by her!'*[29] Mary, the true contemplative, watches continuously in faith and always remains in communion with God. *'In a profound silence, an ineffable peace a divine prayer which never ceases, The soul all overgrown with eternal light stood Night and day Mary, faithful Virgin. Her heart, like a crystal, reflected the divine, The Host who lived there, Beauty without decline. Great communicant, soul completely invaded In a meditation, deep, mysterious and night and day surrendered to her God'.*[30]

Elizabeth had a great devotion to the Immaculate Conception and saw Our Lady as being responsible for her taking the Carmelite Habit, including, of course, the Scapular. *'It was Mary the Immaculate who gave me the habit of Carmel and I asked her to put on this' fine linen dress 'with which the wife adorns herself to go to the supper of the wedding of the Lamb,'*[31]

Elizabeth was very conscious of the vocation of the Carmelite to come into union with God through Love.

> 'To love, for a Carmelite,
> Is to surrender like Jesus
> A true love never hesitates,
> It wishes to always give more and more.
> Let us be a faithful image
> Of our Bridegroom sacrifices,
> Retrace in us the model
> Of this divine Crucified One.
> Looking at him night and day

Let's climb the austere mountain,
It is the home of Love,
His palace and his sanctuary.
In this mysterious temple
Sacrifice ourselves with a happy heart.'[32]

Elizabeth is conscious of living in the presence of God and in union with God. *'I leave you my faith in the presence of God, of the God of all Love living in our souls. I entrust it to you: it is this intimacy with Him 'inside' that was the beautiful sun radiating my life.'*[33] *'May the One who took me be always more the Friend in whom you rest of all. Live in your intimacy as you live with the One you love, in a sweetheart to heart; it is the secret of your daughter's happiness.'*[34] This union with God is all enveloping because it is founded on love, yet it is clear that for her, God, the Trinity lives in her soul, as she wishes God should live in others; *'May the Father cover you with his shadow, let this shadow be like a cloud that envelops and separates you. May the Word imprint on you its beauty, to contemplate in your soul like another himself. May the Holy Spirit, who is love, make your heart a small home that will delight the three divine persons by the heat of its flames.'*[35]

This deep union with God in love culminates in the prayer *'My God, Trinity whom I adore'*[36], in which she used words of deep commitment to God as Trinity *'O my God', 'O my unchangeable', 'O my beloved Christ', 'O eternal Word', 'O my beloved Star', 'O consuming fire', 'O Father 'and finally' O my Three '*. She wants to offer herself entirely: *'forget herself', 'completely given up', 'I give myself to you'*, but this gift of self is motivated and driven by love, the love of Elizabeth which is response to the love of God: *'Trinity God whom I adore', 'My beloved*

Christ, crucified by love, I would like to be a wife', 'consuming fire, Spirit of love'.[36] Thus she becomes *'A praise of His Glory'*. Clearly, for Elizabeth, there is a strong connection between union with Our Lady, the Carmelite Habit and scapular, living in the presence of God, and union with God.

Lawrence of the Resurrection

Finally, what can we say of Lawrence of the Resurrection, who gave us the Practice of the Presence of God?[37] His writings talk of a deep union with God, and he lived the Carmelite Life, wearing their scapular as part of their Habit. His writing is not on our Lady, but only on living in deep union with God, but the truth is this. He lived as a Brother of the Blessed Virgin of Mount Carmel, living in the Presence of God and wearing Our Lady's habit and Scapular. He must have known from his Uncle, a Carmelite Priest, and from his formation as a Carmelite the history and traditions of the Order of Brothers of Our Lady of Mount Carmel; Therefore like all Carmelites, he lived in union with Mary, he Sister and Mother as well as living in the Presence of God.

Conclusion

Hence we can conclude that Emanuele Boaga is correct. For all the Carmelites we have discussed, living in union with Mary is intimately linked with both living in union with and in the presence of God, and also with the fact of being part of the Order of Our Lady of Mount Carmel and wearing its habit and scapular.

References:

1 *'Saint Teresa of Jesus and the Virgin Mary' Updated 04 giu 2003 by OCD General HouseCorso d'Italia, 38 - 00198 Roma – Italia*
2 *Teresa of Jesus Life 1:7.*
3 *Teresa of Jesus Way, Escorial 48:22.*
4 *Teresa of Jesus Relations 36:1.*
5 *Teresa of Jesus Way 26:8.*
6 *Teresa of Jesus Concepts 3:11.*
7 *Teresa of Jesus Relation 58*
8 *Teresa of Jesus Relation 15: 1, 6.*
9 *Teresa of Jesus Relation 25:1.*
10 *Teresa of Jesus See Mansions VI 7:13 and the title of the chapter; 8:6.*
11 *Teresa of Jesus Relation 25.*
12 *Teresa of Jesus Letter to the nuns of Seville, January 13th 1580: 6*
13 *Teresa of Jesus Mansions V: 1:2.*
14 *Teresa of Jesus Life 38:31.*
15 *Br. John-Mary of Jesus Crucified, OCDhttps://discalcedcarmel.org/the-mariology-of-saint-john-of-the-cross/The Mariology of Saint John of the Cross 1918*
16 *'The Virgin Mary, St John of the Cross and other Carmelite authors' Updated 04 giu 2003 by OCD General House Corso d'Italia, 38 - 00198 Roma – Italia*
17 *John of the Cross,Canticle B 20:10; Canticle A 29:7.*
18 *John of the Cross,Ascent III: 2:10*
19 *John of the Cross,Jn 2:3; Canticle A & B 2:8.*
20 *John of the Cross,Sayings of Light and Love 104; See Ascent II:22:3-6.*
21 *John of the Cross,Prayer of the enamored soul.*
22 *Fr. Peter Davis O.Carm, Our Lady's Brown Scapular Sign of Consecration to Marywww.ecatholic2000.com › cts › untitled-328.*

23 *Fr. John A. Hardon, S.J.Devotion of St. Thérèse of Lisieux to the Blessed Virgin Mary https://hardonsj.org/devotion-of-st-therese-of-lisieux -to-the-blessed-virgin-mary/*

24 *Thérèse of Lisieux Autobiography 60*

25 *Thérèse of Lisieux Autobiography 68*

26 *Mary Julian Baird 1958 Edith Stein and the Mother of God*

27 *Emanuele Boaga, J Chalmers, et al. The Lady of the Place: Mary in the History and in the Life of Carmel (Carmelitana), 2001*

28 *Elizabeth of the Trinity Letter 298 , July 1906*

29 *Elizabeth of the Trinity,Heaven in Faith 39-40*

30 *Elizabeth of the Trinity,Poetry 79*

31 *Elizabeth of the Trinity Letter 294 , July 1906*

32 *Elizabeth of the Trinity P94 To Love (1) [for July 29 1905*]*

33 *Elizabeth of the Trinity Letter 333.*

34 *Elizabeth of the Trinity Letter 170*

35 *Elizabeth of the Trinity Letter 278 , of June 10, 1906 to Germaine de Gemeaux*

36 *Elizabeth of the Trinity Prayer 'My God, Trinity whom I adore'*

37 *Lawrence of the Resurrection 'The Practice of the Presence of God*

SIXTY THREE

CARMEL, THE SCAPULAR, AND LOVE

Mark Agius

HAVING DISCUSSED IN DEPTH THE RELATIONSHIP AMONG Carmelites between the union with God, union with Our Lady, and the Scapular, there is another important relationship which needs finally to be discussed. That is love of God and our neighbour and the scapular.

When we discussed union with God and the Carmelites / the scapular, it was very evident from all the quotations which we used on all the Carmelites which we quoted that their experience of Union with God was indeed one not only of Adoration but of deep love of God. What I need to do now is to discuss whether these same persons also demonstrated deep love of other persons and ask whether there is a relationship between this love and their having the Carmelite Ethos.

There is, in fact, no doubt that all of these Carmelites who we have examined showed great love of other persons, and indeed seemed enthusiastic to share with other persons what they had experienced of their relationship with God, which they saw as being the most important relationship of their experience. They shared their experience with great love, enthusiasm, and often good humour.

We can mention a few quotes from each of these Carmelites in order to demonstrate this:

Teresa of Avila

Saint Teresa of Avila was very much in love with God. 'Prayer is an act of love; words are not needed. Even if sickness distracts from thoughts, all that is needed is the will to love.' 'The Lord asks only two things of us: love for His Majesty and love for our neighbour,' 'perfection consists not in consolations, but in the increase of love'. She was committed to be doing all things with love. 'It is love alone that gives worth to all things.' 'Love turns work into rest.' 'The important thing is not to think much but to love much; and so do that which best stirs you to love.' 'Accustom yourself continually to make many acts of love, for they enkindle and melt the soul.' She saw a strong connection between her love of God and her help to her neighbour. 'Christ has no body now on earth but yours, no hands but yours, no feet but yours, Yours are the eyes through which to look out Christ's compassion to the world, Yours are the feet with which he is to go about doing good; Yours are the hands with which he is to bless men now.' Her advice to her nuns was - and this held for both their relationships with each other and with persons outside the monastery - 'Let us realise, my daughters, that true perfection consists in the love of God and of our neighbour, and the more nearly perfect is our observance of these two commandments, the nearer to perfection we shall be.' All was done with good humour, even while talking to God - 'If this is how you treat your friends, no wonder you have so many enemies.' And with other people - 'God save us from gloomy saints!'[1]

Therese of Lisieux

Therese of Lisieux also was committed to love, both to loving God and to loving others. Regarding love of God, she said 'For me, prayer is a surge of the heart; it is a simple look turned toward heaven, it is a cry of recognition and of love, embracing both trial and joy.' She was ready to offer all difficulties in relationships in the convent and all of her personal suffering to Jesus as a gift of love, and this became more evident as she became ill. 'Miss no single opportunity of making some small sacrifice, here by a smiling look, there by a kindly word; always doing the smallest right and doing it all for love'. 'When something painful or disagreeable happens to me, instead of a melancholy look, I answer with a smile. At first I did not always succeed, but now it has become a habit which I am glad to have acquired.' Regarding deeds she did for others, she echoed Teresa of Avila 'Without love, deeds, even the most brilliant, count as nothing.' She loved unstintingly 'When one loves, one does not calculate.' How she related to others was driven by the consciousness that 'A word or a smile is often enough to put fresh life in a despondent soul.'

A final quote links Therese' suffering in illness with her love of Christ; she saw suffering as a way to love God for herself and others; 'to dedicate oneself as a Victim of Love is not to be dedicated to sweetness and consolations; it is to offer oneself to all that is painful and bitter, because Love lives only by sacrifice and the more we would surrender ourselves to Love, the more we must surrender ourselves to suffering'.[3,4,5]

Maria Maddalena de' Pazzi

Maria Maddalena de'Pazzi was extraordinarily in love with God, who she saw as being Love itself; she would in extacy cry out;'Amore, Amore! O Amore, che non sei né amato né conosciuto!.... O anime create d'amore e per amore, perché non amate l'Amore? E chi è l'Amore se non Dio, e Dio è l'amore? Deus charitas est!'. Regarding love of others, she begged God for reform of the Church, and she wanted to help promote it, despite being an enclosed nun., Her deep concern for the Church moved in two directions: outwards, for growth and expansion of the Church; and inwards, for reform and renewal of the life of faith. This led her to write letters to the Pope and to other nuns in other convents about the reform of the church.[7]

Elizabeth of the Trinity

Elizabeth of the Trinity was deeply in love with God. 'May my life be a continual prayer, a long act of love.' 'A soul united to Jesus is a living smile that radiates Him and gives Him.' Elizabeth was extraordinarily committed to sharing her experience of God with others... one can feel the enthusiasm in her letters, thus, for example 'My mission in heaven will be to draw souls, helping them to go out of themselves to cling to God, with a spontaneous, love-filled action, and to keep them in that great interior silence which enables God to make his mark on them, to transform them into himself.'[6]

Lawrence of the Resurrection

Lawrence of the Resurrection did everything for the love of God. 'We ought not to be weary of doing little things for the love of God, who regards not the greatness of the work, but the love with which it is performed.' 'We must know before we can love. In order to know God, we must often think of Him; and when we come to love Him, we shall then also think of Him often, for our heart will be with our treasure.' Lawrence needed to do much work for his monastery, so he did everything for the love of God, thus helping his neighbour, the other friars, by doing his work well. 'My God, since You are with me and since, by Your will, I must occupy myself with external things, please grant me the grace to remain with You, in Your presence. Work with me, so that my work might be the very best. Receive as an offering of love both my work and all my affections.[8]

John of the Cross

Finally we consider John of the Cross. Regarding union with and love of God, John has said 'To love is to be transformed into what we love. To love God is therefore to be transformed into God.' He was committed to love; ' My sole occupation is love.' 'There is nothing better or more necessary than love. 'John was very aware that it is our love of God that prompts us to carry out works of charity thus; 'A Christian should always remember that the value of his good works is not based on their number and excellence, but on the love of God which prompts him to do these things'. For John, it was important to love persons, even if they did not appreciate the love with which we help them; 'Have a great love for those who contradict and fail to love you, for in this way love is begotten in a heart that has no love.' 'Where there is no love, pour love in, and you will draw love out.' 'Love consists not in feeling great things but in having great detachment and in suffering for the Beloved.'However, in the end, what mattered was how much we had loved; 'At the evening of life, we shall be judged on our love.'[2]

Thus, certainly, Carmelites, who wear the scapular, live in union with God and Our Lady and love their neighbour with great commitment, for 'At the evening of life, we shall be judged on our love.' This is how persons who wear the Carmelite Scapular should act.

References:

1 *https://www.goodreads.com/author/quotes/74226.Teresa_of_vila*
2 *www.goodreads.com › author › quotes › 1911605.Juan_de_la_Cruz*
3 *https://www.coraevans.com/blog/article/10-most-powerful-st.-therese-of-lisieux-quotes*
4 *https://www.coraevans.com/blog/article/10-beautidul-st-therese-of--lisieux-quotes-on-love*
5 *https://www.goodreads.com/author/quotes/248952.Th_r_se_de_Lisieux*
6 *https://www.goodreads.com/author/quotes/202324.Elizabeth_of_the_Trinity*
7 *https://maddalenadepazzi.jimdofree.com/english-spanish/the-community-of-florence/*
8 *Lawrence of the Resurrection 'The Practice of the Presence of God'.*

AFTERWORD - CONCLUSIONS FROM THIS BOOK

WHAT CAN BE LEARNT FROM THIS BOOK?

The reader will be aware that the author has meandered across a large number of disciplines; from history to anthropology to theology to elements of psychology. However it is the opinion of the author that the understanding of this story suffers if one or other of these various disciplines is left out. This is because ultimately this has been a story about humanity and the relationship between humanity and in fact a group of persons, and hence the individual persons in that ever growing group and the God, who creates and cares for those persons, mediated by each individual persons' relationship with Mary, recognised by Christians as the Mother of God.

I have deliberately emphasised that in the book I am recording the popular traditions which the devotion to Our Lady of Mount Carmel has developed around the world, because, when talking of the relationship between God and Humanity, popular religion is important, so long as the relationship between God and man remains the most important thing, with popular customs only being an expression of this.

In particular, this story is a Christian one; it assumes the Christian story that Mankind has been redeemed by Jesus Christ and that Jesus Christ was conceived through the Holy Spirit by the Virgin Mary.

So our story develops when, about 1 000 years after Jesus' birth, some western pilgrims and soldiers settled on Mount Carmel in what is now Israel, there, impressed by the beauty of the place, they saw Mary as the Lady of the Place, to whom they owed allegiance, and the beauty of that countryside and the Mediterranean sea, inspired them, and they knew themselves as being both the descendants of Elias and the Sons of the Prophets who has lived there before them, and the sons and brothers of Mary, who they saw as 'The Lady of the Place', because in their church they had an icon of her, and also in a feudal sense. They strengthened their view of their relationship with Mary with many local stories, and in particular the view that Elias saw Mary in the small cloud he had seen rising from the sea. They were given a rule and became a religious order of hermits with a prophetic function called the Brothers of Our Lady of Mount Carmel, or Carmelites. They wore a habit which included a cloak and a scapular.

The wars in the Holy Land led to the Carmelites moving to Europe and becoming Mendicant Friars. Wherever they went they defended their right to be considered the Brothers of Our Lady. Soon, they began to actively defend the concept that Mary had been Immaculately Conceived through the action of the Holy Spirit. In the meantime, they began to give lay persons who wished to be associated with the Order, their scapular as a sign of affiliation with the Order. Over time, this scapular, made small so that lay persons could wear it, became a very popular devotion all over Europe, including the Mediterranean basin.

Throughout all the stages of the spread of the Carmelites across

Europe, including across England, Italy, The Adriatic coast, Spain, France and Germany, the Carmelites set up many convents and churches, and preached about Christ and His Mother Mary. One important way in which the Carmelites appear to have encouraged lay persons to meditate on the life of Christ was to meditate on the Joys of Mary, and this seems to relate to the devotion of Thomas Becket, since Aylesford, the Carmelite Mother House in England was close to Canterbury, and pilgrims to Becket's tomb used to stay at the Carmelite Monastery. This devotion to the Joys was very popular across Medieval Europe, and was gradually substituted by the Rosary. The devotion of the Joys also became linked with the Devotion to The Mother of God the Madonna Bruna, in the Carmelite Church of Naples, which developed into the tradition of the Carmelite Devotions to Mary on Wednesdays. The Wednesdays between Easter and Pentecost became particularly important, especially in Sicily (Sambuca), Rome and Malta. A Carmelite Chaplet of the Joys of Our Lady remains popular and widespread in Italy.

In the meantime, the spread of the Carmelite Order from the beginning in the Holy Land through their spread across Europe, was accompanied at all stages by numerous accounts of miraculous happenings. The most important of these were the Apparition of Our Lady to Saint Simon Stock in Cambridge, where she gave him the Scapular to assert that the Order pertinent to Mary (and the consequent protection from Eternal Fire) and the miraculous healings related to the Madonna Bruna, which brought about the link with devotions on Wednesday (which had in the Mediterranean been previously a fast day to mourn the betrayal of Jesus). We have mentioned many other miraculous events. The traditions about Medieval miraculous happenings are very difficult to prove satisfactorily. However, the Apparition to Saint Simon Stock, though always known within the Order, was to become very important from the seventeenth century onwards. Meanwhile the Miracles of the Madonna Bruna (which may or may not have come directly from the Monastery of Mount Carmel, and which was an icon of Our Lady of Tenderness, probably the most common icon of Our Lady among the Medieval Carmelites) emphasised the Order's devotion to the Mother of God.

Another important issue was the Sabbatine Privilege, which derived from a Vision which Pope John XX was said to have received from the Virgin Mary with a promise of freedom from Purgatory on the Saturday after their death for devotees of the Carmelite Scapular. This was contested in the Holy Office, and it was after the decision of this issue in favour of the Carmelites in the seventeenth century that promotion of the Scapular of Mount Carmel and the Confraternities set up to promote it became extremely popular. Huge numbers of persons across Europe joined the Scapular Confraternities, and these also became extremely popular also in South America and the Philippines. Later, as people from Italy migrated to North America, the devotion became popular there too. It is true that it was mostly the working classes who most treasured the scapular- the fishermen, sailors, builders, soldiers among others. The common iconography of the order changed, showing Our Lady and the child Jesus proffering the miniature scapular to the people, or Our Lady and the Souls in Purgatory as prescribed by the Holy Office, and the feast of the 16th July became extremely popular across the seventeenth to the twenty-first centuries. Carmelite confessors would commute the obligations linked with the Sabbatine privilege to saying the Rosary and abstaining from meat on Wednesdays and Saturdays, thus linking the devotion to Our Lady of Mount Carmel to the Church's devotion to Our Lady on Saturday, which had been developing over the centuries from the Saturday fast of earlier times.

Here I wish to comment that, apart from academic discussion about whether individual documents are authentic or not, one extremely important aspect of both the Simon Stock Apparition and the Sabbatine Privilege is the traditions handed down within our families, from mother to son, about them and the fact that the privileges relating to these apparitions are approved by the teaching authority of the Church. Here, Church approved tradition offers us what we can believe.

Now, from the very beginning of the Order, Carmelites writers had seen the scapular as a special sign of their dedication, or Consecration to the Virgin Mary. This is why they were the 'Brothers of Our Lady of Mount Carmel. Hence the scapular began to be seen as the sign of Consecration to the Virgin Mary both inside the Order and outside of it, for the tertiaries of the Order and for all members of the Confraternities and all devotees who wore the scapular. Preachers of Consecration to the Virgin Mary, such as Grignion de Montfort (in France the Order itself had disappeared as a result of the French Revolution), Claude de la Colombiere and Alfonsus de Liguori saw the scapular as a sign of this Consecration. By the end of the nineteenth century, Consecration to the Virgin Mary was becoming more popular, and linked to the devotion to Our Lady on Saturdays, and this became most popular in the Twentieth Century after the Apparitions of Our Lady at Fatima, which linked Consecration to Our Lady with the Devotion to Our Lady on Saturdays, and also with the Carmelite Scapular, because on the last Apparition, Our Lady appeared dressed as a Carmelite.

But what does Consecration to the Virgin Mary mean and why is it linked with the Brown Scapular? The Carmelites had always seen that their scapular meant that they were linked with the Virgin Mary in a special way- that she was their Mother, sister and Queen thus they lived in union with her. Looking at the documented lives of some well-known Carmelites, it was clear that they all lived in the Presence of or said otherwise, in Union with God, in other words, that through their union with Mary, they also lived in union with her Son. This union with God is also manifested in great love for God and Other Persons.

The principle suggestion of this book, having looked very broadly at the scapular from every point of view, is that if several Carmelites can live thus in the presence, and in union with God, through their union with Mary, then it is for all persons who wear the scapular- that mass movement across the globe including persons of all cultures- from Santiago Chile, to Seville Spain, to Naples Italy, to Valletta Malta, to Haifa Israel to Manilla in the Philippines and everywhere in between – to also live in the same union with Jesus and Mary, simply by virtue of their choice to wear the scapular, and so be affiliated with the Carmelite Order. But to do this, they must necessarily choose to live in the Presence of God, in conformity with his will as Mary did, and this must be shown by action because 'today Jesus has no hands but yours'.

APPENDIX

THE SCAPULAR OF OUR LADY OF MOUNT CARMEL

Issued by the Maltese Carmelite Province in the Marian Year 2001

1251-2001; 750 years of the Carmelite Scapular

'O Mary of Carmel, in your image you appear to us clothed in Honour and Beauty. This beauty comes from the Child Jesus who you hold in your hand, the blessed fruit of your womb, Give us your divine Child. Look on us as we stretch our hands to you to welcome Him and embrace Him to our hearts.' Blessed Titus Brandsma O.Carm.

The Scapular of Our Lady of Mount Carmel witnesses to our faith that we will one day meet with God in eternal life through the help and protection of the Virgin Mary.

The Carmelite Scapular

Given the history and spiritual values of the order, we show honour to Mary in Carmel, through the scapular. Therefore, whoever receives it becomes a member of the family of the Carmelite Order and attempts to live its spirituality according to their state of life. The scapular is a dress or Habit, hence the Italian word for it is 'abito' or dress- habit. In fact, the scapular is a miniaturised version of the Habit of the Order, symbolising that the wearer has, in order to live in obedience to Jesus Christ, has chosen a spiritual life of familiarity with Mary, the Sister, Mother and Model of every Carmelite.

According to a precious tradition, in 1251, during a difficult time, when the Carmelite Order was going through a difficult time, seeking full and firm recognition within the Church, the Blessed Virgin herself, patroness of Carmel, gave us the scapular as a sign of her protection.

Therefore, this year, 2001, which is the 750th anniversary of the giving of the Carmelite Scapular, the Order is dedicating a year to the Mother and Beauty of Carmel, in order to give Her thanks for everything which She has always done for the Order and to encourage a deepening of the understanding and living of its Marian spirituality.

The 'Carmelite Marian Year' Commission Maltese Carmelite Province 2001.

The Catechetical and Pastoral Aspect of the Scapular

Signs in the Life of Mankind

We live in a world made out of things which can be seen, such as Light, Fire and water, all of which have symbolic meanings. In our daily life, there are also experiences which bring persons together, and expressions which show and come to mean more profound realities, such as eating together (a sign of friendship), taking part in a meeting attended by many persons (a sign of solidarity), celebration together of a National anniversary (a symbol of identity).

We human beings need signs or symbols to help us understand or live the happenings of today or of the past and to help us understand who we are as persons or as groups.

Signs in Our Christian Life

Jesus is the greatest gift and sign of love of the Father. He founded the Church as a sign and instrument of His love. The Christian Life also has its signs and symbols. Jesus himself used bread, wine and water to help us to understand greater truths which we neither can see or touch.

In the celebration of the Eucharist and the other sacraments (Baptism, Confirmation, Confession, Marriage, Holy Orders, Sacrament of the sick), all the symbols which are used (water, oil, laying of hands, rings) have their own meanings and help us come into union with God, who is present through them.

Apart from these liturgical symbols, in the Church we also have other signs which are linked with some happening, a tradition, or a person. Among these symbols is the Scapular of Our Lady of Mount Carmel.

The Scapular, a Marian Symbol

One of the traditional symbols of the Church, over the last seven hundred years, is the Scapular of Our Lady of Mount Carmel.

It is a sign of the motherly love that Mary has for Her children.

It is a sign which is approved by the Church and held by the Carmelite Order as an external sign of love for Mary, of the confidence which Her children place in Her, and of the firm determination of Her children to live like Her.

'The scapular' was a piece of cloth which friars in ancient times used to wear over their religious habit during work time as an apron.

Over time this piece of cloth took on a symbolic meaning: that one would carry his cross daily, as the disciples and those who follow Jesus do. Among some religious Orders, among them Carmel, the Scapular became a sign of their identity and their life.

For the Carmelites, the scapular came to show their special union with Mary – the Mother of the Lord, their confidence in Her care for them as their Mother, and their wish to imitate Her in her giving love to Christ and to others. Thus, the scapular became a Marian symbol.

From Religious Orders to the Whole People of God

During the Middle Ages, many Christians wished to become affiliated in some way with one of the Mendicant Religious Orders which had been founded at those times; the Franciscans, the Dominicans, the Augustinians or the Carmelites. They began to affiliate with these orders through lay confraternities.

All the Religious Orders wished to give lay persons a sign of their union and of their share in their spirit and their apostolate. This sign was a part of the habit of the order; a mantle, a cincture or a scapular.

Hence the Carmelites began to distribute a miniaturised scapular to lay persons as an expression of their union with the Order and with its spirituality.

The use and meaning of the Scapular

The scapular has its roots in the tradition of the Carmelite Order, which saw in it the Maternal protection of Mary. Through the experience of such protection over centuries, the scapular took on a spiritual meaning which was approved by the Church:

- It shows our firm commitment to follow Jesus as Mary did. Mary is the perfect example of faithfulness among all the disciples of Jesus. This commitment begins with our baptism which makes us children of God.

The Virgin Mary teaches us:

1. To live with a heart open to the will of God as shown in the happenings of life.
2. To hear the Word of God in the scriptures as applied to our daily lives; we believe it and do what it asks.
3. To pray without ceasing, so as to find that God is present in all things.
4. To live close to our brothers in need and support them.

- It unites us in the Carmelite Family, which is a community of male and female religious which has existed within the Church for more than eight hundred years, and it calls us to live fervently the ideal of this religious family, which is to live in intimate union with God in prayer.

- It reminds us of the example of the male and female saints of Carmel who we see as our brothers and sisters.
- The Scapular of Our Lady of Mount Carmel witnesses to our faith that we will one day meet with God in eternal life through the help and protection of the Virgin Mary.

Practical Rules

- Whoever is enrolled in the Scapular is enrolled only once by a priest or by an authorised person.
- Once a person has been enrolled, he can, instead of it, wear a medal which on one side has an image of the Sacred Heart of Jesus and on the other side an image of Our Lady.
- The scapular encourages us to live as true Christians as the Gospel teaches us, so that we can receive the sacraments and witness to our special devotion to the Blessed Virgin by saying at least three Hail Marys a day.

A short form of Imposing the Scapular:

Take this Scapular as a sign of your special union with Mary, the Mother of Jesus, and endeavour to follow in her footsteps. May it remind you of your dignity as a Christian, of your commitment to serve others, and to imitate Mary.

Wear it as a sign of her protection and as a sign that you are a member of the Carmelite Family, ready to do the will of God and to participate in building a world according to His plan of Union, Justice and Peace.

THE SCAPULAR OF OUR LADY OF MOUNT CARMEL...
IS NOT:

- A magic object or lucky charm,
- An automatic guarantee of salvation
- An excuse for an individual to avoid the obligations of the Christian Life.

Instead it is a sign:

- Approved by the Church for more than seven hundred years,
- Which shows our commitment to follow Jesus as Mary did:
    1. With our hearts open to God and to his will,
    2. Led by faith, hope and love,
    3. Close to other persons who are in need,
    4. Praying without ceasing to experience God's presence in all the happenings of our lives,
- Which unites Christians with the Carmelite Family,
- Which strengthens our hope that we will one day meet with God in eternal life through the help and protection of the Virgin Mary.

Flos Carmeli

Flower of Carmel,
Tall vine, blossom laden,
Splendour of Heaven,
Child bearing, yet Maiden,
None equals you.
Mother so tender
Whom no man did know,
On Carmel's children,
Your favour bestow,
Star of the sea!

Further copies of this book
can be obtained from

Goodnews Books
Upper level
St. John's Church Complex
296 Sundon Park Road
Luton, Beds. LU3 3AL

www.goodnewsbooks.co.uk
orders@goodnewsbooks.co.uk
+44 (0) 1582 571011